Industrial Research Department
Wharton School of Finance and Commerce
University of Pennsylvania

RESEARCH STUDIES
XXXV

PRICES AND INFLATION DURING THE AMERICAN REVOLUTION
Pennsylvania, 1770-1790

INDUSTRIAL RESEARCH STUDIES

I. *Earnings and Working Opportunity in the Upholstery Weavers' Trade in 25 Plants in Philadelphia*, by Anne Bezanson. 1928. $2.50. Out of print.

II. *Collective Bargaining among Photo-Engravers in Philadelphia*, by Charles Leese. 1929. $2.50.

III. *Trends in Foundry Production in the Philadelphia Area*, by Anne Bezanson and Robert D. Gray. 1929. $1.50.

IV. *Significant Post-War Changes in the Full-Fashioned Hosiery Industry*, by George W. Taylor. 1929. $2.00. Out of print.

V. *Earnings in Certain Standard Machine-Tool Occupations in Philadelphia*, by H. L. Frain. 1929. $1.50.

VI. *Help-Wanted Advertising as an Indicator of the Demand for Labor*, by Anne Bezanson. 1929. $2.00. Out of print.

VII. *An Analysis of Production of Worsted Sales Yarn*, by Alfred H. Williams, Martin A. Brumbaugh, and Hiram S. Davis. 1929. $2.50.

VIII. *The Future Movement of Iron Ore and Coal in Relation to the St. Lawrence Waterway*, by Fayette S. Warner. 1930. $3.00.

IX. *Group Incentives—Some Variations in the Use of Group Bonus and Gang Piece Work*, by C. Canby Balderston. 1930. $2.50.

X. *Wage Methods and Selling Costs*, by Anne Bezanson and Miriam Hussey. 1930. $4.50.

XI. *Wages—A Means of Testing Their Adequacy*, by Morris E. Leeds and C. Canby Balderston. 1931. $1.50.

XII. *Case Studies of Unemployment*—Compiled by the Unemployment Committee of the National Federation of Settlements, edited by Marion Elderton. 1931. $3.00. Out of print.

XIII. *The Full-Fashioned Hosiery Worker—His Changing Economic Status*, by George W. Taylor. 1931. $3.00.

XIV. *Seasonal Variations in Employment in Manufacturing Industries*, by J. Parker Bursk. 1931. $2.50. Out of print.

XV. *The Stabilization of Employment in Philadelphia through the Long-Range Planning of Municipal Improvement Projects*, by William N. Loucks. 1931. $3.50.

XVI. *How Workers Find Jobs—A Study of Four Thousand Hosiery Workers*, by Dorothea de Schweinitz. 1932. $2.50.

XVII. *Savings and Employee Savings Plans*, by William J. Carson. 1932. $1.50.

XVIII. *Workers' Emotions in Shop and Home*, by Rexford B. Hersey. 1932. $3.00. Out of print.

XIX. *Union Tactics and Economic Change—A Case Study of Three Philadelphia Textile Unions*, by Gladys L. Palmer. 1932. $2.00.

XX. *The Philadelphia Upholstery Weaving Industry*, by C. Canby Balderston, Robert P. Brecht, Miriam Hussey, Gladys L. Palmer, and Edward N. Wright. 1932. $2.50.

INDUSTRIAL RESEARCH STUDIES

XXI. *Wage Rates and Working Time in the Bituminous Coal Industry, 1912-1922*, by Waldo E. Fisher and Anne Bezanson. 1932. $3.50.

XXII. *Ten Thousand Out of Work*, by Ewan Clague and Webster Powell. 1933. $2.00.

XXIII. *A Statistical Study of Profits*, by Raymond T. Bowman. 1934. $3.00. Out of print.

XXIV. *The Dollar, the Franc, and Inflation*, by Eleanor Lansing Dulles. 1933. $1.25. (The Macmillan Company.)

XXV. *Executive Guidance of Industrial Relations*, by C. Canby Balderston. 1935. $3.75.

XXVI. *Prices in Colonial Pennsylvania*, by Anne Bezanson, Robert D. Gray, and Miriam Hussey. 1935. $4.00.

XXVII. *Earnings of Skilled Workers in a Manufacturing Enterprise, 1878-1930*, by Evan Benner Alderfer. 1935. $1.50.

XXVIII. *Depression and Reconstruction*, by Eleanor Lansing Dulles. 1936. $3.00.

XXIX. *Wholesale Prices in Philadelphia—1784-1861*, by Anne Bezanson, Robert D. Gray, and Miriam Hussey. 1936. $4.00.

XXX. *Wholesale Prices in Philadelphia—1784–1861, Part II—Series of Relative Monthly Prices*, by Anne Bezanson, Robert D. Gray, and Miriam Hussey. 1937. $4.00.

XXXI. *Some International Aspects of the Business Cycle*, by Hans Neisser. 1936. $2.50. Out of print.

XXXII. *Economic Consequences of the Seven-Hour Day and Wage Changes in the Bituminous Coal Industry*, by Waldo E. Fisher. 1939. $2.00.

XXXIII. *Industrial Study of Economic Progress*, by Hiram S. Davis. 1947. $2.75.

XXXIV. *Effective Labor Arbitration—The Impartial Chairmanship of the Full-Fashioned Hosiery Industry*, by Thomas Kennedy. 1948. $3.50.

PRICES AND INFLATION DURING THE AMERICAN REVOLUTION
Pennsylvania, 1770-1790

by

ANNE BEZANSON

assisted by

BLANCH DALEY

MARJORIE C. DENISON

MIRIAM HUSSEY

INDUSTRIAL RESEARCH DEPARTMENT
WHARTON SCHOOL OF FINANCE AND COMMERCE
UNIVERSITY OF PENNSYLVANIA

Philadelphia
UNIVERSITY OF PENNSYLVANIA PRESS
1951

Manufactured in the
UNITED STATES OF AMERICA

PREFACE

MANY VALUABLE STUDIES have been made of the American Revolutionary era both before and since Charles M. Andrews wrote his challenging plea, "We owe it to ourselves, as one of the great nations of the earth, to study our colonial and Revolutionary periods, not as isolated and provincial phenomena, but as phases of a great forward movement, worthy of that creative analysis which the scientist gives to the operations of nature and the scholar gives to other movements that have played their parts in the evolution of the human race."[1] In this rich literature, with many special studies, attention is given in numerous ways to the advance in prices during the Revolutionary War, the difficulties of army and civilian supply, costs of transportation, currency inflation, experiments in price and trade controls, and many innovations, municipal and regional, which had to be tried to meet the constant needs of the community and army.

No extensive archival research, however, has given the historian of these crucial years a continuous record of the movement of prices which would establish a groundwork for other studies, as well as indicate the stage in price advance at which innovations occurred. The primary purpose of this study is to fill that need for a period of swift-moving social and economic change when scattered data of the height of prices of particular commodities lose their significance. The excessive prices of the time, even today, seem staggering; but, as isolated figures, they have limited meaning, since it is mainly the manner in which the interrelated system of prices responded that is helpful in tracing the changes of this formative period or in linking it to the colonial and federal eras.

The stage of dealing with "isolated and provincial phenomena" cannot yet be by-passed, since special studies that would enable one to state how similar were the experiences in all parts of the mainland are still wanting. Because the financial policies of each of the thirteen colonies had been self-determined and because each issued its own currency before Congress acted and even continued to do so afterward, the war started not only with fundamental financial arrangements on a different basis

[1] Charles M. Andrews, *The Colonial Background of the American Revolution*, p. 219.

in each but with the groundwork laid for variations between them in the rate and timing of inflation. Generalizations thus lose their vitality until more specific knowledge of areas can be obtained.

Some background of international price movements has been obtained by the use of *Inquiry into the History of Prices in Holland* by N. W. Posthumus, from which a group of commodities as similar as possible to those for Philadelphia has been transcribed into a comparable statistical index. Since Holland was the leading financial market of continental Europe and was not involved in war until late in 1780, these Amsterdam prices should reflect the conditions of world trade without the direct effects of war and currency problems.

This study of inflation and prices, then, has concentrated on Pennsylvania, where a wealth of manuscript materials made it seem possible to acquire the needed data for detailed study. Even so, the filling in of monthly series for a few staple commodities is by no means an easy undertaking. Some articles were at times so scarce that intermittent sales could be found in only a few accounts. At other times a wide range for the same commodity would prevail among different merchants. Other commodities which became key war items ceased to have a public market and were either allocated by Boards of War or were limited to plants manufacturing or transporting war materials.

Libraries, historical societies, and even private collections have made their materials available. More and more families which have stored business papers and records for generations are gradually placing them where they will be available to students of history. Such family papers have been particularly valuable to this study.

The richest source of Revolutionary War materials for the Philadelphia area is, of course, the Historical Society of Pennsylvania, and a particular debt is owed to its director, R. Norris Williams, 2nd, not only for keeping us informed of acquisitions and gifts of account books and letters but for the opportunity to use the newly available shipping records for the decade before the Revolution, and for his readily aroused and helpful interest. Many and widely scattered libraries, as well, have been consulted: the Manuscript Division of the Library of Congress; the Manuscript Division of the New York Public Library; the New York Historical Society; the Bucks County Historical Society; the Historical Society of Montgomery County; the Haverford College Library; the Historical Society of Berks County; the Massachusetts Historical Society; the Swarthmore College Library; the American-Jewish Historical Society; the John Carter Brown Library; the Princeton University Library; the Girard College collection of Stephen Girard's papers; the Ridgway Branch Library; the University of Pennsylvania Library; and the Library of the American Philosophical Society.

Everywhere, cooperation and assistance have been proffered by those in charge, and while it is hardly practicable to name all of the busy librarians who have assisted, it would not be possible to pass over Miss Catherine H. Miller and Mr. J. Harcourt Givens in the Manuscript Division of the Historical Society of Pennsylvania, who have been patient and helpful these many years.

Mention of manuscripts and merchants within this volume gives, by no means, a complete list of sources searched. Although many accounts of tradesmen, such as printers, tanners, clockmakers, hatters, and silversmiths, have been consulted, attention can be called only to the records which have appreciable length and continuity. The bibliography itself is not a complete catalogue of all material investigated, since the value of many manuscripts was mainly corroborative and only those actually used, either in the final assembly of the price series or in the text, are noted. The swift movement of prices and the disparity of quotations in a single source during a single month often made one question whether the prices were typical. Throughout the study, however, the comments of officials, merchants, iron masters, shipbuilders, diarists, and consumers have been collected as a means of verifying the movement of prices and the impact of inflation.

In a study long in process, though frequently interrupted, credit for aid in the assembly of data is due to many who participated in former price history volumes, as well as to those whose direct contribution in the final stages of preparing this publication is recognized on its title page. Apart from his helpful comment, a debt is owed to Hiram S. Davis for permitting the study to delay others in the Industrial Research Department; for comment on parts of the manuscript, acknowledgment is made to Gladys L. Palmer and George W. Taylor, of the University of Pennsylvania, and especially to Arthur H. Cole of Harvard University.

Financial assistance at a critical stage in the completion of the study was provided by two grants from the American Philosophical Society, one from the Penrose Fund and one from the Reserve Fund. The cost of publication has been borne by the Committee on Research in Economic History.

CONTENTS

TABLES

CHARTS

APPENDIX TABLES

PRICES AND INFLATION DURING THE AMERICAN REVOLUTION

Pennsylvania, 1770-1790

CHAPTER I

INTRODUCTION

LIKE OTHER VOLUMES in the history of prices in Pennsylvania, this study of *Prices and Inflation during the American Revolution: Pennsylvania, 1770-1790,* is based on monthly wholesale quotations of certain staple commodities—some domestic, some imported. In previous volumes, *Prices in Colonial Pennsylvania* and *Wholesale Prices in Philadelphia, 1784-1861,* reliance could be placed on prices current published in the papers or in market reports to form the basic data for a selected list of commodities sold in the regular channels of trade. Only at such times as lists were omitted or published in abbreviated form was it necessary in the study of colonial years to supplement the data or to fill in gaps in the record from the account books of contemporary merchants and from letters to correspondents in other areas or from the prices current appended to their letters.

In contrast, from 1775 to August 1784, the account books of contemporaries and their letters to their clients and families became the sole basic source of data. Normally, a considerable number of different sources had to be consulted before the prices of even a single staple commodity of daily use could be filled in, and a much larger number had to be used to test and verify them. Even the correspondence of merchants gave a less general view of the whole situation of the market or of the causes of short-term fluctuations in prices in the war years than they did before the war, when the arrival of vessels, the loading of ships, and the prices paid for commodities were not only regularly published for the information of all but were matters for frequent discussion among captains, owners, tradesmen, and shipbuilders at their gatherings in the coffeehouses.

The secrecy of the war period, the absorption of many citizens in committee activities, and the migration of merchants to upstate areas left few in a position to take an over-all view of the market or to be well-informed on the extent of its supplies, either actual or potential.

The data in this final volume in the pre-Civil War commodity price history studies for the area of Philadelphia are intended to complement the two previous publications which cover the years 1720 to 1775 and 1784 to 1861. Because the statistics for the intervening Revolutionary years differ in source and coverage from those given in the previous volumes, an overlapping interval of five years is included both for the colonial period and the readjustment which followed the close of the war.

It must not be assumed that the price student of this period can decide upon a well-selected sample of commodities, representative of the varied sectors of the economy, and draw material from a limited number of sources. The filling in of complete monthly prices for even one staple commodity is not only a major undertaking but is dependent upon the regularity of its sale in accounts of those merchants whose records happen to have been preserved. Besides, the accounts of different merchants are often in conflict or represent such a spread in quotations and so few sales that a judgment checked against contemporary comment must be made in arriving at what seems to be a prevailing or modal price.

It is therefore felt to be no small achievement that as many as fifteen commodities can be included in an index of prices for the war years. The commodities complete enough for this inclusion are:

Beef	Flour, Superfine	Rum, West India
Chocolate	Iron, Bar	Sugar, Muscovado
Coffee	Molasses	Tar
Corn	Pepper	Tea, Bohea
Flour, Common	Pork	Wheat

Other important but less complete series included in the discussion and in the Appendix Tables for part of the period are:

Bread, Ship	Leather, Sole	Tobacco, Virginia
Cotton	Rice	Turpentine
Flour, Middling	Sugar, Loaf	Wine, Madeira
Indigo		

Prices of some commodities of great importance, such as salt, gun and cannon powder, shot, lead, cordage, steel, and lumber, had to be omitted. Salt, procured from domestic manufacture and from new areas of trade, lost all semblance of grading and, though it was an item of major use with a wealth of quotations, was peculiarly difficult to classify. Naval stores, except tar, and shipbuilding materials did not pass through the hands of merchants generally, and prices appeared so rarely that even the use of a diversity of obscure sources failed to yield regular monthly price data. Of the commodities complete enough for inclusion in a general index not all were of equal importance at any time nor in use in the same proportions throughout the war years. The index does include staple commodities in daily use and such West India products as were likely to be sold by most merchants.

That there was active trade in West India products may be attributed in part to the increasing commerce with the "foreign" islands before the war. Though direct trade with the British islands, of which the most important were Antigua, Barbados, and Jamaica, was shut off, other British islands captured by French forces, notably Dominica, Grenada, St. Vincent, St. Kitts, Tobago, and Montserrat, occasionally furnished cargoes for North American mainland vessels. The need for strategic materials expanded trade with the French islands of Martinique, Guadaloupe, and the western part of Hispaniola (now Haiti), and with the Dutch island of St. Eustatius and the mainland possession of Surinam. In addition, the Spanish part of Hispaniola (now the Dominican Republic) and, late in the war, Havana contributed important products as did the smaller but well-established commerce with the Danish islands, notably St. Croix and St. Thomas of the Virgin Islands group. In merchant comment, reference is frequently made to the main port, and islands pass under a variety of spellings like Martinico, San Domingo, and Statia.

Chapter II deals with the general course of prices as shown in the currencies in use in the period. It reveals the extent of the total advance brought about by instability of the currency, scarcity of goods, interrupted shipping, the state of crops, the confusion of war, and all the other factors which impinged upon prices in this critical period.

The discussion of the hazardous task of finding a method of correcting the commodity price series for depreciation of "congress money" is deferred until the general trend of prices has been considered. Even if information were not obscure, it would be difficult to apply a formula to translate prices of commodities exchanged for continental currency into something like stable values. Modern methods for detecting the start of inflation or the extent of currency depreciation afford little guidance in the Revolutionary years. Foreign exchange quotations lasted only through 1776, and even in those months were affected by the eagerness for bills of individuals anxious to return to Europe. No open market for dealings in precious metals existed, and the circulation of foreign coins in the absence of any minted in the colonies evolved no agency regularly concerned with recording the premium on coin or bullion. Besides, the small amount of specie in circulation, when it was not hoarded, often passed at higher rates in cash transactions than in fair exchange for goods, especially durables. Until the middle of the war, transactions in which coin changed hands were infrequent enough to serve at best only to date stages in the price advance. Insofar as price controls were at times effective, the movements of some commodities failed to reflect the full extent of depreciation, to say nothing of the dissimilar effects of embargoes, shipping risks, and other barriers to trade.

By some means, the mercantile community had to find ways of protecting itself against a continuous shrinkage in the value of the medium of exchange. In the spring of 1777, the best-informed merchants began to convert the items in their accounts which they had already posted in continental currency by a coefficient assumed to represent the specie rating of paper. Once the relation of paper money to specie became the most important information included in the prices current attached to merchants' correspondence, these scales of depreciation gradually became narrowly limited in range. Whatever their validity, they represent the basis on which trade was conducted and accounts balanced. Their use by merchants, shipowners, artificers, iron-makers, and even public officials long antedated the adoption of legal scales, and gave to the mercantile community a measure of control over the pace of currency devaluation in that they furnished a basis for the markup of goods. More than likely, a corrective used so generally by common consent even influenced actual dealings in specie. Apart from these practices, reviewed in Chapter III, two separate measures have been calculated: the one based on direct exchange of specie for continental money; the other, on commodity transactions in specie. These, along with contemporary comment, are the only devices so far obtainable for deflating the index of prices. All must be used and understood in terms of the events of a period in which parts of the economy were self-sustaining, many persons found ingenious ways of living outside the pecuniary system, and a few, in key situations, even were able to contract for payment in specie.

In a sense, the behavior of the specific commodities making up the total, when considered in relation to other items in the series, reveals more than does the general average. These are interpreted in Chapters V through XIV in the light of comtemporary comment by merchants, commissaries for the army, delegates to Congress, and others in a position to have as informed an opinion as possible of the terms of sale or the supply of a commodity. In addition, in Chapters XV through XVII an impression can be given from less continuous records of the course of prices for important commodities like tobacco, raw cotton, and textile fabrics which played a role in the shipping and affected the merchant organization and activity of the period.

Contemporary opinion has been cited extensively in the discussion of specific commodities. It differs in emphasis according to the role the observer played, his location, and the opportunity he had for forming a judgment. Not all records, whether in the form of accounts or of letters, span the whole period. Prominent merchants of the colonial era, like the Cliffords, Joseph Anthony, Benjamin Fuller, and others, withdrew to the country or in other ways marked time for the whole or a part of the war; others, like Robert Morris, William Pollard, and Henry Hill, engaged in public activity with intermittent attention to trade. As a result, commodity transactions in many accounts were sparse or wholly blank, especially in 1777 and 1778, before a revival of confidence and lack of profits in agriculture began to draw individuals back into mercantile life.

Although many accounts had to be consulted and some yielded useful data, first emphasis was placed on continuous records, particularly on those in which both account and letter books have been preserved, as is the case with Reynell and Coates (later Josiah and Samuel Coates), James and Drinker, and the Hollingsworth family. This last-named ubiquitous group has written a page of as yet not fully explored commercial history, to which the student of prices in these years is especially indebted for continuous records of many agricultural staples, to say nothing of their activity in the tobacco trade, milling, iron manufacture, and importation. With members of the family scattered from Virginia and Maryland through Delaware and Pennsylvania, all communicating with one another and with their clients and suppliers, they have left not only prices current and bulky well-kept accounts but copious comment on contemporary activity and the place of an interrelated mercantile group in it.

While the city of Philadelphia was occupied by the British (September

1777 to June 1778), price quotations were of two types, those within and those without the metropolis. Some merchants whose records were used moved out of the city along with Congress, making it possible to follow, though with increased difficulty, the movement of prices outside the city, where the primary interest of the study during the occupation lies. The account book of the younger Drinkers, John and Henry, along with that of Charles Wharton who remained in the city—the one kept in old Pennsylvania paper and the other in sterling—provide a means of contrasting the prices of some staples within and without the occupied area. For the months of occupation, a great deal of culling of records was necessary to obtain prices of even a few commodities, what with the scattering of supplies, the cutting off of the port and hence of direct imports, and the increasing problem, with a currency made more unstable by adverse military events, of provisioning an army.

For knowledge of the many expedients of the middle years of war, use was made of the accounts and letters of Chaloner and White, Philadelphia merchants, and of the correspondence of Ephraim Blaine and John Davis, all concerned with purchasing army supplies in upstate areas, whose letters have to do with price regulations, quantities of goods available, and the more or less continuous problems of transportation. Within the city, as activity revived, one could rely upon the accounts of Shinkle and Graff for beverages, upon Edward Penington for prices of loaf sugar and of supplies for his refinery, and upon Matthew Irwin, Stephen Girard, and many less-known merchants for both West India and domestic goods.

A notable aspect of the postwar years is the gradual reentry into trade of so many prominent colonial merchants, although not all of them returned to their former specialties. Benjamin Fuller, shrewdly anticipating the likely deluge of dry goods, expanded his West India trade and turned to dry goods only after a stable government had been formed. Even Josiah and Samuel Coates made no importations on their own account in the early postwar years. They expanded their trade with New England and, in accounting for their restraint in pushing trade in other directions, explained, "The precarious state of public and private credit forbids us still from running the risques, which many of our countrymen do to their own great injury, and the ruin of their unsuspecting friends."[1]

The emphasis on the tobacco trade by Robert Morris and his associates

[1] May 26, 1786, Josiah and Samuel Coates to Robert and Henry Coleman & Co.

is well known, as is the activity of Pelatiah Webster in the New England area. The spread-out mercantile organization developed by Peter Kuhn in his concentration upon trade with the southern states is typical of the postwar activity of many other Philadelphia mercantile houses which had expanded geographically in the intervening years. He, too, was interested in the tobacco trade, though he turned to dealings in corn and supplies for the China trade as tobacco was more and more taken up by Robert Morris. Lamar, Hill, and Bisset represent a specialized firm, formerly engaging in wine importation and later in triangular trade. Lamar was in London, Hill in Philadelphia, and Bisset and an agent, Gilliss, in Madeira. Wheat and flour were exported to Portugal, wine and bills of exchange sent to England, and English goods thence to Philadelphia. James and John Cox, whose available letters begin in 1786, were chiefly interested in the West India trade—the import of coffee and molasses and the export of wheat. Just getting himself established in Philadelphia during the war period was Stephen Girard, who, in the early postwar years, dealt largely in sugar and molasses. Robert Henderson, who transferred his dry goods business from New York after the British evacuated that city, may be mentioned as typical of the new merchants. Many other names to be found in later chapters belong to importers well known in colonial trade.

Market customs had changed less from colonial times than one might have expected, and the summary of market practices given by Coates in 1788 might have been made as well before the war as after.

> Remittances may be made to Philadelphia by many different ways: by produce of the West India islands, such as sugar, rum, and molasses, immediately to us which in general commands a quick sale. Remittance is also made by wines from Fayal, Teneriffe, Lisbon and Madeira, being the kind mostly in use, but 'tis to be observed that wines are apt to be very long on hand and afterwards to sell on long credit, which is very discouraging, especially Madeira, which won't sell until it is two or three years old and scarcely ever to profit, and other wines must be very good if they sell at all. Rice from Carolina is brought in quantities to us, but seldom pays a full freight. Bills of exchange are sometimes sent us to advantage. . . . From your port the chief articles that will turn quick into money are rum and molasses, good tow cloth and flaxseed in the fall. Sometimes sole leather, which is now only 13 pence, very good; sometimes candles will answer, though not at present. On receiving such goods, our custom is to advance the amount thereof in our produce to order and to charge on the sales 2½ per cent and on shipments 5 per cent—

storage we seldom charge, unless we hire stores, in which case we always do. All incidental charges, such as porterage, weighing, gauging, and cooperage, duties, etc., you are liable to.[2]

For purposes of comparing prices, the continuance of customary charges in the conduct of business and the survival of many seasoned mercantile houses is as helpful as it is remarkable. It is truly more a mark of the firm basis on which the commercial life of Philadelphia rested than of lack of change in the structure of trade. Throughout the comments, cited in the chapters on individual commodities, there is many a hint that the revival of trade, under way even in the later war years, entailed experimentation, changes in commercial organization, and appraisal of new and untried routes of trade. Some merchants, like Pelatiah Webster, survived the uncertainties of the years of conflict, inflation, loss of vessels, and even migration with their capital substantially intact; some were in a non-liquid position with heavy investments in land; and some, who had turned their attention to the southern trade, notably tobacco, had far-flung organizations and the obligation of underwriting or making loans to the local business houses serving as agents for them. Other profound and more far-reaching changes in the stability of laws, the state of domestic manufacture, and even the credit of men could not be appraised for decades. The statement of Robert Morris, as early as 1782, in a measure summarized the position of many at the beginning of the era of trade revival. "My property," he wrote, "was then and is now very much out of my power—a great part in the hands of other people, the remainder in land. What I had afloat has all been lost, and the amount of that loss, I will forbear to mention, as there might be in it an appearance of ostentation."[3]

The stirring story of the methods by which trade was revived has yet to be written. It can be understood only as part of the general history of a transition period which was regarded even by British observers as one of changes of deep and lasting significance. Contrasting the impact of the two decades between the Peace of Paris of 1763 and the Treaty of Versailles of 1783, a member of Parliament said, "Within that short period, we have seen the most astonishing events and revolutions in Europe, Asia, and America, that the history of mankind can

[2] June 5, 1788, Josiah and Samuel Coates to Faris and Stocker, presumably New England.

[3] July 18, 1782, Robert Morris to Colonel Richard Butler.

produce in so narrow a space of time. We have also seen the discovery of new countries, new people and new planets; and the discoveries in science and philosophy are such as the human mind had hitherto no conception of."[4]

Prices in Pennsylvania, upon which this study is concentrated, furnish but one of the many changing elements in which local manufacturing was being developed and commercial life finding new directions.

[4] *Gentleman's Magazine and Historical Chronicle,* October 1785, v. 55, p. 789.

CHAPTER II

THE GENERAL COURSE OF PRICES

AN OVER-ALL PICTURE, in the form of a combined index of prices for the years 1770 to 1790, can be made continuous only by using quotations in the different kinds of money dominant in the period. From 1770 to 1775, state paper (rated in Pennsylvania at 7 shillings 6 pence to the Spanish milled dollar) and a minor amount of coin furnished the medium of exchange in domestic trade. From 1775 to April 1781, which includes the years of concern about inflation, state paper, although largely supplanted by continental notes, remained in use until Philadelphia was captured in September 1777 and circulated in the city during the occupation. In 1778, after the city was repossessed, the colonial issue was called in. The existence of state paper created no special price problem except insofar as it swelled the amount of currency in circulation, since in general the two forms of paper money depreciated together. From May 1781, after a few months of trading primarily in specie, until 1790, state paper, which at times depreciated mildly, again became the medium in daily use. In all years a small number of business transactions were made in specie and from 1779 onward, especially during the months of extremest inflation, the community enjoyed an increasing circulation of coin.

In a period when a variety of coins and paper money was circulating in trade, the affairs of everyone, whether trader, employer, landlord, workman, or housewife, were affected by the equivalence between the value of the money of account in the different colonies and the foreign-minted coins. The issuance of paper money by the Continental Congress in 1775 added to the confusion, and the citizens' lack of faith in the new currency contributed to the inflation of the subsequent years.

To be sure, the monetary units of pounds, shillings, and pence, in which accounts were kept and in which most of the state issues were made, were continued during and after the war, even though Congress designated its issues in dollars. The rating of the Spanish milled dollar, which differed in each of the colonies, remained unchanged. In Pennsylvania it equalled 90 pence, thereby making for the fractional division of the dollar into ninetieths in that state.

The Basic Trend

A general index for such an era serves to indicate the speed at which depreciation progressed or, in terms of prices, the extent of the spectacular and uneven inflation. It has, at best, limitations, the most serious of which arises from the small number of commodities that can be included in it. Important war materials, for which demand was immediate once hostilities started, are represented only insofar as their influence is reflected in prices of bar iron and tar. The products of local manufacture—stimulated by the war to the point of replacing some former imports, increasing craft employment, and providing some new forms of investment—can rarely be represented even by their basic raw materials. Tools, canvas for tents, and many articles of clothing are missing. As monetary inflation became severe with paper values falling continuously, investors sought safety in purchases of land, city lots, trade in staples of other parts of the continent, and purchases of some durable goods. None of these areas of investment are directly represented in the total price index. From the point of view of its use as an over-all level of prices, the restricted coverage of the best general average of prices that can now be constructed should be noted. The limitations, however, should not be overstressed, since agriculture, iron manufacture, and many of the important articles regularly entering into trade are included and would be sensitive to changes in other parts of the economy.

The major analysis of prices must rest upon the behavior of individual commodities, since during the war years each had, in a sense, its own peculiar supply and price conditions. Only by comparing the movements of particular commodities can an indication of the impact of war and inflation upon different sectors of the economy be gained. Of the fifteen articles for which continuous monthly prices can be constructed by the use of many sources, not all were equally sensitive to inflationary pressure. In fact, at critical times, such a dispersion occurred in the indices of the fifteen items as to obscure any over-all tendency.

As one means of summarizing the varied movements of the individual series, the monthly median of the fifteen items for 1770 to 1790 has been located. This record overlaps the closing years of a period included in a previous study, *Prices in Colonial Pennsylvania.* Before the beginning of the period covered by this study, prices in Philadelphia dropped more than 17 per cent in a comparatively unbroken recession from November 1766 to April 1769,[1] and an advance from the low point then established had not progressed far when, in the spring of 1769, the merchants of Philadelphia joined with those of Boston and New York in an agreement to refrain from importing British goods. This measure, in force for the first nine months of 1770, did not prevent a selective advance in prices of domestic staples, salt, and a few other commodities, which gained momentum as the force of the European demand for grain made itself felt. As a result, prices of domestic staples not only reached the highest peak of colonial years in 1772 but held at relatively high levels until 1774.

The use of 1771 to 1773 as a base for the price indices tends to minimize the extent of the prewar boom and later contractions brought about on the whole by mild and gradual monthly variations. Barring the decline in May 1775, the month-to-month changes from 1770 to the spring of 1776 amounted to little more than 4 per cent, except in six months, and in the main fell below 3 per cent.

By contrast with prewar years, prices advanced briskly in the last nine months of 1776, and by September all commodities were participating in a strong upward surge. The unusual tempo of this rise is indicated by an advance in the median in December 1776 of 25 per cent above the preceding month. Prices were then more than double their prewar average, and doubled again before the next year's end. Once under way, the accelerated rise of prices was at times temporarily checked, but never long halted until, in May 1781, continental currency ceased to circulate. How rare these lulls were is indicated by the movement of the median, which in the 64 months beginning January 1776, without any correction for seasonal variation, showed a decline below the preceding month only nine times and was unchanged only twice.

The largest month-to-month increases occurred in the fall and early winter of 1779 when, in a single month, prices soared more than 45 per cent over the previous month, followed by three months of further rapid expansion. As a result of four years of inflationary rise, average

[1] Anne Bezanson, Robert D. Gray, and Miriam Hussey, *Prices in Colonial Pennsylvania*, p. 308.

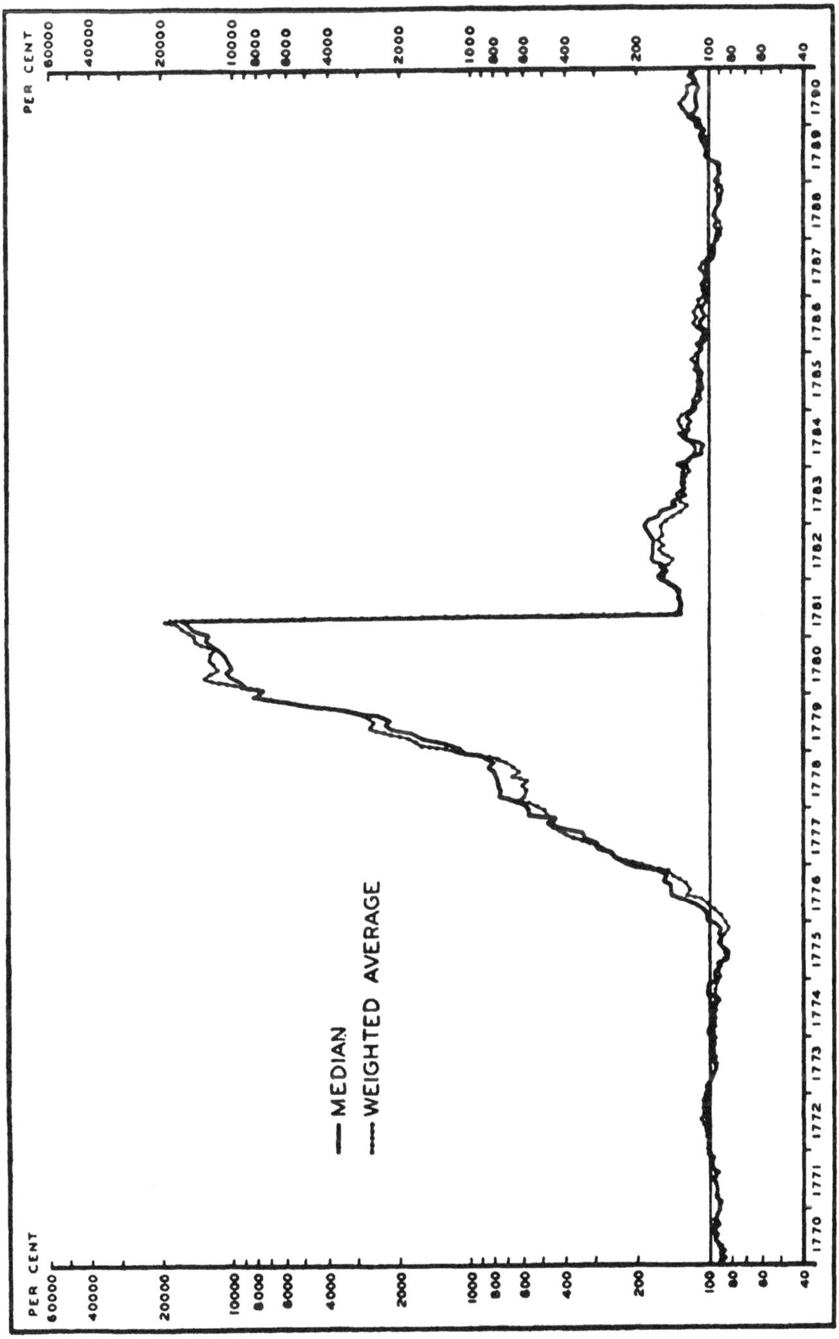

CHART I—MEDIAN AND WEIGHTED AVERAGE OF MONTHLY WHOLESALE PRICES OF FIFTEEN COMMODITIES IN PHILADELPHIA, 1770-1790
(Base—Monthly Average, 1771-1773)

prices at the close of 1779 were more than seven times their level at the beginning of this critical year. The price level by then was so high that later percentage increases from month to month seem small, though the value of continental money continued to sink until the median reached a peak at 16,502 in April 1781, the month of its final acceptance as a medium of exchange.

Commodities of foreign origin and others limited in supply led in the first phases of upswing, and their indices had leaped far ahead before grain and its products had even ended their long declines. As a result, the dispersion of the relatives of the fifteen commodities gradually increased. By October 1777, the average percentage deviation[2] from the median had reached 92, the widest scatter of the whole period. Once domestic articles began to soar, the deviation lessened as lagging items caught up with those first to rise. Such speculation in commodities as the war induced drew its stimulus from the price differential between commodities and the uneven impact of inflation upon articles of unlike origin and sensitivity.

The disappearance of continental currency effected no marked decrease in the percentage deviation of items away from the median. In fact, the dispersion was greater in 1782 than it had been in 1779 and 1780 when grain products especially were leaping upward at an alarming rate. After the peace, the average deviation narrowed suddenly, but once shipping was resumed the demand for grains and the lowered price of imports resulted in crosscurrents in commodity movements and a wider spread between price series than had been typical of prewar behavior.

Obviously, the demise of continental currency had a drastic effect upon the nominal level of prices. In the first four months following April 1781 the median of fifteen series was only about 33 per cent above prewar prices. From the lowest point of these months, July 1781, one might date the beginning of an upswing which, by the close of 1782, had lifted prices 90 per cent above prewar years. At this time, the median not only reached the maximum of postwar years but was higher than in November 1776, when continental paper was said to be the only currency in circulation.

[2] The average deviation expressed as a percentage of the median from which it was derived is referred to throughout the text as the "average percentage deviation."

The gradual downward drift of prices until April 1789 followed no regular pattern. Months of high prices in 1784 were followed by relatively stable movements in the following year. It was not until August 1787 that the persistent decline dropped the median below the prewar level. In terms of the general average, it was six years after Yorktown before prices were as low as they had been before the war. In terms of individual movements among the series, there was no return to prewar patterns within the years covered in this analysis.

Inflationary Pressures

Any summary measure, especially one for a period of disordered currency with prices rising unevenly, not only conceals the wide deviation of items from each other but, in the case of the median, minimizes the influence of the most extreme changes in particular series. A comparison with the weighted arithmetic average supplements the picture of the general course of prices by giving emphasis to products important in daily consumption.[3]

As might be expected, the two measures differ only slightly from 1770 to 1775 when price movements, though variable, were comparatively mild. One might infer from both measures that prices drifted upward slightly from July 1775, though an unbroken rise did not occur before December. From then, the comparative positions of the two indices fall into four distinct periods: (1) from December 1775 to April 1777 the median overtops the average in all but one month; (2) from May 1777 to October 1777 the median, rising less steeply than the average, falls below it; (3) from November 1777 to November 1778 the median again overtops the average; (4) from December 1778 to November 1781, except in four months, the average soars above the median.

These swift changes depict the difference in sensitivity of groups

[3] Weights, more or less arbitrary, were developed on the basis of exports in 1773, the standard set for army rations in February 1778, and army supplies in June 1780. They are:

Beef	10	Flour, Superfine	15	Rum, West India	7
Chocolate	0.5	Iron, Bar	9	Sugar, Muscovado	7
Coffee	3	Molasses	3	Tar	2
Corn	8	Pepper	0.5	Tea, Bohea	2
Flour, Common	15	Pork	10	Wheat	8

of commodities. The median and the average failed to conform in the first period when West India products began a rapid rise while the more abundant domestic staples continued to decline. In other words, in the early stages of the war the effect of inflation upon commodities depended upon the supply situation. Those in which surpluses existed, primarily staple domestic articles, lagged in the first phases of price advance.

The state of supplies had a bearing, too, upon the scope of price regulations. A rising trend in West India goods attracted attention, even before April 1776 when the ports were opened to foreign trade. Until early that year, it had been possible to assume that the Continental Association of October 20, 1774, would, by voluntary agreement supplemented by boycott of violators, prevent an advance in prices above the levels of 1774, except in the case of such admittedly scarce items as salt and military supplies. As prices of West India goods edged upward, a committee of the Committee of Safety began its series of piecemeal controls by placing maximum prices upon a selected list of commodities, primarily those of West India origin. It was hoped that the opening of the ports and the lifting of restrictions on exports would not only bring in much-needed supplies but automatically restore prices to their accustomed levels.

The period from December 1775 to April 1777, during which the median rose more than 200 per cent, includes the last months of voluntary price control and a brief experiment in compulsory control of selected items by local authorities. After April 1776, only green tea and salt remained on the list of regulated items. In the case of salt, it was hoped that by limiting through careful rationing the quantity to be purchased by any one consumer and by uniform sales prices a special committee would be able to achieve regional allocations as well as price stability. By the end of 1776 the control of salt had to be abandoned because there was not enough to allocate.

Contemporary opinions differ on the effect of the short phase of committee control of prices. As prominent a merchant house as Reynell and Coates noted an abrupt rise in prices of West India products as soon as the controls were lifted; others cited abuses resulting from the controls, such as extra charges for containers and services, a general shortening of terms of credit, and the shipment of scarce articles to parts of the continent where prices were higher—in one case as large a shipment as 500 hogsheads of molasses. The claim of alleged abuses, not immediately reflected in prices, was reiterated in later phases of the war as an argument against any reintroduction of price tariffs.

Conclusive evidence on the effectiveness of the first experiments in regulating prices cannot be drawn from statistical records. Many new factors were affecting the price level, some definitely creating an unusual demand for goods and some increasing family spending power. In this stirring period, the beehive of artisan workshops for which Philadelphia and its vicinity was noted was expanded by war contracts and supplemented by gun, gunlock, and cannon manufacture, cloth weaving, frigate building, tent making, and a diversity of other war undertakings. The putting-out system became so general, especially in spinning for the textile plants, that, by the middle of 1776, 4000 women were reputed to be employed in their own homes, thus expanding family income before the price upswing became general. In more direct ways, continental currency, entrusted to the heads of military companies, was distributed among the families of needy "associators," as participants in the war were termed, a practice which as late as 1779 Washington deplored on the ground that such maintenance of the families of soldiers "at the public expense is peculiar to us and is incompatible with the finances of any government."[4]

The use of a currency that circulated freely between colonies, too, was beginning to make itself felt. By March 1776 continental currency was being sent from Connecticut "to purchase sundries" in Philadelphia,[5] and somewhat later from as far as Haverhill, Massachusetts, to pay for supplies.[6] Circulation of the currency, too, was speeded by private trading, large-scale purchases by the state, the measures adopted to divert manpower, and increased local means of consumption. These basic changes connected with conversion to war had a gradual impact compared with the military events at the close of the year which induced a migration of families from Philadelphia and the transport of supplies to outlying areas. It was to this migration and the haste and alarm which accompanied it that Robert Morris attributed the speedy depreciation of the last quarter of 1776, the first full year of war. After the danger of im-

[4] May 10, 1779, General George Washington at Headquarters to Brigadier General Maxwell; Jared Sparks, editor, *The Writings of George Washington*, v. 6, p. 253.

[5] March 6, 1776, Benjamin Marshall and Brothers Waste Book (in Christopher, Jr., and Charles Marshall Ledger).

[6] May 18, 1776, Samuel Souther, Haverhill, Mass., to Reynell and Coates.

mediate capture was over, Morris wrote to the President of Congress, stressing the interrelated factors that had contributed to increasing inflation.

> The removal of Congress from this city had a pernicious effect on the credit of their money. You will consider Philadelphia from its centrical situation, the extent of its commerce, the number of its artificers, manufacturers and other circumstances, to be to the United States what the heart is to the human body in circulating the blood. The continental currency is perpetually passing and repassing through it for commercial and other purposes and it carries with it from hence, wherever it goes some proportion to what it bears here. This is now verified, for since it sunk here the depreciation is gradually extending to the extremities.[7]

The period from May to October 1777 requires little explanation, since it tallies closely with the second movement of metropolitan supplies and migration of inhabitants to the surrounding countryside. In this case, the military danger had been long anticipated. Congress recommended, as early as mid-April 1777, that the Pennsylvania executives "request the commanding officer of the continental forces in this city" to remove to safe and convenient locations all supplies that would aid the enemy or by their loss "distress the continental army."[8] From the movements of the two armies, citizens, too, could anticipate enough to bring about a gradual dispersal of families and movable property. As a result, wagons from the surrounding area were kept in readiness for private and public use. It is, in many ways, surprising that the outlay for storage depots, the necessary disregard of costs, the shortages from transit delays, and the scattering of supplies, coupled with a belief by some that continental money would not be redeemed, raised prices only 49 per cent in these months. The character of the rise is notable, however, since it accentuated the spread in the price level which was carrying imported goods far out of relation to those of domestic origin.

November 1777 to November 1778 includes most of the nine months of British occupation (September 25, 1777 to June 18, 1778) and the readjustment following it. Experiments in price control and support of the currency in this period were directed at specific points of practical difficulty. Within the city the occupying authorities immediately set price maximums and limited unit purchases to small quantities, with

[7] February 4, 1777, Robert Morris to John Hancock, President of Congress, Baltimore.
[8] April 16, 1777, *Journals of the Continental Congress*, v. 7, p. 271.

enforcement in the hands of merchants; outside the metropolis, the powers of control rested with the Council of Safety, but enforcement was for a short period entrusted to commissaries.[9]

Previously, according to Colonel Clement Biddle, during the uncertain movements of the army, temporary supplies and especially forage had "always been paid at different rates according to our situation."[10] With the metropolitan market closed, the procurement problem had shifted from one of civilian to one of army supply, and the commissaries for a time seemed willing to outdo the Council of Safety in their eagerness to avoid an undue price rise in a selected list of domestic staples, in this way initiating a period in which the price of domestic provisions failed to reflect the extent of monetary depreciation.

It is true that the exact limits implied in the original price lists could not always be followed, but on the whole circumstances favored the regulations. An illustration of the process by which control with a measure of flexibility was effected may be drawn from the correspondence of an agent of the Quartermaster in Reading who, on December 5, 1777, wrote, "I have just to inform you that there is positive orders that there is no more than 8 shillings 6 pence to be paid for wheat in our Department,"[11] only to revise his orders two weeks later to: "You had better calculate what grain you will want as I have done and advertise in York and Cumberland to each township to bring in their proportion. It takes with the people here . . . Everything at the old price, except wheat I have raised to 10 shillings."[12] The effect on prices is clear, but the contribution of such methods to the war effort is another matter, and happily by February 1778 the method of appointing state commissioners in every county was adopted and later followed by an advance of about one-third in the prices offered to farmers.

By June 1, 1778, the act of regulating the several articles on the price lists was wholly suspended.[13] Soon a prospect of poor crops, fur-

[9] The Committee of Safety, appointed June 30, 1775, was reorganized and enlarged as the Council of Safety on July 23, 1776. The Council served until December 6, 1777.

[10] November 3, 1777, Clement Biddle to Thomas Wharton, Jr., President of the Supreme Executive Council of Pennsylvania, *Pennsylvania Archives*, 1st ser., v. 5, p. 739.

[11] December 5, 1777, Mark Bird, Reading, to Sirs.

[12] December 21, 1777, Mark Bird, Reading, to Colonel John Davis, Deputy Quartermaster General. Prices approved at Lancaster by the General Assembly on December 26, 1777, and published in the *Pennsylvania Gazette* at Lancaster, January 10, 1778, included a long list of domestic articles.

[13] June 3, 1778, *Pennsylvania Packet*.

ther gradual depreciation of the bills of credit, active demand, and the preparation for French participation in the war combined to raise prices of foodstuffs alarmingly and gradually restored the former relation of the weighted average and the median. To halt the market rise, an embargo was placed on the shipment of provisions out of the state.

In terms of commodities, a steep upswing in prices of imports dominated the first three periods of war inflation. In all, molasses, rum, sugar, and normally pepper and tea were persistently far above the median. Among the domestic goods, in the same three periods, corn, wheat, flour, and pork ranked well below the median. Only beef, among domestic staples, was in active enough demand to be raised above the median in 1776 and the first half of the following year. Thus, the momentum of the advance in the first phases of the spectacular rise in prices was supplied by imported goods and resulted in the widest dispersion in the price levels found at any time in the war years.

Toward the last quarter of 1778, the fourth period and a new era in price behavior began. In August 1778, bar iron, which heretofore had maintained a central position in the series, moved above the median for the first time in these years. Common flour rose so rapidly that by November 1779 it was not only far above the median but had outdistanced products like sugar, coffee, chocolate, and tea. Beef, later joined by pork, displaced other items near the top of the price scales. Only toward the spring of 1780, with soaring prices in which some West India articles led, was there a short period of wide divergence of the median and the average. Their relationship in the final stages of depreciation is only partially attributable to the weight assigned to the chief domestic farm staples. It is also the result of the rise of beef and pork to a place among the commodities with highest prices and the long-delayed upswing in prices of flour which carried it to a rank formerly occupied by less essential commodities.

The later stages of inflation, in which price advances were more serious than before, were characterized by experiments in measures of monetary control which at most were meant to keep the depreciation from growing worse. But even the calling in of two early issues of currency in 1779 created, in the short run, an increased demand for goods. Neither the taxes to be furnished by the states, nor the cumbersome method of allocating "specific supplies" among them, brought speedy enough results to support the war effort efficiently, and by March

1780 Congress had to resort to a drastic official devaluation of all issues.

The extent of the progressive climb in prices may be summarized briefly by comparing the percentage change in the median from April to April of each year.

TABLE 1
ANNUAL PERCENTAGE CHANGE IN MEDIAN
APRIL OF ONE YEAR FROM APRIL OF PRECEDING YEAR

Year	Percentage Change	Year	Percentage Change
1776	+ 24	1779	+131
1777	+153	1780	+489
1778	+156	1781	+ 59

DOMESTIC AND IMPORTED COMMODITIES

Looking more closely at the movements of the war years by the use of separate indices of goods of domestic and foreign origin makes it evident that the phase of unequal advance in the two series lasted until the spring of 1778, when the rise in West India products halted or proceeded mildly for as much as eight months. Meantime, not only did domestic commodities mount higher in every month from November 1777 through May 1779 but the tempo increased in the last nine months of this rise. Both groups were stabilized for a few months in the summer of 1779, only to surge forward in the last quarter of the year. In the month of September alone, domestic goods rose 61 per cent above the preceding month. Two months later, West India goods more than balanced this rise by an increase of 67 per cent above the previous month. Both proceeded at a slower pace for the rest of the period of dealings in depreciated currency. The retreat of both groups, in the summer of 1780, might have been as encouraging to contemporaries as it looks in retrospect were it not certain that in this period the high levels were in no way a reflection of scarcity.

The extent of the spread in prices before 1779 is significant for the indication it gives of the dating of the period of most profitable trading in commodities. Those importers who could keep their ships active in the early years of war, when domestic staples were relatively low and prices of imported products extremely high, must have enjoyed a margin to cover the risks of seizure and increased costs of shipping such as never

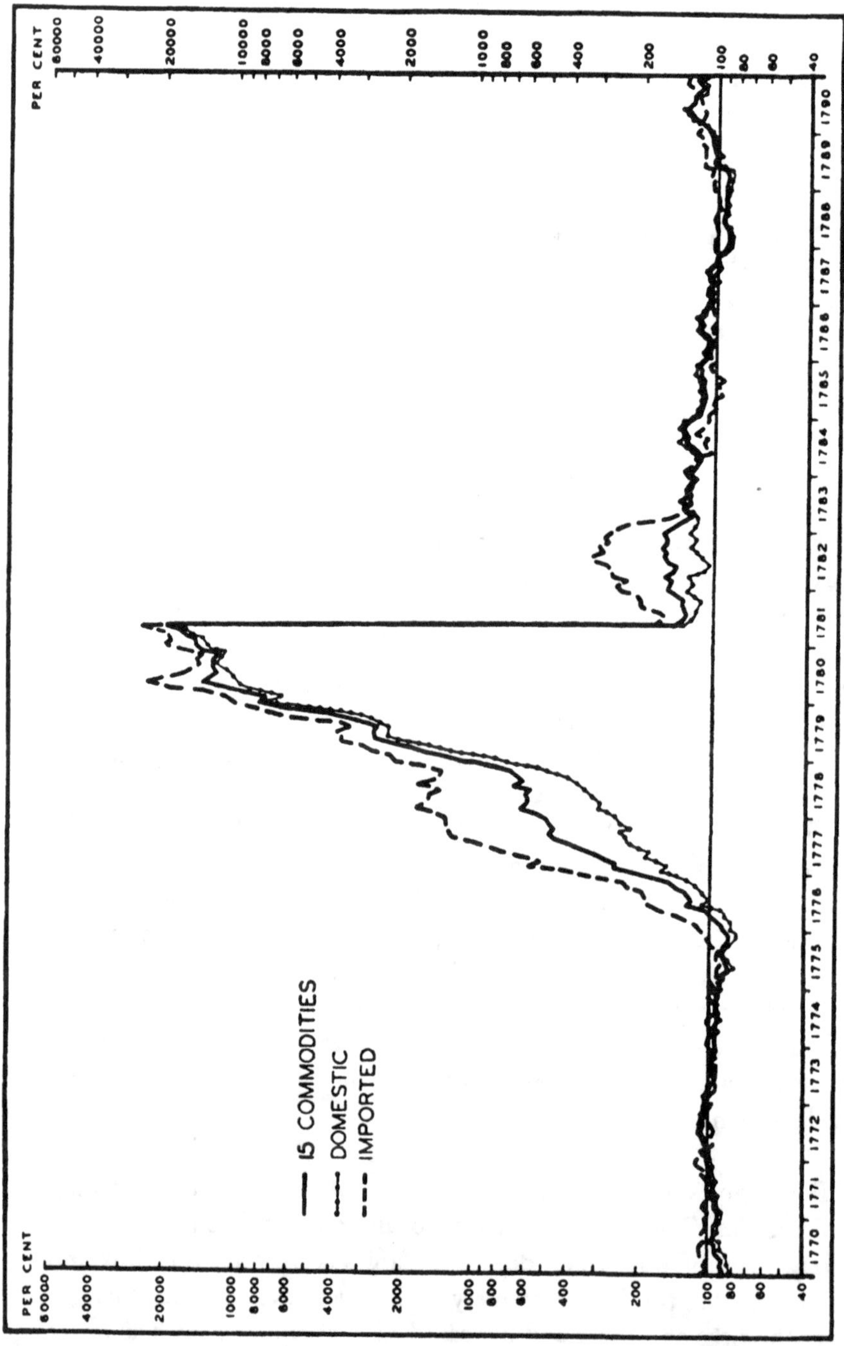

CHART II—WEIGHTED AVERAGES OF MONTHLY WHOLESALE PRICES OF FIFTEEN COMMODITIES AND OF DOMESTIC AND IMPORTED COMMODITIES IN PHILADELPHIA, 1770-1790
(Base—Monthly Average, 1771-1773)

recurred in later stages of the inflation. Confirmation for this inference will be found in the quotations of merchants in the chapters dealing with particular commodities, but that the reversal in opportunity for gain was well enough known to contemporaries to be noted in general terms in the brief of the committee of city merchants late in 1779 is clear in the statement, "A greater part of those lately engaged in monopolizing have been losers and not gainers by the business."[14]

From commodity prices, no conclusion can be drawn about the opportunity for other forms of speculation. In a period when the price level was steadily rising, those merchants holding goods for higher prices would incur little risk. Articles could still be bought in advance of needs, products transferred to other areas where prices were more favorable, funds invested in durables, or advantage taken of the slower pace of depreciation in other states. The significance of the spread in the curves of domestic and imported products is in defining the period when the fanning out of prices would seem to have made the exchange of Pennsylvania's agricultural staples for West India imports especially advantageous, leaving out of consideration all but the terms of local exchange.

All the sudden fluctuations in prices in these unsettled years cannot be connected with war currency. A marked cycle in prices of imports, after continental currency ceased to circulate, must be attributed to captures and other disturbances in the islands. It started at a low index of 164 in July 1781 and reached a peak of 323 in July 1782, with no counterpart in domestic goods. Drastic contraction began with the circulation of rumors of peace.

This general picture of the course of prices from 1770 to 1790 includes the changes of two decades in the level of world prices, a notable episode in currency depreciation, and the additional costs of a war in which commodities had to be transported "from the extremes of the continent."[15] An attempt to isolate some of these factors involves attention to the impact of the period on commodities representative of particular sectors of the economy and the methods devised to accommodate to it.

[14] September 10, 1779, *ibid.*

[15] September 10, 1779, *ibid.*

CHAPTER III

MERCHANT PRACTICES AS EVIDENCE OF INFLATION

EVIDENCE of the early stages of inflation, other than the movement of prices, is at best fragmentary. Occasionally the premiums on half johannes (a Portuguese gold coin, much used in the colonies, rated at 60 shillings Pennsylvania currency, and generally referred to as a "half joe"), and on a variety of other coins in use, were cited. Rates of sterling exchange, though available throughout 1776, were at some times only nominal and at others influenced in the same way as the value of coins, by scarcity and the bidding of those anxious to leave the colonies. Only the most indirect statements could be expected from contemporaries, since many of them viewed the rise in prices as normal, at least until quotations passed the exceptionally high levels enjoyed by domestic producers in the trade of the early seventies. Had all commodities participated at once in the advance, or had the community not shared beforehand in the benefits of a period of boom in prices of staples, more alarm might have accompanied the first stages of the upswing.

Official scales of depreciation, used retroactively in settling accounts,[1] gave no attention to the inflation clearly evident in the index of prices in the last part of 1776. Only from qualitative evidence, such as preference for investment in durable goods and in land rather than in currency, unwillingness of dealers to sell non-perishable goods, unaccustomed adjustments in wages, changes in terms of sale of commodities, occasional transactions in coin, as well as contemporary comments, can even a risky estimate be made of the role played by unstable currency in price enhancement.

Two contemporary scales of depreciation beginning with January 1777 have long been available: the legal ratios for converting continental accounts to an equivalent in specie, tardily adopted by the Pennsylvania Assembly; and ratios derived from merchants' accounts

[1] See Table 3, Chapter IV, p. 65.

by Pelatiah Webster. The official scale of depreciation adopted by the Pennsylvania legislature in April 1781 for the settlement of all claims against the state had been preceded by a scale of depreciation developed in October 1780 for rating the certificates of pay due to the Pennsylvania soldiers, which was ordered to be kept up to date and the depreciation so ascertained published monthly in the Pennsylvania papers.

As early as 1778, Pelatiah Webster urged that a scale or table of exchange as accurate as possible be calculated to serve as a guide in all dealings involving paper and specie. In his essay published in August 1779, he deplored the general unwillingness of public officials to admit the extent of currency depreciation and advised that a scale of the relation of currency to specie be established and hard money received and paid into the continental Treasury according to it. At least as early as September 1779, merchants were using a table of depreciation prepared by Webster. His figures were derived from the accounts of a merchant who had regular dealings in specie, checked against the accounts of some other merchants. His weekly summary was the average of the highest and lowest rates of exchange between the two currencies. As Webster believed that the rise in prices before October 1776 could be attributed to the circumstances of the war and the depreciation of the last quarter of that year disregarded, he began his scales in January 1777.

Except in January and April 1777 and April and May 1779, the two tables of exchange are alike until January 1780, when they begin to differ substantially. All evidence of the extent of depreciation found in the course of this study, then, has been placed beside these contemporary scales with a view to modifying or confirming them. Attention must first be given, however, to any manifestation in 1776 of a fall in the purchasing power of currency.

Rates of Exchange on London in 1776

A premium of 4 per cent for the half johannes was referred to in Congress in the course of a debate on December 15, 1775, on a motion of Robert Morris to "consider of ways and means to bring in gold and silver and keep it in the country."[2] At that time, exchange rates on London were at the highest point of the year, though usually it was expected that bills of exchange would fall, once produce came plentifully to

[2] December 15, 1775, Richard Smith Diary, *Letters of Members of the Continental Congress*, v. 1, p. 276.

market. The appreciable decline in July and August and the rise in September and October 1775 brought the ratio close to the "par of exchange" of £166⅔ Pennsylvania currency for £100 sterling, usually referred to by merchants as 66⅔ with or without a percentage notation. It was, therefore, an unusually high rate for the close of a year that a Philadelphia merchant cited in December 1775 when he reported, "Bills are 73 to 74 per cent and likely to rise to 75 if not higher, according as opportunities offer to remit them,"[3] a forecast that was borne out in the movement of the following year.

TABLE 2
STERLING EXCHANGE RATES

Month	Monthly Average 1776	Monthly Average 1766-75	Percentage deviation 1776 from 10-year average
January	174.7	165.5	+ 5.6
February	176.0	163.6	+ 7.6
March	180.3	161.3	+11.6
April	180.0	163.5	+10.1
May	182.5	163.8	+11.4
June	188.8	164.0	+15.1
July	188.8	164.5	+14.8
August	190.0	163.4	+16.3
September	193.4	163.0	+18.7
October	195.0	163.8	+19.0
November	225.0	163.5	+37.6
December	250.0	161.2	+55.1

The sources of the quotations for 1776 deserve emphasis. Citations, which are frequent enough in the first three months to make the averages dependable, for the remainder of the year rest on no more than one or, at most, two quotations in the course of a month. The firm of Reynell and Coates, quoting rates of exchange to its New England clients in every month except one until August, commented in April, "Bills still continue very high, we believe 80 or upward,"[4] and by July, felt that the rate of 87½, which they cited, was nominal.[5]

[3] December 12, 1775, Reynell and Coates to Stephen Hooper, Newburyport.
[4] April 6, 1776, the same to the same.
[5] July 1, 1776, the same to William Teel, Newburyport.

Another indication of the sharp advance in rates on London is found in the correspondence of the agent of the Penn family about his difficulties in transmitting funds. In June 1776 he wrote, "Our exchange is high and tempting being 90 per cent."[6] He was less cheered in September to enclose bills of exchange "for a small sum only, . . . but small as they are, I can assure you I was glad to meet with them, though they cost 98 per cent. I have tried all in my power to get more bills, but they are actually not to be had. I have heard of some extravagant rates of exchange being offered for them far exceeding what I gave."[7] At this time, Robert Morris was sending bills of exchange to Martinique to preserve the credit of William Bingham, when produce could not be forwarded.[8]

Since the advance in exchange would be influenced by insurance, risks, freight charges, and other factors unconnected with the content of the currency, any quantitative conclusion as to the course of depreciation would be unsafe. A direct transfer of £19 in "currency money of Pennsylvania" for £10 sterling in September 1776, for the purchase of land, not only conforms to the direction exchange was taking but establishes a differential of 14 per cent between currency and specie in effecting the transaction.[9] If one may take the allowance made by Samuel Inglis, of the firm of Willing and Morris, of 1¼ to one in October and November 1776,[10] as a close estimate of the stage depreciation had reached, the contemporary scales might well be extended backward for at least four months.

The report of Robert Morris to the Commissioners in Paris after Congress moved to Baltimore giving a darker picture of the currency situation than most of the data so far cited should be discounted as a general description of the market. It was made during a period of great confusion and reflects both the strain of war and concern about depreciation. After referring to those who refused to take continental currency, Morris wrote, "Those that do receive it do it with fear and trembling, and you may judge of its value even amongst those when I tell you that £250 continental money, or 666⅔ dollars, is given for a bill of exchange of £100 sterling, sixteen dollars for a half johannes, two paper dollars for one of silver, three dollars for a pair of shoes, twelve dollars for a hat

6 June 11, 1776, Edmond Physick to Lady Juliana Penn, England.

7 September 17, 1776, the same to the same.

8 September 27, 1776, Willing and Morris to William Bingham, Martinique.

9 September 30, 1776, Edmond Physick receipt to Cadwalader Jones.

10 Samuel Inglis' Virginia Account with Willing and Morris.

and so on; a common laborer asks two dollars a day for his work and idles half his time."[11]

The Search for Stable Values

The qualitative evidence of depreciation is of many kinds. As early as October 1776, an essayist in the *Pennsylvania Evening Post* pointed out that the likely consequence of a quantity of continental currency greater than would be necessary as a medium of exchange would be a demand for durable goods or, as he phrased it, "People will choose to have their estates vested in any good of intrinsic value rather than in money."[12]

A hint that merchants were anxious to spend the paper money in their possession is furnished by a purchaser of tobacco who conditioned his purchase upon the acceptance of continental money in payment, "and as there is scarcely any other money passing amongst us we desire you will omit making the purchase unless it can be done payable in that money."[13] That there were tobacco growers who rated their product above the going prices, if paid in paper, was clear in the report, "Some will not take paper money, but say they would rather keep their tobacco."[14]

Since land had always been a common form of holding by Philadelphia merchants, one would not cite its purchase in relation to depreciation, had the buyer not stated his own motives. The explanation of a purchase of durables, of which there was little but land to choose, was given in December when General Howe's army was threateningly near.

> The company of Reynell and Coates having more continental money than at present they have any use for in this place, and having no prospect of laying it out, unless at a great loss, I take the liberty to send thee on their account . . . 2000 dollars of that currency which I desire thee to dispose of in the purchase of any article (excepting flour and those goods which are liable to perish in a short time by laying by) . . . Uncle Reynell also sends by this opportunity 3200 dollars to dispose of in like manner.[15]

[11] December 21, 1776, Robert Morris to Commissioners at Paris; Francis Wharton, editor, *The Revolutionary Diplomatic Correspondence of the United States*, v. 2, pp. 234-35.

[12] October 5, 1776, *Pennsylvania Evening Post*, reprinted in Pelatiah Webster, *Political Essays on the Nature and Operation of Money, Public Finances, and Other Subjects*, p. 3.

[13] September 3, 1776, Samuel Pleasants to Robert Pleasants & Co., Va.

[14] October 16, 1776, John Harper, Alexandria, to Abel James.

[15] December 18, 1776, Reynell and Coates to William Hartshorne, Va.

Adjustments in non-commodity prices took place along with, if not before, the resort to official price control. Their progress was marked by a series of gradual changes. In March 1776, the cost of subsistence for those in the marine service was raised from 7 shillings 6 pence to 10 shillings, or 33 per cent. In May, a shoemaker, advertising for journeymen, claimed that the piece rates he offered were 6 pence per pair above those offered by any other masters. At the same time, he hoped that the patrons who "favor him with their custom will consider the rise of every material he works with and pay 12 shillings per pair for bound shoes and 11 for plain."[16] The managers of the House of Employment concluded in June 1776 "that the wages hitherto given for spinning is not now equal to or sufficient for the maintenance of people so employed" and determined to give "one shilling per dozen for spinning good flax yarn"—a scale adopted also by the managers of the manufactory moving from "the corner of Ninth Street to the corner of Elbow Lane in Market Street."[17] Good flax was, by then, selling for 14 pence a pound, or double the price of February when the calculations of the managers were originally made.

In November, when the publishers of newspapers increased the annual subscription price 50 per cent, they cited "the extraordinary advance in the price of paper and other materials in the printing business."[18]

The pervasive character of the advance is indicated, too, by the willingness of well-informed officials to make adjustments, coupled with the decision of General Washington, on the basis of his own knowledge and "also by advice, to promise officers and men, that their pay shall be augmented *twenty-five per cent.*"[19]

Hoarding of old Pennsylvania paper, along with specie, which had begun with the issues of continental money, could be accounted for by the dislike of pacifist groups for a currency issued for the sole purpose of financing a war. Only a belief that the British would capture the city and accept the state currency as its medium of exchange would account for a preference for the "old paper currency of this Province" or would

[16] May 30, 1776, *Pennsylvania Evening Post.*

[17] June 25, 1776, *ibid.*

[18] November 6, 1776, *Pennsylvania Journal.*

[19] December 20, 1776, General George Washington to John Hancock, President of Congress; Jared Sparks, editor, *The Writings of George Washington,* v. 4, pp. 232-33.

make anyone offer "£300 Congress for £150 Pennsylvania currency,"[20] but the likelihood that continental money would not be redeemed if the British captured the city was a prospect which for a time seemed real enough to most observers.

An appraisal of many bits of evidence forces one to conclude that the decline in value of the medium of exchange in 1776 cannot be disregarded. Despite the downward trend of important staples like wheat and flour until the last quarter of the year, the speed and character of the uneven rise in other articles completely changed the established relation of products of one sector of the economy to the other. By the beginning of 1776, paper currency would buy 4 per cent less than specie. In July it would buy 8 per cent less, in September 14 per cent less, and by October and November, about 25 per cent less.[21]

It is not surprising that export staples failed to respond in the first stages of currency instability. Even without the curtailment of trade, grain and flour would have enjoyed a less active market in 1776 in southern Europe than they had a few years before. According to Parr and Bulkeley, shippers did not lose much in the first months of embargo. By November 1775, these consignees were meeting difficulties in disposing of freight already carried to Lisbon. "Prices of wheat and flour are very low," they reported, "and supplies from the Western Island, England, etc., are daily dropping in, so that if trade was not interrupted nothing to advantage could be done from the continent."[22] The downward course of prices of grain through June 1777 at Amsterdam not only confirms this opinion but pictures the extent of the European recession.[23] More important evidence is found in the middle Atlantic area in the huge supplies of wheat and its products, so in excess of demand that even in 1777 wheat of the growth of 1775 was being advertised for sale in Philadelphia and Baltimore. In the light of these supplies, only marked depreciation, speeded by unfavorable military events and accompanied in 1776 by reports of light crops, could have reversed the trend of grain prices.

[20] December 21, 1776, Francis Johnston to Brigadier General Thomas Mifflin, *Pennsylvania Archives*, 1st ser., v. 5, p. 125.

[21] See Table 3, Chapter IV, p. 65.

[22] November 18, 1775, Parr, Bulkeley & Co., Lisbon, to Reynell and Coates.

[23] N. W. Posthumus, *Inquiry into the History of Prices in Holland*, Table 1.

Depreciation in 1777

By the beginning of 1777, though the speed of the price advance moderated, it was widely recognized that some means had to be devised to support the credit of continental money. Congressional action took the form of making the currency a legal tender in the payment of taxes and debts and of passing strict laws against premium dealings in specie in sales and contracts. Though the regulations were an indirect recognition of depreciation, the attempt to ignore the differential between the value of coin and paper complicated the settlement of estates. Stephen Collins soon sought advice about taking continental money for debts due to the Barrell estate which he was engaged in settling.[24] His concern was shared by others even before the President of Congress admitted, "The depreciation of the continental currency having been for some time past a most growing evil, it became absolutely necessary to provide some remedy against it."[25] Merchants, when possible, put part of their funds in land and other durable materials and the best-informed among them began to keep their accounts in ways that would insure something like stability of values. At first the methods in use were not uniform, but from the spring of 1777 there was a growing use of formulae for converting totals in continental money at a ratio which was assumed to be the price at which specie could be purchased.

That not all transactions were made with awareness of the decline in the buying power of paper may be inferred from the purchase of flour in January 1777 for hard money at 21 shillings 6 pence a hundredweight, or slightly less than it averaged in October 1776 in currency.[26] For a time old state paper, too, held a value above the continental, as the superintendent of the state salt works informed the Council of Safety by concrete illustration in his statement, "I can buy pork for 4 pence old money and 7 pence continental, wheat 6 shillings the old and 8 shillings continental, rye 4 shillings old, 5 shillings continental, corn 3 shillings 6 pence old, 5 shillings continental,"[27] a set of comparisons which would rate the two currencies, in January 1777, from 1¼ to 1¾ to one.

24 January 15, 1777, Stephen Collins to Jonathan Amory, Boston.

25 January 14, 1777, John Hancock to Maryland Assembly, *Letters*, v. 2, pp. 217-18.

26 January 15, 1777, Charles Humphrey Ledger.

27 January 18, 1777, Thomas Savadge to Council of Safety, *Pennsylvania Archives*, 1st ser., v. 5, p. 194.

For most of 1777, data for determining the stage of depreciation are limited. In February, Stephen Collins found little open to him in the way of durable investment. "There is no such thing," he wrote, "as bills of exchange to be bought here at any rate, and it is out of my power to invest the paper money on hand in any article of remittance whatever, almost at any price, except perishable commodities."[28] At the same time, Reynell and Coates, who in 1776 sent their surplus to the southward, were authorizing the use of £2500 Virginia currency (£3125 Pennsylvania) to purchase a lot there "which in thy opinion will bring the same money when trade revives again."[29]

The rarity of specie transactions makes significant a settlement on February 8 of £2741 9 shillings 3¾ pence sterling for £6853 13 shillings 3¼ pence in paper currency—a rate of £250 Pennsylvania currency for £100 sterling. At the former par of exchange, the total in Pennsylvania currency would have been £4569 4 shillings. The actual exchange basis tallies with the 1.5 for one which Webster accepted in his scale of depreciation for this date.

Only three kinds of data of the extent of depreciation in this critical year can be assembled, namely, the ratio used by merchants in converting transactions to what they felt to be stable values, the prices paid for occasional purchases of specie, mostly coin, and commodity transactions in specie for which the continental currency value is known. The average of the monthly ratios used by merchants in their accounts differs slightly from those given by Webster. On the assumption that the amount of paper given in purchases of specie would be the most sensitive indicator of depreciation, the three types of evidence have been separated and the results summarized in the chapter following this discussion of contemporary practices.

The ratios derived from commodity transactions in specie, though more variable than the accounting formulae, tend to fluctuate with them. They are influenced by non-uniform practices among merchants and variations in ratios in converting small amounts. For instance, for January 1777, for which Webster cited a depreciation of 1.25 and the Assembly later arrived at 1.5 to one, ratios of 1.75 were found in sales of pork, 1.25 in rye, 1.33 in wheat, and 1.43 in corn. In February, when 1.5 was typical in merchants' accounts, a ratio of 2.05 appeared in sales

[28] February 3, 1777, Stephen Collins to Jonathan Amory, Boston.
[29] February 4, 1777, Reynell and Coates to William Hartshorne, Va.

of bar iron. Such differences in converting currency can be expected in any period and they are cited mainly to show how hazardous a general ratio derived after the event may be in months in which the number of transactions for which we have information is limited.

In settling the account of Willing and Morris, at a later date, Inglis accepted 2 and 2.5 for one for March and April 1777 respectively. By April, Hollingsworth had adopted a 3 for one basis, though later in the year he conformed to the practices of others. Other evidence is inconclusive. On March 12, Congress was willing to pay 7 shillings 6 pence currency for woolens which cost one shilling sterling, or about 3.75 to one, allowing for the customary markup of 100 per cent on sterling cost.[30] On the other hand, Irish linens, calculated on the same basis, sold for about 2.25 to one.[31] Since early March, General Washington had expected the British army to "make a push for Philadelphia, so soon as the roads will allow them to move,"[32] and it is not surprising that merchants were speculating about "the effect . . . upon the paper money (if they should succeed) in Philadelphia."[33]

Observers throughout this period viewed the depreciation as one that could still be corrected by some forceful move by Congress. Such an attitude was in the mind of William Duer when he wrote, "The depreciation of the continental money is astonishingly rapid, and I see with concern that no attempts are made to check so fatal a measure."[34] In May 1777, the owner of a woolen factory complained that since he undertook his contract less than a year previously, the cost of producing a yard of cloth had increased 37.5 per cent. In fact, cloth that he contracted to supply at 18 shillings a yard now cost him more than 25 shillings, and worse still, the prospect was that prices of raw wool would soon advance.[35] John Adams, at this period, looked upon the "redun-

[30] A markup of 100 per cent, as used in the period, covered the conversion to Pennsylvania currency plus an allowance for expenses.

[31] March 12, 1777, Francis Lewis, Baltimore, to the New York Convention, *Letters*, v. 2, p. 298.

[32] March 6, 1777, General George Washington, Morristown, N. J., to William Duer; Sparks, *op. cit.*, v. 4, p. 353.

[33] March 27, 1777, Reynell and Coates to Stephen Hooper, Newburyport.

[34] April 17, 1777, William Duer to Abraham Ten Broeck, President of New York Convention, *Letters*, v. 2, p. 331.

[35] May 16, 1777, Samuel Wetherill, Jr., to Board of War for Pennsylvania, *Pennsylvania Archives*, 1st ser., v. 5, p. 342.

dancy of the medium of exchange" as only one of three misfortunes which were felt at once. It was accompanied by a decrease in the supply of goods at market and an increase of demand "occasioned by two large armies in the country."[36] Merchants, impressed by the advance on first cost for dry goods "at vendue," were attempting to find a stable basis for comparisons by keeping each other informed of the markup on sterling cost. For instance, a Philadelphia merchant, who prepared a prices current for staples the first week in June, reported "dry goods in general very high from 800 to 1000 per cent on the first cost from Europe,"[37] a ratio in fact not unlike that noted in March at vendue in Baltimore.

Were it not for speculation in coin, the extent of depreciation in June 1777 could be established directly by the rating of various coins in exchange for continental paper. The half johannes, which contained 9 pennyweight and had exchanged for £3 in Pennsylvania throughout prewar years, continuing to pass in most transactions at that rate until May 1776, was reported to have exchanged in June 1777 for £15 to £20; the English guinea, weighing 5 pennyweight 6 grains, which was rated at £1 15 shillings in May 1776, had reached £6; the Spanish milled dollar, the "piece of eight," rated at 7 shillings 6 pence in Pennsylvania, was now £1 10 shillings, or a rate of 4 to one.[38] These ratings exceed the depreciation of 2.5 to one accepted in Webster's scale and followed by other Philadelphia merchants. On the other hand, a lower rate of depreciation was agreed upon between Philadelphia merchants buying one-fourth of a vessel in Curaçao, "We to pay at the rate of twelve shillings continental currency for every piece of eight they may cost at Curaçao."[39] It may be that the lack of uniformity in the allowance for depreciation in midsummer can be laid to the threatening position of the armies, the movement of goods and families out of the area, and the hasty preparations to protect the city, along with a general overrating of coin.

About the time that Alexander Hamilton was warning Gouverneur Morris of the shock an adverse military event would be to faith in the

[36] May 26, 1777, John Adams to Thomas Jefferson, *Letters*, v. 2, p. 375.

[37] June 2, 1777, Alexander Abrahams to Michael Gratz, Fredericksburg; William Vincent Byars, *B. and M. Gratz, Merchants in Philadelphia, 1754-1798*, p. 165.

[38] June 22, 1777, James Lang, Lancaster, to Board of War for Pennsylvania, *Pennsylvania Archives*, 1st ser., v. 5, pp. 396-97.

[39] June 1777, Christopher, Jr., and Charles Marshall Ledger.

currency,[40] a transaction in which an ounce of silver exchanged for 26 shillings, instead of 8 shillings 6 pence, indicates a relation of currency to silver of 3 to one, in agreement with the practice of Hollingsworth and the scale of Webster.[41] August brought still further depreciation.

There is little evidence in the first months after the city was occupied by the British to check against the merchants' scales. Within the city, old Pennsylvania paper, which the non-associators had hoarded, was reported to be depreciated and Elizabeth Drinker recorded in her journal the payment of 3 half johannes for £60 of continental money, an emergency rating of nearly 7 to one.[42] Areas outside the city, from which the prices of commodities were drawn during the occupation, gave the currency a higher rating. Most specific are three detailed transactions of Samuel Wetherill, in which continental and specie exchanged at 4 for one, the rate given by Webster for the close of this year.

By November 1777, two months after the British occupied the city, the median of commodity prices was 480 per cent above the prewar average. The movement of the government out of Philadelphia was accompanied by a period of price control, limited to domestic commodities essential for the use of the army, enforced through action of commissaries, and made effective by lack of a metropolitan market. In the next months, the fixing of maximum prices on what were termed "material articles" prevented the index of prices from showing the full extent of currency depreciation. At times, merchants refer to sales at "the price the continental commissary pays"[43] in explaining variations from the agreed-upon price limits. Authority for deviations was given by President Wharton of the Pennsylvania Assembly in transmitting the prices to be paid for wheat, rye, corn, beef, and pork, in his instruction, "You will, however, be able from time to time to judge best of this matter, and perhaps will be under the necessity of varying occasionally."[44] Prices of particular articles, notably wheat, had to be sub-

[40] July 22, 1777, Alexander Hamilton to Gouverneur Morris; John C. Hamilton, editor, *Works of Alexander Hamilton*, v. 1, p. 31.

[41] July 26, 1777, John Ross account book.

[42] November 22, 1777, Henry D. Biddle, editor, *Extracts from the Journal of Elizabeth Drinker, 1759-1807*, p. 66.

[43] October 26, 1777, Charles Humphrey Daybook, 1772-1790.

[44] October 26, 1777, Thomas Wharton, Jr., President of the Supreme Executive Council of Pennsylvania, Lancaster, to Colonel William Buchanan, Commissary General of Purchases, *Pennsylvania Archives*, 1st ser., v. 5, p. 711.

stantially increased in November, but in the main the lack of any concentrated market made control of domestic commodities effective while prices of uncontrolled imported goods soared.

A concession in the transport of supplies, important for the precedent it set for other occupations, was contained in the order of November 1777 that "the pay of the county waggon master be twenty-two shillings and six pence per day, and the pay of the deputy waggon masters be twenty shillings per day for every day, in *actual specie* [author's italics]."[45]

That the price control of this period was arbitrary may be inferred from the reiteration of positive orders that limits be adhered to, and the bitter comment, "If the farmers does not like the prices allowed them for this produce let them choose men of more learning and understanding the next election."[46]

At the close of 1777, the value of continental money in merchant practice was not more than 5 shillings to the pound. Bills of exchange were rarely obtainable. To Lady Juliana Penn, Edmond Physick explained,

> I have since [May 19, 1777] employed my utmost endeavors by frequent journeys to Philadelphia to invest more of your son's money in bills, but have failed in every attempt and do assure you I am much distressed to get this money out of my hands which consists of about £300 in sterling specie, upward of £2000 in paper money on the old legal establishment which I collected, exchanged and hoarded with great pains, and I suppose about £1000 in continental money, the comparative value whereof to sterling is about 10 to one [6 to one Pennsylvania].[47]

The detailed discussion of practices in 1777 serves to show how general was the search for ratios, often based on little more than acquiescence, that would facilitate dealings on a more stable basis than the medium of exchange afforded.

Depreciation in 1778

In the first half of 1778, the advance in prices was gradual. Merchants rated continental currency at 5 to one in April and May and did not

[45] November 14, 1777, *Minutes of the Supreme Executive Council of Pennsylvania, Colonial Records*, v. 11, p. 371.

[46] December 5, 1777, Mark Bird, Quartermaster General, Reading, to Sirs.

[47] December 12, 1777, Edmond Physick, Lansdowne, Pa., to Lady Juliana Penn, England.

give it as poor a rating again until midsummer. Ratings in commodity sales in April varied from 4.25 to one in bar iron to 6.5 to one in soap, but tended in the ensuing months to follow the depreciation subsequently developed by Webster.

The action of Congress in January in setting a basis for supplying clothing to the commissioned officers of the army might be interpreted as inflationary when they agreed to a "rate of two-thirds of a dollar [5 shillings Pennsylvania currency] for one shilling sterling cost thereof, in Europe, estimating American manufactures at the prime cost of European articles of the same species and qualities."[48] According to Robert Morris, there was then

> no such thing as bills of exchange now passing or negotiating amongst us. I bought at different times £12 to £14,000 sterling before I left Philadelphia and have above one-half of them returned protested. I cannot get them renewed and the drawers and endorsers wanting to avail themselves of certain resolutions of Congress and laws of their states for settling sterling debts want to pay them off at 166⅔ per cent, although I gave 200 to 300 per cent for many of them. I never will submit to this iniquity and the bills remain so much dead stock on my hands and of course afford no encouragement to buy more, either on your account or mine, but if I was disposed to make such purchase I do not know where to find the bills.[49]

Congress recognized only a rate of 3 to one as "the present exchange" in February 1778 in settling an account with a French officer,[50] and in March agreed to a similar rate in adjusting the account of Beaumarchais.[51] Negotiations over a contract with a local cannon manufacturer indicate that there must have been considerable doubt about the allowance for depreciation when in April it was resolved "that the depreciation of the currency be left to arbitration, and Daniel and Samuel Hughes allowed such price for their cannon as the said arbitrators may adjudge to be equal to the original price contracted for."[52]

In May, Edmond Physick complained not only about the earlier law of the Assembly making £155 Congress money a tender for a debt of £100 but about "another law to disable every person from selling land

[48] January 1, 1778, *Journals of the Continental Congress*, v. 10, p. 11.
[49] January 12, 1778, Robert Morris, Manheim, Pa., to William Bingham, Martinique.
[50] February 16, 1778, *Journals*, v. 10, p. 174.
[51] March 23, 1778, *ibid.*, p. 281.
[52] April 4, 1778, *ibid.*, p. 307.

or suing for a debt who would not take an oath of fidelity to what is now called the state."[53] He was then forwarding a bill of exchange for £100 "bought with hard money of my own for which your account is charged with £600 Congress money."[53] His whole explanation of the disordered currency and his puzzled sense of responsibility deserves further stress.

> If I could possibly get a bill on the same terms for the few hundred pounds of Congress money still in my hands, I would gladly do it, but Mr. Franks to whom I have applied refuses to draw for less than after the rate of £850 Congress for £100 sterling, which he says has been the usual course of exchange since November last. . . . When this sort of money is disposed of I shall have a pretty large sum remaining of legal, now commonly called old, paper money issued in New Jersey, Pennsylvania and Maryland and do assure you I have been much perplexed to know what to do with the Pennsylvania part of it in particular, for by a law lately passed here all persons who have any in their possession are required to carry it into a public office, and there get it exchanged for Congress money on or before the 1st of next month, or otherwise it is declared irredeemable. The old paper money was formerly accounted in value equal to gold and silver and £850 of it would have purchased bills to the amount of £500 sterling or more. When the Congress money was first issued it passed equal to other paper money but began soon to depreciate and now £850 of it will not purchase a bill for more than £100 sterling. . . . This being the case, I know of some who will rather take the risk of future events than exchange their old money for that which is already reduced so much in value and I cannot think you will blame me for following their example whatever the consequence may be.[53]

Throughout the summer, continental notes were appraised at 4 or 5 to one in hard money. Transactions at ratings as low as 5 to one appeared in June in the accounts of Hollingsworth, though as disadvantageous a scale was not generally used before August. Meantime, almost as soon as price regulation on domestic products was suspended, the making of whiskey from grains was prohibited and an embargo placed on the export of foods.[54]

Textile prices in 1778 were disturbingly high. According to a summary made by Chaloner and White, they were selling "from 12—1500% on the sterling cost."[55] Since merchants frequently noted the advance on sterling cost as a means of stating the price of dry goods, the

[53] May 28, 1778, Edmond Physick, Lansdowne, Pa., to Lady Juliana Penn, England.
[54] September 7 and 10, and November 17, 1778, *Statutes at Large of Pennsylvania.*
[55] August 11, 1778, Chaloner and White to William Buchanan, Baltimore.

quotation would place the rise between April 1777 and August 1778 at 200 to 300 per cent—a more rapid advance than that of the general average before the spectacular increase, just making itself felt in grain prices, was well under way. This increase offset the encouraging appreciation in the currency manifest in money transactions, and soon Congress had to adopt drastic measures to check the rise, calling upon the states for a census of their food resources,[56] and calling in the continental emissions of May 1777 and April 1778.

Depreciation was rapid at the close of the year. In November gold and silver were exchanged at 5 to one—a month in which the Pottsgrove Iron Works, Morris, Hollingsworth, and Paschall, like Webster, were following a rating of about 6 to one. Silver exchanged for 7 to one in December. The growing use of specie is evident in the tobacco accounts of Hollingsworth, who settled a balance of nearly £534 in gold and silver.[57] The analysis of these many transactions results in ratios that differ slightly in 1778 from contemporary scales in that the scales seem to overstate somewhat the depreciation in the first half of the year and understate it in the last quarter. The ratios computed on commodity transactions exceed the scales from October to December and those on coin in December only.

Depreciation in 1779

By 1779 the practice of converting and posting accounts in both paper and specie became general and transactions in hard money frequent. Officials still hoped to prevent further depreciation. In January, when James Duane described the proposals of Congress for controlling the pace of inflation by borrowing abroad for clothing, arms, and ammunition, by taxing at home, and by calling in two previous emissions, he mentioned the ratio of 5 to one as the basis on which continental notes had passed "during the last ten months," in this way minimizing the acceleration of the close of 1778.[58]

That there were variations in scales of conversion is not surprising, since no open market in specie existed. Uniform rates of conversion between coin and bills of credit could arise only from accord among

[56] November 11, 1778, A Committee of Congress to the Several States, *Letters*, v. 3, p. 489.

[57] December 2, 1778, Levi Hollingsworth Cashbook.

[58] January 3, 1779, James Duane to George Clinton, Governor of New York, *Letters*, v. 4, pp. 2-3.

merchants or adherence to the practice of someone whose judgment was accepted. Webster's ratio of 8 to one in January 1779 coincides with that given by Samuel Fisher to his brother in New York, when he quoted flour at 30 to 35 shillings per hundredweight. Elaborating later, he held that his statement "clearly showed I owned no other money than gold and silver, for it was well known that flour at that time was from £12 to £14 per hundredweight."[59] From the diary of Christopher Marshall, it can be inferred that the half johannes was at £24 in February, though the evidence of appreciation to £18 which he also recorded is hard to find.[60] Such improvement in sentiment as seems to have prevailed arose from a decline in prices of West India goods, especially sugar and rum, and from a few months of more moderate advance in other prices.

Bills of credit had deteriorated since the close of 1778, when there was an official admission by the Supreme Executive Council of a depreciation of 6 to one in arriving at the charge for wagons of the army of the United States "passing the bridge over Schuylkill at 7 shillings 6 pence each wagon, which is not an improper advance on the old price of 1 shilling 3 pence each."[61] At the beginning of February and again toward its close, merchants took credit at the rate of 10 to one for gold and silver which they paid out. On the whole, the rating of notes fell in March. Penington, Charles Humphrey, and the manager of Pottsgrove Forge rated them at 10 to one; Chaloner and White toward the end of the month quoted 10 to 11 in currency as equal to one in gold and silver; Hollingsworth adhered to a ratio of 11 to one, exchanging, on March 23, 1779, £14 15 shillings for £162 5 shillings in currency. The 10.5 adopted by Webster may be taken as a conservative figure, typical of the practice of the previous month and effective only for a short time in March.

Webster makes up for any lag in this March ratio by using 16.1 to one in April. That a sudden and major change took place is indicated by the unusual month-to-month advance in the median of prices from January to May. Other testimony is not uniform. From the correspondence of Silas Deane, who wrote on April 6 to his brother, "Everything

[59] February 19, 1779, Samuel Rowland Fisher to Jabez Fisher, explained March 31, 1779, *Pennsylvania Magazine of History and Biography*, 1917, v. 41, pp. 157, 161.

[60] February 20, 1779, Christopher Marshall Diary.

[61] January 22, 1779, *Minutes of the Supreme Executive Council of Pennsylvania*, *C.R.*, v. 11, p. 674.

is at present rising most rapidly and the currency depreciating which is the same thing,"[62] it would seem likely that values slipped considerably within a short span of days. A bill of exchange for £100 sterling bought on the first day of April for £900 continental currency would be useful in marking the stage of depreciation if succeeding rates could be established.[63] On April 7 Hollingsworth equated the two currencies at 12 and 13 to one in two separate hard money transactions. A half johannes exchanged on April 21 at 20 for one.[64] Debts at this time were being settled in most involved ways, some of which placed the risk definitely upon the payee. For instance, the manager of the Pottsgrove Forge entered in his accounts an obligation for the amount due on an old account "to be paid as money formerly was worth"; that due in current money "to be paid him when called for equal to exchange at 10 for one, that is if the value of money rises he is to deduct, if it fall I am to make it equal to that exchange."[65] It was a high value for the time of the record by contrast with a detailed prices current furnished April 27, 1779, to a Boston merchant in which the markup on dry goods was given as 3000 on the sterling cost, and that on hardware 4000. Coin was listed at 15 for one.[66]

Since it has been frequently stated that the official scales tended to understate the depreciation, one would lower them only on the basis of clear evidence. A complexity in evaluating the information from diverse sources is the speed of the depreciation. The ratios in April 1779 as published some time afterward were:

April	1	12½ to one
	14	14
	27	16
	30	22[67]

which would average 17, the Assembly rate, only by placing undue weight on the last three days of the month. From the records still existing, one would be inclined to modify the scales of Webster for April and May 1779 from 16.1 and 23 to 15 and 20.

62 April 6, 1779, Silas Deane to his brother.

63 April 1, 1779, Elias Boudinot to Elisha Boudinot, *Pennsylvania Magazine*, 1905, v. 29, p. 198.

64 April 21, 1779, Christopher Marshall Diary.

65 April 26, 1779, Pottsgrove Forge Daybook.

66 April 27, 1779, Kuhn and Kuhn to Benjamin Joy, Boston.

67 January 20, 1780, *Pennsylvania Packet*.

There is reason to infer from contemporary comment that toward the end of April few goods were changing hands. Kuhn advised his correspondent in Boston on May 3, "No change in our markets has taken place . . . trade very dull and almost at a stand, owing to the idea that some people entertain of goods lowering." At the same time he added, "Coin from 16 to 17 for one."[68] Mrs. Galloway, a week later, cited, "Continental money from 17 to 20" for one.[69] On the 17th, the operator of Durham Furnace exchanged silver at 15 to one. Most surprising of all the entries are Pelatiah Webster's own accounts on May 25 and again on July 4 giving a ratio of 20 continental to one hard money, in contrast to the 23 for one for May which he computed from the accounts of other merchants.

The evidence of strain in this period, arising from an increase in the prices of staples and from resistance to measures to control prices, was summarized by a county commissioner: "I am doubtful very little of anything will be got in this county for continental money without force as it is regarded as worth nothing."[70]

In June the ratio of 20 to one, noted by Mrs. Galloway, was the one accepted by Reed and Forde, Paschall, and Humphrey. Durham Furnace adjusted its accounts at 15 and Hollingsworth at 18 until late in the month. Barring these exceptions, the accounts follow the 20 for one, finally arrived at by Webster, and continue it until September.

A greatly accelerated price movement initiated in August gained momentum in the next four months. Methods for "the appreciation of our money" were continually under discussion. In August a New York delegate in Congress reported "a dollar is rated here in the purchase of necessaries equal to three pence of the old currency." Like other delegates, he was concerned with the effect upon daily living, illustrating his concern by pointing out that "in the years 1775 and 1776 board and lodging were at four dollars per week exclusive of liquors, it is now at 100 dollars per week."[71]

Merchants were still rating the currency at 20 to one, or 4.5 pence

[68] May 3, 1779, Kuhn and Kuhn to Benjamin Joy, Boston.

[69] May 10, 1779, "Diary of Grace Growden Galloway," *Pennsylvania Magazine*, 1931, v. 55, p. 79.

[70] May 19, 1779, David Grier, York, to Colonel John Davis, Deputy Quartermaster General, Carlisle.

[71] August 18, 1779, Francis Lewis to George Clinton, Governor of New York, *Letters*, v. 4, p. 382.

to the dollar. But whatever the rating, the report of the commissioners in York County that people had not faith enough to accept it was verified in other areas. President Reed found that "tobacco is not to be obtained in many parts of Virginia or Maryland but for gold and silver, and of course a barter is introduced that will, if not checked, soon give the money its fatal stroke."[72] Congress, already alarmed, had, in the words of Henry Laurens, "determined a fortnight since and more, to make no emissions beyond 200 million dollars. We are verging fast to that amount, yet not one solid step trodden in the road of future ways and means for replenishing our treasury and carrying on the war."[73] This succession of rapid steps in discrediting paper money led a purchaser to conclude, "We are now in the kingdom of imagination."[74]

It is not surprising to find a diversity of opinion about the extent of depreciation in a month in which prices advanced 45 per cent above the previous one. Durham Furnace, Charles Humphrey, Reed and Forde, and Paschall posted their accounts at the 24 to one rate given by Webster. Before the month was over, Clarkson and Morrison adopted a 30 to one rate which became general practice in October.

In November, rates were slipping almost daily. The weekly summary of the ratio of continental paper to specie, published early in the next year, indicates the change in tempo in one of the most critical stages of the period:

November	8	32 to one
	15	33⅓
	20	40
	25	40
	30	45[75]

There is no way of escaping the effect of these ratios on prices. They were the basis on which goods were marked up, contracts and purchases made, accounts posted, and specie bought and sold. An indication of the usage is given in the correspondence of Michael Gratz, who in November 1779, when 38.5 for one was the accepted ratio, was informed,

72 September 7, 1779, Joseph Reed, President of the Supreme Executive Council of Pennsylvania, to General George Washington, *Pennsylvania Archives*, 1st ser., v. 7, p. 686.

73 September 26, 1779, Henry Laurens to Jonathan Trumbull, Governor of Connecticut, *Letters*, v. 4, p. 441.

74 September 28, 1779, Nicholas Pouquet, Fredericksburg, to Stephen Girard.

75 January 20, 1780, *Pennsylvania Packet*.

"Mr. Levy told me yesterday that half joes sold for £120 and will in all probability be more. The paper money is next to nothing, few people caring to touch it since this account from the south,"[76] in this way emphasizing how greatly the defeat of Count d'Estaing in Georgia speeded the reduction in the value attached to the currency. No attempt was made by Owen Biddle to give a quantitative appraisal when he wrote to his brother, "Continental money goes on depreciating at a rapid rate." His concern was with the pervasive effect on prices with "no prospect of the price reducing under the present situation of our funds."[77] Business continued to resort to barter arrangements of various types, like the agreement Deborah Morris had to make in renting two of her houses at the same rentals "as in former times," the tenant agreeing "to work for me at the old rate by jobs or 5 shillings per day."[78]

In December, for which Webster arrived at a rate of 41.5, Hollingsworth and Reed and Forde adhered to a rate of 40 continental for one hard money. Not all exchanges were made on this basis. On December 15, the operators of Pottsgrove Furnace paid £6750 continental for £150 in hard money, or 45 for one—just 2 pence for the dollar. Congress voted to sell £75,000 of the bills on Jay and Laurens at the rate of 41.67 continental for one sterling.[79] By the time the action was taken, the price rise had halted and a short period of appreciation brought a rating of 38 to one before the year closed.

Depreciation in 1780

The median of prices for January 1780 declined slightly as a result of a temporary drop in domestic goods and a slackening in the rate of advance in West India staples. Among the merchants, a diversity of depreciation ratios from 40 to 45 to one may be found, according to the part of the month in which the transaction occurred, the prevailing practice favoring the rate of 40.5. The attempts to effect an appreciation by indirect measures, such as the regulation of prices by action of a convention of the states then meeting, attracted much attention. "They talk of the appreciation of our paper into real Spanish dollars," Benjamin

[76] November 22, 1779, Colonel George Croghan, Lancaster, to Michael Gratz.

[77] November 30, 1779, Owen Biddle to Clement Biddle, *Pennsylvania Magazine*, 1892, v. 16, p. 313.

[78] November 1779, Deborah Morris, Account of Rents, Repairs, etc., 1777-1793.

[79] December 27, 1779, William Graham Sumner, *The Financier and the Finances of the American Revolution*, v. 1, p. 251.

Rush, who opposed price regulation, wrote, "as a matter to be performed as easily as an army is to be raised or defeated by a single resolution of Congress."[80]

The case for regulation of prices by law, if all states adopted it, was stated to Joseph Reed as a hopeful measure, if coupled with the retrenchment of expenses and the laying in of grain in public magazines at regulated prices.[81] The members of the convention, handicapped by the absence of authorized representatives from some of the states, were agreed at first on only one opinion—"that any measures for regulating prices, adopted without the concurrence of all the states, proposed by the convention at Hartford, might prove ineffectual."[82]

The change, contemplated at the close of 1779, in the method of obtaining supplies for the army by calling upon the states to furnish specific quantities, forced upon Congress the determination of a basis for pricing. While the matter of using the Spanish milled dollar in accounting for the commodities was under discussion, 65 guineas exchanged in Philadelphia for £5118 15 shillings, or at 45 to one.[83] Hollingsworth used a ratio of 46 on the very first day of February 1780, Reed and Forde 50 during the month, and Durham Furnace 47.5, the latter ratio being the one adopted by both Webster and Paschall. Ratings were uncertain enough to lead the North Carolina delegates to inform their governor, "The currency is no longer capable of procuring any given quantity of supplies." They felt satisfied that, in its call for specific supplies, Congress allowed "liberal prices for every article and all as near as could be in the same proportions. The prices of the year 1774 were assumed from the best information that could be obtained, and fifty per cent were added in consideration of the particular circumstances of the war. The whole indeed will operate as a loan from the staple states to the whole union of which they must afterwards be charged with their proportion and be creditors for the surplus."[84] Low as was the value of continental money, the state of Pennsylvania had

[80] January 19, 1780, Benjamin Rush to Dr. James McHenry, *Pennsylvania Magazine*, 1905, v. 29, p. 63.

[81] January 24, 1780, John Armstrong, Carlisle, to Joseph Reed, *Letters*, v. 5, p. 13.

[82] February 7, 1780, *Journals of the House of Representatives of the Commonwealth of Pennsylvania*, v. 1, p. 422.

[83] February 8, 1780, George Nelson Diary.

[84] February 29, 1780, North Carolina Delegates to Richard Caswell, Governor of North Carolina, *Letters*, v. 5, p. 55.

none in its treasury with which to attempt to draw supplies. Just before Congress announced its decision to devalue continental money, it had varied ratings. On March 18, Nelson wrote, "For some time past the minds of people have been much disturbed on account of our public affairs, the money having depreciated 60 for one and the blame of it charged principally on the House of Assembly who have fixed their wages with the wages of all the officers of government in wheat, by which means they have given a finishing stroke to our continental money."[85]

Confusion over New Issues

On March 18, 1780, Congress resolved to call in the old notes and with the aid of the states to issue a new currency at 40 of old for one new, implying that the new would be equal to specie, although the ratio selected had ceased to be current in Philadelphia two months before. In this month, Penington was exchanging at 50, Reed and Forde at 60, Paschall and Durham Furnace at 61.5, though the latter before the month ended used 73 to one in some conversions.

Had the states accepted fully the plan laid down by Congress, the period of transition would have been confusing enough. To carry out the plan, instructions and price lists had to be sent to all commissary officers on the assumption that the new currency would circulate on a par with coin. At a time when the army was in dire need of supplies, the commissary general learned, "Flour is offering for sale every day and Chaloner and White have no money to purchase."[86]

Not only were transactions in specie increasing but the conversion rates between the paper and specie became, for a few months, more uniform in most accounts. The explanation of the uniformity as given by the trustee in settling the account of Henry Hill with Meredith and Clymer was, "The depreciation on the several amounts before 1st September 1779 are struck without any certain rule, the payments until that time made to Mr. Hill rather anticipating than falling behind M & C's receipts. The depreciation on the amounts since that date are taken from Pelatiah Webster's Table of Depreciation, and the mediums,

[85] March 18, 1780, George Nelson Diary.

[86] March 23, 1780, George Morton to Colonel Ephraim Blaine, Commissary General of Purchases.

especially with respect to the receipts on account of the goods sold, accurately fixed."[87] From the middle of 1778, as depreciation intensified, the rate of conversion of paper to specie had become the most important price information in the market. Many large transactions were deferred until a comparison of ratios in practice could be made. Thus it is impossible to decide whether the merchants' conversion ratios were forcing the price level upward or were adjusting to its previous rise.

Uniformity in procedure was essential once payment to employees "working for hard money"[88] became common. In April 1780 a comment in the forge book of the Durham Furnace recognizes the practice in the payment of blacksmiths and in the entry "hard money at 60 for one being paid to persons who have agreed for hard money,"[89] the rate Girard, Collins, and others were using and that at which English guineas were exchanged.

Even before it was clear that some states had started "rejudging the expediency" of the financial plans of Congress, the Board of War was warned "that the Congresses new money will not without the help of policy enter the world with that repute it ought to do."[90] Before the end of May, instructions had reached the county purchasers in Pennsylvania "revoking," as one wrote, "my former instructions as to prices to be offered, and acquainting me that the House had rescinded the resolutions for fixing the money at 40 for one."[91]

From March to June, exchange fluctuated around 60 to one, the ratio at which the state of Pennsylvania was accepting continental notes for specie or for its own emission of £100,000 authorized March 25, 1780, to purchase provisions for the army. The same basis was followed by the agents selling confiscated estates.[92] In June, when the merchants undertook to advance funds on their own credit to supply the temporary needs of the army, the depreciation, as given by Webster, was 60 to one, though some accounts used higher rates.

[87] March 24, 1780, Henry Hill in account with Meredith and Clymer.

[88] April 10, 1780, Durham Furnace Forge Book.

[89] April 22, 1780, *ibid.*

[90] May 5, 1780, Chaloner and White to the Board of War for Pennsylvania.

[91] June 5, 1780, Nicholas Lutz, Reading, to Joseph Reed, *Pennsylvania Archives*, 1st ser., v. 8, p. 301.

[92] June 21, 1780, *ibid.*, p. 345.

Only in rare instances, mostly in official dealings, was the 60 for one rate continued into July. Early in the month Clarkson and Morrison exchanged hard money for continental at 63 for one. Later, Shinkle and Graff reckoned it at 65, and Hollingsworth at 68, the differences being largely an indication of the speed of decline in the value of paper. The idea still persisted that state paper was on a par with coin. The commissioners of purchases, claiming that flour had now a more settled price than formerly, pointed out that "the state money has got into very general and easy circulation, especially since it became receivable in taxes."[93]

The merchants' complaint, on the other hand, as voiced by Hollingsworth, was of "a scarcity of cash from the sums taken for taxes, militia fines, subscriptions to the army, bank, etc. [so] that few of our retailers are able to buy a hogshead of sugar."[94] More serious than buying in small parcels was the evidence that "our paper money is again depreciating on account of the demand for specie with the French vessels now in port."[94] In the next month, when ratings for continental reached 70 for one, Hollingsworth insisted that the prices he supplied were only nominal as "cash is too scarce to say they are current."[95]

Financially the operation of the plan of March 18, introducing the new paper, was discouraging. According to Ezekiel Cornell, it "meets with so many obstructions I almost despair of the credit it will have in the states that comply with the resolution."[96] Actually the estimates for a monthly quota from the states could have produced the necessary supplies only on the assumption of stable prices or immediate collection of the tax. Neither was likely. Besides, when the quotas were set Congress had meagre information about regional prices in 1774 for the commodities it called for and still fewer data on the supplies available in each state.

The slowness in replacing the old currency and the lack of means for gaining acceptance of the new called for recognition of the increased depreciation of the old money in circulation. During the first week of September, the Pennsylvania Assembly had to take some action on the petition of the wagoners. President Reed was informed, "They expect to have the exchange fixed at the present difference between hard and

93 July 24, 1780, *ibid.*, p. 441.

94 July 20, 1780, Levi Hollingsworth to Marsden and Smith, Va.

95 August 8, 1780, the same to John Sterrett, Baltimore.

96 August 13, 1780, Ezekiel Cornell to Nathanael Greene, *Letters*, v. 5, p. 323.

continental money, which is fluctuating between 70 and 75 for one."[97] The ratio requested by the wagoners conformed to merchant usage. Shinkle and Graff, before the middle of the month, were converting at 70 to one, Humphrey and Paschall at 72, and Irwin, Coates, and Reed and Forde at 75 to one. In October adjustments were made at 77, at 78, and even 80 to one in different accounts, the lower ratings for the value of continental notes falling at the end of the month. The timing deserves emphasis since, for the rest of the inflationary period, the official scale adopted by the Pennsylvania Assembly understated the depreciation and coincides with a troublesome time in making contracts as artisans sought to protect the purchasing power of part of their earnings by demanding one-half their pay in advance at the time their services were engaged.[98]

The attempt during the summer to adhere to a standard price in purchases for the army meant that winter supplies were unduly low. Nor had the mercantile community reason to regard the period as a profitable one. In a pessimistic mood unusual in his correspondence, Hollingsworth, referring to dealings in sugar, wrote, "The state of our market and the depreciation of our currency since the commencement of this business hath proved very disadvantageous to the concern." He attributed the rise in the prices of imported goods and the decline in "the paper currency in equal proportion"[99] to the landing of British troops in Virginia. The outlook of President Reed of the Pennsylvania Assembly was no less gloomy when he informed the Deputy Commissary General and Treasurer of Lancaster County, "We are in the greatest distress for money, exchange daily rising as well as goods and little or no money coming into the treasury from the counties."[100] It is not surprising to find a diversity of exchange ratios, ranging from 80 to 100, scattered throughout November 1780, or to find agreements for payment in specie along with an increase in the number of specie transactions. The New Hampshire delegate to Congress was summarizing a general situation

[97] September 7, 1780, David Jackson to Joseph Reed, *Pennsylvania Archives*, 1st ser., v. 8, p. 544.

[98] September 22, 1780, Colonel Ephraim Blaine to the Board of War for Pennsylvania.

[99] November 4, 1780, Levi Hollingsworth to Carter Braxton, Va.

[100] November 10, 1780, Joseph Reed to William Henry, *Pennsylvania Magazine*, 1887, v. 11, pp. 502-3.

when he reported, "The exchange here is from 85 to 110."[101] No average rate of depreciation could have much meaning when the accounts of a merchant like Matthew Irwin varied from 80 to 90 for one on a single day. Quotations of 75 to one appear after the Treasurer of Pennsylvania, by resolve of the Executive Council, was directed "not to issue any of the state money otherwise than at the rate of 75 for one,"[102] which followed a meeting of the merchants on November 20 at which it was "determined to fix the exchange at £75 currency for 1 specie."[103] Commodity transactions conform to the 100 to one ratio followed by Girard and others, but the net effect on pricing is obscure.

Contemporary opinion leads to the impression that while the ratio of exchange among the various media was uncertain, only small quantities of goods were changing hands. The effect on the army was to make it as short of rum and some other imports known to be plentiful and falling in price as it was of meats and breadstuffs, which were advancing despite the semi-barter arrangements for their procurement. General Washington, in his plans for winter quarters for the army, was cutting down as much as possible the demands for forage and, as usual, cautioning that "the state of our magazines of provision requires also every attention to frugality and economy."[104]

Officials felt relieved when the merchants associated to stabilize the scale of conversion then in use. With beguiling faith, Madison wrote, "The association of the merchants for fixing the depreciation seems likely to prove a salutary measure. It reduced it from 90 and 100 to 75 at once, which is its present current rate; although it is observed that many of the retailers elude the force of it by raising the price in hard money."[105] Other observers averred that the merchants merely substituted one form of inflation for another by action which "satisfied the Assembly and Congress for a season,"[106] an allegation which would not be easy to substantiate, since specie prices of some important commodities, notably bar iron, had advanced as early as October. Throughout De-

[101] November 15, 1780, John Sullivan to Meshech Weare, President of New Hampshire, *Letters*, v. 5, p. 449.

[102] November 25, 1780, *Minutes of the Supreme Executive Council of Pennsylvania*, *C.R.*, v. 12, p. 552.

[103] November 20, 1780, Levi Hollingsworth to Marsden and Smith, Va.

[104] November 27, 1780, Instructions to Brigadier General Wayne; Sparks, *op. cit.*, v. 7, p. 311.

[105] November 28, 1780, James Madison to Joseph Jones, *Letters*, v. 5, p. 461.

[106] December 3, 1780, John Sullivan to Meshech Weare, *Letters*, v. 5, p. 473.

cember 1780 some accounts were settled at the official rate of 75 to one, but Girard, who in general was conservative in his rate of conversion, followed a rating of 105 to 110.

The whole tone of the commodity market at the close of 1780 changed with the arrival of vessels from St. Eustatius and from Cape François and news that the embargo on exportation of flour would be lifted. The imports lowered the price of wines and other luxury items and increased the supply of needed dry goods. "Every day produces either prizes or arrivals of our own," Hollingsworth wrote, "in most of which Blair McClenachan, that son of fortune, [is] capitally interested. These arrivals stagnate the sales of goods."[107] But they did not remove the urgent demand, "Let me know . . . what is the correct exchange in town,"[108] which had to be answered before purchases were likely to be made.

Already the artificial character of the legal scale of depreciation was manifest in the terms of dealings. "Specie in all bargaining 75," Hollingsworth informed his correspondent, "though to buy it they ask 90 to one."[109] Dry goods were then priced "out of all reason, though plenty."[110] Toward the close of December, the exchange rate of continental for specie, for the first time since the merchants had intervened to stabilize it, was given at 100 for one,[111] a rating which conforms to the opinion of a New England delegate to Congress that "the practical discount is 100 for one." He went on to explain, "This has been principally produced by the vast influx of money from the southward." The state had not only made its own issue of "Island money" a legal tender "equal in value to specie, but . . . put the new bills, issued according to act of Congress, on the same footing,"[112] though none of the new were yet issued. The plan met some resistance, as President Reed indicated in his elaborate explanation to Congress, in which he held that "the refusal of the officers to receive any but the old money not only militates strongly against our publications on this subject but induces the people to set an additional value on the old money which will be likely in consequence to appreciate and introduce as destructive a speculation as

107 December 5, 1780, Levi Hollingsworth to Samuel Harrison.
108 December 6, 1780, Henry Howell, Mount Holly, N. J., to Stephen Girard.
109 December 12, 1780, Levi Hollingsworth to George Anderson, Richmond.
110 December 19, 1780, the same to Henry and Thomas Brown, Smithfield, Va.
111 December 26, 1780, the same to Andrew Leiper, Richmond.
112 January 2, 1781, Oliver Wolcott to Oliver Ellsworth, *Letters*, v. 5, p. 510.

that of depreciation."[113] The new money was just then getting into circulation[114] and it was too early to decide whether the tender act of the state would accelerate or impede circulation.

Merchants, at this time when the general level of prices dipped, distinguished carefully between exchange for specie, which was 100 for one, and exchange for state money, "which latter passes current in this city" at 75 for one.[115] There was a spread in quotations and some diversity of opinion when James Lovell wrote, "Money is exceedingly scarce here, yet exchange is from 100 to 115 old for silver."[116] There can be little doubt that continental was worth less than a penny to the dollar when loaf sugar was sold for 2 shillings 6 pence in specie or 36 dollars in currency.

The general practice by merchants of rating Congress money to specie at 100 for one in January 1781 was not continued in the following month. It is true that Josiah Hewes exchanged gold for notes in both months at 100 for one, and Irwin, at the beginning of January, made a transaction in specie at 90 for one, but Hollingsworth used a scale of 100 to one only through the first week of February, and by the seventh was quoting 110 to one. Others adopted the 110 even earlier. Almost over night the basis changed in a way evident to members of Congress. A delegate wrote on February 8, "Our prospects as to money do not brighten. You may be assured that 115 were yesterday given for one and this at a time when everybody complains of the want of old bills."[117] By the middle of the month a rating of 120 to one was reached and seems to have held for a few weeks, though the legal rate of 75 to one in exchange for state paper crops up in sales and in the settling of balances. The ramifications of the two bases in business transactions may be illustrated by the notation of a diarist: ". . . paid me the balance of one year's rent amounting to £1 14 shillings 6 pence or 345 dollars,"[118] instead of 552 dollars which specie would have purchased at 120 to one.

The net effect on prices of impaired currency values appears in an

[113] January 15, 1781, Joseph Reed to the Delegates in Congress, *Pennsylvania Archives*, 1st ser., v. 8, p. 703.

[114] January 16, 1781, Oliver Wolcott to Tapping Reeve, *Letters*, v. 5, p. 538.

[115] January 22, 1781, Levi Hollingsworth to James Leatch, Lyons Creek.

[116] January 23, 1781, James Lovell to Samuel Holten, *Letters*, v. 5, p. 542.

[117] February 8, 1781, the same to the same, *ibid.*, p. 565.

[118] February 28, 1781, George Nelson Diary.

advance in the median of more than 17 per cent in a single month, the largest month-to-month increase since the previous February, when the price level was lower. To the army in need of clothing, both in the south and in the north, the rise in dry goods was most serious.

In March few exchanges of continental for specie were made under 125 to one, and at as favorable a rate as that only in the first week. Hollingsworth quoted a range of 125 to 130 per milled dollar[119] to his correspondent in Baltimore on March 6, and two weeks later informed another, "Exchange for hard money 130 to 135,"[120] the upper limit being higher than any really adopted. Girard, who—as already noted—was always conservative in the ratios he used, had in this month a range of 115 to 125. Congress, meantime, was considering the repeal of all tender laws, which were claimed to be hindering purchases by the quartermasters. The confusion faced by citizens when offered payment in paper not worth its nominal value was multiplied by the various courses followed by adjoining states when the rate of exchange was 130 to one between continental and specie. When Pennsylvania insisted that old bills be called in at 75 dollars for one of the new emission, New Jersey held that they should be called at their current value compared with specie; Maryland followed a different practice, passing a law which, in effect, nullified the bills of the old emission at the end of the period in which they should have been recalled by taxes.[121]

Only by the confidence expressed in the appointment of a superintendent of finance did the passage of time introduce an element of stability. On the same day that Madison reported "the exchange between specie and the old paper here is about 135 for one,"[122] Hollingsworth found "exchange between paper and hard money £140 for one."[123] A week later he reported, "Dry goods have risen 25 per cent." By then the whole character of the market was rapidly changing. "French bills," he continued, "have risen from 75 to 90 dollars and appear on the rise. Sugars have also got up to £480 per hundredweight. This is partly owing to the fall in paper money which hath within

119 March 6, 1781, Levi Hollingsworth to William Buchanan, Baltimore.

120 March 19, 1781, the same to John Sterrett & Co., Baltimore.

121 March 11, 1781, New York Delegates to George Clinton, Governor of New York, *Letters*, v. 6, p. 23.

122 April 3, 1781, James Madison to Thomas Jefferson, Governor of Virginia, *Letters*, v. 6, p. 43.

123 April 3, 1781, Levi Hollingsworth to Isaac Smith, Fredericksburg.

10 days depreciated to 150 to one, in fact no exchange can now buy hard money and partly owing to the want of arrivals of vessels."[124]

Equally troublesome was the depreciation in the value of state issues. In previous months state paper had been privately adjusted to specie at 1⅓ to 1¾ for one, but in April 1781 differentials of 2 and 2⅓ for one afforded evidence of the resistance to its official rating of which the quartermasters complained. The action of the Pennsylvania Assembly in authorizing an issue of £500,000 on April 7 was criticized for the effect it was likely to have on the new continental issues.[125]

On April 18 Hollingsworth quoted the exchange of continental paper for gold at 160 for one[126] and three days later, in explaining the rating of state paper, he wrote, ". . . the money daily sinks in value and now sells at 2⅓ for £1 hard and 'tis my opinion will be lower, perhaps 3 for one next week when the money is promised by Mr. Biddle."[127] It was a conservative appraisal. In reporting the arrival of vessels from Havana and Martinique, Josiah Hewes cited continental paper at 170 to one specie and added, "Most kind of goods rise with the money."[128] The effect of the fresh supplies of West India goods and the quantity of specie they carried was a matter of contemporary speculation. "What influence," Hollingsworth reflected, "the many arrivals at this port will have on our markets and money a few days will show."[129] He was then rating hard money at 175 to one.[129] President Reed, at the same time, wrote to General Washington, "The confidence of the people in paper money is so shaken that the produce of the country is furnished to the commissioners with much reluctance, and even of this money we have but a very incompetent sum, when compared with the amount and value of the supplies. Credit may be said to be at an end; the innumerable certificates granted by the quartermaster and commissary department and by the authority of the state having extinguished all confidence."[130]

[124] April 10, 1781, the same to Henry Armistead, Fredericksburg.

[125] April 16, 1781, John Mathews to General George Washington, *Letters*, v. 6, p. 57.

[126] April 18, 1781, Levi Hollingsworth to Isaac Smith, Fredericksburg.

[127] April 21, 1781, the same to John Sterrett & Co., Baltimore.

[128] April 24, 1781, Josiah Hewes to Aaron Lopez, *Commerce of Rhode Island, 1726-1800*, v. 2, p. 132.

[129] April 24, 1781, Levi Hollingsworth to John Sterrett & Co., Baltimore.

[130] April 24, 1781, Joseph Reed to General George Washington, *Pennsylvania Archives*, 1st ser., v. 9, p. 99.

A detailed statement of the steps in depreciation serves to show that in practice the rate of exchange between continental dollars and specie had reached 175 before the order of May 2, 1781, by the General Assembly, which made 175 continental dollars equal to one of the new emission. This order of the Assembly set up the additional requirement of regular monthly publication of the exchange between continental and specie and made the state paper a legal tender.[131] It was the fictitious rating of state paper that first attracted comment. Hollingsworth explained:

> Our executive council have on Wednesday last passed a resolve making continental currency 175 for one of the state money or of the quota of the Congress new money uttered by this state, so that old Congress money will not buy anything in this city nor even pass since said resolution, and the quantities of it sent to Boston to buy bills with are also returning as not passable in that city but for their taxes. . . . Exchange here is so uncertain that we can have no dependence of purchases to be made in anything but hard money, nor do I believe any other currency will pass in ten days time. There are but few articles that could be bought with paper before this resolution of Council, and that hath thrown the people into great resentment against the paper currency.[132]

For some months, many commodities had been priced in specie and, in his further comment, Hollingsworth stressed the likelihood of its increased use, "Exchange between state money and hard money is now 3 for one and looks likely not to pass many days longer though made a legal tender."[132] The measure was more disturbing to the community at large than to the mercantile part of it, whose purchases were already largely on a specie basis. A diarist noted, "Great murmuring in town amongst the generality of people at the Council's fixing the old continental money at 175 for one of the new emission."[133] Delegates to Congress hastened to inform their states in order to warn them of the likelihood that the old currency would be shipped to them. On the situation in Philadelphia, Madison wrote, "The effect of this declaration has been a confusion among the people of this city approaching nearly

[131] May 2, 1781, *Minutes of the Supreme Executive Council of Pennsylvania*, *C.R.*, v. 12, p. 716.

[132] May 4, 1781, Levi Hollingsworth to Henry Armistead, Fredericksburg.

[133] May 4, 1781, George Nelson Diary.

to tumult, a total stop to the circulation of the old money, and a considerable stagnation and increased depreciation of the new."[134]

After an explanation by the Council, Nelson noted that "people in general seemed more easy, but it caused the state money to depreciate as 4 to one which is full as alarming,"[135] or, as Madison phrased it, "The difference between the latter [new money] and hard money is at present vibrating from 4 to one downwards."[134]

Belatedly, the Council sought information on the price of commodities "distinguishing the difference if any between sale in hard money, new continental money, or state money properly so called."[136] It was too late. Continental money, old or new, was being "received here by few persons."[137] Hollingsworth had to pay hard money to his wagoners. Already "convention bills" were not passing and "old continental currency [was] totally out of use."[138] Joseph Reed soon was informed that the millers were in general so "supplied with hard money from the merchants that I need not pretend to do anything but at tennor of the law and that I doubt will be attended with bad success. Everything that's to be purchased is five times the sum that hard money would be and then the people not free in taking of it."[139] Finally, he informed Congress, "For above a month past paper of all kinds has been pretty generally refused in payment for flour. The trade in this article being now carried on in actual specie."[140] It was June before all state laws making all continental notes a legal tender were repealed, and a tax laid to assist in redeeming the state notes of March 1780 and April 1781, which slowly raised their value.

The detailed discussion of the years when the Revolutionary War was being financed by diluting the purchasing power of money shows that business enterprisers tried every device they could think of to protect themselves against a continually growing depreciation. The devices varied. At times, when the value of paper currency was shrinking rapidly,

[134] May 5, 1781, James Madison to Thomas Jefferson, *Letters*, v. 6, p. 79.

[135] May 5, 1781, George Nelson Diary.

[136] May 8, 1781, Joseph Reed to Colonel Jacob Morgan, Jr., *Pennsylvania Archives*, 1st ser., v. 9, p. 127.

[137] May 8, 1781, John Sullivan to Meshech Weare, *Letters*, v. 6, p. 84.

[138] May 8, 1781, Levi Hollingsworth to Henry Armistead, Fredericksburg.

[139] May 15, 1781, William McCalla, Bucks County, to Joseph Reed, *Pennsylvania Archives*, 1st ser., v. 9, p. 136.

[140] May 22, 1781, Joseph Reed to Samuel Huntington, President of Congress, *ibid.*, p. 162.

isolated exchanges can be found that seem to be wholly unrelated to general practices. Yet there is no reason to think that the rates used in exchanging paper for coin, or in the sale of commodities for specie, are wholly free from the influence of the remedial formulae which merchants used in posting their accounts. As currency shrank in value, information about the prevailing ratio of depreciation was the most important figure in the prices current which merchants supplied to each other.

CHAPTER IV

SPECIE EQUIVALENTS

MANY MAJOR INFLUENCES unconnected with instability of currency are combined in the general curve of prices for the Revolutionary War years. Since commodities were following divergent trends before the war started, it would be difficult from prices alone to date even the beginning of the rise attributable to currency depreciation.

Between April 1775 and April 1776, all series in the index of 15 commodities advanced, except chocolate, corn, common and superfine flour, and wheat; the change was slight in iron in contrast to items like pepper, tea, and rum, in which it was especially striking. From the fact that a majority of the series were involved early in this upswing, one could argue that by the end of April 1776 inflationary influences were ascendant, especially as the qualitative evidence seems to confirm the statistical account. Already manifest were wariness about extending credit, experiments in selective price control, and the weakening of the provisions of the Continental Association.

Attention can now be given to the major factors affecting the general level of prices: the movement of world prices; the costs, scarcities, and wastes of the war; and the continual shrinkage in the purchasing power of an inconvertible currency. Obviously, the dominant element can be separated only if a satisfactory method can be devised for adjusting the index of prices for currency depreciation.

Prices at Amsterdam as Indicative of Trends in World Prices

World prices, except in the middle stages of the war, followed a relatively mild course. They can be depicted by use of the readily available data for the Amsterdam market which typify the price trend in a northern European center not directly involved in the war until continental currency was nearing the end of its use as a medium of exchange.

For purposes of comparison, a group of commodities, as nearly identical with the Philadelphia series as possible, was selected from the data published by N. W. Posthumus in his *Inquiry into the History of*

Prices in Holland. The median of the index numbers of this group, computed on the average of 1771-73, is used as an indicator of changes in the level of world prices. In general, the Amsterdam index was declining from July 1775 to February 1777, when the decline gave way to an irregular rise which dominated the movement of prices until November 1781 and raised the index, in all, about 18 per cent above the prewar average. Part of the rise, even in Amsterdam, may have been an indirect effect of the war in North America, since the total includes West India products as well as those of European origin. Neither the Philadelphia nor the Amsterdam total includes tobacco, indigo, or salt, important in the trade of the war years.

Not all commodities participated equally in the upswing in Amsterdam. In November 1781, chocolate was 22, tea 51, coffee 76, molasses 95, and sugar 111 per cent above their average prewar prices. On the other hand, by the same month, corn, Prussian rye, pork, and wheat had fallen far below their prewar rank.

Even before the war, the movements of the Philadelphia and Amsterdam series were not synchronous, and in the postwar years the early readjustment of prices to conditions of peace was completed on the Amsterdam market in 1785 and was followed, after the spring of 1786, by marked recovery. Thus, in 1787 and 1788, while prices in Philadelphia continued their long postwar decline, prices in Holland had been stabilized and were about 14 per cent above their own prewar level. This lack of conformity had some effect upon the many efforts to develop trade with the continent in these years.

It is, however, the downward trend in the median of Amsterdam prices until February 1777, in months when Philadelphia prices mounted, that is here of significance. Notable, too, is the timing and extreme rise in major tropical products, which soared early and were sensitive to change throughout the war. Although much of the advance in Revolutionary War years was attributed in America as often to speculation as to depreciation, the rise in Amsterdam of 101 per cent in molasses and 111 per cent in sugar before the close of 1781 may be considered as evidence that, even in areas unaffected by a redundant currency, international factors should be considered in accounting for part of the extreme behavior of prices of West India goods. Comparisons between the two markets should be limited to the period when Amsterdam prices were not directly affected by the war. Since the Dutch became embroiled before the close of 1780, it is with the previous advances in prices that comparisons should be made. Between January 1777 and October 1778, prices of molasses on the Amsterdam market rose 80 per cent, and between April 1776 and February 1779, prices of sugar rose 67 per cent. Between the same dates, the advances in Philadelphia were 728 per cent for molasses and 1962 per cent for sugar, on top, of course, of earlier enhancements in their prices.

Adjusting the Philadelphia Series for Currency Depreciation

In addition to the devices evolved by merchants for converting their accounts to specie equivalents, described in the preceding chapter, all other data likely to be useful in separating the part of the rise in prices induced by a redundant currency from that brought about by other factors have been assembled in the course of this inquiry. They are, necessarily, rather limited, and the detailed discussion has already shown how numerous were the factors that would influence any correction for currency variation in a period of swift and erratic price movements.

On the assumption that the most reliable measure of depreciation would be found in the amount of continental currency paid in purchases of specie and in notations of the changing valuations of foreign coins in circulation, rates at which the two currencies exchanged were computed for each transaction and the monthly averages are referred to as "specie ratios" in this discussion. A second measure of depreciation was sought by isolating commodity transactions in specie, when the price in continental currency from the same or other merchants' accounts was known. The third source, described in the preceding chapter, was the formulae used by merchants in settling balances and posting accounts, and frequently sent to correspondents along with lists of commodity prices.

It was to the ratios of merchants dealing in specie that Pelatiah Webster turned in his calculations of the extent of decline in the purchasing power of continental money. His scale differs for short intervals, though less often than might have been expected, from those evolved in the course of this study. The review of all such methods for reducing the inflated indices of prices would not be so necessary if it were certain that specie and commodity transactions were free from the influence of these contemporary judgments.

As might be expected, both specie and commodity transactions suffer from some erratic quotations, arising from a sparse number of entries,

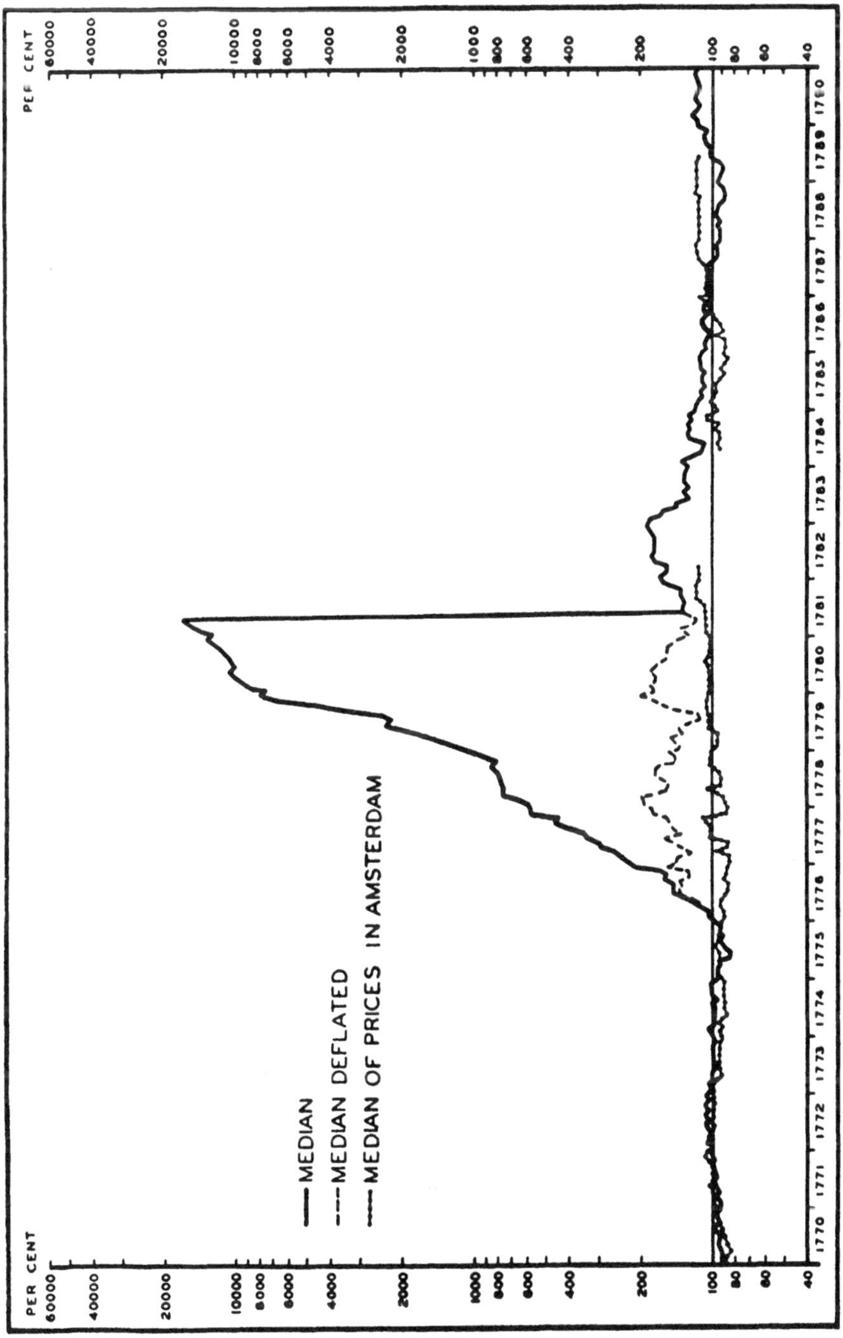

CHART III—INDICES OF MONTHLY WHOLESALE PRICES IN PHILADELPHIA AND IN AMSTERDAM WITH PHILADELPHIA INDEX ADJUSTED TO SPECIE EQUIVALENT, 1770-1790
(Base—Monthly Average, 1771-1773)

from differences in individual practices in periods when no prevailing ratio of exchange was generally recognized, from slowness of communication between trading centers, and from eagerness to acquire gold or silver. The differences arising from uncertainties of the rate of exchange between currencies would be expected to average out only if the number of transactions were larger than is likely ever to be available.

The sort of odd valuations that may occur even in specie transactions may be illustrated by a letter sent in May 1778 from Lancaster to a correspondent in Boston. " I have come purposely to this town this day," Thomas Bond wrote, "to write to you and advise you to be very cautious in the articles you bring for us. I think the prices of goods will be very precarious here. Gold and silver have fallen exceedingly. I bought half joes this day for £9 a piece and T. Lawrence authorized me one week agone to give £16 10 shillings a piece for them for his mother and I am since told they may be bought 2 for one [£6 each]."[1] Only a day later, after he had time for further inquiry, he was able to forward the more accurate report, "Half joes are bought here at £7 10 shillings."[2] The ratio of 2.5 continental money for one in specie cited in the second letter would not have been an uncommon rate in Pennsylvania between February and April 1778, and even the 3 for one paid on the previous day was moderately close to the prevailing rate. On the other hand, the 5.5 for one which Bond was authorized to pay was an extremely low rating for continental money in specie transactions before November. It is worth pointing out, however, that a Philadelphian in a position that made acquisition of specie urgent to him did pay the exorbitant rate of 5 for one in May 1778, and some merchants were then converting their accounts to specie equivalents on the same basis.

Special forms of irregularity occur in some commodity transactions. More specie seems to have been paid in the purchase of butter and beef than for other commodities when they were especially scarce, but here the range in quality might account for what seems to be a variation in practice. Occasionally steel, for which prices seldom reflected differences in quality, was exchanged at ratios far out of line with general practices, and offerings of wheat at extremely low prices in specie may be accounted for by the eagerness of farmers to hold a currency that could

[1] May 19, 1778, Dr. Thomas Bond, Jr., Lancaster, to John Reed, Boston.

[2] May 20, 1778, the same to the same.

be kept safely for the season when they most needed supplies. None of these irregularities make for persistent differences and, as one might have expected, the commodity ratios and the formulae for converting accounts at most times conform closely.

A choice of a divisor for reducing the price index to specie equivalents narrows, then, to (1) the specie ratio in money transactions, (2) the average of merchant and commodity ratios, and (3) the scales developed by Webster or (4) some combination of the three. All have been smoothed by the use of a three-months moving average, and the effect of their use summarized in Table 3. A preference for the ratios evolved in the course of this study rests primarily on the fact that they apply to the accounts from which the price series were obtained.

Theoretically, the specie ratios should be more defensible than other divisors. It seemed to William Graham Sumner, at the time he made his study, *The Financier and the Finances of the American Revolution*, that the best gauge of depreciation would be found in the amount of continental paper given in purchases of specie, as it doubtless would be were it not for overvaluation of specie at times when the military outlook was gloomy[3] or purchasers were in circumstances that made specie balances particularly advantageous. Besides these inescapable drawbacks, the specie ratios suffer from some months with lacunae and others with a limited number of clearly identifiable money transactions. Since they conform, in general, so surprisingly to the other ratios until late in 1780, there is no reason to assume that one series introduces a bias not found in the others. In the six months November 1780 to April 1781, when the scales of the Pennsylvania Assembly are valueless, other evidences of depreciation are especially copious.

Contemporary judgments and formulae often partake of the outlook of individuals. For instance, Stephen Girard, Peter Kuhn, and at times Edward Penington made milder reductions for depreciation than did

[3] The overvaluation from fear that the colonies would be defeated was less likely after 1779 than before. An interesting evidence of the shift in opinion in the middle years of the war is found in the comment, "As to matters respecting the war, both sides at present are quiet in their different camps, except in Georgia where there have been many skirmishes with different success. Sometimes one party get the better, sometimes the other, but nothing decisive in that quarter and as to conquest, I am sure it is out of the question; neither do I believe at this time the British Court expect it." April 22, 1779, Samuel Morris, Jr., to William and S. Buckley, St. Eustatius.

Levi Hollingsworth or Josiah Hewes, though in the main disparate practices were matters more of the speed of adopting a changed rate than of long-run, persistent differences. They deserve to be stressed because, from the time inflationary forces became ascendant, the mercantile community, within limits, signaled, if it did not wholly determine, the rate of depreciation. The conversion rate thus became a salient, even at times a causal, force in influencing the level of prices.

Whichever ratio is applied, the Pennsylvania index reduced to a specie equivalent presents, by contrast with the orderly advance of prices at Amsterdam, a series of marked cyclical movements during the period when continental currency was in use. Another of similar type occurred in the two and a half years after it was abandoned. The first of these movements in the reduced series reached a peak in January 1777, indicating that increased purchases of food, military equipment, and supplies for the starting of enterprises in the early stages of the war, brought a rapid response in price. At the beginning of 1777, the price level, reduced to specie equivalents, was 50 per cent or more above prewar. From then on the tension on prices eased, and by July 1777 they were approximately 30 per cent above prewar, whether corrected by the commodity ratios evolved in the course of this study or by Webster's scales, and considerably lower if corrected by the specie ratio. As in the later price swings, the difference introduced by the choice of divisors is largely in the intensity of high and low points and rarely in direction or timing. In this first extreme movement, the divergence of the index reduced by the specie ratios from the markedly similar results of the other measures arises largely from sparsity of specie items.

The upswing after July 1777 corresponds closely with the period when military operations were in or nearing the vicinity of Philadelphia, large numbers of the residents migrating, and stores and workshops being gradually moved to outlying areas. The mounting prices lasted until March 1778 and raised the index on a specie equivalent basis 98 to 144 per cent above prewar.

The irregular decline from these levels, broken for a few months in midsummer, continued not only through 1778 but through the first seven months of 1779. In this movement, Webster's scale gives a somewhat different price trend in the early months of 1778 from either the specie or commodity ratios assembled in the course of this study. From December 1777 through May his figures seem to overstate the depreci-

TABLE 3

THE RELATION OF CONTINENTAL MONEY TO SPECIE

December 1775-April 1781

	Ratios			Median corrected by three-months moving average			Ratios			Median corrected by three-months moving average		
Year & Month	Webster Merchants	Specie	Commodity	Webster Merchants	Specie	Commodity	Webster Merchants	Specie	Commodity	Webster Merchants	Specie	Commodity
1775							1779					
Dec.		1.04										
1776												
Jan.							8.0	8.00	7.99	141.0	136.7	138.5
Feb.							10.0	9.91	9.95	138.9	143.0	134.5
Mar.							10.5	9.77	11.50	130.9	150.4	127.2
Apr.					110.4		16.1	12.17	16.21	106.5	137.5	117.8
May					120.6		23.0	16.46	17.12	108.9	139.0	120.5
June					135.5		20.0	17.67	20.07	111.8	128.9	111.2
July		1.08			136.1		19.0	19.62	25.12	112.9	112.9	94.8
Aug.					133.4		20.0	21.72	25.10	117.2	116.1	95.8
Sept.		1.14	1.75		136.0		24.0	22.24	26.82	144.7	144.8	132.8
Oct.		1.25	1.75		126.0		30.0	30.00	28.68	154.4	161.9	158.0
Nov.		1.25			126.0		38.5	36.00	34.88	176.8	179.7	178.1
Dec.		1.50	1.50		151.8		41.5	42.22	45.60	193.9	200.9	191.9
1777							1780					
Jan.	1.25		1.44	171.4	154.0	142.4	42.5	40.00	43.30	169.9	178.6	166.7
Feb.	1.5	1.50	1.85	157.2	150.5	139.5	50.0	45.25	47.73	174.1	183.9	181.7
Mar.	2.0	2.00	2.06	139.7	127.8	124.1	62.5	61.50	57.51	167.0	171.5	176.5
Apr.	2.0	2.50	2.26	137.1	134.0	137.7	60.0	61.21	57.98	170.4	170.5	176.0
May	2.5		2.16	128.4	107.2	144.5	60.0	59.67	61.20	178.9	181.8	180.6
June	2.5	3.72	1.80	125.8	112.7	159.2	60.0	56.30	59.10	167.1	171.9	163.6
July	3.0	3.06	2.36	123.0	97.0	136.5	62.5	61.38	66.08	161.5	165.7	157.0
Aug.	3.0		3.50	138.0	123.6	148.4	70.0	70.00	72.87	154.9	157.8	151.6
Sept.	3.0	3.00	2.50	154.7	139.4	151.2	75.0	72.33	73.08	149.4	156.5	149.1
Oct.	3.0	3.00	3.22	148.3	151.3	155.0	77.5	70.00	76.98	145.6	154.0	148.5
Nov.	3.0		2.90	174.2	186.0	175.8	90.0	86.87	87.68	141.2	147.3	146.1
Dec.	4.0		3.78	158.1	204.3	178.5	100.0	99.54	93.74	137.9	138.0	142.8
1778							1781					
Jan.	4.0		3.08	138.4	213.2	191.4	100.0	103.33	98.54	122.7	124.5	128.5
Feb.	5.0	2.71	2.54	141.6	212.0	196.3	110.0	102.50	103.72	132.0	134.7	137.0
Mar.	5.0		4.50	144.4	243.6	198.4	127.5	125.00	123.02	113.7	123.1	125.7
Apr.	6.0	2.28	4.60	142.8	221.2	153.8	167.5	146.67	139.74		118.3	
May	5.0	3.53	5.74	153.3	234.5	152.7						
June	4.0	4.00	4.72	178.3	201.1	158.5						
July	4.0		4.16	182.9	195.0	171.0						
Aug.	5.0	4.17	5.00	174.3	185.4	172.4						
Sept.	5.0		5.00	171.6	195.5	167.3						
Oct.	5.0	4.00	5.40	152.7	165.8	145.9						
Nov.	6.0	5.72	6.34	155.2	159.4	145.0						
Dec.	6.0	6.84	6.47	157.4	153.3	151.5						

ation during part of the critical months of the British occupation. It is true that formulae similar to those cited by Webster appear in some accounts, and it is possible that prices drawn from the same sources as Webster used for his ratios would have conformed more closely than does our index, since these months are particularly difficult ones in which to assemble either prices or depreciation ratios.

In the light of qualitative data and the customs of the period, it would be difficult, however, to believe that a genuine decline in prices could have occurred before the early spring of 1778. Normally some upturn in prices toward the close of the year, though varied in timing according to the openness of roads, arose from the typical provision for winter living that characterized the mode of life in colonial years. Customarily, merchants laid in stocks for sale during the winter, just as families filled their cellars when crops were garnered. It is well known that, during the war, these previsions at the same time that military purchases were most concentrated often interfered with the securing of adequate supplies for the army. Even in 1778, when the army was better provided for than usual, Chaloner and White complained to the commissary general, "All kinds of merchandise have risen in value here within these few days. The speculators have laid in for winter sale; and should we want any foreign articles before the month of March, we expect to pay dearly for them, unless our exports this month should exceed our expectations, or some other event turn up in favor of us."[4] As in any inflated economy, the opprobrium of speculation is here applied to customary foresight, once it becomes difficult to say where prudence ends and speculation begins. In 1778, activity by commissary agents purchasing earlier in the season than usual changed the normal pattern of upsurge in the autumn to a peak in late summer.

In the first half of 1779, all ratios devised for reducing the price series to a specie equivalent show a decline ending before August—a phenomenon the less surprising, since, even in terms of continental money, prices of certain commodities like molasses, pork, sugar, superfine flour, and rum fell in some months in this period and others were stabilized for a time. Pelatiah Webster noted that some articles had dropped below prewar terms of sale and even Chaloner and White re-

[4] November 10, 1778, Chaloner and White to Colonel Jeremiah Wadsworth, Commissary General of Purchases.

ferred to the price advances made to offset the depreciation of currency as advantageous "in idea only."[5]

In purchasing power, specie was assumed in many situations to have retained its customary worth. For instance, Thomas May, managing Elk Forge for the Hollingsworths, contracted for his "salary superintending the company business, one year April 9, 1778 to April 9, 1779, £100 specie or the exchange."[6] The next year's contract, which ran to April 1780, was made at the same rate, so that one would assume that a marked advance in prices in specie terms was not anticipated.

The peak of the third cycle in the reduced index, reached in December 1779, was 92 to 101 per cent above the prewar average, according to the ratio chosen for adjustment, and relatively high prices prevailed in the following months. In this movement, except for the extreme peak, all the ratios give remarkably similar results.

Had the above comparisons been made on the basis of the weighted average, the highest prices of the war years would be placed in March to May 1780, owing to the justifiably heavy weight assigned to breadstuffs and meats, which had been rising markedly in this and the previous year. Thus the real increase in the cost of living created by mounting prices of domestic staples in the last half of 1779 and in 1780 is emphasized more clearly in the weighted series than in the median.

After continental currency ceased to circulate, a swing in prices occurred not unlike the three movements of earlier war years, with the familiar end-of-the-year peak in 1782, in which the weighted average was 65 per cent above prewar in September and the median about 90 per cent above in December. This movement, free from any doubt about the validity of divisors for reducing the series, strikingly resembles earlier swings in the specie equivalent series.

Since the results of the use of each of the three ratios have been compared in this summary, some choice among them should be indicated. For 1776, the ratio evolved in the course of this study is a composite of specie and commodity ratios and the only one available. In 1777 and 1778, the commodity ratio, which is based on a larger number of transactions than the specie, seems preferable to it. From 1779 onward, preference would be for the specie ratios, though in these years all, including

[5] April 18, 1779, the same to Colonel Ephraim Blaine, Deputy Commissary of Purchases.

[6] Thomas May, Elk Forge Accounts.

Webster's scale, give markedly similar results. Since Webster's scale purports to be based on the specie transactions of one merchant checked against the practices of some others, it was hoped that his might be paralleled by or combined with our specie ratios, but the divergence in 1777 to 1778 precludes such a use of the data.

As in all attempts to eliminate the influence of one factor from a price index, there is in these calculations the danger that the most likely normal accompaniment of emergency conditions will be obscured. Regardless of the monetary system in use in these years, even if supplemented by orderly taxation, it is unlikely that a war, undertaken without preparation and carried on in one form or another for nearly a decade, could have been waged without some change in legal tender that would result in price inflation. In an over-all correction, this usual inflationary concomitant of war is all attributed to currency influences. The basis for so treating the general index is that the accounting of the period and much of the public policy rested on the premise that the effect of currency depreciation could be dissociated from other factors.

Barring the year-end peaks in prices, when consumer purchases, merchants' provision for winter sales, and army buying were concentrated, Congress was not far astray in its estimate of March 1780 that an average of 50 per cent in specie terms above the prices of 1774 would offset the additional costs of the war on most staple items. Hollingsworth estimated in December 1780 that the advance in house rent in specie terms was 50 to 75 per cent.[7] Such estimates do not, however, take account of the fact that the incidence of the rise in the first phases of war was greatest in products which the consumer could forgo and in later phases involved the most essential items in family living.

Individual Commodities

A check upon the conversion ratios may be made on individual commodities sold for specie. On this basis, bar iron reached its highest specie prices, except for one month in 1780, between April 1778 and June 1779 when it sold for £40 a ton, or more than 54 per cent above its prewar average. The highest prices for coffee, for which there are few specie quotations in the early years and continuous ones later, occurred in the first six months of 1780, with the peak about 89 per cent above prewar. Common flour, at its peak in the first quarter of 1779, sold in

[7] December 12, 1780, Levi Hollingsworth to George Anderson.

specie for 33 shillings a hundred, or about 75 per cent above prewar. It dropped abruptly during the summer of 1779, but fetched 50 per cent or more above prewar in the last half of 1780 and in some months in 1781. Superfine flour, for which specie prices are infrequent, was at most 20 to 30 per cent above prewar in the first four months of 1781, when continental money was still in circulation.

Loaf sugar, a luxury item for which transactions in specie occur frequently, was 111 per cent above prewar from August to November 1776, and thereafter rose irregularly until by March 1779 it sold for 3 shillings 6 pence a pound, or 268 per cent above its average in 1771 to 1773. Though more moderate prices prevailed afterwards, loaf sugar sold in specie until March 1781 for 111 per cent more than before the war.

Since muscovado sugar reached the market in many grades, its specie prices are difficult to follow. Its most spectacular rise occurred early in the war, with the highest specie price found in the course of this study recorded before November 1778, when it sold for £11 a hundredweight in hard money, or 339 per cent above prewar.

These direct comparisons of the sale prices of individual commodities in specie indicate how varied was the actual rise of different products, both in extent and timing. The swift changes in price movements and the divergence of commodities from each other, which were the special features of this era, can be charted as well in terms of the currency in use as in specie. The reduction of the index to specie equivalents was undertaken to provide a link with the periods which preceded and followed it.

The unevenness of the advance in prices would make it unlikely that the relatives of individual commodities adjusted by use of a ratio computed from a diversity of products, many not included in the general index, would conform closely to their indices based on actual specie sales. The lack of conformity, however, should not always be in the same direction.

As a test of the results, the index of specie prices and an adjusted index in continental money are shown for loaf sugar, flour, corn, bar iron, and coffee—all commodities dissimilar in speed and time of price advance. The adjusted relatives of loaf sugar are consistently above the specie index in 1776 and 1778 except in June, when specie prices were rising rapidly, and more nearly conform to it from 1780 to 1781 when the trend of specie prices was generally downward. On the other hand, before 1780 the adjusted index of common flour tends to fall below the specie series, and that of bar iron to conform in general to it. Like those of loaf sugar, the adjusted relatives of common flour, from 1780 on, conform reasonably well to its specie relatives, and in 1781 the two are almost identical for superfine flour.[8] Corn, in which the adjusted index falls below the specie in some months and rises above it in others, provides an indication of the suddenness with which the new crop could lower specie prices of a commodity which, during the extreme inflation, advanced less than other farm products included in the general index. Bar iron offers as interesting a comparison as any in the group, since the adjusted relatives tend to conform to the specie index in the first phases of rise and, from October 1779 through September 1780 when specie prices were firm, are consistently above the specie series. After October 1780, with specie prices advancing, the adjusted index again falls below. Prices of coffee, in adjusted terms, tend to fall far below its index based on specie sales, especially from April to July 1780. Like corn, the sudden decline in specie prices seems to be connected with the entry of new supplies.

These comparisons serve to show that the bias of the commodity ratios is not all in one direction. A choice among the different measures for adjusting the general index must still be made.

The result of a reconsideration of all data available for reducing prices to a specie equivalent, that is, separating the part of the advance in prices that can be attributed to unstable currency from that connected with the additional demands and costs of war, provides ratios which differ significantly only in three intervals from the scales of depreciation made available by Webster from his analyses of merchants' accounts. These occur from July to December 1776, from January to June 1778,

[8] The specie and adjusted indices of superfine flour are:

	Specie	*Adjusted*
1780		
January	135.2	160.8
December	121.6	125.2
1781		
January	121.6	125.1
February	130.7	131.2
March	120.2	125.7
April	113.8	125.5

Table 4

Indices of Specie Prices and of Continental Currency Prices Adjusted by Commodity Ratios

Selected Commodities

August 1776-April 1781

Year & Month	Loaf Sugar		Common Flour		Corn		Bar Iron		Coffee	
	Specie	Adjusted	Specie	Adjusted	Specie	Adjusted	Specie	Adjusted	Specie	Adjusted
1776										
Aug.	210.7	291.4								
Sept.	210.7	323.5								
Oct.	210.7	295.0								
Nov.	210.7	295.0								
1777										
Feb.							92.8	107.0		
1778										
Feb.	241.3	569.7								
Mar.	231.8	475.3					154.7	149.5		
Apr.	239.2	384.5					154.7	132.8	198.2	240.2
May	197.0	312.1							178.1	177.4
June	263.4	216.4								
July		409.7								
Aug.		334.9								
Sept.		369.7								
Oct.	263.4	311.6								
Nov.										
Dec.	192.8	380.1								
1779										
Jan.			174.7	127.3						
Feb.			172.0	118.7						
Mar.	368.8	251.9	174.7	88.6						
Apr.				106.3			153.2	195.4		
May			116.4	107.1			154.7	169.1		
June				91.7			154.7	157.0		
July				81.3						
Aug.				74.2						
Sept.			119.1	112.9						
Oct.				169.9			116.0	133.3		
Nov.				203.6			120.6	151.4		
Dec.				214.1			108.3	179.7		
1780										
Jan.	228.7	208.2		150.3	130.7	95.6		172.6		179.8
Feb.		191.6		181.7		105.6		156.4		152.7
Mar.		174.3		176.5	128.3	93.4		162.0	112.0	138.9
Apr.		161.0	203.8	156.9	123.4	109.7	112.2	148.7	220.0	126.2
May		179.5		152.8	130.7	127.1	116.0	161.6	189.0	112.3
June	263.4	190.8		143.1	130.7	144.9	112.2	163.6	181.4	91.2
July	210.7	205.9	158.8	140.0	163.2	142.6	112.2	166.4	189.0	95.3
Aug.		208.0	146.7	136.0	87.1	128.7	108.3	168.5		91.3
Sept.		212.7		139.2		131.9	108.3	142.8		82.6
Oct.		226.0		124.1		117.5	121.4	138.8		79.5
Nov.		205.4		128.8		118.9	164.4	135.4	103.2	122.7
Dec.	219.2	245.7	132.3	124.1	116.1	108.9	135.4	124.5	119.7	119.2
1781										
Jan.	219.2	218.3		128.5	116.1	88.3		116.4	126.0	110.7
Feb.	210.7	193.1		140.3	108.9	96.4		120.4	126.0	104.6
Mar.	222.3	179.7	128.4	123.8		73.7		103.7	131.2	111.7
Apr.	192.8		111.7	111.6		75.5	135.4	110.1	105.0	101.7

and in May 1779. There are, besides, minor variations in some months in 1780 and in 1781. From the beginning of 1780 to April 1781, Webster's scales or the ones provided by the new computations of this study are preferable to the legal rates adopted by the Pennsylvania Assembly, which after August 1780 ceased to have any validity.

CHAPTER V

WHEAT, FLOUR, AND BREAD

DURING the entire colonial period, wheat, flour, and bread held a predominant place over all other commodities in the trade and growth of Pennsylvania. Prices of all were closely linked and followed each other in the succession of cyclical movements of the era from 1720 to 1775. Toward the end of the period, three grades of flour were current in the market: superfine flour was favored for the export trade, and middling and common flour were dominant in the mainland trade, in home consumption, and in the purchases of local bakeries which furnished bread for ships at the port and a surplus for part of the demand of New England fishing fleets. At times the prices reflect the uses. An embargo in the port might decrease the price of superfine flour, just as a period of active trade might raise it, disproportionately to the price of common.

Prices of wheat and its products dipped to low levels in the severe depression which marked the spring of 1769. All swung upward before the year ended. Thus the year 1770, when this study starts, found wheat and its products in the early phase of an expansion to a peak in 1772 so pronounced that the leading staples of Pennsylvania sold at the highest prices of colonial years.

Prewar Rise in Grain Prices

In January 1770, wheat was selling for 5 shillings 6 pence a bushel, common flour for 14 shillings 6 pence a hundredweight, and ship bread for 13 shillings a hundredweight. To the surprise of Philadelphia merchants, prices of provisions continued to rise. They traded cautiously when they might have been daring because they feared that the port of Lisbon would be overstocked "when all the ships arrive that are gone of late . . ."[1] The demand for breadstuffs in Madeira brought the statement to a Philadelphia house trading there, "We have only about 100 moys [of wheat], and of the 200 barrels of flour from New York and

[1] May 9, 1770, Thomas Clifford to Parr and Bulkeley, Lisbon.

100 barrels by Kerlin, we have only twenty remaining on hand, so that in a short time we shall have of neither of these articles at market, unless you should have engaged some of our friends on the continent to adventure this way."[2]

As late as September, merchants felt that the price of wheat, then at 6 shillings 1 penny a bushel, was nominal. Benjamin Fuller, complaining of the increased prices, commented, "The farmers are rich and loath to part with it at that, and the millers are afraid to give it, for any large quantity. I think it must be lower, the crop being great and good . . ."[3] During the rest of the year, wheat continued to rise and by December sold for 6 shillings 6 pence a bushel, a price which was felt to be too high for either the Lisbon or West India markets.[4]

The rise of prices continued in 1771. Requests for wheat and its products brought such laconic replies as "Wheat, none to be had,"[5] or "Flour has been advanced very high of late."[6] Nothing in the correspondence indicates the shortage of crops in northern Europe from inundations at Hamburg, Brussels, and Berlin, nor the rising prices which caused the Court of Session at Edinburgh to order "the ports to be opened for the free importation of all kinds of grain."[7] Flour was coming "very slow to market"[8] in September, and by October it was "in so great demand and so exceeding scarce, 'tis impossible to be attentive to the quality. We are now obliged to buy if it will pass the inspection or to go without."[9] In this year of avid demand for grain, two-thirds of the exports of wheat from Philadelphia went to southern European ports. Toward the end of the year, Clifford explained to his correspondent in Lisbon, "Wheat this year amongst us is lighter than common and not so great a quantity." He added that "flour is high and discourages many people from adventuring."[10]

In 1772, when breadstuffs reached the highest prices of colonial years, Philadelphia exporters referred to the prices they were paying for grain as "most extravagantly dear," "exorbitantly high," or higher "than

[2] June 30, 1770, Joseph Gilliss, Madeira, to Henry Hill.

[3] September 5, 1770, Benjamin Fuller to John Scott, Jr., Armagh, Ireland.

[4] December 22, 1770, Thomas Clifford to Lancelot Cowper, Bristol.

[5] April 24, 1771, Reynell and Coates to John Wood, Newburyport.

[6] June 17, 1771, the same to the same.

[7] August 1771, *Gentleman's Magazine and Historical Chronicle*, v. 41, pp. 373 and 375.

[8] September 18, 1771, Reynell and Coates to Nathaniel Gorham, Charlestown, Mass.

[9] October 17, 1771, the same to Samuel Souther, Haverhill, Mass.

[10] November 12, 1771, Thomas Clifford to Parr and Bulkeley, Lisbon.

I have known them." They eagerly awaited the new crop which would begin to come in before July.

In the meantime, the clearest indication of scarcity came from Europe in the petitions from various parts of England for the free importation of grain, in the reports that the Dutch were in "utmost distress for want of bread corn,"[11] and in the public discussions of the steady increase in the price of provisions. In June, when wheat was slightly over 8 shillings a bushel, Clifford explained to a Bristol inquirer, "Our last crops were but indifferent and the country being much drained of wheat occasions it being very high." He added, optimistically, "The price will be down after harvest no doubt."[12] By the next month he had to admit to the same correspondent that "no wheat comes to market to be had at any price."[13]

The new crop of 1772 reached the market slowly enough to cause a delay in filling orders, especially those with price limits set months before. In October, Drinker explained to correspondents in London and Genoa, "Our present prices for wheat is from 8 shillings to 8 shillings 3 pence [a bushel] and we do not foresee any material change therein, at least not before the time our winter generally sets in. The last crop, though not the most plentiful, is of an excellent quality."[14]

Prices of wheat, flour, and bread declined moderately in the fall of 1772, but it was not till November that Drinker informed his correspondents in Leghorn of "a decline in the price of wheat within a few days past."[15] "Contrary to our expectation, and that of many others," Drinker wrote on the same day to another correspondent, "the price of wheat has had a sudden decline within a few days so that we were enabled to purchase on the 14th instant upwards of 9000 bushels of a good quality to average about 7 shillings 6 pence."[16] An equally "unexpected demand," brought about by hurricanes in the West Indies, was given as a cause for persistence of high prices.[17]

Toward the end of the year, a merchant, aware that the abnormal foreign demand could not last, commented on the internal effect of the

[11] January 1772, *Gentleman's Magazine*, v. 42, p. 44.
[12] June 22, 1772, Thomas Clifford to Thomas Franks, Bristol.
[13] July 15, 1772, the same to the same.
[14] October 21, 1772, James and Drinker to Zachariah Philip Fonnereau & Sons.
[15] November 16, 1772, the same to Chabanel Uhthoff & Co., Leghorn.
[16] November 16, 1772, the same to Zachariah Philip Fonnereau & Sons.
[17] November 17, 1772, the same to John Jeffrey, Joseph Randle, and Thomas Street.

boom in grain, "The country's growing rich from the exorbitant prices that the produce of all kinds have borne for some years past. The last crop good, yet flour keeps up at 20 shillings and wheat in proportion. Fear seems to possess all lest the markets to the eastward should fail next spring. I take it that the calamities of poor Poland has been the true cause of enriching this country and whenever that kingdom recovers itself a change will certainly take place here." He held that the effect on the scale of living was, "Luxury has greatly crept in among us—a small family that in your time could have subsisted genteelly on £300 per annum cannot now live in the same manner for £500 per annum."[18]

The high prices for grain products which persisted throughout the following year were of the "greatest concern" to the British Parliament,[19] to the northern mainland colonies,[20] and to southern Europe. Meantime, the acreage under wheat cultivation had been extended until that of 1773 far exceeded any previous year.[21] The crop was plentiful, but late in October there was still a scarcity of flour to load the many vessels in port.[22] Surprisingly, to contemporaries the markets of this year seemed unsettled.

The momentous year 1774 opened with the river full of ice, "scarcely any business stirring," and little flour "at market."[23] It was then felt that flour would rise in price as soon as navigation opened. In the light of good crops in Pennsylvania, the unknown factor was the state of foreign demand. "It was expected in the spring," Reynell explained, "that freights to the eastward might be readily obtained; but accounts (via Lisbon) signify that flour, etc., in England is in great plenty, and 'tis thought will be exported from thence so as to affect our eastern markets. The advice has put our shippers to a stand, as they had great hopes of advantage, and they wait with impatience for the January packet's arrival, when they will learn the English prices."[24] The news brought by the packet turned out to be less discouraging than had been expected.[25] Instead of a slackening in demand, the problem in March was how to

[18] December 26, 1772, Benjamin Fuller to John Scott, Jr., Armagh, Ireland.

[19] February 1773, *Gentleman's Magazine*, v. 43, p. 66.

[20] February 9, 1773, Simeon Perkins Diary, Liverpool, Nova Scotia.

[21] May 6, 1773, William Pollard to Thomas Earle, Liverpool.

[22] October 26, 1773, Reynell and Coates to William Teel, Newburyport.

[23] January 22, 1774, the same to William Wyer, Newburyport.

[24] February 4, 1774, the same to the same.

[25] March 13, 1774, the same to the same.

procure freights for the 73 vessels which arrived in the port of Philadelphia. Prices of wheat and its products were well sustained in the spring months. A merchant then explained, "The Lisbon and Streights markets being high occasions our markets to keep very high also. Some of our vessels have met a great market at Alicant."[26] In May, neither a vessel nor wheat to load it could be obtained at the limits set by the client for a cargo to Leghorn, as "the Lisbon and Cadiz, etc., markets have been so favorable that all our vessels are fully employed."[27]

Decline in Grain Prices

The drop in wheat prices in the summer of 1774 is closely linked to the discussions which preceded the calling of the First Continental Congress. In May, Thomas Wharton warned his brother in England that "politicians talk of again entering into a non-importation agreement."[28] Even before it was known whether the deputies from the colonies would meet in Philadelphia or New York, Drinker informed his suppliers in London that there could "scarcely be a doubt"[29] that a general nonimportation agreement would be pressed for. At the same time he added, "We have the prospect of the greatest crop of wheat ever known; if good weather continues two or three weeks it will be all cut and got in. Advise us frequently prices of wheat and flour at London and what harvest you may have."[29]

Only a week later the seriousness of the political situation, which could not fail to bring repercussions, was related by Thomas Wharton to his brother. Anxiously he wrote, "Since my last, great have been the commotions on this continent, occasioned by the act of Parliament for shutting up the port of Boston and the prospect of other acts relative to that unhappy place, and be assured the whole continent will hereby be united in a stronger and more firm union than anything which has heretofore happened could possibly effect."[30]

Along with the disturbing events at home, merchants felt a lack of certainty about the state of crops and the movement of prices abroad.

26 April 4, 1774, William Pollard to Peter Holme, Liverpool.

27 May 16, 1774, the same to Thomas Earle, Liverpool.

28 May 17, 1774, Thomas Wharton to Samuel Wharton, England, *Pennsylvania Magazine of History and Biography*, 1909, v. 33, p. 335.

29 June 29, 1774, James and Drinker to Pigou and Booth, London.

30 July 5, 1774, Thomas Wharton to Samuel Wharton, England, *Pennsylvania Magazine*, 1909, v. 33, p. 435.

At about the height of the wheat harvesting season, Drinker apprised his Mediterranean shippers that wheat and rye crops in Pennsylvania "promise to be larger than we have known, but," he added, "the prices will be governed very much by your crops and the demand from France, Italy, Spain and Portugal."[31] Prices of common flour dropped slightly during the summer on the basis of information that the markets at Lisbon were low, but at the same time superfine flour was scarce and "in demand for Jamaica."[32] All accounts from Europe for some months had been discouraging to traders in wheat and its products, "England and Ireland excepted."[33] In September, Drinker summarized the uncertainties for the London office of his Genoa and Leghorn correspondents, "Advices from Portugal, Spain and Italy for some time back brought most discouraging accounts to the adventurers that way, but latterly the intelligence from those countries particularly Spain and Italy have been more favorable. This added to an expectation now raised of a demand in England will be likely to keep up the prices of wheat and flour, at least for 2 or 3 months to come."[34]

In the fall of 1774, during the discussions of the First Continental Congress and before the result of the proceedings was known, prices dropped "so low that the farmers would not thrash out or bring their wheat to market."[35] The price of flour declined proportionately less than that of wheat because it continued difficult to get. Even at the close of the year, an inquiry from Newburyport had to be answered, "it is very uncertain whether we can find the 10 barrels of superfine [flour]."[36] Many vessels were then in the river to compete for cargoes of flour. The year 1774, in which 200,000 bushels of wheat, 280,000 barrels of flour, and 50,000 barrels of ship bread were reported to have been exported from the port of Philadelphia, was admittedly a peak in colonial supply of wheat and its products to world markets.[37] In all, 816 vessels entered the port, 103 from southern European ports—a total slightly above the arrivals from the British Isles.

British economists did not fail to appraise the significance of this

[31] July 8, 1774, James and Drinker to Zachariah Philip Fonnereau & Sons.

[32] August 13, 1774, Reynell and Coates to all clients.

[33] August 17, 1774, James and Drinker to Henry Trotman, West Indies.

[34] September 5, 1774, the same to Zachariah Philip Fonnereau & Sons.

[35] November 6, 1774, Thomas Clifford to Thomas Frank, Bristol.

[36] December 3, 1774, Reynell and Coates to William Wyer, Newburyport.

[37] July 5, 1775, *Pennsylvania Journal.*

colonial trade in grain. Coombe, in revising and completing Anderson's *Origin of Commerce,* remarked that "Mr. Arthur Young in his Political Arithmetic has very ably proved that in the year 1774 the American farmer could not only supply the West India market with flour much cheaper than the English farmer could do, but even exclude the English farmer from supplying the domestic markets of Britain."[38]

Shippers, who had traded with great caution for four years of high grain prices, vied with each other in the early part of 1775 in an effort to ship as much as they could get vessels to carry. Drinker, spurred by the high rate of exchange with "the encouraging advices we had of the markets at Leghorn and [the] strong desire in our own minds to have as much of effects on their way to our friends in England as we could forward," advised the Barclays that a ship loaded with wheat was on its way to "our friends Belli and Fonnereau at Leghorn."[39]

Colonists had enough experience with the effect of embargoes to anticipate that the restrictions would cause a drop in the prices of domestic staples and an increase in foreign goods. A shipper who bought nearly 1000 bushels more wheat than the ship he was loading would hold explained, "This circumstance would not be uneasy to us, if we did not apprehend that the intelligence received yesterday from England would throw a general damp on trade and tend to reduce the price of provisions very considerably."[40] A few weeks later, exportation to Halifax, Newfoundland, and the fishing coasts was suspended.[41] As further restriction was anticipated, "millers were hurrying their flour to market."[42]

Throughout the confused events of the summer of 1775, prices fluctuated in response to rumors and alarms from home and abroad. In May, when wheat had declined to less than 6 shillings a bushel, one of the best-informed merchants in Philadelphia hoped that the port would "continue open to 10th July, if not to 10th September."[42] With markets unsettled and prices sensitive to minor changes in shipping, it was difficult to accumulate cargoes without incurring unusual risks. Illustrative of the uncertainty is the comment of Drinker to a British purchaser, "Wheat got down to 5 shillings and 5 shillings 3 pence, but

[38] Anderson, *An Historical and Chronological Deduction of the Origin of Commerce,* v. 6, p. 696.

[39] January 2, 1775, James and Drinker to David and John Barclay & Co., London.

[40] April 12, 1775, the same to Joseph Glover.

[41] April 29, 1775, the same to John Geffrard & Co.

[42] May 30, 1775, Thomas Clifford to Thomas Frank, Bristol.

as the alarm arising from the measures adopted on your side subsided, the markets advanced so that after much pain and thought we obtained 5 shillings 10 pence for the wheat purchased in at 6 shillings 6 pence."[43] By August, the fear that led to the willing assumption of unusual risk had become a certainty, for a Bristol merchant was given the news, "The hurry in our port is very great on account of the resolution of the Congress not to export after the tenth of next month and the pushing for loads to forward many vessels before that time hath advanced the prices of several articles very much. Common flour as high as 19 shillings per hundredweight."[44] A few days later he reported the new wheat crop as "more in quantity and equal if not superior in quality to any former year." Flour was then selling above "the general proportion it bears to the price of wheat owing to the great demand therefor for many ships to be sent away before the tenth of next month."[45]

The curve of prices of wheat, with the period when continental currency was in use shown in relation to pre- and postwar levels, indicates that wheat continued an irregular decline from the middle of 1774 which was not interrupted until August 1776. At the trough of this contraction, wheat was selling at 4 shillings a bushel, or about one-half the level of 1772, the high price of colonial years, and flour, though proportionately higher, had declined equally.

Farmers seem to have been less concerned about getting the good crop of 1775 out of the country than were the merchants. At any rate, Clifford reported that "numbers of the country people" either did not believe the ports would be closed or would not "put themselves out of their usual course of business to bring their produce to market."[46] Their delay was not fatal, since before the year ended Congress was "taking into consideration the propriety of opening the ports of the United Colonies after the first day of March next."[47]

Before the beginning of 1776, the market had been narrowed to the needs of the colonists, plus such special shipments as Congress permitted. Regular prices current no longer were printed in the newspapers, and merchants became more dependent than before upon the information

[43] July 1, 1775, James and Drinker to Joseph Glover.

[44] August 26, 1775, the same to Lancelot Cowper, Bristol.

[45] August 31, 1775, the same to Joseph Sanders.

[46] September 4, 1775, Thomas Clifford to Thomas Frank, Bristol.

[47] December 26, 1775, *Journals of the Continental Congress*, v. 3, p. 457.

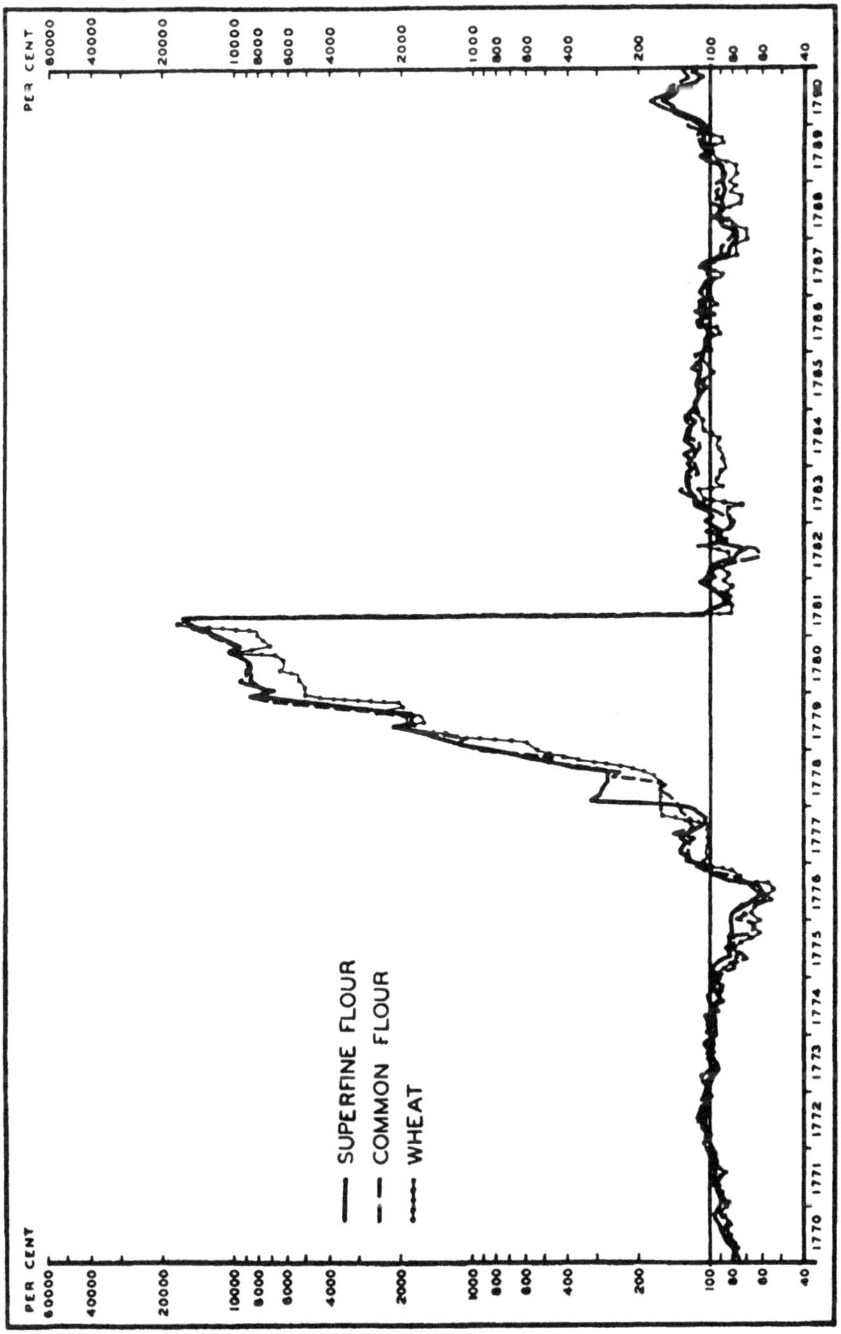

CHART IV—MONTHLY RELATIVES OF WHOLESALE PRICES OF WHEAT AND FLOUR IN PHILADELPHIA, 1770-1790
(Base—Monthly Average, 1771-1773)

supplied by their own correspondents. About the middle of January, Reynell wrote in detail to an inquirer in Newburyport,

> [Flour] is now 14 shillings 9 pence to 15 shillings and the fall of it very uncertain; there is but little made and the demand greater than was expected. Several New England vessels are loading, and some others by permission of Congress, some we believe on account of the continent. One large ship had upwards of 4000 barrels on board. It being uncertain what other vessels they may permit to load makes it difficult to judge what the market may be. It has not been under 13 shillings that we know of these 8 weeks and we rather doubt if it will be as low this winter again.[48]

Ten days later he advised the same correspondent, who had already dispatched a vessel to Philadelphia, "Flour is now at 14 shillings and the Congress buying."[49]

Flour continued at 14 shillings until "The rumor of 20 sail of our vessels being seized and carried to the West Indies stopped the buyers of flour, the beginning of this week, and it fell to 13 shillings 6 pence at which price we bought upwards of 400 barrels."[50] Only a week later the purchaser of flour was advised, "The Congress have stopped all trade to Great Britain, Ireland and the English West Indies; the consequence is the fall of flour which is now 13 shillings 3 pence to 13 shillings 6 pence."[51] By April, flour was "much lower" and few were willing to run the risk of shipping it.[52] Late in the same month Reynell wrote, "Flour is very plenty and no buyers that we know of. We could purchase at 12 shillings . . . but could not get a single hundred pounds insurance."[53] The matter of insuring grew more difficult as the year passed, "it being thought scarcely possible for a vessel to go and come safely" to the West Indies.[54] Having been deprived, by Congress or by extreme risk, of all but home markets, flour had been too long on hand and "the greatest part of the flour at market" was "but mean."[55]

Reversal of the Price of Breadstuffs

The whole trend of prices was reversed as the lightness of the new

[48] January 13, 1776, Reynell and Coates to Stephen Hooper, Newburyport.
[49] January 24, 1776, the same to the same.
[50] February 21, 1776, the same to the same.
[51] February 28, 1776, the same to the same.
[52] April 12, 1776, the same to the same.
[53] April 29, 1776, the same to the same.
[54] July 1, 1776, the same to William Teel, Newburyport.
[55] August 6, 1776, the same to Stephen Hooper, Newburyport.

wheat crop became generally known.[56] Prices of wheat in September 1776 advanced 33 per cent over those of the previous month. Reynell, in answer to a complaint about flour, admitted, "We are afraid from the present prospect of the badness of wheat and the length of time that most of the flour in the country has been kept for want of a market that we shall be in worse credit next winter than ever."[57] By the end of September, he was willing to predict, "Flour will continue at its present price if it doth not rise much higher . . . and believe it will be difficult at any rate to get it."[58]

The reversal of prices of wheat in September, of bread in November, of superfine flour in August, and of common flour as early as June, marks the end of a long cycle in prices of wheat and its products. In four of these years, at the height of prices, Pennsylvania was supplying grain from bumper crops to a broadening market and to outlets that reached even Central Europe.

New factors accompanied the upswing in prices in the closing months of 1776. Not only had much of the nearby wheat crop been ruined, but what was going to the millers was "thought to be from 15 to 20 pounds lighter per bushel than the preceding crop,"[59] making it likely that the flour supplied to other colonies, now the main markets, would bring complaints of poor quality. Once started, the upward movement, measured in the paper currency of the period, was not effectively checked until the spring of 1781, when continental currency was abandoned.

The first year of rise was in no way alarming. Until October 1777, when wheat rose to 10 shillings a bushel, it was not quoted at as high prices as in the peak of 1772. The next month it rose to 12 shillings and held this level through June 1778, when an uninterrupted rise began which carried it, by May 1779, to 150 shillings a bushel. The climb in the following years was interrupted by occasional mild breaks, but the spiral of rising prices continued until January 1781, when farmers would no longer take continental currency for wheat. Enhancement in quotations of flour preceded that in wheat. Prices of the three grades of flour—common, middling, and superfine—followed each other closely enough in the period of currency depreciation to provide some verification of the course of the advance.

56 August 27, 1776, the same to the same.
57 September 2, 1776, the same to the same.
58 September 30, 1776, the same to the same.
59 November 8, 1776, the same to the same.

By an advance in every month from May 1776 through March 1777, common flour not only overcame all the decline of 23 months but rose above the maximums of colonial years. At an early stage in the upswing, shippers of flour began casting about for ways of investing in durable goods instead of holding their surpluses in paper. Reynell made it clear that "the near approaches of General Howe's army has thrown us into very great confusion."[60] Robert Morris, who stayed in the city when Congress moved to Baltimore, was assembling flour and indigo "both on public and private account"[61] for a sloop which he was to dispatch to William Bingham at "Martinco." When the invoice for the cargo was forwarded and flour was selling at 24 shillings a hundred, he wrote that he expected a "ministerial fortune" from the adventure, but apprised Bingham, "Flour is very scarce and dear here and will continue so, as the last crops were the worst ever known and the consumption and destruction of two armies is immense."[62]

Scarce as the crop seemed to contemporaries, it is noteworthy that prices of flour and wheat did not advance in the remainder of 1777 until after the city was occupied by the British. By then, the record divides into the struggles of those who remained in the city and of those who had to find supplies for an army at Valley Forge with Congress at Lancaster and York. There is no conformity between prices in the two areas. By the middle of November, when Mrs. Drinker was recording in her journal, "Flour, what little there is, at £3 per 100"[63] and some of the inhabitants "by permission of Washington" were going to the mills at "Pennapack . . . for flour at 40 shillings per hundredweight,"[64] common flour was being sold outside the city at 24 shillings 9 pence. As supplies in the vicinity of the army headquarters became exhausted, prices of wheat and its products rose sharply.

Purchasing Supplies in 1778

In 1778, when wheat held at 12 shillings a bushel, flour continued a gradual rise that had started in the closing months of the previous year. The concern about food for the army and fodder for animals at a

[60] December 18, 1776, the same to William Hartshorne, Va.

[61] February 12, 1777, Robert Morris to William Bingham, Martinique.

[62] February 26, 1777, the same to the same.

[63] November 12, 1777, "Journal of Mrs. Henry Drinker," *Pennsylvania Magazine*, 1889, v. 13, p. 301.

[64] November 23, 1777, "Diary of Robert Morton," *ibid.*, 1877, v. 1, p. 31.

time when it was doubtful that six weeks' supply of flour for the army could be found[65] brought instructions to the millers about receiving and bolting grain which may well have introduced a change in grade.[66] In this emergency, the Assembly of Pennsylvania in February passed a law appointing commissioners "in every county of the state with full power to purchase or to seize, at stated prices, all provisions necessary for the army."[67] Meantime, the Board of War had been given authority by Congress "to purchase twenty thousand barrels of flour and other provisions necessary for the army." Such uniformity of price as was maintained during the hurry to collect produce must be attributed to the county commissioners who had to reconcile contradictory instructions and overcome the competition of other agents in their territories.[68]

In June, when rumors that the British were preparing to evacuate Philadelphia were being relayed to Congress in York, an embargo was laid on all provisions "both with a view to our own supply and the enemy's distress."[69] The resolution passed by Congress June 8, 1778, put an embargo on "the exportation of wheat, flour, rye, indian corn, rice, bread, beef, pork, bacon, live stock and other provisions from any of these United States, from and after the tenth day of June instant, until the fifteenth day of November next."[70]

Throughout the summer of 1778, the army commissaries were more worried about forage than breadstuffs. As prices soared, Congress attempted to meet the problem by appointing a committee to consider the question of depreciation. At first, neither the commissaries nor Con-

[65] January 5, 1778, Jonathan Bayard Smith, York, to Timothy Matlack, *Letters of Members of the Continental Congress*, v. 3, p. 15.

[66] January 11, 1778, Instructions to millers, *Pennsylvania Archives*, 1st ser., v. 6, pp. 303-4.

[67] February 14, 1778, John Henry, Jr., to Thomas Johnson, Jr., Governor of Maryland, *Letters*, v. 3, p. 85.

[68] Typical of their statements was that of one of the agents in Berks County, who wrote to President Wharton that his orders sanctioned "a higher price than was fixt by the late Act of Assembly which I presume is the rates I am to pay." (March 9, 1778, John Lesher of Berks County to Thomas Wharton, Jr., President of the Supreme Executive Council of Pennsylvania; *Pennsylvania Archives*, 1st ser., v. 6, p. 347.) At the same time, Colonel Grier stressed the lack of uniform procedure when he wrote, "I have got some grain at 12 shillings, but the people are informed that Captain Rippey is giving 15 shillings at Shippensburg and they now expect that price and will not sell under." (April 20, 1778, Colonel David Grier to Colonel John Davis, Deputy Quartermaster General.)

[69] June 9, 1778, James Lovell to Horatio Gates, *Letters*, v. 3, p. 285.

[70] June 8, 1778, *Pennsylvania Archives*, 1st ser., v. 6, p. 585.

gress was willing to attribute the rapidly mounting prices of grain to scarcity, though there is evidence that in some areas little was for sale. "The old grains are nearly exhausted," the deputy quartermaster wrote to Colonel Cox, "and the farmers have not begun to thrash out their new crops and the prices of what are to be sold are extravagantly high. The farmers won't sell under 3 dollars [22 shillings 6 pence] per bushel and the distillers are now offering 25 shillings per bushel (Colonel Bird informs me he can sell all the grain his mills brings in at that price)."[71]

Prices of wheat averaged 25 shillings in the next month and mounted steadily in every succeeding month until June 1779. Flour advanced more rapidly than wheat as instructions reached agents that a "very large demand will be made on our Department in a very short period for flour" with the injunction added, "Don't risk a sufficiency for want of price."[72]

Before the end of September, price limits for grain had to be disregarded. Agents were not only free to get supplies at such prices as they could but were warned, "The fluctuating price of wheat is such that we cannot with any degree of safety limit you."[73] On the same day, Owen Biddle, deploring the "uncommon, very rapid rise in the price of grain," wrote to John Davis at Carlisle, "You are hereby instructed to give the current price for grain and corn for forage, let it be what it may, rather than the army should suffer which you have to supply and the intended expedition be retarded for want of it."[74]

In this manner, the necessity of placing stores at strategic points along the line of march of the army came to outrank the necessity of putting a check on the depreciation of the currency. Both concerns had claimed the attention of Congress, but for the short run the getting of stores had precedence. Early in November, Ephraim Blaine, the Deputy Commissary of Purchases, instructed Chaloner and White immediately to "proceed to Cantwell's Bridge and fix upon a proper person to take in

[71] September 4, 1778, Colonel John Davis to Colonel Cox. Robert Morris, in a formal address in Congress, claimed that at the time supplies were desperately needed "flour was daily exported" from Maryland, "under, or under the idea of, tobacco." (September 10, 1778, Henry Laurens, President of Congress, to Rawlins Lowndes, President of South Carolina, *Letters,* v. 3, p. 407.)

[72] September 16, 1778, Chaloner and White to Robert McGermont, Dover, Del.

[73] September 25, 1778, the same to George Eichelberger, York.

[74] September 25, 1778, Owen Biddle to Colonel John Davis, Carlisle.

wheat. . . . Should the prices I have fixed not be sufficient to command the market you will exceed it, one shilling per bushel weight, but would rather continue at the prices fixed as I am of opinion the people will comply, and in a few days be well satisfied with the price."[75] Congress, in need of information about resources, called upon the governors of the states for an informal census of the "articles of consumption" in their areas, particularly "flour, wheat, rye, barley, oats, corn and rice, beef, pork, working oxen and horses, cyder and vinegar."[76]

Prices of flour, at the close of 1778, were mounting so rapidly that instructions were likely to be out of date before they reached the agents. For instance, Chaloner and White, convinced that prices were so high that provisions of "engrossers" would be seized, quoted flour, on December 1, at 107 shillings 10 pence.[77] Four days later, Reynell and Coates, evidently dealing in superfine flour, wrote to Newburyport, "Flour is very high with us at £8 10 shillings per hundredweight and a very considerable part of what we do get is a bad quality, the wheat being greatly injured by the fly so that we see no prospect of supplying your wants."[78]

It could have been that the discussion of a motion in Congress "to take out of circulation all the emissions of May 20, 1777, and April 1778"[79] added to the lack of faith in continental notes at a time when depreciation and depletion were joint factors in the mounting prices. At this time the President of Congress, John Jay, in an effort to have rice released from South Carolina for the French fleet, emphasized the temporary shortage when he explained,

> The middle and eastern states cannot supply more wheat this year than the inhabitants and army will consume. New York, New Jersey, and Pennsylvania have been so much embarrassed and injured by military operations, as to afford at present but a small proportion of their usual supplies. The crops

[75] November 3, 1778, Colonel Ephraim Blaine, Deputy Commissary of Purchases, to John Chaloner.

[76] November 11, 1778, A Committee of Congress to the Several States, *Letters*, v. 3, p. 489.

[77] December 1, 1778, Chaloner and White to Colonel Jeremiah Wadsworth, Commissary General of Purchases.

[78] December 5, 1778, Reynell and Coates to William Wyer, Newburyport.

[79] December 16, 1778, John Fell Diary, *Letters*, v. 3, p. 536.

now in the ground indeed are great and promise plenty the next season. The wheat in Maryland and Virginia, and I may add North Carolina, has been so destroyed or spoiled by a fly which infests those countries that but little flour and that in general of a bad quality can be procured there.[80]

Critical Rise of Breadstuffs in 1779–1780

By January 1779, the Executive Council, spurred by stormy protests from consumers, tightened the restrictions on "monopolizers and forestallers" and two private committees attempted rigid control of prices. The goal was to push prices back to the levels of May of the previous year, but the machinery did not get fully under way until May 1779. If the objective were attained, wheat selling above 120 shillings a bushel would be reduced step by step to 12 shillings; flour then at 360 shillings would be gradually lowered to about 30 shillings. Whatever prospect there was of containing prices depended on the extent of inventories of grain in the country, of which no one had precise information. All the measures adopted at this time indicate that scarcity, lack of information, and currency depreciation were hopelessly blended in creating a price advance. The favorite device of the commissaries, especially when obtaining fodder crops, was to contract with a great number of farmers for the market price at the time of delivery to be fixed "at the most favorable part of the season for lowering the price."[81]

In the first half of 1779 it was the opinion of officials and merchants that wheat and its products were scarce. Demand was then general. The Assembly of Massachusetts requested that the embargo on shipping grain to the eastward be lifted and Rhode Island was in "great want of flour"[82] at the very time when the President of Congress cautioned the Governor of New York that "the scarcity of bread in the East and South is become a serious subject."[83] It was information of the same type which a Philadelphia merchant gave to his brother in New York in the much-quoted letter which caused his arrest when he wrote, "The prospect of there not being sufficient of grain for bread till harvest seems well

[80] December 18, 1778, John Jay, President of Congress, to Rawlins Lowndes, *Letters*, v. 3, p. 541.

[81] January 31, 1779, Nathanael Greene, Quartermaster General, to Colonel John Davis.

[82] February 1, 1779, John Fell Diary, *Letters*, v. 4, p. 53.

[83] February 19, 1779, John Jay to George Clinton, Governor of New York, *Letters*, v. 4, p. 75.

founded. Flour now sells from 30 shillings to 35 shillings per hundredweight,"[84] in hard money.[85]

The advance in the price of flour to 220 shillings in February was attributed to "the many persons engaged in purchasing."[86] Though the quartermasters were urging that not more than 240 shillings be offered to the farmers,[87] the following day the agent who received the instructions noted "flour looks up as high as 17 pounds 10 shillings."[88] In the light of the evidence of those most informed about supplies in the spring of 1779, prices rose less than might have been expected.

In their eagerness to get supplies for the army, the agents overbought. By April, they were refusing to give the asking prices to holders of wheat and flour as "we do not think the necessity great enough to justify an advance price."[89] Flour prices, limited by consent among the agents at 500 shillings,[90] did not reach that level in merchant quotations until September. Fodder, on the other hand, was so urgently needed that agents were directed to "Purchase . . . all the rye, oats, spelts, barley and corn you can in your neighborhood on as low terms as possible but the grain we must have, let the price be what it will."[91]

The rise of flour prices in April and May was attributed to the activity of the French consular agents in getting stores for their squadron at Martinique, "not so much from the quantities they bought as from the idea their attempts to purchase made on the holders of flour of their necessity."[92] Once it was known that the crops were "promising throughout the continent"[93] and the Commercial Committee expected "the finest crops, both as to quality and quantity that has been known for many years,"[94] Chaloner and White, a trifle optimistically, wrote, "The crops

[84] February 19, 1779, Samuel Rowland Fisher to Jabez Fisher, New York, *Pennsylvania Magazine*, 1917, v. 41, p. 157.

[85] March 31, 1779, Journal of Samuel Rowland Fisher, *ibid.*, p. 148.

[86] February 22, 1779, Colonel Ephraim Blaine to Mr. Ewing.

[87] February 27, 1779, the same to Chaloner and White.

[88] February 28, 1779, Chaloner and White Papers.

[89] April 18, 1779, Chaloner and White to Colonel Ephraim Blaine.

[90] April 29, 1779, the same to the same.

[91] May 18, 1779, Colonel John Davis, Canedoguinet, to Colonel David Kennedy.

[92] May 22, 1779, Chaloner and White to Gouverneur Morris, Chairman of Committee of Congress.

[93] June 14, 1779, Daniel of St. Thomas Jenifer to Thomas Johnson, Jr., *Letters*, v. 4, p. 267.

[94] July 19, 1779, Commercial Committee of Congress to Oliver Pollock, *ibid.*, p. 330.

of wheat in this state, Maryland and to the northward are exceedingly fine."[95]

A new factor influencing purchases was introduced with the decision to export flour to pay for necessary clothing for the army. The instruction to the assemblers of flour was, "Wherever there has been any agreement of the people fixing a price we would not have you exceed it, and when there has been no such agreement we would not have you exceed the price at this market; which is £20 per hundredweight."[96] As the maximum was set higher than the average prevailing in the summer months, the agents tried an experiment in lowering prices. "We made a rule among ourselves," the agent in Lancaster County wrote, "to lower the prices of wheat and rye 10 shillings per bushel weekly and inferior grain in proportion, which had the desired effect as it reduced the prices of wheat and rye from 10 pounds to 7 pounds 10 shillings per bushel,"[97] a statement which implies higher quotations for wheat than were general in the city. By chance, the agents had a few months favorable to their experiment, as is clear from the report of the committee appointed by Congress to superintend the commissary department that there was "on hand in the Public Magazines, pork, beef, and flour in greater quantities than the armies can consume before it will become perishable."[98] Thus the stage seemed to be set for a recession, or at least an end to the upswing in prices.

On the strength of a temporary lull, the ports were opened for the export of flour to the French West Indies and produce from the abundant stores of the army was shipped to the French forces in San Domingo. Soon a demand arose for a renewal of the embargo to offset the activities of merchants and traders who were believed to be "already making contracts for flour."[99] By the next month the purchasers of flour were resorting to tied-in sales, "salt . . . to be sold to the inhabitants [of Berks County] at £15 per bushel, giving preference to those who supply flour and will receive two-thirds of the money at £20 per hundredweight—one third in salt . . ."[100]

[95] July 20, 1779, Chaloner and White to William Aylett.

[96] July 10, 1779, Joseph Reed, President of Supreme Executive Council of Pennsylvania, to purchasers of flour, *Pennsylvania Archives*, 1st ser., v. 7, p. 548.

[97] July 21, 1779, Colonel Philip Marsteller, Lebanon, to Joseph Reed, *ibid.*, p. 567.

[98] July 24, 1779, Commercial Committee of Congress to the same, *ibid.*, pp. 579-80.

[99] August 11, 1779, Joseph Reed to the Delegates in Congress, *ibid.*, p. 639.

[100] September 8, 1779, the same to purchasers of flour, *ibid.*, p. 692.

Wheat prices doubled between October and November, the most extreme advance in a single month in Revolutionary years. Common flour more than doubled, but the increase was spread over a three-month interval. At this time, the commissioners at Lancaster could do no better than set the price of wheat at 300 shillings a bushel and that of flour at 840 shillings a hundredweight.[101] Chaloner and White felt that these maximums were already being exceeded and "if the millers continue as they have done for a month past 30 pounds will not procure a bushel of wheat a month to come."[102] Their fears, though exaggerated, were not unwarranted, as wheat was selling at 375 shillings before the year ended.

Congress at once recommended the laying of an embargo in all states where one was not already in effect.[103] The factors in the gradual progress of depreciation, stressed by Reed to General Washington, were, "The crops in this state are very far from being so plentiful as was believed some time ago. The supply of the French fleet and the draught of our flour to Baltimore and Wilmington, where the embargo has not been executed with the same strictness as in this port, has also very much lessened our natural stock."[104] On the basis of price movements, however, there is little evidence of lack of resources at the start of 1780, one of the most critical years of the war.

The acute problem which dominated all others in the discussions of Congress in that year concerned the means to draw in supplies, or as one Philadelphian wrote to Blaine, "Flour is offering for sale every day and Chaloner and White have no money to purchase."[105] Toward the end of March, Blaine tentatively informed the President of Congress, "If the contracts my people have made for flour are complied with (which I have reason to think the disappointment of money has induced some people to hold back) there will be sufficient of flour and indian meal to serve the army up to the middle of June."[106]

From April through June 1780, the average prices of flour declined.

101 October 20, 1779, *Minutes of the Supreme Executive Council of Pennsylvania, Colonial Records*, v. 12, p. 142.

102 November 13, 1779, Chaloner and White to Colonel Jeremiah Wadsworth.

103 December 15, 1779, Samuel Huntington, President of Congress, to Thomas Johnson, Jr., *Letters*, v. 4, p. 536.

104 December 22, 1779, Joseph Reed to General George Washington, *Pennsylvania Archives*, 1st ser., v. 8, p. 55.

105 March 23, 1780, George Morton to Colonel Ephraim Blaine, Commissary General of Purchases.

106 March 29, 1780, Colonel Ephraim Blaine to Samuel Huntington.

During this period, the purchasers of flour were apprising the farmers of the prices to be paid under the plan of redeeming the old currency, issuing a limited amount of new, and depending upon the states to raise quotas of supplies apportioned to them. An agent in Reading began contracting for provisions at what he understood to be the agreed-upon prices "assuring the people at the same time that the merchants would take the new money at the same rate as specie and also that in case higher prices were given in other counties, they should have the same," when he received a letter "revoking," as he said, "my former instructions as to prices to be offered, and acquainting me that the House had rescinded the Resolutions for fixing the money at forty for one."[107]

The merchants were associating in a plan to speed the return of the old continental bills to the loan offices, to be replaced by new bills at "the exchange established by the Resolution of Congress."[108] They had also undertaken to relieve the temporary necessities of the army by their own credit.[109] Already the lure of specie had had an effect. Late in June a purchaser in Lancaster County wrote to President Reed, "My opinion as to the price of flour and wheat is that flour may be had from 20 shillings to 22 shillings 6 pence, and wheat at 7 shillings 6 pence, hard money, which prices, I think, will purchase all the grain and flour which can be spared in the county."[110]

Compared to those of the two previous years, prices of common flour, which fortunately can be assembled continuously from the same accounts, rose only moderately until the closing months of 1780. It was the progressive advance in prices already fantastic that made the rise notable. The circular to the commissaries of purchases stated that flour "having now a settled price or at least one much more so than formerly, we hope you will be able to forward a considerable quantity. The Philadelphia

[107] June 5, 1780, Nicholas Lutz, Reading, to Joseph Reed, *Pennsylvania Archives*, 1st ser., v. 8, p. 301.

[108] June 11, 1780, Elbridge Gerry to Robert Morris, *Letters*, v. 5, p. 205.

[109] "Our greatest hopes of being able [to] feed them are founded on a patriotic scheme of the opulent merchants of this city who have already subscribed nearly £3,000,000 and will very soon complete that sum; the immediate object of which is to procure and transport to the army 3,000,000 lbs. of rations and 300 hhds. of rum." June 23, 1780, James Madison to Thomas Jefferson, Governor of Virginia, *Letters*, v. 5, p. 235.

[110] June 25, 1780, Colonel Philip Marsteller, Lebanon, to Joseph Reed, *Pennsylvania Archives*, 1st ser., v. 8, pp. 362-63.

price at present is £80 continental money and so in state money at the rate of 60 for one which you are authorized to give."[111]

In the confused currency situation of the last quarter of 1780, prices of flour and wheat advanced rapidly. The merchants' efforts in November to peg the ratio of paper to specie at 75 to one created at most a temporary lull of limited effect. By mid-December, the rating of specie in commodity dealings differed from the price at which specie could be purchased with continental money.[112]

The unwillingness of farmers to sell except for hard money is shown clearly in dealings in wheat. Such prices as can be found quoted in paper follow the relatively mild but cumulative advance shown in flour. In the main, quotations from April 1780 on are in specie. The peak and final price of wheat in continental currency was found in January 1781 at 600 shillings a bushel, when it could be purchased with specie for 6 shillings 6 pence. Millers seem to have accepted currency, though it was rapidly depreciating, through April 1781, when common flour averaged 2830 shillings and superfine flour more than 3737 shillings a hundredweight. Toward the end of the attempts to keep paper in circulation when the value of state paper was being pegged, a purchaser of flour explained, "On account of the rapid depreciation that our money hath got, I can purchase flour for twenty-two shillings and six pence per hundredweight hard money or five times that sum state money. The millers in general is supplied with hard money from the merchants that I need not pretend to do any thing but at tennor of the law . . ." The prospects not only seemed poor and prices in paper far above those in hard money but "the people not free in taking of it."[113]

Prices after the Withdrawal of Continental Money

The analysis of price behavior of 1781 is complicated by the sudden disuse of continental currency and the shift in May to a few months of dealing substantially in hard money. On this basis, prices of superfine flour declined from February 1781 to August and those of common flour to September. Wheat held its lowest price of this decline from May

111 July 24, 1780, Circular [of the Supreme Executive Council] to Commissaries of Purchases, *ibid.*, p. 441.

112 See Ch. III, Merchant Practices as Evidence of Inflation, p. 50.

113 May 15, 1781, William McCalla, Bucks County, to Joseph Read, *Pennsylvania Archives*, 1st ser., v. 9, p. 136.

through August and returned to that low again in November. After these adjustments, there was a short, erratic, one-year swing in prices with a peak in December 1781 and a corresponding low point in June or July 1782 in all products of wheat. From the trough of mid-1782 began one of the most surprising phases of price behavior of the postwar years. Prices of superfine flour rose irregularly from July 1782 to March 1784 and held at high levels to the close of that year. Common flour followed though less steadily, indicating how much the strength of the upswing was attributable to export rather than to internal demand.

The decline in price from this gradual rise was never abrupt. For instance, after about two and three-quarter years of mild decline, superfine flour had been reduced from the peak prices of 1784 only 21.2 per cent and common, only 19.8 per cent. Wheat, in the four years following the close of 1783, had two rather pronounced cycles.

In accounting for the price movements of this period, one cannot overlook the blow that trade suffered in the early months of 1781 by the capture of "no less than seven fine vessels . . . taken out of an outward bound fleet."[114] One source of the demand for superfine flour was the shipment of it to Havana in return for specie. The preference for specie was, according to President Reed, stimulated by these shipments. Purchases of flour had to be made with state paper at "a great depreciation, which increased to three and four for one."[115] In continuing his explanation to Washington, Reed wrote, "But on the last arrivals from the Havannah and before any declaration of exchange by public authority, the purchases immediately stopped, no flour could be had but for money; and so it has continued ever since, the late supplies having been procured chiefly on an exchange for salt. We then had recourse to the law directing one-third to be delivered to the state; but here again we were disappointed. The merchants would not deliver the one-third for paper money, but at a *depreciation destructive* of the money, and many wholly declining it."[115] Admittedly there was no scarcity of supplies, as Reed concluded, "This city has now an abundance for exportation, though we cannot obtain a barrel with our money, this commodity being only attainable for specie."[115]

The same type of information was communicated by others. On May

[114] January 16, 1781, James Madison to Edmund Pendleton, *Letters*, v. 5, p. 539.

[115] May 17, 1781, Joseph Reed to General George Washington, *Pennsylvania Archives*, 1st ser., v. 9, pp. 145-46.

28 a member of Congress from Maryland wrote, "Yesterday and today arrived from the Havannah eight sail of vessels with hard money. The merchants I am told pay very little regard to the embargo law, indeed the state has not money to purchase the third of any vessel's cargo even were it to be offered to the President and Council."[116] Once payment in specie was resorted to, Reed stated, "The people of the country as well as in the city universally demand gold or silver for their produce and merchandise, and will not part with either for paper money but at a most unreasonable depreciation."[117]

Sales in specie were accompanied by a decline in prices and a general speeding up of trading. Robert Morris informed General Washington,

> All our ships have been and continue to be constantly employed in carrying flour to the French and Spanish Islands, our port is filled in return with West India produce, some European goods and many Spanish dollars, and flour remains so plenty that there has not been a day in which I could not buy 5,000 to 10,000 barrels in this city and the price has fallen from 28 and 30 shillings which was asked and given at first to 17 shillings which is now asked, but I think 15 shillings or two hard dollars will buy 112 pounds very soon.[118]

The prospect of "a most plentiful harvest"[119] and the belief that confidence was fast being restored led the President of the Executive Council of the Commonwealth of Pennsylvania to conclude that "our public affairs in general wear a favorable aspect."[120] Active as trade was, Hollingsworth believed that "the scarcity of cash is also too great to suppose a rise in goods."[121] To a dealer in Virginia he wrote, "Paper money of all kinds are out of use here and hath been since May, which is the principal reason of a stagnation in the price of produce."[122]

Toward the close of the year, prices of breadstuffs started a mild advance. Shippers, however, alarmed by the capture and necessary "de-

[116] May 28, 1781, Daniel of St. Thomas Jenifer to John [Hall], *Letters*, v. 6, p. 101.

[117] June 7, 1781, Joseph Reed to Speaker of Assembly, *Pennsylvania Archives*, 1st ser., v. 9, p. 197.

[118] July 2, 1781, Robert Morris to General George Washington, *Collections of the New York Historical Society for the Year 1878*, v. 11, p. 465.

[119] July 14, 1781, Thomas McKean, President of Congress, to General George Washington, *Letters*, v. 6, p. 145.

[120] August 27, 1781, Joseph Reed to Thomas Scott, Washington County, *Pennsylvania Archives*, 1st ser., v. 9, p. 375.

[121] August 13, 1781, Levi Hollingsworth to Low and Russell.

[122] August 21, 1781, the same to Marsden and Smith, Va.

tention of vessels at the French and Spanish West India"[123] islands, found little reason to hope for a strong export market. Sales of flour in the domestic market were feeling the first effect of the shift from procurement by state quotas supplemented by purchases on commission to supplying the army by contract.

Rumors of a truce, circulating out of New York,[124] added uncertainty to an already dull market, and introduced a cautious tone in all trade comment. As a result, the lowest prices for superfine flour in postwar years were reached in July 1782, the culmination of six months of steady decrease. The decline was not wholly a local market situation. Late in September, Chaloner and White reported that the incoming vessels from Havana brought news that flour had fallen there "in consequence of which the few vessels loading here are discharging for other cargoes. Flour I have bought this day at 16 shillings 6 pence per hundredweight and I expect it will be under that price."[125]

The news that changed the direction of prices came from other sources. Toward the close of 1782 a British merchant, formerly one of the partners in a trading house in the Madeira Islands, began to reopen his trading and wrote to the Philadelphia partner, "The failure of the last crops almost in every part of Europe having been greater than was ever known to be, and being very desirous to avail ourselves of the high prices that wheat and flour will undoubtedly bear two or three months hence, we hope it will be in your power to furnish the House with a cargo . . . consisting of the above articles to about the amount of £1000 to £1200 sterling as soon as your ports shall be opened or you can obtain a license for it."[126]

The advance in breadstuffs from July 1782 was the beginning of a major cycle which, at its peak, raised the prices of superfine 29 and common flour 38 per cent above their prewar averages. The movement resembled the upswing of the early seventies in smoothness and sustained aspects. The postwar rise differed, however, not only in the speed with which maximums were attained but in the persistence of moderately high levels. Amid all the uncertainties of postwar adjustment, it is notable that the decline in flour prices from the close of 1784

[123] April 23, 1782, the same to Henry Hollingsworth, Head of Elk.

[124] May 7, 1782, Pelatiah Webster to John Perit, Norwich, Conn.

[125] September 25, 1782, Chaloner and White to Jeremiah Wadsworth, Baltimore.

[126] December 5, 1782, Thomas Lamar, London, to Henry Hill.

until September 1787 was not only orderly but relatively mild. Prices of wheat fluctuated more than flour but advanced less steeply.

Postwar Trade in Grains

There was world interest in 1783 in the state of the harvests in the Middle Atlantic region. In January the *Gentleman's Magazine* recorded, "Some private advices from Philadelphia say that the harvest has been so remarkably plentiful in the middle provinces that wheat was sold at New York from 15 to 13 shillings the quarter."[127] It was then at the low price of 6 shillings a bushel in Philadelphia. By contrast, the Lord Mayor of London complained the next month "the price of wheat was so excessive, and that of barley so exorbitant, that it almost amounted to a prohibition of the use of it."[128] The "low state" of Scottish crops[129] offered no relief. Shippers in the middle states were informed of the temporarily favorable outlook for their ample supplies at a time when other countries were forced to purchase. Putting both factors together, Pelatiah Webster, with his capital more nearly intact than that of many other dealers, showed his readiness to trade in his comment, "We have large quantities of country produce on hand, much more than our own vessels can export and harvest is near. We hear the European markets for flour are very good."[130] Before long, flour was found to be "scarce and in high demand."[131] It was not expected "to be lower soon . . . as there is so many vessels here and harvest time approaching, which is a very busy season in the country."[132] About the same time, another prominent merchant reported in more detail: "Common flour is at 40 shillings to 43 shillings. Superfine 47 to 48 shillings 6 pence per barrel. Scarce and difficult to be got owing to the great number of shippers having engaged the factors to supply all that they receive."[133]

Already the dull market for dry goods and the disparity between low prices of West India produce and rising prices for domestic goods had attracted attention. As usual, merchants distrusted the stability of the prevailing prices, especially the upswing in flour. "There has been no

[127] January 1783, *Gentleman's Magazine*, v. 53, p. 84.
[128] February 1783, *ibid.*, p. 108.
[129] February 1783, *ibid.*, p. 110.
[130] April 23, 1783, Pelatiah Webster to Benjamin Goodhue.
[131] June 25, 1783, Stephen Collins to William Gray, Salem, Mass.
[132] June 25, 1783, the same to the same.
[133] June 27, 1783, Chaloner and White to ———.

market to induce this price," Stephen Collins warned his New England client, "except with you and that can't hold long, but our port is crowded with shipping and everyone must load with something though with a prospect of loss. . . . flour I think must be down very considerably as soon as harvest is over, but it will not before."[134]

Merchants, counting heavily on the returns from the new crop in satisfying their customers and easing the terms of purchase, differed little in the factors they were considering. Clifford had the state of crops and shipping facilities in mind when he wrote to his brother in midsummer, "There is a prospect of a very great crop of grain this harvest, which I am in hopes will reduce the price of that article. Flour is now very high, more owing to the great number of vessels in port than the price abroad."[135] Shippers to Madeira knew that the islands were being supplied with grain from Portugal and that the scantiness of the vintage would not encourage the purchase of more American flour than had been shipped.[136] Throughout the summer, they were puzzled that flour "rather rises than falls,"[137] which, by the latter part of August, was held to be "principally owing to the want of water at the mills."[138]

Only by a survey of the prices of other commodities could it be known that beef, corn, rice, and some less staple commodities diverged further from the average prices of all commodities than did wheat and flour. At the close of this year, the editor of the *Origin of Commerce* not only expressed surprise "that the prices of all things have been uncommonly high in the United States since the peace" but found the prevailing prices of December 1783 in Philadelphia, converted to sterling, nearly as high as the current London rates.[139] He included prices of common flour, fine flour, beef, and pork in his comparisons at rates which tally closely with those in our price tables. Robert Proud, then resident in the city, believed that "the expense of living here is about double of what it was ten years ago,"[140] a statement that would be difficult to verify. Careful commentators agree, on the whole, with the conclusions in Anderson's history. For instance, in giving his impressions

[134] July 2, 1783, Stephen Collins to William Gray, Salem, Mass.

[135] July 8, 1783, John Clifford to Thomas Clifford, Jr., Bristol.

[136] July 15, August 2, September 20, 1783, Joseph Gilliss, Madeira, to Henry Hill.

[137] August 4, 1783, Stephen Collins to William Gray, Salem, Mass.

[138] August 20, 1783, the same to the same.

[139] Anderson, *op. cit.*, v. 6, p. 696.

[140] October 16, 1783, Robert Proud to William Proud, Hull.

to a friend in London soon after his arrival, Poultney wrote, "I was much surprised at the dearness of several things in this country. House rent is dearer than in London; meat nearly the same price; butter much dearer and bread as dear." Like others, he found the market for European goods dull "and but a few I believe will yield much profit to the speculators."[141] The description brings out the difficulty of picturing the postwar situation by any general statement. It looked adverse to the articulate group of dealers in dry goods whose lack of sales colored their outlook on the whole economy. Dealers in grain, lumber, staves, or tobacco gave a different emphasis and even the householder who had to purchase cordwood found it had nearly doubled in price.[142]

Flour and wheat held at high levels longer than some of the other products. At times their behavior induced caution which turned out, in the light of later events, to be overdone. Swanwick, acting for the firm of Willing and Morris, concluded in the spring of 1784 that flour and wheat would not answer at any foreign market.[143] Robert Morris shared his sentiment when he wrote, "I am glad to find that wheat had met with a check not that I expect anything can be done in it, for some how or other our farmers and millers have so completely got the game in their own hand that they play *alone* and will do so until bad markets abroad and large quantities at home half ruin them."[144] These comments were made during the period of the lowest prices of the year, when other observers felt that wheat and flour were "in great abundance at market,"[145] a situation that changed with the arrival of vessels for spring freights. By midsummer, a price of 9 shillings a bushel for wheat was not unusual.[146] The fact was, the shippers had no reliable appraisal of the prospects in European markets, as Robert Morris readily admitted in his own statement,

I think Mr. Swanwick cannot answer the questions you propose respecting wheat. The fate of the European crops cannot be ascertained so as to know the

141 December 15, 1783, Joseph Poultney to Robert Dixon, Jr., London, *Pennsylvania Magazine*, 1928, v. 52, p. 95.

142 February 14, 1784, Jacob Cox Parsons, editor, *Extracts from the Diary of Jacob Hiltzheimer*, p. 61.

143 April 8, 1784, Willing, Morris, and Swanwick to Tench Tilghman & Co., Baltimore.

144 April 20, 1784, Robert Morris to Tench Tilghman, Baltimore.

145 May 4, 1784, Chaloner and White to Wadsworth and Church.

146 July 3, 1784, John Clifford to Thomas Clifford, Jr., Bristol.

demand or the prices in that country, neither can he know what calls will be made on the House for supplies, and whilst prices remain so dear in America I do not wish much concern in the exportation, experience having taught me how very hazardous such enterprises are.[147]

Others were cheering their clients with the news that though "wheat keeps up yet . . . the large quantity put in the ground for next summer, with our present plentiful harvest, must certainly bring it down."[148] Of more importance were the efforts to draw supplies of wheat from states to the southward,[149] which could be done only if the orders for wheat and flour were not placed at too rigid price limits.[150]

The market for wheat was sustained at this time, according to Clifford, by what appeared to be "a scarcity in Spain and Portugal. There has already been several cargoes shipped to Lisbon."[151] For a time the demand for shipment so affected the differential between grades of flour that superfine was raised more than 9 shillings per barrel above common.[152] Complaints continued that "the exports of this country are all kept up at such extravagant prices as to render every speculation in that way extremely precarious."[153]

There is no way of indicating how much of the caution expressed by shippers was a desire to please purchasers, how much the reflection of distress of merchants in other lines, and how much uncertainty about commercial regulations. In retrospect, there would seem to be little evidence of irregularity in the prices of wheat and its products. On the Amsterdam market, Koenigsberg wheat rose steadily in these postwar years until June 1785, reaching then the highest peacetime price since the middle seventies.[154] In Pennsylvania, prices of wheat followed a more irregular course, but prices of flour, for nearly two years, were subject only to minor variation. Such direct comparisons were not open to contemporaries and from the correspondence it is clear that exporters had to act on indirect knowledge of the way crops in one region affected

[147] August 3, 1784, Robert Morris to Tench Tilghman, Baltimore.
[148] August 23, 1784, William and John Sitgreaves to Thomas Bramall, Liverpool.
[149] October 26, 1784, Kuhn and Kuhn to James Finlay, Port Royal, Va.
[150] November 23, 1784, Robert Morris to Tench Tilghman, Baltimore.
[151] January 8, 1785, Thomas and John Clifford to Amos Hillicar & Son, Bristol.
[152] February 22, 1785, Josiah and Samuel Coates to William Teel, Newburyport.
[153] March 10, 1785, John Clifford to Thomas Clifford, Jr., Bristol.
[154] N. W. Posthumus, *Inquiry into the History of Prices in Holland*, Table 1.

markets in another. For instance, toward the close of 1785, Robert Morris suggested to his Baltimore partner, "You will find that the weather in England proved bad for the harvest; prices were rising in consequence of it and I believe Barcelona will be a pretty good market for wheat."[155] Other merchants felt that domestic prices were edging toward a change, as is evident in the typical summary of Clifford: "The prices of our produce will fall though I cannot join with Mr. Randle's friends in saying it has already taken place."[156] Among his other activities in Virginia and Maryland, Morris was urging the purchase of superfine flour to be shipped from Norfolk and of 5000 to 7000 bushels of "good sound wheat" for the Lisbon and Barcelona markets.[157] Thus the activity of Philadelphia shippers was disseminating to other continental areas the effect of the international demand for grain.

The strong demand in the beginning of 1786 was for wheat, which Clifford found "selling at 8 shillings to 8 shillings 4 pence per bushel" and did not "see much prospect of its falling,"[158]—a sentiment shared by Morris, who had information that "flour bears a good price in Cadiz."[159]

The over-all situation as seen by members of Congress was, by contrast, gloomy. The Connecticut delegates, in looking ahead, wrote to their governor,

> Our affairs seem to indicate the approach of some great crisis. Our trade in a very distracted situation, Britain watching for some opportune season to revenge her smarts, the fickle Indian nations ready to join those who best can supply their wants, and jealous of the approach of the Americans so near their territories, the states unwilling or neglecting to adopt almost any one measure which can be proposed to them by Congress so as to act jointly and efficaciously for mutual benefit.[160]

Trade practices reflected a change in sentiment long before a decline was felt in prices of flour and wheat. While shippers of flour were urging that their consignments be sold immediately, not "kept for a market,"

[155] November 28, 1785, Robert Morris to Tench Tilghman & Co., Baltimore.

[156] December 4, 1785, John Clifford to Thomas Clifford, Jr., Bristol.

[157] January 3, 1786, Robert Morris to Tench Tilghman & Co., Baltimore.

[158] February 27, 1786, Thomas and John Clifford to Amos Hillicar & Son, Bristol

[159] March 2, 1786, Robert Morris to Tench Tilghman, Baltimore.

[160] April 12, 1786, Connecticut Delegates in New York to Matthew Griswold, Governor of Connecticut, *Letters*, v. 8, p. 339.

merchants who had turned to retailing to avoid extending credits were being forced to accept state paper money or make no sales, and bankruptcies and lack of punctuality in payment were adding impetus to a general slowing down of trading.

The strength of prices of grain in the first half of 1786 was attributable to a poor crop in the previous year. A new harvest held the prospect of a decline, but no immediate influence could be reflected in prices, especially as fall rains delayed threshing, cleaning, and milling.[161] Damage to mills from severe storms affected the Baltimore supplies[162] and flour kept at levels which were held to be too high for West India markets.[163] In attempting to supply choice flour, merchants were calling attention to the inclusion in their shipments of mill brands which were assumed to represent the best grades, such as Canby, Newlin, Lewis, Robeson, and Downing.[164] Late in the spring of 1787 the contrast between supplies on hand and the minor decline in price was frequently noted. At the end of March, a merchant with continuous dealings in West India goods wrote, "Flour is very plenty here, but still continues high to ship to the West Indies."[165] Two months later he retailed the even less encouraging news, "Flour has started in price here, and there is every appearance of scarcity of that article soon, as the wheat is almost run out. Superfine flour is now brisk at 42 shillings per barrel, and we expect it will be at ten dollars [75 shillings] in the course of a few days."[166] In this prediction, he was mistaken. There were only a few months of brisk demand before the new and "very large" crop of wheat made lower prices certain. Levi Hollingsworth, who in mid-July found flour "at present very scarce,"[167] revised his estimate before the month ended to "flour is on the fall with us and I apprehend will be at 35 shillings to 37 shillings 6 pence for superfine and common in proportion." He was not so certain about wheat prices because "the farmers hold up their crops to 7 shillings 6 pence [a bushel] . . ."[168]—a practice

[161] September 26, 1786, John Clifford to Dom. d'Oliveira Abz, Jr., Madeira; and October 7, 1786, James Cox to Thompson and Rowlandson, Barbados.

[162] October 28, 1786, James Cox to John Cox.

[163] November 2, 1786, the same to the same.

[164] February 26, 1787, the same to the same.

[165] March 30, 1787, the same to Charles Hagart & Co., St. Thomas.

[166] May 26, 1787, the same to the same.

[167] July 19, 1787, Levi Hollingsworth to Philip Marchinton, Halifax.

[168] July 30, 1787, the same to Murray and Samson, New York.

which could last but a short time since it was soon reported, "The wheat harvest this season has been as fine and abundant as it was ever known in this country."[169]

The combination of unusual supplies and changes in demand and terms of shipping brought to an end the long period of mildly declining but relatively minor price fluctuations in grain and its products. In these years, the average annual price of superfine flour was about 28 shillings in 1784; 25 in 1785; 24 in 1786; 21 in 1787—a gradually declining trend which, in every summer including 1787, recorded prices above 24 shillings a hundredweight. After the abrupt decline of the last five months of 1787, superfine flour sold by December for 17½ shillings, or about the price of the opening months of 1770 and nearly 5 shillings below the prewar average.

Soon a merchant house which had been active in shipping flour to the West Indies and was hopeful of a turn in local prices felt at a loss to know how to keep its vessel going as "the late restrictions of the British government have stopped every avenue to these islands. They have so deranged us that we are quite at a loss what to do with our brig. We have laid her up for the present in hopes that we may sell her."[169] On the other hand, one of the largest dealers in the market felt more concern about the diversity in terms of purchase and sale than about prices. His emphasis was, "Flour has fallen to a reasonable price, but as it is a cash article and all West India produce [are] sold subject to a credit, I would recommend your shipping specie in general which commands flour on better terms considerably than the produce of the Island."[170] Knowing that large shipments both from the Delaware and the Chesapeake would be made to St. Eustatius, a shipper with a brig regularly in that trade urged selling flour immediately upon its arrival.[171] Political as well as economic factors were disturbing to trade. For a time, merchants showed more interest in disposing of their vessels in ports of the West Indies than in operating them. They were marking time until a stable home government and greater certainty about the commercial policies of foreign governments could be had.

Before grain prices turned downward, one might infer from the ability

[169] August 5, 1787, James and John Cox to Thornton, Baillie and Campbell, Grenada.

[170] August 10, 1787, Levi Hollingsworth to Hankinson and Barrow, Kingston, Jamaica.

[171] August 18, 1787, Benjamin Fuller to Henry Ash, St. Eustatius, and to Robert Totten, Trinidad.

of farmers to withhold crops that agricultural areas enjoyed a measure of prosperity. It is less easy to arrive at the effect upon merchants, who complained of the depreciation of the state paper, high prices of exportable goods, and variable markets. The insistence upon drawing up balances at the end of each year and the attempt to calculate the profit from keeping vessels in regular routes, noted in the correspondence of Benjamin Fuller, James and John Cox, and Peter Kuhn, reflect care in accounting practices induced by narrow margins and other uncertainties. Benjamin Fuller and the Coxes, in these years, dealt primarily in breadstuffs in return for West India staples. Fuller, formerly an importer of dry goods, had withdrawn from the city early in 1775. Though he returned soon after the British evacuated in 1778, he claimed to have done little business before March 1780 or thereabouts. His return was "to pursue business having suffered the loss of the greatest part of my fortune by the unhappy contest." His own appraisal, in 1788, of the success of his trading, largely to the Islands though in a diversity of items, was, "Providence has remarkably blessed my endeavors since my recovery [March 1780] and I have in some measure repaired my great loss, but am still obliged to be industrious and careful."[172] Kuhn expanded his business in the southern areas, but was not peculiarly an exporter of Pennsylvania staples as were Fuller and the Cox brothers. The experience of Robert Morris in the export of flour to Europe, on his own evidence, seems to have been unrewarding.

Wheat and flour reached their lowest postwar prices in the first quarter of 1788, and recovered only slightly before the close of the year. About the time of the reversal in the trend of staples, general sentiment was undergoing a change. Hollingsworth wrote in April 1788, "Great quantities of wheat are shipping off for Portugal and flour for Spain and I flatter myself that on the Federal government taking place a new spring will be given to trade and agriculture."[173] Clifford gave similar information to his supplier in Bristol[174] and Robert Henderson, one of the slowest to find cause for optimism, reported a change in prices of breadstuffs.[175] A month later, Cox in reporting the rise in flour

[172] April 8, 1788, Benjamin Fuller to Mrs. Judith Sober, Barbados.

[173] April 21, 1788, Levi Hollingsworth to Mark Pragers, London.

[174] April 26, 1788, John Clifford to George Watson, Bristol.

[175] April 26, 1788, Robert Henderson to David Lamb, Charleston.

referred to the "European demand for it," which, he predicted, "it is probable will continue high till October."[176]

As large shipments of wheat left the port for England as well as southern Europe, purchasers began to take note of the condition of nearby crops. The appraisal was not reassuring. Coates, writing to Rhode Island early in June, found, "Our crops in Jersey are like to be very bad, and some in Bucks County on the river Delaware, many thousands acres of wheat being wholly destroyed by the Hessian fly—is expected to do as [much] mischief as the Hessian army."[177]

The activity of spring shipping reduced inventories of grain. By mid-summer Cox was stating, "Our market for flour is very high at present owing to the old wheat being nearly expended and the new not yet at market."[178] That the advance in grain prices was mild in the fall may be attributed to the fact that light crops were not general throughout the country. Virginia reported an especially good crop of wheat. Around Philadelphia, by contrast, crops had "in many instances fallen short and [been] in great degree injured by the heavy rains during harvest."[179] The situation favored speculation in southern wheat, a prospect so obvious that one trader would have liked to apply "every shilling to that use."[180] But as the year advanced, the lighter demand from Europe than had been indicated in the spring found adequate supplies of grain.[181] Just before the period of shipping ended, a dealer in staples wrote, "Flour is plenty here at present but the price has got up to 35 shillings per barrel, owing to a demand in the Mediterranean."[182]

A complete reversal in the grain market appeared in the spring of 1789. Flour rose above its prewar average in May; wheat rose in the same months, but first exceeded its prewar average in July. Merchants profited in the beginning of the strong market for wheat by taking advantage of a differential between Philadelphia and Virginia wheat prices.[183] Contracting for a considerable quantity seemed to Kuhn to

[176] May 20, 1788, James and John Cox to Charles Hagart, St. Thomas.

[177] June 3, 1788, Josiah and Samuel Coates to Moses Brown, Providence.

[178] July 14, 1788, James and John Cox to Gilloch and Ker, Grenada.

[179] August 15, 1788, Kuhn and Risberg to William French & Co., Fredericksburg.

[180] August 18, 1788, the same to the same.

[181] November 24, 1788, the same to the same.

[182] December 10, 1788, James and John Cox to Charles Hagart, St. Thomas.

[183] January 8, 1789, Kuhn and Risberg to William French & Co., Fredericksburg.

be taking a minor risk, especially as even higher prices in the Philadelphia market were anticipated.

"A price [for flour] scarce ever passed"[184] was reached in Madeira by February. Wheat, according to Kuhn, "never before gave more flattering prospect of advantage . . . both the West India and European French ports are open for flour and wheat and in the latter a great bounty is given for American wheat."[185] Before the advance made much progress, shippers to St. Eustatius feared flour had already risen too high for that market and felt the demand for Europe "will keep it up here all the summer."[186] Others were generally informing their clients of the upswing in wheat and flour.

Uncertainties were added to trading by speculation about the way the new duties would affect the price of goods and, more important, the individual interests of each state. Coates had both problems in mind when, late in April 1789, he described the activity in the Philadelphia market. He wrote,

> Demand now continues [for vessels] to carry wheat and flour to France and Spain and flour to Portugal. Five shillings to five shillings and six pence sterling has been given for flour per barrel to France and Lisbon and one shilling for wheat per bushel. Thus the prospect is fair. This demand for ships has occasioned produce to rise; and that may possibly discourage. If any vessel is to come we recommend great expedition in getting them off. We should suppose the eastern states may be benefited by the duties the Congress may lay on foreign bottoms; but the southern states not being so much engaged as you are in building ships will follow their interest and oppose such a duty unless it be a moderate one.[187]

In spite of high freight rates, vessels were delayed in loading because it took an undue time to get flour.[188]

Buyers, for the time, seem to have disregarded the advance in price. A merchant, corresponding with Moses Brown in Providence about freight rates, expressed surprise over the strength of the offers for produce. "We had hopes," he wrote, "flour would not rise above

[184] February 9, 1789, Lamar, Hill, Bissett & Co., Madeira, to Henry Hill.
[185] February 18, 1789, Kuhn and Risberg to William French & Co., Fredericksburg.
[186] March 14, 1789, Benjamin Fuller to Henry Ash, St. Eustatius.
[187] April 22, 1789, Josiah and Samuel Coates to Stephen Hooper, Newburyport.
[188] April 23, 1789, Robert Henderson to David Lamb, Charleston.

33 shillings, but it suddenly did rise to 34 and 35 shillings. At the latter price much was bought."[189] Before his letter could possibly be received, flour was selling for 40 shillings a barrel in an upswing that continued for the next twelve months. A shipper to the West Indies found flour "getting very scarce here as the harvest approaches." He added, "I could now sell every barrel superfine flour on board the brig at 42 shillings 6 pence per barrel."[190]

That the marked upswing in breadstuffs was at all gradual may be attributed to the volume and quality of the incoming wheat crop. As the new flour appeared, an exporter found the differential between common and fine flour so slight that he forwarded only the best grades as "the wheat is so very good this year that I expect there will be no common flour made."[191] Not only had European demand been active but the year brought "a very great market in all the ports of Hispaniola."[192]

In accounting for the sustained high prices of superfine flour, a merchant estimated that there was "a larger number of vessels here than has been at one time since fall, '84. There is," he continued, "a good deal of flour about to be shipped to Britain."[193] Troubles in France and the state of crops in Europe were the chief explanations merchants gave to each other for the activity. Thus, as news arrived, it is not surprising to find such warnings as "There being great crops in Europe and a large crop here, we cannot but believe flour must fall."[194] Undoubtedly Philadelphia was enjoying better trade than it had for many years.[195] It was puzzling, in the light of the news of European crops, to have all expectations changed "by large orders just received from England to load with wheat and flour without limitation of price."[196]

An astute observer, probing beneath the day-to-day shipping situation, and drawing his conclusions from the unsettled happenings in France, warned his correspondent at Cape François, "You may rest assured that the troubles in Old France will not speedily end. How they may

189 May 18, 1789, Josiah and Samuel Coates to Moses Brown, Providence.
190 June 17, 1789, James Cox to John Cox.
191 September 2, 1789, the same to the same, Grenada.
192 September 5, 1789, the same to the same, Grenada.
193 October 7, 1789, Robert Henderson to David Lamb, Charleston.
194 October 21, 1789, Josiah and Samuel Coates to Moses Brown, Providence.
195 November 5, 1789, John Lewis to James Jones, New Orleans.
196 November 30, 1789, Josiah and Samuel Coates to Moses Brown, Providence.

affect the colonist I will not take upon me to determine, but I cannot help believing that property in all the French colonies is very insecure." At the same time he saw "no reason to expect a fall while the demand continues for the European market."[197]

Exports of flour from Philadelphia increased in every year in which volume is reported from 1786 to 1793. The 369,000 barrels of flour exported in 1789,[198] marking an increase of 68 per cent over the previous year, account for such a statement by a cautious merchant as "There never was so much [wheat and flour] . . . exported in one year since Pennsylvania has been known,"[199] an opinion shared by a long-established merchant, who wrote,

> The exports this fall exceed anything I ever remember. A great number of foreign vessels have come to load with wheat and flour and both those articles are bought up as fast as they come to hand, the former at 8 shillings 6 pence and the latter superfine 45 shillings per barrel, the wheat is so good this year there is little but superfine comes to market. There has been so great an export pushed this fall both here and in the Chesapeake that there will not be so much left in the country in the spring as usual after such a crop as last, added to this circumstance the supply which our market received usually from up the Delaware on the breaking up of the waters in the spring being totally cut off for the next season, and I am persuaded if the demand for Europe should continue as it has been the price will be still higher.[200]

Some indication of the hectic European demand for grain is given by the character of the Amsterdam market where prices rose in the first seven months of 1789 and receded only slowly in 1790.[201] The new year brought no decline in interest in grain in the port of Philadelphia. In fact, it was soon evident, according to James Cox, that "the demand for wheat and flour in Europe seems to increase. Flour has risen to 47 shillings 6 pence per barrel and expected to get to 50 shillings. Every vessel that can be procured here or at New York are taken up to carry wheat and flour to Europe. The consequence of this is that bills of exchange are very plenty and selling at a low exchange."[202] Scarcely any grain

[197] December 14, 1789, Benjamin Fuller to George C. Schroeppel, Cape François.

[198] Edward P. Cheyney, *Commerce, Navigation and Ship-Building on the Delaware River*, p. 9.

[199] December 12, 1789, Robert Henderson to David Lamb, Charleston.

[200] December 29, 1789, John Clifford to Thomas Clifford, Jr., Bristol.

[201] Posthumus, *op. cit.*, Table 1.

[202] January 8, 1790, James Cox to John Cox, Grenada.

could reach the city on account of bad roads, but that did not prevent orders being "lodged here for large quantities and the agents are not limited."[203]

No one knew fully the supplies that farmers might be induced to spare at unusual prices. The information sent by Clifford to his brother was as specific as possible.

> It is supposed that the western shores of Maryland and Virginia, the Delaware state and the county bordering on the navigable rivers have generally sent their wheat to market and that there is but little more than sufficient left for their own use until next harvest. This is a circumstance that has rarely happened heretofore and will doubtless occasion flour to keep up its price. There is but little comes to market and now readily commands 50 to 51 shillings per barrel, wheat 10 shillings 6 pence per bushel. Our dependence now principally rests on the western country and I do not expect there is any considerable quantity remaining there. It appears to me as if flour will still rise and I think it not improbable but it may get to 8 dollars [60 shillings] per barrel.[204]

Such reports were as likely to stimulate buyers whose needs, to experienced observers, seemed to be "much more than this country can possibly supply,"[205] though news from northern Europe in the spring indicated that grain and flour were falling there.[206] No immediate easing in prices resulted, nor could result as long as owners of vessels were competing with each other for cargoes. Such was the situation Clifford had in mind when he wrote, "The port is as full of shipping as I remember to have seen it except when the British army was here. I don't know what they can do for cargoes. Grain and flour continue at their high price, say flour 62 shillings 6 pence to 65 shillings per barrel; wheat 13 shillings per bushel."[207] The underlying difference was not in price, but in direction of trade. Practically all the shipment of grain in the spring of 1790 was for Lisbon and the West Indies.

Elements of uncertainty in direct trading to the West Indies, as summarized by Levi Hollingsworth, were: "To the Danish or Dutch Islands you have a privilege of carrying any produce at present; the French Islands are open on payment of small duties, but this is only on

[203] January 25, 1790, Josiah and Samuel Coates to Moses Brown, Providence.

[204] February 1, 1790, John Clifford to Thomas Clifford, Jr., Bristol.

[205] March 24, 1790, Benjamin Fuller to Robert Totten, Trinidad.

[206] April 5, 1790, John Clifford to Thomas Clifford, Jr., Bristol.

[207] May 12, 1790, the same to the same.

sufferance and may be taken off before your vessel arrives. At the English and Spanish Islands you cannot be admitted."[208] Had the rules of commerce been more settled, his advice against seeking West India outlets would not have differed much, as he was already convinced "no markets in the West Indies or the world will allow of these prices and you will lose by shipments abroad."[208] Few observers were in a position to be as well informed as Hollingsworth. The decline in prices of superfine flour already suffered at Baltimore could be detected in Philadelphia only by a slackening in volume of sales as high wheat prices persisted.

Only in May 1790 was the maximum of the steep rise in breadstuffs reached, long after cautious merchants had become wary. Some even feared that purchasers were likely soon to regret their activity. "I think it probable," Clifford commented in spite of the fact that he had earlier been warned by his brother in Bristol of the expectation of a Spanish war, "there will be a great deal of money lost by the shipment of wheat and flour for this four or five months past. As the shipments have been made principally for houses in Europe, the loss must center there."[209] That the loss was not confined to European houses was evident from the speedy return of protested bills of exchange to prominent houses in Philadelphia, Baltimore, and New York.[210] Besides, flour was "tumbling down very fast" with the European market "at an end and the news of peace hourly expected."[211]

Farmers at first resisted the decline. As a merchant interpreted it, "The late high prices have had such an effect on the farmers they will not bring out their wheat for some time, in hopes by holding back the price will keep up."[212] Shippers continued to stress the reluctance of farmers as they reflected on low prices and the likelihood that prices would "fall considerably in the spring."[213] As it turned out, the farmers, in bringing only small quantities of their crop to market at a time, anticipated better than the merchants. It is true that the fall shipments were "mostly for the West Indies, and some to different ports of the United

[208] May 21, 1790, Levi Hollingsworth to Thomas Nuglett & Son.

[209] June 14, 1790, John Clifford to Thomas Clifford, Jr., Bristol.

[210] August 10, 1790, James and John Cox to Charles Hagart, St. Thomas.

[211] August 18, 1790, Benjamin Fuller to Robert Totten, Trinidad.

[212] September 25, 1790, John Clifford to Thomas Clifford, Jr., Bristol.

[213] November 4, 1790, James Cox to John Cox, Grenada; November 5, 1790, Robert Henderson to Thomas Pinkerton, London.

States,"[214] but the demand from Europe, even in the winter months, reversed the trend of grain prices. In the light of the next five years, the decline in the last six months of 1790 appears only a minor check to the spectacular advance of grain prices that accompanied the Revolution in France.

Reversal of Ratio between Wheat and Flour

The outstanding characteristic of prices of wheat and flour in colonial years was the succession of periods of high and low prices, movements which appeared almost simultaneously in wheat, flour, and bread. In these fluctuations a close relationship in value between flour and wheat was strikingly maintained. Over the 55 years from 1720 to 1775, there was a slight tendency for wheat to become dearer than flour, and in the last twenty years of the colonial era slightly less than three bushels of wheat would be required to buy a hundredweight of flour. In 1773, when prices of wheat were said to be disproportionate to flour, the unsually low quantity of 2.55 bushels would buy 112 pounds of flour.

Farmers, millers, and even the mercantile community relied upon the persistence of these customary relationships in their buying and selling. Important, too, was the reference to the price of wheat or flour in payment for a day's work in agricultural or other employment.

Table 5

Number of Bushels of Wheat Required to Purchase One Hundredweight of Flour

Year	Common	Superfine	Year	Common	Superfine
1770	2.65	3.25	1781	2.77	3.29 (4 months)
1771	2.58	3.11	....	2.74	3.25 (8 months)
1772	2.62	2.98	1782	2.45	3.06
1773	2.55	3.02	1783	3.16	3.85
1774	2.60	3.09	1784	3.10	3.72
1775	2.59	3.40	1785	2.74	3.16
1776	2.96	3.50	1786	2.76	3.21
1777	2.81	3.16	1787	2.87	3.20
1778	3.22	4.49	1788	2.91	3.32
1779	3.87	4.17	1789	2.90	3.24
1780	3.70	4.20	1790	2.75	2.92

[214] November 18, 1790, Report of James Read, Flour Inspector, to the Supreme Executive Council of Pennsylvania, *Pennsylvania Archives*, 1st ser., v. 11, p. 756.

Did the pattern of colonial years outlast the inflation or did the inflation of 1776 to 1781 change the ratio of exchange between wheat and its products? Did the millers, the dealers in flour, or the growers gain relatively most in these critical years? A comparison on an annual basis of the amount of wheat that would have to be exchanged to buy a hundredweight of flour indicates that in the early stages of inflation the trend of colonial years was reversed. In this shift it was flour that became dearer than wheat. In 1776 it took nearly three bushels of wheat to buy a hundredweight of common flour, and considerably more than three bushels was needed from 1778 through 1780, the terms of exchange being most disadvantageous to growers of wheat in 1779. Lower ratios than during the drastic depreciation, though still above three bushels, held in 1783 and 1784. In 1781 and from 1785 onward less than three bushels of wheat, but more than in the five years before the war, would exchange for 112 pounds of common flour. Superfine flour, which before the war had closely approximated three bushels in exchange for wheat, gradually changed until four and a half were required to effect an exchange in 1778 and more than four in 1779 and 1780.

Clearly the inflation altered the former terms of exchange between groups concerned with growing and distributing the dominant product of the Pennsylvania economy. The position of wheat in terms of its product—flour—temporarily approached its former basis of exchange in 1781 and 1785, but even in postwar years the old relation of common flour to wheat was not fully restored, an important element in the delayed reversal in relationships being that the over-all trend of grain prices was strongly upward in the late colonial period and persistently downward in postwar years.

CHAPTER VI

CORN

IN COLONIAL YEARS, fluctuations in the price of corn rarely conformed closely to those of wheat. The decade preceding the Revolutionary War was no exception. Crop conditions in 1769 and 1770 accounted for a steep upswing in prices of Indian corn. By the spring of 1771 a rise in wheat prices, along with a sharp contraction in those of corn, brought the two series into close relation. After 1775, the urgent demand for fodder raised the price of corn rapidly, the upswing beginning as early as January 1776, while wheat was still declining. Throughout 1777 and 1778 not only was the gap between the indices of the two grains especially marked but even up to the close of 1780 the climb in corn prices generally was steeper than that in wheat.

Both before and after the war, crop conditions and spurts in international demand account for short-term fluctuations in prices of corn. The sharp rise in 1770 was attributed to vigorous buying for export to Lisbon at a time when local supplies were scarce.[1] Throughout the shipping season, small quantities, along with flour and bread, were sought for the Madeira Island trade.[2] The new crop created little if any surplus, and late in November 1770 a correspondent in St. Christopher was informed that no corn was available in the market.[3] With the close of shipping, corn dropped sharply from its maximum price of colonial years to a level in conformity with wheat. Both sold at high rates in the next two years.

The character of the demand for export easily accounts for the strength of prices in earlier years of the colonial period. Except in 1752 and 1761, the annual export of corn from Philadelphia was normally less than 60,000 bushels. In 1768 and 1769, shipments more than doubled the previous average. In 1771, the peak year for exports of corn, the total, exclusive of corn meal, reached 259,441 bushels. Though

[1] April 14, 1770, Thomas Clifford to Parr and Bulkeley, Lisbon.

[2] August 28 and October 31, 1770, Joseph Gilliss, Madeira, to Henry Hill.

[3] November 26, 1770, Thomas Clifford to William Smith, St. Christopher.

smaller amounts were shipped in the immediately following years, the total exports of 140,000 bushels of corn even in the lowest year were well above those of any year before the seventies.

Throughout 1772, country produce was felt to be high enough to discourage shippers, even though wheat, flour, bread, rice, corn, and other provisions were needed in Europe in quantities often not to be had. In June 1772, Henry Drinker wrote to an English inquirer, "It is many years since our produce has been at the extreme high prices they commanded this year, and we hope and expect it will not so happen again suddenly unless some fatality should attend our crops which at present there is no probability of."[4] Only a month later when corn was quoted at 4 shillings a bushel, he ventured the comment, "We have no doubt but wheat, Indian corn, and beeswax will bear great prices these 12 months to come, also pork and flaxseed."[5] Soon 4 shillings became the minimum in all quotations until late in the fall. In November, Drinker, loading for Leghorn, was able to call a client's attention to the fact that "Indian corn at present is the cheapest article being about 3 shillings 2 pence per bushel."[6] The break in prices was temporary and, before shipping closed, corn could not be bought for less than 3 shillings 6 pence.[7]

During the next two years although corn never dropped as low as it had been before 1768, it was often available at as much as 4 pence below 3 shillings. It was "higher than usual" at the close of 1774, according to Thomas Clifford, and "worth from 3 shillings to 3 shillings 3 pence."[8] After navigation stopped, domestic produce dropped in price, and by mid-January "large quantities of Indian corn might be purchased at about 3 shillings per bushel."[9] Quotations fluctuated slightly throughout the year in response to the arrival of vessels[10] and the "pushing for loads"[11] before the ban on foreign shipping should become effective.

[4] June 22, 1772, James and Drinker to Philip Robin, via Liverpool.

[5] July 22, 1772, the same to Captain Joseph Jones.

[6] November 23, 1772, the same to Richard Ford & Co., London and Barcelona.

[7] December 26, 1772, the same to Captain Joseph Jones.

[8] December 20, 1774, Thomas Clifford to Thomas Frank, Bristol.

[9] January 17, 1775, the same to the same.

[10] July 21, 1775, Reynell and Coates to Stephen Hooper, Newburyport.

[11] August 26, 1775, James and Drinker to Lancelot Cowper, Bristol.

Effect of War

Like those of other domestic staples, prices of corn dropped with the embargo on foreign trade. It was quoted in March 1776 at 2 shillings 7½ pence, an unusually low price. No regular publication of market prices was then being made, but the information exchanged by merchants indicated that corn prices turned upward a few months before those of wheat and in the last quarter of 1776 shot up rapidly. The speed of its advance is illustrated by occasional quotations at 3 shillings 2 pence in the last week in August and the sale of it in November as high as 4 shillings 11 pence a bushel.

Once the price reached 6 shillings a bushel, an effort was made to prevent its further rise by acquiring "with as much secrecy as possible . . . a quantity of good, merchantable Indian corn"[12] for the army from the crops of Virginia. The price accepted as equitable at the time was actually the prevailing one for the next three months and recurs in official quotations and even in merchants' estimates late in 1777, though the sales of midsummer were made at higher rates. Soon after the city was occupied, the British commissary office established the price of 4 shillings a bushel as the amount to be paid for corn "delivered at Willing and Morris's stores . . . which will be paid for in gold and silver at 7 shillings 6 pence per dollar . . ."[13] Outside the city the Council of Safety recommended 6 shillings 6 pence to the commissary general as a price not to be exceeded in purchasing.[14] Though the offer was lower than any selling prices that can now be verified, it is notable that the rapid rise in corn prices was temporarily checked.

In February 1778, an official rate of 9 shillings was recognized and was not exceeded until July, when prices soared to more than 14 shillings a bushel. As other produce shared in the upswing, a thirty-day embargo was placed on exportation of grain and other foodstuffs "to any parts or places beyond the sea."[15] Toward the end of August, the report from "York Town" was that there was no forage "to be purchased now at or near this place under 3 dollars [22 shillings 6 pence]

[12] February 5, 1777, *Journals of the Continental Congress*, v. 7, p. 92.

[13] October 11, 1777, *Pennsylvania Evening Post*.

[14] November 5, 1777, *Minutes of the Council of Safety of Pennsylvania*, *Colonial Records*, v. 11, p. 336.

[15] August 4, 1778, *Pennsylvania Packet*.

per bushel,"[16] and a month later the army was still "much distressed about forage."[17] Rye, oats, and all other grains were rising and little could be purchased.[18]

Though no complete series for these substitute grains can be assembled, it is evident that prices of oats doubled their prewar levels before the city of Philadelphia was occupied by the British. By February 1778, when corn was selling for 9 shillings a bushel, oats brought 7½ shillings or more than three times the prewar price. In the search for grain, prices of oats more than doubled between February and November, in this way following the lead of corn. Oats was then quoted at 18 shillings 9 pence a bushel and was procurable only in small parcels.

Supplies were no easier to purchase in adjoining states than in Pennsylvania. Diligent reconnoitering for grain brought the discouraging report from Hanover, "I have been riding this three days down on the edge of Maryland for Indian corn and . . . only purchased 125 bushels which I got for 20 shillings per bushel—but farmers will not sell for any price; the chief I saw that had any to sell asked 25 shillings."[19] The prices cited tally closely with the averages furnished by the Hollingsworth account books, the most continuous source for prices of corn in this and the following years. Congress had, at this time, no reliable data to aid it in tapping the areas of surplus: the commissaries hoped to make "examples of all those who attempt to engross, also those who are disposed to hold back from sale."[20] The combination of competition among purchasers, scouting in all directions for supplies, and the lack of any incentive to sell in the light of distrust of the future value of continental bills of credit kept relative prices of corn, from April to September 1779, above the median of the group. Though the upswing was still in progress, the report of bumper crops of corn slowed it in the last quarter of the year relative to that in other commodities. The Massachusetts Board of War, which had been purchasing grain in the southern states, was informed in September that the crop of corn

[16] August 28, 1778, Colonel David Grier, York, to Colonel John Davis, Deputy Quartermaster General, Carlisle.

[17] September 4, 1778, Colonel John Davis to Colonel Cox.

[18] September 28, 1778, Owen Biddle to Colonel John Davis, Carlisle.

[19] November 20, 1778, Alexander McDowell, Hanover, to the same.

[20] February 27, 1779, Colonel Ephraim Blaine, Deputy Commissary of Purchases, to Chaloner and White.

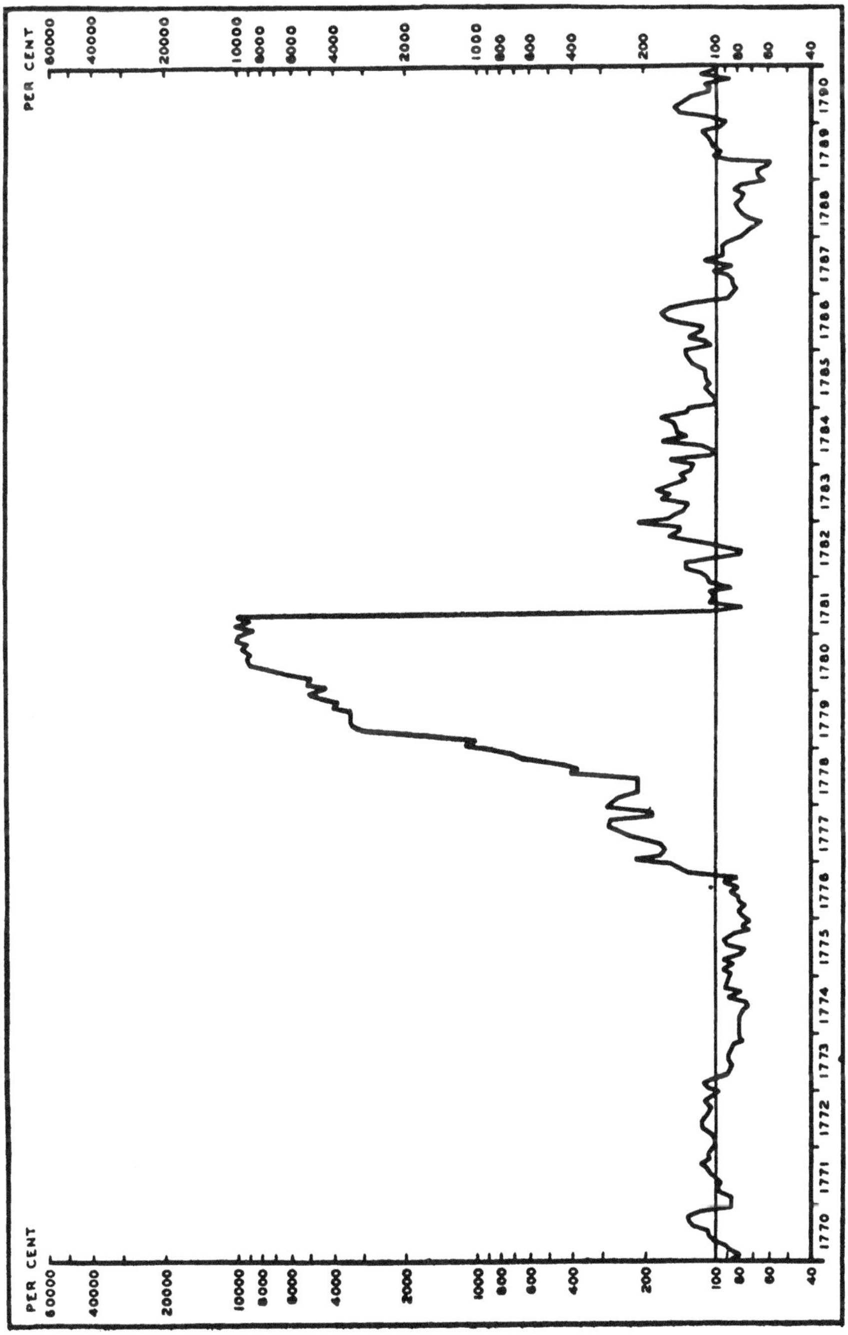

CHART V—MONTHLY RELATIVES OF WHOLESALE PRICES OF CORN IN PHILADELPHIA, 1770-1790
(Base—Monthly Average, 1771-1773)

in Maryland and Virginia was "much more than twice the usual quantity."[21]

That much of the price advance was illusory may be illustrated by converting to a specie basis the 157½ shillings a bushel paid for corn in November 1779, even admitting that specie itself was greatly overvalued. Half joes, which always passed for £3 before depreciation, "sold for £120 and will in all probability be more."[22] Applying this ratio to the prevailing price of corn places its specie price at about 3 shillings 11 pence, a quotation not unusual in prewar years.

The administrative discussions throughout 1780 concerned: (1) ways of regulating prices by law, (2) economies in expenditure, and (3) laying in grain in public warehouses at limited or regulated prices. By then it was generally admitted that any measures for regulating prices must have the concurrence of all the states. In the call for "specific supplies" the specie price arrived at for the purchases of corn in Pennsylvania was 4 shillings a bushel, about 41 per cent above the average prices of 1774. Some corn was exchanged in April 1780 at 4 shillings 3 pence, against transactions in continental currency at 222½ shillings. By June, when the average price was 310 shillings in continental currency, the purchasers were authorized to contract for it at 5 shillings 6 pence per bushel, exclusive of carriage and containers, giving the sellers of corn, as of other produce, the assurance "that the merchants would take the new money [the issue authorized March 1780] at the same rate as specie, and also that in case higher prices were given in other counties, they should have the same."[23] At this time the northern areas had not the advantage of drawing supplies of corn from Virginia[24] though, in the light of its prewar export, the quota of 200,000 bushels assigned to Pennsylvania should not have been a heavy drain upon the area from which the port drew its supplies. Between June 1780 and the disappearance of dealings in continental currency, it is notable that prices of corn did not keep pace with the currency depreciation, confirming in an indirect way the complaints of the county agents that people were "paying

[21] September 25, 1779, Samuel and Robert Purviance to Samuel Phips Savage.

[22] November 22, 1779, Colonel George Croghan, Lancaster, to Michael Gratz.

[23] June 5, 1780, Nicholas Lutz, Reading, to Joseph Reed, President of the Supreme Executive Council of Pennsylvania, *Pennsylvania Archives*, 1st ser. v. 8, p. 301.

[24] June 18, 1780, Philip Schuyler to General George Washington, *Letters of Members of the Continental Congress*, v. 5, p. 224.

their assessments in the ordinary kind of grain and green corn" and thus making it difficult to obtain wheat or "the quantity of flour required."[25]

Prices of oats, though alarmingly high in the minds of contemporaries, rose less than corn. The steps in their climb in paper money terms may be judged from the quotations of 100 shillings in November 1779, 120 shillings in April, 150 in August, and 165 in December 1780. In these 14 months the maximum price given in specie terms was little more than 3 shillings 9 pence or at most about 50 per cent above the prewar average.

The course of prices in 1781 in both paper money and specie is the best evidence for concluding that, toward the close of the war, there was no lack of corn in Pennsylvania. The specie price was but 6.5 per cent above the prewar average in May 1781, the last month of firm quotations in continental currency with corn about 392 shillings in that medium. For the rest of the year, corn sold for 3 shillings to 3 shillings 9 pence a bushel on what was substantially a hard-money basis. Numerous comments in this period tally with that of Hollingsworth—"We have no money in use but gold and silver"[26]—or of the Connecticut delegates, who reported that paper was "but little used here in any trade or dealing and not at all in the market."[27] Later in the year, Hollingsworth commented, "We have all hard money in circulation and hope never to see paper money in use again."[28] Thus, fluctuations in prices of corn in the last half of 1781 and the first six months of the following year reflect mainly the influence of seasonality. Not even the lifting of the embargo on exports served to advance corn prices. The army was now supplied by contract and bidding in country districts greatly lessened.

Postwar Fluctuations

An upswing in corn prices began before the news of peace reached the city. It was the beginning of a marked cycle in which corn reached a peak of 7½ shillings a bushel in December 1782 and held at high levels

[25] November 12, 1780, Colonel Ephraim Blane, Commissary General of Purchases, to Samuel Huntington, President of Congress.

[26] June 15, 1781, Levi Hollingsworth to Henry Armistead, Fredericksburg.

[27] July 12, 1781, Connecticut Delegates to Jonathan Trumbull, Governor of Connecticut, *Letters*, v. 6, p. 142.

[28] September 8, 1781, Levi Hollingsworth to Marsden and Smith, Va.

throughout the next two years. Part of the upswing may be explained by the demand for and relatively high prices of pork. The sustained character of corn prices was attributed by contemporaries to crop conditions and to scarcity,[29] but it was a period when prices of grains and other domestic staples were well sustained.

The general behavior of prices, once international dealings were resumed, was not unlike that of the early seventies, with domestic staples relatively high and dry goods dull. But the demand for agricultural staples responded in part to the demand of other mainland areas. A New England shipper learned early in July that flour was exceptionally dear and likely to remain so, while the port was "crowded with shipping and everyone must load with something."[30] Corn, especially, was felt to be "very scarce and high."[30] In mid-July 1783 the same New England correspondent was informed, "Corn has been selling this week at 6 shillings 2 pence to 6 shillings 3 pence and scarce any to be got."[31] All reports indicated that the harvest of grain would be abundant, but from the number of vessels in port it was predicted that corn would be "here a dollar a bushel soon. It is almost impossible to get any."[32] The stress was temporary.

After fifteen months of irregular fluctuation, prices shrank until in February 1785 corn sold for 3½ shillings a bushel. Just as most of the decline was suffered in a few months, so the low quotations lasted only until spring shipping opened. The expansion in prices of corn from February 1785 to August 1786 lifted them over 70 per cent above the prewar average. Prices of wheat advanced in the same period by reason of a "scarcity in Spain and Portugal."[33] Shippers throughout the year complained that "the exports of this country are all kept up at such extravagant prices as to render every speculation in that way extremely precarious,"[34] or, more directly, "Our produce continues high."[35]

Indices of corn, beef, pork, and superfine flour were all above those of other domestic foods and most imports in our series when the "House of Assembly" of Pennsylvania was debating the postwar return to an

[29] June 1, 1783, Stephen Collins, prices current.

[30] July 2, 1783, Stephen Collins to William Gray, Salem, Mass.

[31] July 15, 1783, the same to the same.

[32] July 22, 1783, the same to the same.

[33] January 8, 1785, Thomas and John Clifford to Amos Hillicar & Son, Bristol.

[34] March 10, 1785, John Clifford to Thomas Clifford, Jr., Bristol.

[35] April 9, 1785, Kuhn and Risberg to Lars Kahra & Co., Gothenburg, Sweden.

issue of paper currency. According to the "Advices from America" in the *Gentleman's Magazine*, it was a "very unpopular step; but as the public creditors were clamorous, it was necessary."[36] As early as June, merchants commented, "Some depreciation has already taken place which as an opinion is like to continue."[37] Apart from the discount on currency, the state of the harvest and rising prices in Europe influenced the sensitivity of prices of grain. Old Indian corn sold by the close of the year for 4 shillings 8½ pence a bushel and supplies from Virginia then found "ready sale" in Pennsylvania.[38] The strength of grain prices can be attributed to the meagreness of the previous year's crop which made barley and other substitutes almost as scarce as corn. "The crops of Indian corn," Clifford wrote to his brother in England, "have turned out bad last year; they say in general about half a crop . . . Jersey corn has already advanced to 5 shillings per bushel."[39]

Amid the distracted state of trade and growing indications of the approach of a severe depression, merchants continued their quest for corn in Virginia and Maryland. In March, Peter Kuhn wrote to Fredericksburg, "We are pleased to learn that Mr. McKinley continues taking in corn . . . it will in all probability be very high in 6 or 8 weeks."[40] In this appraisal he was right; corn was reported "scarce and very high"[41] in April and continued to mount in price until the new crop came in. By autumn, the trend was reversed, as a result of unusually abundant crops. In September, Clifford reported, "Our crops of all kinds of grain for this time past have been less than before the late revolution; the present one appears more plentiful."[42] Other grains remained high for a time because of a wet harvest season with rains that soaked oats and wheat in the fields.[43] Thus, when prices of some grains held, corn was subjected to a long and severe recession, which persisted until April 1789, when it sold 40 per cent below its prewar average.

By the middle of 1787, corn accumulated in Maryland was being shipped to Charleston in exchange for rice. The whole continent shared

[36] May 1785, *Gentleman's Magazine and Historical Chronicle*, v. 55, p. 396.
[37] June 4, 1785, Josiah and Samuel Coates to Thomas Rutter, Bristol.
[38] December 7, 1785, Kuhn and Risberg to William French & Co., Fredericksburg.
[39] February 27, 1786, John Clifford to Thomas Clifford, Jr., Bristol.
[40] March 23, 1786, Kuhn and Risberg to William French & Co., Fredericksburg.
[41] April 2, 1786, John Clifford to Thomas Clifford, Jr., Bristol.
[42] September 4, 1786, the same to the same.
[43] September 26, 1786, the same to Dom. d'Oliveira Abz, Jr., Madeira.

in the slump in corn prices. "At Boston," Kuhn wrote, "corn is not so high and to the utmost commands only 4 shillings per bushel that currency."[44] Some was shipped to Madeira but met with "very poor encouragement indeed,"[45] but despite the surplus it was a year before prices of beef and pork reflected the low prices of corn. As harvest reports began to appear, it was clear that wheat would be "uncommonly productive over the whole continent."[46] Other grains were no less ample. In August, Benjamin Fuller wrote, "The crops generally over the continent are immense and very fine in quality"[47]—a fact that was confirmed over and over in the autumn.

By the beginning of 1788, merchants with corn on hand found it unprofitable to wait with the hope of recovering the purchase price. In a communication sent to Maryland, a Philadelphia holder urged, "We shall be glad to learn the sale of the corn as it is better to take two dollars per barrel than suffer longer advance, particularly when it is considered that West India produce has been for the chief part given therefor. Of course every day that it remains on hand adds to our loss and disappointment."[48] Two months later he was insistent that he would rather take 11 shillings a barrel for corn than risk further delay as "we can now purchase it here for 2 shillings 9 pence per bushel and should apprehend . . . from the great and constant intercourse from this large trading city to the West Indies that great quantities would be shipped from hence if it afforded even a freight, whereas it is a mere drug here and in no demand."[49] The difficulty of distinguishing between temporary fluctuations and a change in the trend of prices is clear from a sudden brisk demand for corn which soon induced the same merchant to urge its purchase,[50] basing his action largely on damages to other grains from a wet season and "heavy rains during harvest."[51]

Unlike that of wheat, the raising of corn for export was a localized activity. Hollingsworth, explaining its importance in the trade of Philadelphia, wrote, "Corn is generally lower here than with you. The Dela-

[44] June 5, 1787, Kuhn and Risberg to William French & Co., Fredericksburg.

[45] June 13, 1787, James Searle, Bordentown, to John Searle & Co., Madeira.

[46] July 31, 1787, Kuhn and Risberg to Jacob Kuhn.

[47] August 18, 1787, Benjamin Fuller to Robert Totten, Trinidad.

[48] May 12, 1788, Kuhn and Risberg to William French & Co., Fredericksburg.

[49] July 29, 1788, Kuhn and Risberg to Jacob Kuhn.

[50] August 4, 1788, the same to William French & Co., Fredericksburg.

[51] August 15, 1788, the same to the same; also September 17, 1788, Josiah and Samuel Coates to William Bartlett.

ware State raises more of that article for exportation than all America, besides which corn is chiefly sent here for sale."[52] Unexpectedly, in the spring of 1789, prices of corn advanced. Early in the year it was in demand in Madeira.[53] Later it shared in the strong demand for grain, particularly wheat and its products, for European continental markets, when contrary to usual trade practice, orders received from England were without limitation of price.[54] Corn was quoted to an English merchant in the spring of 1790 as high as 5 shillings 6 pence,[55] the maximum reached in this major upswing.

The change in the direction of price was attributed to many causes, though most explanations amounted to little more than "the great demand in Europe for flour and corn has raised the prices of these articles to a most uncommon rate."[56] The bidding for cargoes not only kept the port busy but benefited the farm areas. According to Clement Biddle, "The great quantity of our produce exported, which was last year beyond anything ever known before or since the war in quantity besides the addition in price has also thrown a greater plenty of money into circulation."[57] Crop reports, however, at this time were unpromising and it was believed the country might face a shortage of grains. Instead, prices of corn declined mildly in the last half of 1790.

In the two decades 1770 to 1790, corn had assumed a more important role in export trade than it held earlier. According to Tench Coxe's view of the whole United States, the quantity of corn shipped at the end of the period was nearly four times that of 1770, in spite of an increase in wheat, buckwheat, rye, and other grains.[58]

[52] November 15, 1788, Levi Hollingsworth to Thomas Contee.
[53] February 9, 1789, Lamar, Hill, Bisset & Co., Madeira, to Henry Hill.
[54] November 30, 1789, Josiah and Samuel Coates to Moses Brown, Providence.
[55] March 24, 1790, John Clifford to Thomas Clifford, Jr., Bristol.
[56] April 1, 1790, James and John Cox to Charles Hagart, St. Thomas.
[57] May 23, 1790, Clement Biddle to Richard Smith, London.
[58] Tench Coxe, *A View of the United States of America*, p. 225.

CHAPTER VII

BEEF AND PORK

PRICES OF MEATS had turned sharply upward in the year before this study begins. In September 1769, when the advance was checked, beef sold for 65 shillings and pork for 95 shillings a barrel. By the beginning of 1770, prices had declined to 50 shillings for beef and 75 shillings per barrel for pork.[1]

Scarcity of beef, to which the advance of 1769 was attributed, was not again an influence in the prewar years. Except for an upswing in 1772, prices were relatively stable until February 1776 and fluctuations primarily seasonal. By contrast, pork prices, always more variable than beef, had a marked cycle between the close of 1770 and December 1775, which is also evident in the ham or gammons series.

Before pork rose to a maximum price of 102 shillings a barrel in September 1772, contemporaries discouraged orders for its shipment. One Philadelphia merchant predicted to a Liverpool correspondent, "Pork will be at £5 per barrel if wanted before December, when the new begins to come in, which may reduce it to £4."[2] Its period of high prices was not expected to be as temporary as that of beef, which rose "owing chiefly to the very cold raw weather we have had."[3] In the expansion phase of the cycle in pork prices, gammons advanced about 33 per cent in 28 months. When they were selling at a peak price of 9 pence a pound, Clifford wrote to a purchaser in Barbados, "The hams cost a very extravagant price but as they are good hope they may please. They are very scarce and believe there is none such to be had now at any price."[4] Later in the same month, James and Drinker informed a merchant in Bristol, "It is very doubtful if hams can be had a few months hence. They are now very scarce at 9 pence per pound . . . Bur-

[1] The weight of the two differed slightly before March 1789, when both were standardized at 200 pounds; previously, a barrel of beef weighed 225 pounds, one of pork 217¼ pounds.

[2] May 16, 1772, William Pollard to Peter Holme, Liverpool.

[3] May 20, 1772, the same to George Whitehorn Lawrence, Montego Bay, Jamaica.

[4] September 7, 1772, Thomas Clifford to Jonas Maynard, Barbados.

lington pork keeps pace with the advance on other provisions, from 100 shillings to 105 shillings per barrel."[5]

Only once in the colonial era had prices of pork been as high as they were in this year of generally active demand for staples, and then only for a few months in 1764 after the close of the Seven Years' War. Although prices of all agricultural commodities were high in 1772, by September the prices of pork were proportionately higher than those of wheat and flour. The persistence of demand at such levels led James and Drinker to remark, "These prices much enrich the farmers but we can't see where the merchant can be advanced by them."[5] Prices of pork eased as the new supplies came in, but even in November a well-informed merchant wrote to Liverpool, "Pork is also at the high price of £5 5 shillings to £5 7 shillings 6 pence, but I expect in three weeks that article will be as low as £4 5 shillings,"[6] an estimate that must have had especial significance to an English merchant because the price of provisions in Britain had become a matter of official concern. Before the year was out, a bill was introduced in Parliament "for importation of salted provisions from Ireland, and for salt beef, pork, and butter, from any of His Majesty's plantations in America."[7]

After July 1772, the decline in quotations for beef was rapid until it reached 53 shillings. Twice in the next two years prices dipped as low as 50 shillings, but, in the main, were maintained with notable stability. In 1773 prices of pork receded slowly, the best grade, Burlington, being quoted at 90 shillings through the spring, though a slackening in demand is evident from the lack of call for the lower-priced Carolina and Lower County pork.[8] Toward the end of June, best hams dropped to 7 pence a pound,[9] and by October best pork fell a trifle below 75 shillings a barrel. A new note began to appear in merchants' comments, especially among those who had been trading cautiously in the years of high prices for domestic goods. "Provisions of most kinds," Drinker commented, "have lately declined in price and from the best information we have obtained from the several markets in Europe, which are generally supplied with quantities from hence, we are induced to think that provisions

[5] September 22, 1772, James and Drinker to Lancelot Cowper, Bristol.

[6] November 11, 1772, William Pollard to Peter Holme, Liverpool.

[7] December 14, 1772, Proceedings of Parliament; *Gentleman's Magazine and Historical Chronicle*, 1773, v. 43, p. 51.

[8] April 14, 1773, James and Drinker to Samuel Cornell.

[9] June 22, 1773, the same to John Clitherall.

must be yet lower here to promote our furnishing those markets under any prospect of advantage."[10] In these calculations doubtless prices of grain and its products claimed more attention than meats. Yet Liverpool merchants were informed about the supplies of new pork expected in the Philadelphia market before the end of November,[11] and early in December other purchasers from Liverpool learned that "pork is low this season, say 70 shillings."[12]

Except for a seasonal peak in May, orders for pork throughout 1774 could have been filled at an average of 70 shillings a barrel. Such uncertainties as the year produced came from factors other than prices. Late in the spring, when shipping was active, a Philadelphian explained his dilemma to a Bristol merchant: "About the time we were filling up the ship . . . a doubt arose with some persons whether salted provisions from America could be imported into England duty free and what raised the doubt was an article in the Bristol papers, and also in the *Gentleman's Magazine* under the date 14 March mentioning a motion made by Sir Joseph Mawbery for revising an act of the last session for the free importation of salted provisions which after a short debate was put to vote and carried in the negative."[13] At most, the doubt about terms of admission of goods had only a temporary effect upon prices of meats. By midsummer 1774, pork and beef were being shipped to Dominica[14] and the demand for hams in other parts of the Indies kept their price, at 7 pence a pound, somewhat out of line with that of pork.[15] The fresh supplies of pork coming to market in December dropped its price to nearly 60 shillings a hundredweight, which in the first half of 1775 remained its prevailing price. It was then in demand in Bristol, but Drinker explained that the changed terms of trade from the lack of importation made it "extremely difficult to raise money" on bills. "The article of pork," he wrote, "is now 60 shillings to 62 shillings 6 pence, but as exchange has got down about 155 to 157½ [per cent] it is not likely to answer."[16] Seasonal increase of supplies at the close of the

[10] October 30, 1773, the same to Peter Street.

[11] November 18, 1773, William Pollard to Peter Holme & Co., Liverpool.

[12] December 9, 1773, the same to Thomas and Clayton Case, Liverpool.

[13] May 23, 1774, James and Drinker to Lancelot Cowper & Co., Bristol.

[14] August 23, 1774, Reynell and Coates, invoices of cargo of Schooner *Polly* for Dominica.

[15] August 25, 1774, James and Drinker to Samuel Welsh.

[16] March 27, 1775, the same to Lancelot Cowper, Bristol.

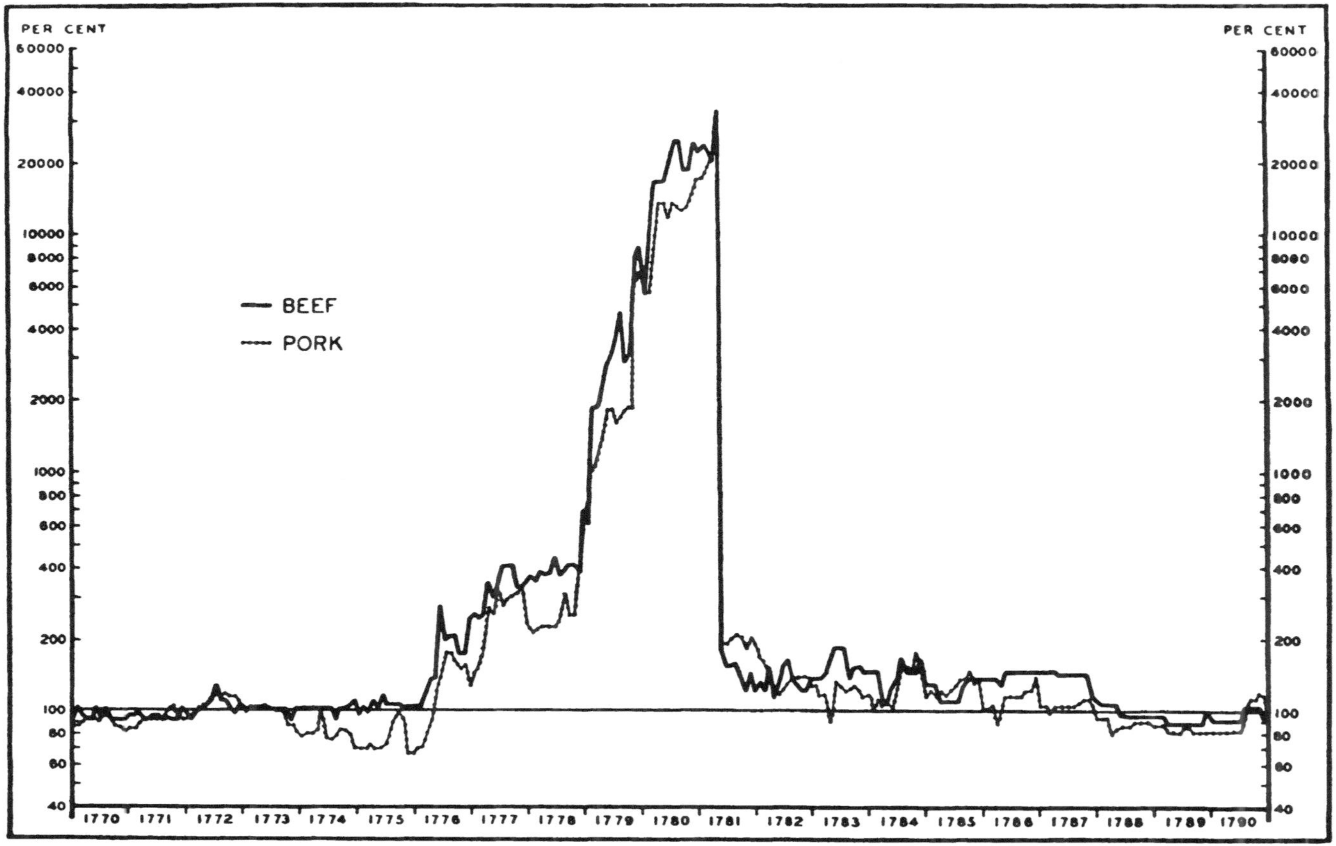

CHART VI—MONTHLY RELATIVES OF WHOLESALE PRICES OF BEEF AND PORK IN PHILADELPHIA, 1770-1790
(Base—Monthly Average, 1771-1773)

year lowered the quotations until beef and pork sold at about the same price per barrel.

Methods of procurement and changes in the location of the war, to say nothing of difficulties in preserving and transporting meats, changed the method of their distribution. The introduction, before the close of 1775, of the practice of supplying the army with part of its meats by driving animals to camp and butchering and salting there, brought it about that prices in what was then the largest single market for meat cannot be made strictly comparable with the quotations of barreled provisions in prewar years. The driving of hogs "on the foot" to the army, initially assented to by Congress in September 1775 as an economy,[17] had to be continued on account of the chronic shortage of salt.

Scarcity of Meats Brings Embargo

In 1776, the shipment of live animals including "horned cattle, sheep, hogs" as well as lumber for making casks was banned, even to vessels importing powder and arms, such as those loading for Martinique and Hispaniola.[18] By February, prices of meats began a sharp advance. At this time the report to the Committee of Safety read, "No pork to be had in Bucks County, but bacon may be got."[19] It was "scarce" in March and quoted in merchants' prices current at 70 shillings to 72 shillings 6 pence.[20] Thus, by March 1776, pork was selling at the average of 1774, having made up all that it had lost in the decline of the previous year. Beef, meantime, rose proportionately more than pork.

Prices of pork soared in the next few months. Some part of the advance was attributable to the provisioning "with all possible despatch"[21] of the continental army in Canada. Congress felt that the demand came from other sources and proceeded to deal with one of the persistent avenues for black market operations. Its order of June 1776, when pork was at 120 shillings a barrel and beef at 150 shillings, read that "Whereas it has been represented to this Congress that great quantities

[17] September 15, 1775, Eliphalet Dyer to Joseph Trumbull, *Letters of Members of the Continental Congress*, v. 1, p. 197.

[18] February 8 and 13, 1776, *Journals of the Continental Congress*, v. 4, pp. 120, 130-31.

[19] February 17, 1776, "Extracts from the 'Minute' Book of Committee of Safety, 1776, of Pennsylvania," *Pennsylvania Magazine of History and Biography*, 1915, v. 39, p. 233.

[20] March 6, 1776, Reynell and Coates to Stephen Hooper, Newburyport.

[21] April 24, 1776, *Journals*, v. 4, p. 303.

of salted beef and pork have been purchased for exportation which, if not restrained, may render the supplies of the army difficult," none except for the use of the crew should be exported "until the further order of this Congress."[22] Merchants interpreted the order to apply to shipping between states. In July, when a long prices current was sent to William Teel in Newburyport, Reynell added, "Pork £6, but not to be exported only for ship use."[23] As the supply of pork continued to be limited throughout the summer, the same merchant cautioned another New England correspondent, "Don't depend on us for salt provisions if it is possible to get it with you. We have the utmost difficulty in procuring it here."[24]

The advance in meat prices was not steep enough to obscure completely the normal seasonal pattern, and prices of beef and pork declined as the fall supplies came in. Congress, however, strengthened its export regulation, including processed by-products of slaughtering in its order that no bacon, salted beef, pork, soap, tallow, and candles "be exported from any of the United States after the 5th day of January next, until the first day of November next, or until Congress shall take further order therein."[25] The disparity between the quotations of various sources in the closing months of 1776 can be explained by the circulation of two currencies of unequal purchasing power without any distinguishing specifications. Pork averaged about 126 shillings 9 pence in continental currency and slightly less than 72½ shillings in specie when both provincial and national authorities were resolving to keep the two at parity.

In February 1777, the rise in prices seems to have been speeded by the adjustments which the Provincial Council made in its contract for supplying the navy and the artillery of the state with beef. A price of £3 a hundredweight was agreed to for a commodity which was current at £4½ a barrel of 225 pounds.[26] Yet there was enough dispersion in meat prices to make any basis of adjustment uncertain. The Council of Safety knew from the manager of the Pennsylvania Salt Works that provisions were "scarce to be had without old money." Referring to his former experience, he wrote, "Then I could find enough beef. [Now]

22 June 14, 1776, *ibid.*, p. 441.

23 July 1, 1776, Reynell and Coates to William Teel, Newburyport.

24 August 20, 1776, the same to Stephen Hooper, Newburyport.

25 December 30, 1776, *Journals*, v. 6, p. 1054.

26 February 10, 1777, *Minutes of the Council of Safety of Pennsylvania, Colonial Records*, v. 11, p. 119.

I can get none, yet have got but 1800 pounds of pork—that at 5 pence, don't know that I can get any more."[27]

Between January and April 1777, prices of pork increased more than 80 per cent. Two months later the Committee of the Treasury had to adjust prices of provisions taken early in January in the Jerseys for the use of the army. For the satisfaction of the owners, the purchases of pork were settled at £7 per barrel, a price well above that generally current the first of the year. Other commodities were rated closer to the January market.[28]

Salt for preserving was the major limiting factor in meat supplies throughout most of the war years. Uncertain prices, however, were important, and, in the summer of 1777, beef in Pennsylvania was said to be higher than in other areas. Finally the Committee of the Treasury, acting on a report of Matthew Irwin that "the price of cattle in Pennsylvania is most exorbitant," concluded "that it is advisable to direct the Commissary General to suffer as few as possible to be purchased in that state."[29]

At this time pork was advancing faster than beef and the range in quotations was especially wide. For instance, when the Pennsylvania Salt Works was purchasing pork, presumably of New Jersey origin, at 220 shillings a barrel, Hollingsworth was selling it at 240 shillings and participating in assembling army supplies for the Head of Elk, and Robert Morris was quoting "pork from £14 to £15 per barrel,"[30] or about 290 shillings, a higher price than was current a year later. Disparate quotations might be expected when plans were ready for the removal of livestock "into the interior parts of the country, whenever the arrival of the enemy's forces at the Capes shall announce the necessity and propriety of such a measure"[31] and when wagons were ordered to repair to the city for the purpose of removing stores and provisions.[32]

[27] February 10, 1777, Thomas Savadge, Pennsylvania Salt Works, to Council of Safety, *Pennsylvania Archives*, 1st ser., v. 5, p. 218.

[28] June 26, 1777, *Journals*, v. 8, p. 499.

[29] June 27, 1777, *ibid.*, p. 504.

[30] July 22, 1777, Robert Morris to Mr. I—— H——, *Pennsylvania Magazine*, 1884, v. 8, p. 431.

[31] July 30, 1777, Resolution of Congress, *Pennsylvania Archives*, 1st ser., v. 5, p. 468.

[32] July 31, 1777, Thomas Wharton, Jr., President of the Supreme Executive Council of Pennsylvania, to William Henry, Lancaster, *Pennsylvania Magazine*, 1898, v. 22, p. 106.

Experiments in Price Control

By September, when Philadelphia was occupied, pork was selling for nearly 263 shillings and beef for 245 shillings a barrel. Diaries kept within the city during the first months of occupation give scattered illustrations of small sales at scarcity prices.[33] Outside the city, there was a curious attempt to lower prices of meats by setting maximums which applied to purchases for both the army and navy. Before the instructions were circulated, President Wharton pointed out that the price set for pork was rather low and desired that it be reconsidered.[34] In relaying the order to the Commissary of Naval Armament, the Council of Safety stated, "As the Commissary General of Purchases, Mr. Buchanan, has fixed the prices of beef and pork, the former at 10 dollars per hundredweight [£7 10 shillings per barrel] sinking the fifth quarter, as he terms it, and six dollars per hundredweight for pork [£4 7.27 shillings per barrel] the same prices must govern your purchases, and in future you are not to give a greater price than they allow for the necessaries wanted for the army. It is proper to mention to you that the price he has fixed for pork, we have hinted to him is in our opinion too low and desired he would reconsider it."[35] Three days later, the Commissary General explained to his own satisfaction his theory of pricing. An extract from his somewhat lengthy statement gives his reason for introducing a disproportion into the already disparate behavior of prices. William Buchanan wrote to President Wharton:

> I acknowledge the price proposed by me for pork, though higher than usual, is not in proportion to that of beef, or many other articles . . . Six dollars is not only a generous price, but far above what has been customary. Pork is yet in the hands of the original owners by whom I may expect to have it as cheerfully and readily brought to market for 6 dollars, being early informed that that price will not be exceeded, as they would for 8 or 10. A high price holds up the idea of scarcity, of which mankind are too apt to take advantage and to withhold the article in expectation of one still higher. An extravagant price

[33] October 16, 1777, "Good beef sells for 2 shillings 6 pence"; "Diary of Robert Morton," *ibid.*, 1877, v .1, p. 19. November 12, 1777, "Poor beef is now sold for 3 shillings per pound"; Henry D. Biddle, editor, *Extracts from the Journal of Elizabeth Drinker, 1759-1807*, p. 63.

[34] October 16, 1777, Thomas Wharton, Jr., to Colonel Ephraim Blaine, Deputy Commissary of Purchases, *Pennsylvania Archives*, 1st ser., v. 5, p. 677.

[35] October 17, 1777, Council of Safety, Lancaster, to William Crispin, *ibid.*, p. 681.

for beef has so long been submitted to, that to lower it very suddenly to a proper one, I feared might occasion a kind of convulsion, and also ruin many well-disposed persons, who in the way of their very useful business (of grazing and feeding) have been in some measure compelled to buy in poor cattle at a very high price. In fact the market for beef has been grossly abused. That of pork is not yet meddled with.[36]

If such an order could have been enforced, the market for beef might have been eased. As it was, delay and confused orders to procurement officers and farmers affected the assembling of provisions for the army. The maximum established for beef conformed closely to prevailing rates and may have been a factor in its relatively stable prices in the closing months of 1777 and for 11 months of 1778. If put in force at all, the maximum for pork could not long be maintained. On October 26, President Wharton supplied the Commissary General with a list of articles in which beef was quoted at the 10 dollars already established and pork was raised to 8 dollars or more than 116 shillings a barrel instead of the 87 shillings announced at first. More significant than the increases was the added suggestion, "You will, however, be able from time to time to judge best of this matter, and perhaps will be under the necessity of varying occasionally."[37] Still another order was sent to the Commissary General in November suggesting that he allow 7 dollars per hundredweight [£5 1.8 shillings per barrel] for good pork.[38]

It is only in official communications and in the rarity of sales that any trace can be found of the effect of these limitations upon prices of pork. The series, though drawn from few sources, shows a seasonal decline in December 1777 and lower prices in the first six months of 1778 than had been paid in most of the previous year. Meantime, there is evidence of meagre supplies in all the area from which two armies were purchasing. Early in the year, Blaine had given instructions that beef be bought in Pennsylvania, mentioning no price but giving certificates for it. At the close of the year, Francis Lee of the War Office, in an effort to get cooperation in procurement, proposed that the government of Pennsylvania act lest the committee "be obliged to give orders for the taking,

[36] October 20, 1777, Colonel William Buchanan, Commissary General of Purchases, York, to Thomas Wharton, Jr., *ibid.*, p. 690.

[37] October 26, 1777, Thomas Wharton, Jr., to Colonel William Buchanan, *ibid.*, p. 711

[38] November 5, 1777, *Minutes of the Council of Safety of Pennsylvania, C.R.*, v. 11, p. 336.

conveying, and driving all cattle, hogs, pork, flour and grain fit for their consumption to the army, the persons employed for this purpose giving certificates to the owners expressing as nearly as possible the weight and quality of them and agreeing to pay for them at such prices as shall be settled by the convention of committees from the several States who are to meet at New Haven the 15th of January next agreeable to a Resolution of Congress of the 22d November last."[39] After various experiments, Pennsylvania appointed commissioners in every county to buy or seize at stated prices "provisions necessary for the army."[40]

By June 10, Congress had to lay an embargo on the exportation of provisions "from any of these United States,"[41] though even the President of Congress, Henry Laurens, feared that the prohibition would be evaded in Pennsylvania and Delaware.[42] Prices of pork rose in July, the month after the city was repossessed and, although Delaware banned all exports of produce except to Pennsylvania, Maryland, and Jersey,[43] an exceptionally sharp advance occurred in November. Both beef and pork soared in December, an unusual occurrence at a time when new supplies normally lowered the average. In December, when pork averaged 480 shillings a barrel, Chaloner and White wrote, "No pork is taken in here as yet—but little comes to market and for that 3 shillings 3 pence [a pound] is given. The purchasers in the country are taking [it] in at 2 shillings and we thought it best not to rise the market here to their prejudice,"[44]—a range in terms of sale of a staple commodity from 434 to 706 shillings a barrel.

The flexibility in offering prices and successful purchasing in the country in 1778 procured needed winter supplies wanting in the previous year. By contrast with 1777, too, the advance in prices was attributed to currency depreciation. James Duane, concerned with decreas-

[39] December 30, 1777, Francis Lightfoot Lee to Thomas Wharton, Jr., *Letters*, v. 2, p. 603.

[40] February 14, 1778, John Henry, Jr., York, to Thomas Johnson, Jr., Governor of Maryland, *Letters*, v. 3, p. 85.

[41] June 8, 1778, Resolution of Congress, *Pennsylvania Archives*, 1st ser., v. 6, p. 585.

[42] October 6, 1778, Henry Laurens, President of Congress, to Rawlins Lowndes, President of South Carolina, *Letters*, v. 3, p. 441.

[43] November 10, 1778, Chaloner and White, Delaware Proclamation.

[44] December 24, 1778, the same to Colonel Jeremiah Wadsworth, Commissary General of Purchases.

ing the amount of continental currency in circulation, reported that it had been exchanged for more than 5 to one during the previous ten months.[45] Yet the upswing in meats in 1778 was moderate compared with that of 1779 when commissaries were scouting still more avidly for supplies and local committees were attempting to lower prices and limit all chance of sale to favored purchasers.

On the basis of a report to the Commercial Committee of Congress, it became known that those purchasing for the army had, by mid-1779, found the public magazines well supplied. It was "therefore recommended by the commissarial committee, with the concurrence of the minister of France that the Commercial Committee immediately order for shipping to the island of St. Domingo, two thousand barrels of pork, one thousand barrels of beef, and one thousand barrels of flour, for the supplying His Most Christian Majesty's forces on that island, the Minister having promised that the same shall be paid for at the market prices there."[46]

Prices, despite an attempt at local controls, were a matter of controversy during most of 1779, and the embargo on exports from Pennsylvania "to parts beyond the sea" put on in October and "extended November 15, 1779 for 30 days and no longer"[47] indicates the concern about winter supplies. At any rate, beef and pork soared to fantastic prices in November and December.

There is no reason for surprise at the recurring shortages of these years, since salted provisions, though increasing in later colonial years, had never been a major export from Pennsylvania. In 1773, a year of high meat exports, only 8587 barrels of beef and pork were shipped. During the war the direct purchases from farms meant that little came regularly to the city, and, even so, in January 1780, the army was not only "at very short allowance of both bread and meat" but was depending on Connecticut for most of its supplies of beef.[48]

[45] January 3, 1779, James Duane to George Clinton, Governor of New York, *Letters*, v. 4, pp. 2-3.

[46] July 24, 1779, Commercial Committee of Congress to Joseph Reed, President of the Supreme Executive Council of Pennsylvania, *Pennsylvania Archives*, 1st ser., v. 7, pp. 579-80.

[47] October 11 and November 15, 1779, *Minutes of the Supreme Executive Council of Pennsylvania*, *C.R.*, v. 12, pp. 126, 171.

[48] January 11, 1780, Roger Sherman to Jonathan Trumbull, Governor of Connecticut, *Letters*, v. 5, p. 5.

Critical Shortage of Meats in 1780

In May, when the army was faced with a critical shortage, Pennsylvania pork was selling for £580 and beef for more than £450 a barrel. "A few days," Ephraim Blaine wrote, "will consume all the salt provisions in our magazines; little in this part of the country and no money to buy it with. The severity of last winter and backwardness of the spring will deprive of any fresh beef till the latter end of July or beginning of August."[49] Summer brought no improvement. In October, after desperate efforts to procure meats, Blaine complained that "the army . . . have been scantily supplied all summer with beef. They are now without one day's provisions at camp."[50] In more detail he reviewed the handicaps under which the procurement officers were working even when purchasing with specie.

> The resolutions of the 25th February last confine the price of beef delivered before the 1st of December to five dollars and a half the neat hundred, a price for which I cannot obtain a single bullock. The French agents, I have been informed, have made considerable contracts for cattle, five or six hundred of which, I believe, was delivered yesterday and have given from fifty to fifty-five shillings per neat hundred. The butchers who are buying for themselves and merchants exceed that price, therefore it will be in vain for me to attempt to purchase without giving what others are. I beg that Congress would immediately consider this matter as the delay of a day or two may lose me the offer of a considerable number of good cattle.[51]

Other purchasers, too, were offering hard money as Blaine was "adopting every possible measure to lay up small magazines of flour and beef to prevent the like distress the army experienced last winter."[52] In early November he was able to write to General Washington that he had on hand about 1000 head of cattle. It was hoped that New York could supply West Point with flour and that the eastern states could furnish the 1000 head of cattle a week which Congress had requested for a period of ten weeks.[52]

No such ready compliance with regulations could well be expected. The commissary complained that people in Pennsylvania were paying

49 May 27, 1780, Colonel Ephraim Blaine, Commissary General of Purchases, to Thomas Sim Lee, Governor of Maryland.

50 October 24, 1780, the same to Colonel Henry Champion.

51 October 31, 1780, the same to Samuel Huntington, President of Congress.

52 November 10, 1780, the same to General George Washington.

their assessments with most ordinary grain; the better grain was said to be "loading for shipment." Concretely, Blaine had information of three vessels "loading off Wilmington."[53] Beef could not be procured, though it was proportionately far above pork in price. When Blaine finally had to resort to the currency others were offering, he informed the President of Congress, "I have purchased 450 head of cattle at about £8 10 shillings hard or the exchange; those cattle will come about the price fixed by Congress, but the villainy of persons who are daily engaged in depreciating the paper currency has engaged me in disputes with all the people I have been dealing with about the exchange."[53]

None of these quotations indicate the cost of prepared meat. To the army expenditure for live animals must be added the cost of grazing, slaughtering, and, when salt could be had, pickling and barreling. It is little wonder that toward the end of this year the commissary stated forcefully, "Our army will never be properly fed until the public magazines afford a barrel of well cured salt provisions for every man who is entitled to draw rations; to hold up the idea of feeding them with fresh beef is absurd and this continent cannot furnish it, and there remains no certain method but by using every exertion in the fall season when grass, beef, and pork is plenty to procure as amply as our exigencies may require."[54] Originally the driving of livestock to the army had effected some short-run economies, especially when supplies could be drawn from areas surrounding the camp. As the war progressed and the whole resources of the country had to be utilized, it became clear that the system was both expensive and uncertain.

No change in methods could be introduced before the next autumn. Yet there was no marked change in prices during the four months of 1781 when continental currency was in use. Pork sold in January 1781 at £750 a barrel in continental currency and at £9 in specie; beef at £650 in continental and £4½ in specie. After March, the quotations of both commodities appear only in specie. Both declined mildly as the specie basis became general.

Change in Method of Procurement

Before the plans for summer purchasing were put into use, the commissary was notified that a change had been made in the method of

[53] November 12, 1780, the same to Samuel Huntington.
[54] November 20, 1780, the same to Thomas Sim Lee.

procurement, "Mr. Morris having undertaken to supply all the continental posts in this state."[55] Morris was soon confronted with lack of hogsheads and high prices. Empty molasses and rum hogsheads, used to pack beef, were commanding 15 shillings each, while beef barrels were costing 9 or 10 shillings. He concluded, "These prices appear very extravagant and I must enquire further."[56]

Evidence of willingness to take a risk on the movement of prices rather than to continue the method of army slaughtering with all its problems of pasturage and forage is apparent when Morris acted on information that "the price of fresh pork is broke at 6 pence per pound." He reflected, "I think it better to sell the salt and take the chance of buying salted pork, when wanted, which will probably be cheaper then than now."[57] It was a safe decision because, in specie terms, the peak of a cycle in pork which began about April 1780 and ended in May 1782 was reached in January 1781, when it sold for 180 shillings a barrel.

When the contraction phase of the pork cycle was nearly over, Hollingsworth wrote, "Pork though nominally high is a very dull sale."[58] The contracting system which Morris favored in buying army supplies had introduced an element of stability into prices. Hollingsworth, in explaining the new system, wrote, "The army is now supplied by contract for each ration and 4½ pence per pound is the price calculated for pork."[59] Salted provisions were bringing a higher price, however, than the standard cited. From Hollingsworth's own accounts it is clear that pork sold for 120 shillings per barrel or about 6⅔ pence per pound from August to November 1782, and in 1783 fell only as low as 81 shillings or 4½ pence a pound in months of purely seasonal dips.

Well-Sustained Prices after the War

The news of impending peace in 1783 affected prices of beef and pork less than might have been expected, though in the language of Webster it "knocked all business into stagnation and things are fast getting down to a peace price."[60] They soon rebounded. Ships arriving

55 July 23, 1781, Joseph Reed to David Duncan, Fort Pitt, *Pennsylvania Archives*, 1st ser., v. 9, p. 306.

56 November 3, 1781, Robert Morris Diary.

57 November 17, 1781, *ibid.*

58 March 4, 1782, Levi Hollingsworth to Humphrey Richards.

59 March 9, 1782, the same to Hoffman and May, Baltimore.

60 April 16, 1783, Pelatiah Webster to W. Charles Miller, Boston.

from Europe in the haste in which everyone hoped to revive trade were likely to force down the prices of imported goods and keep those of produce high.

At the close of 1783, when pork was at the lowest price of postwar years, there was much comment by observers on both sides of the Atlantic on the immoderate prices in the United States, particularly in Philadelphia. Meats were felt to be high even before a rise in the autumn months carried beef and pork to their maximum postwar levels.

Merchants were marking time or waiting "sometime longer" during the relatively stable prices of the next two years. In March 1786, when pork was selling for 75 shillings a barrel, Drinker cautioned a New York correspondent, "Pork is not likely to be wanted."[61]

In retrospect, prices of meats seem to have been amazingly well sustained until 1788, and even in the closing years of the decade the decline was more marked in beef than in pork. Contemporaries had to consider insurance and exchange, both of which they judged to be unfavorable. Besides, the war had stimulated the trade between states, and a small increase in supplies could affect the general downward direction of what was termed a dull market.

Hollingsworth, an unusually competent observer, basing his opinion upon an over-all view of the market, wrote, "I . . . am informed that New England beef is selling by the single cask at 62 shillings 6 pence and expect to be lower. . . . Pork is expected to be low. I sell Carolina at 65 shillings; Burlington is higher. Very little new pork have yet come to market but from the dull appearance of trade and the real scarcity of cash I apprehend all kinds of provisions will rather fall, as the quantity will be great."[62]

Prices of pork followed a generally downward course for the next two and a half years. At the time of its first sharp decline, Hollingsworth reported, "Pork plenty though rather early in the season. Beef a perfect glut, both New England and of our own putting up. It may be bought in any quantity at 52 shillings 6 pence or 50 shillings."[63] Early in the next year, Philadelphia merchants, confronted with poor business, had difficulty in suggesting articles that could safely be consigned to them

[61] March 25, 1786, Henry Drinker to Embree and Shotwell, New York.

[62] November 1, 1787, Levi Hollingsworth to Robert Bowne, New York.

[63] December 27, 1787, the same to Murray and Sansom, New York.

from other markets. "It is hard," Coates confessed to a merchant in Newburyport, "to give any opinion, which may eventually be erroneous; but if we hazard it, we should suppose that beef, barley, hops and shoes will not do at all."[64] In May of the same year, Hollingsworth noted the continuance of the 50 to 52 shillings 6 pence for beef and added "the quantity . . . at this market this spring is very great and Irish beef hath generally had a preference of 5 to 10 shillings per barrel, but in future I apprehend there will be none imported from that country."[65]

Other markets, too, were less open. A Philadelphia shipper was unable to send the items listed in an order from Barbados, explaining, "Neither can any kind of salted provisions [be sent] or any kind of manufacture whatever, so tight is the English Government on the people of their own plantations."[66]

Prices of beef were unchanged from July to December. Philadelphia dealers tried to discourage its shipment to the port from other areas, as once the weather grew cool enough to put up home-grown beef, "the sales of New York and Connecticut beef will be very small, our meat being generally fatter than that put up with you. Your inspector is not so careful as he should be in the inspection of beef particularly."[67]

A new standardization of containers and methods of packing made difficulties for shippers of pork, admittedly of good quality but purchased from areas uninformed of the regulations. "No pork," Hollingsworth wrote to a dealer, "can be shipped from this port or sold to shipping but must be inspected and branded by the pork officer."[68] Until the regulations were generally known, merchants frequently had to repack and put new pickle in the barrels not actually condemned.[69] Worse still, there were few buyers. Late in November, Henderson narrated his difficulties with a shipment of beef from New York. He wrote,

> I have not been able to sell any more of the beef. There is no demand [and] any vessels that wants beef purchases it in market and puts it up themselves. I have offered it for 50 shillings per barrel but cannot get an offer of any kind—I was witness this day to the sale of nine barrels of as good beef as you

[64] February 15, 1788, Josiah and Samuel Coates to William Bartlet, Newburyport.

[65] May 21, 1788, Levi Hollingsworth to Robert Bowne, New York.

[66] August 27, 1788, Benjamin Fuller to Mrs. Elizabeth R. Carter, Barbados.

[67] September 18, 1788, Levi Hollingsworth to Nathaniel Hazard, New York.

[68] October 9, 1788, the same to Robert and George Service.

[69] November 5, 1788, Robert Henderson to James Scott & Co., New York.

could wish for and in good order at the Coffee House; it sold from 26 shillings 6 pence to 30 shillings per barrel. Before I would sell yours at that I would let it lie over the winter.[70]

Meantime the final standardization of containers came in March 1789 when the sizes of the beef and pork barrels were adjusted to hold the same weight: 200 pounds. The prices for the rest of our period are therefore not those published in the price lists, but are adjusted in proportion to the previous container. The prices of both series of meats declined in early spring. In April, Coates wrote, "We would not advise thee to send beef as there is no sale for that article."[71]

It was late in 1790 before any encouraging comment began to be made about the meat market. By September, Hollingsworth was cheerfully admitting, "Pork . . . is scarce here and will be higher,"[72] and Henderson, reporting on beef to a Charleston correspondent wrote, "As to the beef, there is no half barrels to be got of mess beef, and as to the meat out of the market it will not keep above four or five days in salt at this season—about a month hence you may get what quantity you please put up as then it will keep."[73]

Summary

In the colonial period a gradual, but powerful, upward trend in meat prices reached a climax in 1763 for beef and in 1764 for pork. In general in these years pork fluctuated more than beef, rising above it in years of high prices and falling below it in recession. In the closing months of 1774 an irregular upswing started in quotations of beef, far in advance of any similar movement in other domestic products. Pork, by contrast, except for seasonality, rose little before February 1776 and in the early stages of the advance lagged behind beef.

During the war, the provisioning of the army with meats drawn from all parts of the continent reversed the usual relation of prices of the major staples to each other. For most of the war years, beef maintained its early lead and reached relatively greater heights than pork. By April 1781, the index of beef at 33,113 exceeded the height reached by any

[70] November 22, 1788, the same to the same.

[71] April 2, 1789, Josiah and Samuel Coates to Henry West, Haverhill.

[72] September 3, 1790, Levi Hollingsworth to Jacob Nothlett.

[73] September 14, 1790, Robert Henderson to Lamb and Montgomery, Charleston.

other important commodity, except rum, while pork at 24,451 was surpassed only by rum and molasses.[74]

In the postwar years, the length of time involved in replenishing farm stock is evident in the contrast in the two main meat products. Pork dropped to prewar levels in December 1785 and kept continuously below them from December 1787 through July 1790. Beef never fell to its prewar price until May 1788 and, once lowered, remained below prewar even at the close of 1790, despite a few months of higher quotations after the middle of that year.

[74] To be sure, pepper, an article of minor use and always sold in small quantities, rose to extravagant heights, above all others.

CHAPTER VIII

SALT

EVEN FOR colonial years when grades of some commodities were more or less carefully specified, the assembling of continuous series of prices for coarse and fine salt was not easy. Since they served different needs, however, it was frequently possible to determine which grade was involved in a transaction originally reported without exact designation. The two grades became, in the main, hopelessly indistinguishable in the Revolutionary War years. There is no lack of quotations, for salt as a scarcity item reached inordinate heights which created comment and inconvenience throughout the war years. Though it was one of the most urgent of necessities and early subject to regulation, its prices were disparate even in the records of a single merchant. All notation of quality disappeared and, whenever sold, except in rare cases, it appears under the simple description "salt."

Before the Revolutionary War, the prices of two grades of salt regularly imported, usually from Liverpool and Lisbon and infrequently from Turks Island, bore no continuous relation to each other. Nor was the weight of the bushel of fine and of coarse salt the same. With the great multiplicity of quotations in some months during the war years, followed by a month in which only one or two sales of salt were found, any artificial means devised either for obtaining a single salt series or for continuing the two grades naturally produced prices of arbitrary choice. Since, during the war, salt was often the limiting factor in supplying the army with meat, the general movement of prices serves to indicate its importance. In 1769, prices of both fine and coarse salt were relatively low. They had risen before the period of this study begins and by January 1770 coarse salt was selling for 1 shilling 6 pence a bushel and fine for 2 shillings. For the next three years, little conformity can be found in the movements of the two price series, with fine salt definitely contracting.

In August 1770, when both grades of salt were at the same price, the partner of Henry Drinker then travelling in England was engaged in chartering a vessel at Bristol to "carry salt to Philadelphia, where she was bound, [and was] induced to speculate in that article from the scarcity and dearness of it at Lisbon from whence we did usually get our supplies."[1] He was bringing it to a market already so supplied with salt that what could not be shipped to other ports along the coast was being stored. Later in the year, a Philadelphia merchant wrote to Bristol, "Salt will not answer, the market being quite overstocked."[2] Toward the end of the year, when prices of both grades of salt were lower, he wrote to the same Bristol correspondent, after a shipment arrived, "The length of her passage has been a great disadvantage to us in the sale of the salt. No purchasers now at almost any price. Are shipping a quantity of it round to Baltimore as we hear it will do better there. Expect to store the remainder."[3]

Prices of salt spurted abruptly in the last quarter of 1772 to quotations seldom found except in wartime. The unexpected demand appeared late in the shipping season. About the middle of October, the change in outlook was reported to Bristol by Drinker and James who wrote, "Within these few days fine salt has taken a considerable start and as none can now be ordered to come in this fall, it is probable a supply early in the spring might sell to some advantage."[4] Merchants well supplied with fine salt were able to sell for double the midsummer price during this flurry, which originated in New York, according to a merchant writing to Liverpool who had just sold a cargo of salt "for the high price of 2 shillings 3 pence per bushel; this is 3 pence per bushel more than the last cargo from Liverpool sold for about a week ago."[5]

In the tense situation of these last months of 1772, coarse and fine salt reached identical levels, but the demand for fine salt continued through the spring months of the next year. Prices of coarse salt declined abruptly and continued to contract until, by September 1774, it sold for one shilling a bushel.

The disparity in the movements of the two grades of salt in the spring of 1773 led Pollard to discourage its shipment from Liverpool with the comment, "Salt is now at 16 pence per bushel and I fear it will

[1] August 9, 1770, Abel James, Bristol, to Frederick Pigou, London.

[2] October 24, 1770, Thomas Clifford to Lancelot Cowper, Bristol.

[3] November 5, 1770, the same to the same.

[4] October 13, 1772, James and Drinker to the same.

[5] October 17, 1772, William Pollard to Peter Holme, Liverpool.

be lower."[6] Inquiries were coming to other Philadelphia merchants for coarse salt which the ships participating in the active grain trade with the south of Europe were bringing to Philadelphia from Lisbon. Illustrative of the close price limits on these orders is a request to Levi Hollingsworth for a shipment of "the largest Turks Island salt. If that is not to be procured then good Lisbon fine if it can be got from 1 shilling 6 pence to 1 shilling 10 pence a bushel."[7]

Fine salt rose in the fall of 1773 and sold as high as 2 shillings 4 pence a bushel, but, in late October, Pollard wrote, "A great deal is soon expected in."[8] Later in the month he had to accept a lower price and informed the same Liverpool correspondent, "I do not believe I could obtain 2 shillings for another cargo."[9]

Despite a horizontal trend in salt prices in the colonial period, sudden changes in response to interruptions in shipping, seasonal demand, and temporary shortages would lead one to expect both erratic and diverse fluctuations in war years. Throughout 1774, only mild changes and a downward drift were evident. Toward the end of November, Clifford, then selling fine salt, wrote to Bristol, ". . . have sold the salt for 2 shillings 6 pence per bushel."[10]

Early Rise in Salt Prices

The minor changes of these years may account for the underestimation of the demand of the next. Even in 1775, prices of coarse salt declined until April. In May, when the direction had changed, a cargo of about 2500 bushels of salt was sold promptly at sacrifice prices because of faulty anticipation. "We were all," Thomas Wharton wrote to his brother, "of opinion that it would be most for thy interest to sell the salt though at the poor price of 10½ [pence] per bushel."[11] Prices of fine salt doubled between April and September, and were only slightly reduced to the inordinate price of 4 shillings 9 pence by December. Coarse salt advanced more gradually, and closed the year at 2 shillings 9 pence a bushel. Meantime, an exception to the nonexportation rules permitted a Philadelphia merchant to export Virginia produce for salt.

[6] May 6, 1773, the same to the same.
[7] July 22, 1773, William Rumsey to Levi Hollingsworth.
[8] October 25, 1773, William Pollard to Peter Holme, Liverpool.
[9] October 30, 1773, the same to the same.
[10] November 28, 1774, Thomas Clifford to Thomas Frank, Bristol.
[11] May 6, 1775, Thomas Wharton to Joseph Wharton, London.

The abrupt rise in prices of salt and the dependence upon importation induced a motion in Congress, at the close of 1775, recommending the encouragement by the several assemblies of salt manufacture. At the same time, Robert Morris gave information of a person ready "to establish salt works on the Jersey coast if the Congress will lend him £200."[12] By March 1776, prices of fine salt were regulated at 5 shillings a bushel and coarse at 4 shillings;[13] in April, Congress resolved that "the Secret Committee be empowered to import cargoes of salt on the continental account."[14] From this time on, it is rarely possible to distinguish between the two grades of salt.

The advance between March and May 1776, coupled with a belief that stocks were being withheld, led to a request by the Committee of Safety to Samuel Howell that he keep "for the use of this province, the whole quantity of salt that he has now for sale, and that he be allowed 7 shillings 6 pence per bushel for the same."[15] In the months ahead, salt ranked with gunpowder among the prime necessities of the war. Late in May, Congress recommended that its price be so regulated in all the united colonies "as to prevent unreasonable exactions on the part of the seller, having due regard to the difficulty and risque of importation."[16]

From merchants' comments it may be inferred that prices of coarse salt were pegged at 7 shillings 6 pence until September. If so, fine salt must have advanced to 9 shillings in May and still higher in the following months. Early in September 1776, when the cargo of a prize ship was being sold, Reynell, in giving the sale prices, added, "Coarse salt limited at 7 shillings 6 pence per bushel—a sloop this day arrived with about 2000 bushels, as reported; and another below with salt and some gunpowder."[17] The limitation was taken off coarse salt, and prices reached 14 shillings before the month ended.[18]

Complaints reaching the Council of Safety (formerly the Committee of Safety) led them to believe that whole cargoes of salt were in the

[12] December 29, 1775, Richard Smith Diary, *Letters of Members of the Continental Congress*, v. 1, p. 290.

[13] March 6, 1776, Christopher Marshall Diary.

[14] April 17, 1776, *Journals of the Continental Congress*, v. 4, p. 290.

[15] May 21, 1776, *Minutes of the Committee of Safety of Pennsylvania*, *Colonial Records*, v. 10, p. 577.

[16] May 30, 1776, *Journals*, v. 4, p. 404.

[17] September 7, 1776, Reynell and Coates to Stephen Hooper, Newburyport.

[18] September 30, 1776, the same to the same.

hands of monopolizers and engrossers. The Council, in October 1776, resolved to "allow the generous price of 15 shillings per bushel for every bushel of salt that may be imported into this state and delivered to them [the Council], until the 15th day of November next."[19] All salt thus delivered was to be sold to the public in small parcels and importers were to report their inventories and all new supplies. So urgent was the demand that a comment by Zebulon Hollingsworth may be cited as typical: "Our neighborhood," he wrote, "is in distress. It will sell here for 20 shillings per bushel."[20] In November, permission was given for products to be shipped to Turks Island "to bring in a load of salt from thence,"[21] and small quantities were sent to the several counties less well supplied than the city and liberties of Philadelphia.[22] It is clear that the Council succeeded in distributing salt to upstate counties. On the other hand, it failed to bring uniformity into prices. In November, quotations are dotted all along the scale from 15 to 22 shillings a bushel. The whole attempt to contain prices of salt ended in December with the announcement by the Council of Safety that the controls would be discontinued.[23] The committee on salt had reported to Congress,

> It is found upon trial, either from the artful conduct of interested persons not discovered, or from the impossibility of the thing itself, that the remedy has been ineffectual; and, on the contrary, salt continues scarcer and dearer in this port, than where no regulation has been tried: therefore, *Resolved*, that it be recommended to the Council of Safety of Pennsylvania to take off all restraint upon the sale of salt; and give public notice that it shall be lawful for any person to import and sell it in such manner and at such price as he shall find voluntary purchasers.[24]

Dire Shortage in 1777

In itself, the lifting of all limitations on salt was an admission that supplies were too scarce to permit any regular allocation. It was followed by months of sparse sales and erratic price quotations. A difficult

[19] October 12, 1776, *Minutes of the Council of Safety of Pennsylvania, C.R.*, v. 10, p. 751.

[20] October 24, 1776, Zebulon Hollingsworth, Head of Elk, to Levi Hollingsworth.

[21] November 8, 1776, *Journals*, v. 6, p. 935.

[22] November 23, 1776, *Minutes of the Council of Safety of Pennsylvania, C.R.*, v. 11, p. 13.

[23] December 9, 1776, *ibid.*, p. 41.

[24] December 9, 1776, *Journals*, v. 6, pp. 1014-15.

purchase of a single bushel is recorded in January 1777, followed in the next month by larger amounts at half the price.[25] Prices in merchants' accounts in the first quarter of 1777 vary from 25 to 40 shillings a bushel as each succeeding month brought higher prices.

Complaints about the enormous price asked for salt were as rife in Maryland as in Pennsylvania.[26] Both states tried to ease the tension by erecting salt works, which at best would increase supplies but slightly, and the critical shortage lasted throughout the summer. As clear an indication as can be given of the need of this period is found in the journal of Margaret Morris. Unexpectedly the family received a few luxury items, among them a bushel of salt of which "we thought it our duty to hand out a little to the poor around us who were mourning for want of salt; so we divided the bushel."[27] By June, prices of salt were double those of February, and Congress urged each state to employ one or more vessels for the importation of it.[28] In the next month, when a cargo of salt arrived, the Supreme Executive Council of Pennsylvania was willing to purchase the whole shipment at the high price of 75 shillings a bushel (10 dollars in continental currency).[29] A week later, salt was advertised at Baltimore in the cargo of a vessel just in from St. Eustatius.[30]

When, in August, the Moravians reported 22 dollars a bushel as the price paid for a lot of salt, they were really recording the prevailing price of the next two months, 165 shillings a bushel.[31]

The capture of the city temporarily made priceless such supplies as could be produced at the state salt works at Toms River, especially for the supply of a reinforced army. "Salt," John Chaloner wrote, "is an article we want, and daily consume a large quantity of. Have wrote James White to purchase of the makers in Jersey, for the consumption

25 January 28 and February 9, 1777, "Bethlehem during the Revolution—Extracts from the diaries in the Moravian Archives," *Pennsylvania Magazine of History and Biography*, 1888, v. 12, p. 397.

26 April 1, 1777, *Maryland Journal and Baltimore Advertiser.*

27 June 14, 1777, "Journal of Margaret Morris," *Bulletin of the Friends Historical Society*, 1920, v. 9, pp. 109-10.

28 June 13, 1777, *Journals*, v. 8, p. 461.

29 July 22, 1777, *Minutes of the Supreme Executive Council of Pennsylvania*, C.R., v. 11, p. 249.

30 July 29, 1777, *Maryland Journal and Baltimore Advertiser.*

31 August 12, 1777, "Bethlehem during the Revolution—etc.," *Pennsylvania Magazine*, 1888, v. 12, p. 402.

of the camp, and keep the imported for preserving provisions."[32] Soon a party of soldiers was detailed to seize all salt at Egg Harbor and forward it to a "place of safety."[33]

There is no reason to think that supplies of salt within the occupied city of Philadelphia were at first more plentiful than outside. Early in the occupation, prices as high as 4 dollars or 30 shillings a bushel in hard money were reported[34] and the regulations of the commanding general provided that "not over one bushel of salt was to be sold to a customer without special permission."[35] Outside the city, from the scant data available, it can be deduced that prices of salt in the last quarter of 1777 were as high as 150 shillings a bushel in continental currency.

Advance Checked in 1778

After twenty months of dire shortages in which prices rose from 2 shillings 9 pence a bushel in April 1776 to the just-mentioned 150 shillings before the close of 1777, the behavior of prices in 1778 gives an appearance of stabilization at these high levels. Our prices in the first half of the year are from army suppliers and from the domestic salt works at Toms River and a new undertaking at Egg Harbor, both of which created problems for the state and their operators.[36]

The cause of the lull in the upswing in 1778 was explained to Robert Morris by a correspondent at congressional headquarters in York. "The demand for salt," he held, "is not so great; at least the speculators in that article have got frightened on account of the price lowering at Baltimore where I am told it has got down to £4 and £5 per bushel. The retailers here tho' keep it up at £12 per bushel for country make and I have been offered £10 for that of yours."[37] A temporary easing in the quotations of other imports with the opening of the shipping season led the Treasurer of the United States to apprise Franklin of his hope that the situation would "soon mend, many foreign articles being

[32] October 3, 1777, John Chaloner, Camp at Skippack, to Colonel Ephraim Blaine, Deputy Commissary of Purchases.

[33] October 18, 1777, Colonel Ephraim Blaine to Joseph Hugg.

[34] October 27, 1777, Joseph Reed to Thomas Wharton, Jr., President of the Supreme Executive Council of Pennsylvania; William B. Reed, *Life and Correspondence of Joseph Reed*, v. 1, p. 331.

[35] Willard O. Mishoff, "Business in Philadelphia during the British Occupation," *Pennsylvania Magazine*, 1937, v. 61, p. 169.

[36] January 20, 1778, Samuel Cooper to John Litle, New Mills, *ibid.*, 1886, v. 10, p. 37.

[37] February 23, 1778, John Brown, York, to Robert Morris.

already more reasonable than they were some time ago. Salt at Baltimore has fallen from £18 to £4 and I hear where it is made on the shore it is sold 30 to 40 shillings."[38]

In the spring, a Lancaster dealer was able to offer Liverpool salt at wholesale or retail.[39] The army purchasers found supplies of it at about the prices that had been forecast by Baltimore reports, and by midsummer were able to bargain over a few shillings a bushel when it was offered to them for 85 shillings,[40] about the lowest quotation of the year.

Coarse salt retailed in Baltimore during August 1778 at 100 to 120 shillings.[41] The Philadelphia average was lower, but it conceals a wide dispersion in the quotations, the usual sign of an upswing. Part of the range can be explained by variable sources of supply and of course lack of grading. Soon after an advance was noted, a Baltimore merchant explained, "Salt continues to rise; we mean the white allum salt. It was sold this day at £7 10 shillings per bushel. . . . With respect to French salt, there is yet no market for it, as it is a hard matter to sell a bushel of it when there is any allum to be got—however we believe it will now bring 80 shillings."[42]

Country salt, from the works at Egg Harbor, was selling in Philadelphia at £8 in October[43] when the average prices of all grades, from several merchants' accounts, was 150 shillings or about the price of the closing months of the previous year. At this time, coarse salt, suited to curing meats, overtopped fine in price by a wide margin, as is clear from instructions to sell coarse salt for £10 and fine for £7 per bushel.[44]

Prices eased with the fall arrival of vessels. Chaloner and White passed the news joyfully to the commissary agents, "We are happy in telling you," they wrote, "that the holders of salt began to be alarmed; that some of them have been so humble as to offer the best rock salt at 20 dollars [150 shillings Pennsylvania currency]. This [drop] from £12

38 March 17, 1778, Michael Hillegas, York, to Dr. Benjamin Franklin, Versailles.

39 May 13, 1778, *Pennsylvania Packet*, advertisement of Levy Marks.

40 July 1778, Chaloner and White to Colonel Ephraim Blaine.

41 August 21, 1778, David Moore, Baltimore, to Levi Hollingsworth.

42 September 25, 1778, Woolsey and Salmon, Baltimore, to Samuel Beall, Williamsburg.

43 October 1778, Stephen Cooper to John Litle, *Pennsylvania Magazine*, 1886, v. 10, p. 41.

44 October 6, 1778, Colonel John Davis, Deputy Quartermaster General, Carlisle, to James Davis, Sherman's Valley.

was affected by the arrival of one vessel from France. . . . The salt we need was received at . . . £5 per bushel."[45]

The next month the best Liverpool fine salt was advertised at £6 per bushel.[46] Other merchants sold coarse for £7 10 shillings[47] and imported fine salt for £5[48] at the close of the year.

The behavior of prices in 1778 offers one of the few illustrations of the checking of a progressive upward price movement in a commodity of prime necessity and wide use by the entry of new supplies. French vessels entering at Baltimore effected the first lull in the upswing. By the same means, Pennsylvania was supplied and prices substantially, though erratically, lowered.

Shortage Again in 1779

Only in the last five months of 1779 did the rise in prices of salt again become explosive. In January, imported salt was advertised for sale among other items by a number of dealers,[49] or in exchange for the emissions of currency of May 20, 1777, and April 11, 1778, which were being called out of circulation.[50] A whole cargo of salt was offered for sale in the same way in mid-February.[51] The relatively adequate supply eased the work of commissaries in procuring salted provisions.[52] French salt reaching the port was offered for sale direct from the vessel for £6 a bushel[53] at a time when prices of coarse salt began to fan out with Turks Island quoted by Matthew Irwin as high as £9 a bushel.

August 1779 marked the end of 20 months of fluctuating but gradually rising salt prices. Suppliers of the army, feeling that the efforts of local committees to control prices were responsible for shortages in some much-needed commodities, complained that "the committee has laid such impediments in the way of purchasing that neither rum, salt or flour can at present be procured here."[54] Soon prices of salt began to soar. In

[45] November 1, 1778, Chaloner and White to Colonel Ephraim Blaine.

[46] December 8, 1778, *Pennsylvania Packet*, advertisement of John Wilcocks.

[47] December 12, 1778, Clifford Diary.

[48] December 14, 1778, Christopher Marshall Diary.

[49] January 7, 12, and 14, 1779, *Pennsylvania Packet*.

[50] January 16, 1779, *ibid*.

[51] February 18, 1779, *ibid*.

[52] April 14, 1779, Chaloner and White to Colonel James Copperthwaite.

[53] May 3, 1779, Agreement with LaCaze and Mallet, in Robert Morris Papers.

[54] August 22, 1779, Chaloner and White to Colonel Jeremiah Wadsworth, Commissary General of Purchases.

September, when a thousand bushels were being offered from the vessel of a French merchant to the President of the Supreme Executive Council of Pennsylvania at the exchange of 2½ bushels of salt for a barrel of superfine flour, sailors from the same vessel were selling their part of the venture for £20 to £24 per bushel, and it was reported that the inhabitants "would readily have given a barrel of superfine flour for two bushels thereof."[55] Though prices of both commodities were soaring, the offer came when the state, in an effort to procure flour for the army without raising prices, was giving the preference to those who would sell flour at £20 per hundredweight and receive one-third of the price in salt at £15 per bushel.[56] In explaining the plan, President Reed commented, "It is supposed £15 will be the current price of salt, but if the state pay less the people will have the benefit of it."[56]

Had the incoming vessels in the last quarter of 1779 been as loaded with salt as they were with sugar, the plan of distributing supplies without advancing prices might have succeeded. Instead, only eight of the 22 arrivals carried any salt. Those from St. Thomas and St. Eustatius had small parcels, totaling merely 900 and about 1800 bushels respectively.[57]

By October, salt from the state store was released to the Commissary General of Purchases at £30 per bushel.[58] The action gives an indication of the crucial shortage which, coupled with the alarming pace of currency depreciation, carried prices of salt to £75 a bushel before the end of the year. In the meantime the state salt works were advertised for sale[59] and steady imports or successful private operation became even more necessary than before.

Imports Relieve Shortage Early in 1780

It was the arrival early in January 1780 of a vessel with 6231 bushels of salt[60] that not only halted the rise but lowered prices of coarse salt,

[55] September 1, 1779, John Holker to Joseph Reed, President of the Supreme Executive Council of Pennsylvania, *Pennsylvania Archives*, 1st ser., v. 7, p. 675.

[56] September 8, 1779, Joseph Reed to purchasers of flour, *ibid.*, pp. 692-93.

[57] November 18 and December 16, 1779, *Pennsylvania Packet.*

[58] October 16 and 21, 1779, *Minutes of the Supreme Executive Council of Pennsylvania, C.R.*, v. 12, p. 133.

[59] November 13, 1779, *Pennsylvania Packet.*

[60] March 18, 1780, *ibid.*

then double those of fine.[61] Most of the other arrivals in the spring months had part of their cargo in salt. As a result, in spite of the ever-decreasing purchasing power of continental currency, the average prices were lower in 1780 than they had been in the last quarter of the previous year. Yet, throughout the active discussion of ways of controlling prices and preventing engrossing, salt and flour were the two most-mentioned commodities.[62]

At least 20,000 bushels of imported salt reached the port in the first half of 1780, two-thirds from St. Eustatius.[63] There is now no way of deciding how adequate the total was in terms of consumption. It is known that early in July an observant contemporary noted that "rum, sugar, salt, coffee, plenty, but rising daily."[64] In fact, sales were reported by a prominent merchant only a few days before at £45 a bushel,[65] which became the prevailing price until the last two months of 1780 when the usual seasonal demand for meat packing created a sudden upsurge in prices.[66] Throughout the summer, domestic salt manufacturers, operating with serious handicaps from the use of green wood or lack of wood, shortage of woodcutters, and inability of cutters to work in the heat and mosquitoes of a New Jersey summer,[67] complained of stoppages and low production.

Colonel Blaine was "adopting every possible measure to lay up small magazines of flour and beef to prevent the like distress the army experienced last winter."[68] The drawbacks from the recurring need of salt led Blaine to decry the whole method of supplying the army with meat and to urge "using every exertion in the fall season when grass, beef and pork is plenty to procure as amply as our exigencies may re-

[61] January 12, 1780, Commissioners for Procuring Flour to Joseph Reed, *Pennsylvania Archives*, 1st ser., v. 8, p. 84.

[62] March 11, 1780, *Pennsylvania Packet*.

[63] March 18 and June 17, 1780, *ibid.*

[64] July 8, 1780, Christopher Marshall Diary.

[65] July 5, 1780, George Clymer to Samuel Meredith.

[66] July 31, 1780, the quota of salt required of Pennsylvania for the use of the Board of War was 14,189 bushels, or slightly less than the direct importations of the first six months, credited at an estimated hard money price of £1 2 shillings 6 pence. Board of War to Joseph Reed, *Pennsylvania Archives*, 1st ser., v. 8, p. 473.

[67] August 14 to September 12, 1780, "Journal of Thomas Hopkins of the Friendship Salt Company," *Pennsylvania Magazine*, 1918, v. 42, pp. 47-55.

[68] November 10, 1780, Colonel Ephraim Blaine, Commissary General of Purchases, to General George Washington.

quire."[69] The seasonal rise at the close of each year in meats and in salt for curing them add weight to a conclusion based on hard experience.

From November 1780 to April 1781, prices of salt in paper currency increased each month over the preceding one. Even in hard money at the end of 1780 it was quoted as high as 40 shillings a bushel. The importation of 8279 bushels in the early winter,[70] much of it coming from St. Eustatius, failed to halt the upswing. Despite the arrival of two vessels from Turks Island it had reached £200 to £250 a bushel by mid-March,[71] though such a high price was not much quoted before April.

News that the British had "declared war against the Dutch and taken St. Eustatia, Curaçao, and 60 vessels in the Texel"[72] was not reassuring to a community which had received its main supplies of salt from the Dutch islands. The effect is obscured by the adjustment which accompanied the return to specie. From April to June a wide range of specie quotations indicates both the preference for hard money and the diversity of formulae used in equating the value of paper money to coin. Finally, prices stabilized for the summer months at about 33 shillings a bushel, approximately 19 times the average prewar price of coarse salt.

In October, a break in the relatively high quotations permitted the army for the first time in war years to accumulate its meat supplies at a time when prices of salt were steadily declining. The reversal of trend accompanied by a decline in prices of pork led to Robert Morris's decision, when prices were about 21 shillings a bushel, to sell what he had on hand "and take the chance of buying salted pork, when wanted."[73]

Prices of salt manifest a marked cyclical character in the remaining years of the period. The steep rise to a peak in April 1782 may be attributed to hazards of shipping. Early in March, Levi Hollingsworth reported, "The loss of many vessels . . . will affect the price current for general articles."[74] Others reported the coast "infested by the enemy," with heavy losses which would bring an advance in all West

[69] November 20, 1780, the same to Thomas Sim Lee, Governor of Maryland.

[70] January 6, 1781, *Pennsylvania Packet.*

[71] March 19, 1781, Levi Hollingsworth to John Sterrett & Co., Baltimore.

[72] March 20, 1781, James Duane to Mrs. Duane, *Letters*, v. 6, p. 31.

[73] November 17, 1781, Robert Morris Diary.

[74] March 4, 1782, Levi Hollingsworth to Cumberland Dugan, Baltimore.

India goods.[75] Premature rumors of peace,[76] "British frigates in our bay,"[77] and the prolonged stay of vessels in the safety of West India harbors sustained the prices of most West India goods until August, when the Havana fleets finally arrived with supplies. By then, imported salt was quoted at 25 shillings and country salt as low as 10 shillings a bushel. The whole market was inactive. "All wait," Stephen Collins wrote, "until further advices from Europe."[78] To a long price current, in which he quoted West India salt at 25 shillings, French salt at 15 shillings and Spanish at 18 shillings, he attached the caution, "Markets are now so fluctuating that there is but little dependence, even [for] one or two months time."[78] Despite fluctuation, the average prices held during the months when confirmation of the news of peace was awaited.

Postwar Collapse in Prices

Dull as sales were, salt prices collapsed with the news of peace. So drastic was the readjustment that a commodity quoted at 18 shillings in July 1783 was selling for 3 shillings the following month. In the summer, when incoming ships from many parts of the world crowded the port, salt approached its prewar levels. "The retailers are full of Liverpool salt," Chaloner and White wrote, "and blow on us. I offered it at 2 shillings 3 pence but could not obtain it; though Liverpool is plenty it commands 2 shillings 6 pence per two or three hundred bushels and 2 shillings per the cargo. Coarse salt is risen from 2 shillings 3 pence to 2 shillings 6 pence per the quantity. Thus situated, I thought it best to buy French at 1 shilling 1 penny."[79] This detailed comment was made at the nadir of the first postwar readjustment in salt prices.

The expansion phase of the marked postwar cycle lasted until the spring of 1785. Early in the recovery, a Philadelphia merchant in answer to an inquiry wrote, "There is now no St. Martins or Turks Island salt at market."[80] The speed of the advance and the lack of supplies which affected it appear in such a typical comment as Stephen Collins made in December 1783, "There is now no rock salt at market. It has been sold lately at 3 shillings 3 pence per bushel and as the

[75] April 15, 1782, Pelatiah Webster to W. Charles Miller, Boston.
[76] May 7, 1782, the same to John Perit, Norwich, Conn.
[77] May 21, 1782, Levi Hollingsworth to Smith, Bowdoin and Hunter.
[78] August 21, 1782, Stephen Collins to ———.
[79] September 14, 1783, Chaloner and White to James Bowne & Co., Hopewell, N. J.
[80] October 17, 1783, Stephen Collins to Thomas Pearsall, New York.

season draws late suppose it is pretty much out of the question."[81] In the next nine months, prices more than doubled, as can be gleaned from the eagerness of a Philadelphia trader to acquire a lot of 1800 bushels known to be stored in Maryland. "Concerning the salt," he wrote, "we are very desirous that the purchase should be made of the whole quantity and should you not be willing to hold a concern therein, in that case to be held for our own account as a speculation, being convinced of that article rising with you, any quantity would bring 6 shillings per bushel here and doubt not its being that price with you in less than 6 weeks."[82]

As usual, cautious merchants began to distrust an advance in a staple commodity when prices of others were fluctuating in Europe and signs of recession were evident even in their own market. Before contraction began in prices of fine salt, a merchant warned his brother in Bristol, "Salt . . . is an article so variable in price that I should not think of encouraging thy shipping of it even suppose it was 10 shillings. Two weeks might reduce it to 1 shilling 6 pence. . . . The cargo . . . will be more likely to sell for 2 than 3 shillings. Large quantities are hourly expected and large Turks Island salt is preferred for fish."[83] When the salt landed, he complained, "Had [the vessel] arrived three weeks ago her salt would have sold well, perhaps 4 shillings to 4 shillings 6 pence per bushel. It is now daily coming in small parcels and has reduced the price."[84] Three weeks later, with a decline of 50 per cent in a single month, the discouraging news that "salt has made a most rapid fall"[85] had to be reported and still later that it was only by selling at retail that as much as 2 shillings 6 pence a bushel was salvaged.[86]

Salt, the most sensitive of staple articles of trade in the irregular contraction of prices in the spring of 1785, dropped in May to one-half the price it sold for in March. Neither the future direction of prices nor the quantity likely to be available for sale could be foreseen. Prediction upon which long-distance orders had to be based was made no easier by the action of the Pennsylvania Assembly, hard-pressed to meet long-standing claims against it, in issuing £150,000 in paper money, which actually did not come into circulation until June.

[81] December 1, 1783, the same to Pearsall and Glover.

[82] October 19, 1784, Kuhn and Kuhn to James Finlay, Port Royal, Va.

[83] March 10, 1785, John Clifford to Thomas Clifford, Jr., Bristol.

[84] April 8, 1785, the same to the same.

[85] April 30, 1785, the same to the same.

[86] May 25, 1785, the same to the same.

The combination of pump-priming and vigilance induced one merchant to write cheerfully about his supplies of Liverpool salt, "Salt has an appearance of looking up and I hope before the fall vessels come in will be up to 3 shillings 6 pence and 3 shillings 9 pence per bushel. I have sold 300 to 400 bushels in different parcels at 2 shillings 6 pence. Believe I shall not sell any more at that price."[87] In this he was mistaken and soon had to report, "A cargo of salt arrived a few days ago from Liverpool, which has stopped the rise of it."[88]

The uncertainties, the slender knowledge upon which plans were made, and the assumption that only seasonal factors were influencing prices is clear in the preceding illustration from the correspondence of a prominent and experienced merchant, writing when a major depression, uneven in impact, can now be seen to have been in progress. Fine salt declined to the low price of 1 shilling 4½ pence a bushel by the summer of 1788, and, despite a slight upturn, did not sell again as high as 2 shillings a bushel until the last quarter of 1790.

Coarse salt was a more seasonal item than fine. According to Peter Kuhn it was "consumed here in great quantities and in great demand at the end of October and April in every year."[89] Of the various grades, he rated St. Ubes as "most saleable."[89] Even this preferred grade was shipped from Philadelphia to New England in the depressed summer of 1786 at 19 and 20 pence a bushel.[90]

It was expected that both fine and coarse salt would be subjected to a duty which might prevent their entry in the spring. A merchant with a large inventory of fine salt on hand reasoned that "there is so much salt in store that it cannot affect the price greatly."[91] Many were surprised with the enactment of a duty of 6 pence, one-half what was anticipated.[92] Initially the duty seems to have released supplies and lowered prices. "The price of Cadiz salt . . . ," Hollingsworth wrote early in March, "will be from 18 to 26 pence if good. . . . [There are] large quantities on hand. The duty intended by our Assembly on salt was over-rated by the back country members—this was a disappointment

[87] July 5, 1785, the same to the same.

[88] July 31, 1785, the same to the same.

[89] September 16, 1785, Kuhn and Risberg to Schon & Co., Stockholm.

[90] June 16, 1786, Josiah and Samuel Coates to Jonathan Call; July 27, 1786, to William Bartlett, Newburyport.

[91] December 27, 1786, John Clifford to Thomas Clifford, Jr., Bristol.

[92] January 2, 1787, the same to the same.

to the dealers in that article who had large magazines laid in, in hope of a rise."[93] Since consumers, who could be selective in their purchases of salt in these years as in colonial years, rated Lisbon above Cadiz,[94] and both above the sources they had been depending upon, heavy shipments of wheat and flour to southern Europe in the spring of 1788 and 1789, with salt a likely item in return cargoes, contributed to keeping prices low.

In 1788 merchants showed little interest in salt and made no efforts to push its sale. An inquiry for a preferred grade in the spring of 1789 elicted the answer, "There is no Turks Island salt or allum salt in town. Lisbon may be had at the above price [2 shillings 4 pence to 2 shillings 6 pence per bushel]."[95] At this time, the likelihood of an increase in the duty on salt, once the state levies were superseded by federal ones, interested merchants more than its price.[96] Clearly, any small increase in cost would create resistance to the purchase of a commodity which had proved unprofitable to its importers for four or more years. A competent importer, expressing his concern when he learned that a brig was on its way from Bristol with a cargo of salt, wrote, "Salt is very low. I do not expect what she brings will pay any freight. As we have suffered so much from storing salt I shall be for selling the Roebuck's cargo at what it will bring."[97]

Only a few months later a new note that prices would "mend in the fall" appeared in the correspondence, based on the theory that "the additional 6 cents per bushel expected to be added by Congress and the low price it has been selling for will discourage its being brought in,"[98] a prediction which anticipated the marked upswing in the last quarter of 1790 in prices of both fine and coarse salt.

Regrettably, no continuous series of prices of salt can be made for the war years, despite an abundance of records of sale and comment by merchants, special committees, the Council of Safety, and consumers. The gap is serious because salt was one of the most volatile of all items in common use. Its inclusion in the price group would, no doubt, have

93 March 14, 1787, Levi Hollingsworth to Henry and John Thompson, New York.

94 June 2, 1788, Josiah and Samuel Coates to William Coombs.

95 March 4, 1789, Levi Hollingsworth to Richard Graves, Christiana Bridge, Del.

96 April 22, 1789, Josiah and Samuel Coates to Moses Brown, Providence; and April 24, 1789, Clement Biddle to brother and sister in Berne, Switzerland.

97 March 3, 1790, John Clifford to Thomas Clifford, Jr., Bristol.

98 June 23, 1790, the same to the same.

materially raised the general index. A consecutive record of prices would be particularly illuminating in connection with the experience in importing, distributing, and limiting the prices of salt. It was one of the few commodities on which both price limits and allocation of supplies were attempted, the latter at a time when the commodity was too scarce to be held long enough to accumulate any quantity that could be equitably distributed. Nor would the story of salt be fully stressed even by a suitable average of its prices. It was so desired by farmers that the endorsement of an exchange of salt for their produce would often release, for the army, supplies that could not be procured for any currency but specie. The wide range of prices evident in merchants' accounts indicates that salt was a prime item of interest to speculators and one which could be hoarded in ways that defied all methods of control.

CHAPTER IX

IRON

NO DEVELOPMENT of the colonial era could be said to have more importance in the war years than the operation of iron forges and furnaces. Before the war, these manufacturing units not only found an expanding home market in the workshops of the towns along the Atlantic seaboard—and notably in Philadelphia—but shipped regularly some part of their output of pig and bar iron to British markets. At times, too, small quantities of steel and nails made part of a cargo to other areas, though larger quantities were regularly imported. During the war, the same forges and furnaces cast cannon and supplied camp kettles and utensils of many kinds, in addition to the raw materials for such weapons as were produced by gun factories and other makers of armament.

Other scholars, notably Professor Arthur C. Bining,[1] have thoroughly described the evolution of these industries and their place in the colonial economy. For purposes of this study it is necessary to stress only the prewar state of the industry and the impact of war and expansion upon its prices. Monthly prices of manufactured products of iron cannot be pieced together for the crucial years 1776 to 1783. Even in prewar years, iron products were too varied to be reported in published prices current. Once imports were shut off, both production and use were too local to furnish data standard enough for price series. A reliable series of monthly prices of bar iron from January 1776 to the middle of 1785, when general market reports were unavailable, has been assembled from forge and furnace records and from accounts of such merchants as McBay, Hollingsworth, and Webster. The scattered prices for other iron products serve merely to indicate the extent to which these crucial war materials followed the trend of bar iron.

Prewar Markets

Like most colonial commodities, iron shared in the recession which preceded the decade of the seventies. The prices of bar iron dropped

[1] Arthur C. Bining, *British Regulation of the Colonial Iron Industry.*

from £25 a ton in 1767 to a low of £23 before the spring of 1769. Prices of pig iron in the same period declined £2 a ton to £7 10 shillings. There was no recovery from the levels established in 1769 until late in 1770, when it was clear that the ban on importation from Great Britain would be lifted.

Prices of both forms of iron advanced in 1772, bar iron to a maximum of £28 and pig iron to £8 10 shillings a ton. The rebound in prices came at a time when shippers could take little advantage of the opening of trade, finding, as Clifford did, "Iron is so scarce I would not make terms of consignment, being glad to have it."[2] Even in the spring of 1772 he answered an urgent request from Bristol, "Bar iron is at too high a price and there is no pigs to be had on freight."[3]

Throughout the summer, when all business had been a "little brisker than usual," another Philadelphia merchant, engaged in loading a vessel to return to Bristol, stressed his difficulties in buying iron. "Many material obstacles," he wrote, "have occurred of late, particularly in the article of iron, of which we know not where to purchase ten tons in this city, or if we did, it would be from £8 10 shillings to £9 per ton for Batsto and Etna,"[4] two of the grades of pig iron most sought for the Bristol trade. Later in the month, when the cargo was being loaded, he was able to report "about 8 tons of Etna pigs" and 40 tons of Batsto on board.[5]

Products of iron, such as nails and steel, which might be expected to advance with the raw materials, were not ordered by the merchants. It was not until prices of nails reached their peak that James and Drinker replenished their stock. "Our sales of nails," Drinker belatedly wrote, "have not encouraged our sending forward an order for that article ere this. We now request your shipping the quantity mentioned."[6] Country steel sold in the spring of 1772 for 50 shillings a hundredweight; the quotations for English steel were higher, but, as far as can be determined from the sparse data, prices of steel had passed their peak before those of bar iron.

The shortage of iron was attributed by Clifford to the closing of some

[2] November 16, 1771, Thomas Clifford to Thomas Frank, Bristol.

[3] May 16, 1772, the same to the same.

[4] August 4, 1772, James and Drinker to Lancelot Cowper, Bristol.

[5] August 22, 1772, the same to the same.

[6] September 17, 1772, the same to Finch and Laugher.

furnaces and the lack of ore at others.[7] He continued to refer to difficulties in purchasing iron for shipment, noting that the scarcity arose from "so many of the iron works being out of blast or turned into farms,"[8] until the last months of 1772, when his comments suggest a combination among the owners of iron largely concerned with shipping "to keep up the price at home."[9] This puzzling comment is not explained until two years later. Meantime, Henry Drinker gave to a well-known Bristol firm a detailed and gloomy picture of the state of the iron industry at a time when it was obviously beginning to recover from the depression that followed the Seven Years' War and when he was ready to invest in it.[10]

Once launched as the proprietor of an iron works, Drinker explored the possibilities of shipping his iron to West India markets. He wished to be advised "what quantity may be likely to sell in Kingston in a year and the sizes they will want," also "whether great quantities of grating bars are wanted in Jamaica and what sizes they should be."[11]

While these plans for extending the export markets went on, other shippers found high prices sustained and little iron for sale. Typical of the comments of this period is that of Reynell and Coates to a merchant

7 September 22, 1772, Thomas Clifford to Thomas Frank, Bristol.

8 October 21, 1772, the same to the same.

9 November 27, 1772, the same to the same.

10 "It appears that most of the iron works which have for some years past furnished this place with pig iron are either worked out or dropped. Durham has been done for some time as also Pine Grove. Deep Creek is in a very declining and discouraging situation as we are informed. Etna is out of blast and the furnace is sold to be pulled to pieces, and never can be resumed again for want of ore. Batsto it seems agreed on all hands are near their last shifts for want of both wood and ore, so that we know not of any iron works that will or can furnish this place with pig iron at any moderate expense, except one we have lately become possessed of, that is three-fourth parts thereof, which we had an opportunity of purchasing on pleasing terms and we think has advantages annexed to it superior to any that has been worked in this or the neighboring provinces from the great quantity of ore of approved quality, plenty of wood, moderate expense in bringing the iron to market, and the small distance being about 28 miles from this city and about half thereof water carriage. From these pleasing circumstances and our having 12 to 14,000 acres of land, in general well timbered, and all joining the iron works, we have a prospect of erecting a furnace that may be making iron either in this fall or early next spring, so that we shall be much interested in the price both at home and abroad. At present we make it into bar iron to a tolerable profit at a forge we purchased with the land, etc., some of which we have formerly sent thee called Atsion iron." May 15, 1773, James and Drinker to Lancelot Cowper, Bristol.

11 June 18, 1773, the same to Cadwalader Morris, Kingston, Jamaica.

in New England, "The great scarcity of bar iron prevents us from a chance of choosing so good as we could wish."[12]

Price Stabilization Agreement

It was not until the summer of 1774 that an explanation of the mystifying behavior of iron prices, at a time when shippers were vigorously trying to expand their capacity and markets, was given by Henry Drinker. A group of proprietors of iron furnaces were attempting to maintain the level of prices in the colonial market by apportioning exports among them and shipping iron at prices that would cover commissions and afford "brisk sales." Drinker, in a letter to his Bristol correspondent, solicited a market for the product of his own works. He wrote,

> Some time since we desired your continued and best advices respecting the article of pig iron as we were concerned in erecting a furnace under superior advantages to any we know and as she has been in blast some time and made several hundred tons of pig iron of an excellent quality. . . . Lately it has been intimated to us that iron was likely to rise in England. Be that as it may the present advanced state of your exchange to 174 and 175 per cent, the character our smiths give of the bar iron made of our pigs . . . together with the desire we have of establishing the quality and character of said pigs with you, led us to ship a handsome parcel in this vessel. . . . The latter is shipped in conformity to an agreement our iron masters entered into some time past, that each works should export to England a certain proportion of what they annually made so as to leave for the American consumption no more than would be called for and thereby prevent a fall in price.[13]

Prices of bar iron held at relatively high levels through 1774 and the first four months of 1775 in contrast to those of agricultural staples, which were sensitive to the discussion of nonimportation agreements. Late in November the order of a merchant in Newburyport could not be filled. To the inquiry for bar iron, Reynell and Coates wrote, "David Potts, the largest iron dealer by far of any in the city, has none to sell. He is engaged to the Whartons for the run of next week at £26 per ton. Other people are so much engaged at £27 per ton that we could not procure a good quality at that price and from the great demand for this

[12] July 22, 1773, Reynell and Coates to John Moffatt, Portsmouth, N. H.
[13] August 4, 1774, James and Drinker to Lancelot Cowper & Co., Bristol.

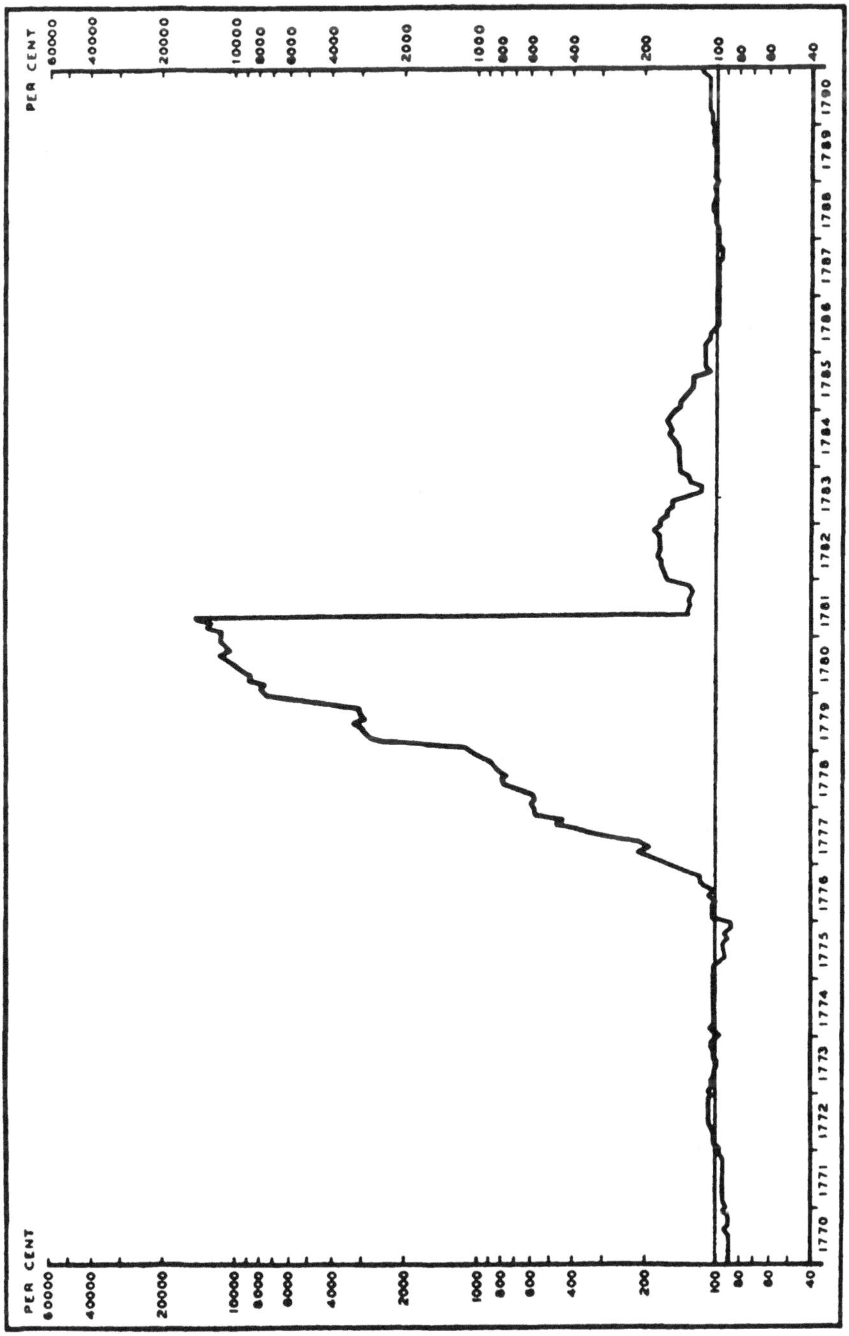

CHART VII—MONTHLY RELATIVES OF WHOLESALE PRICES OF BAR IRON IN PHILADELPHIA, 1770-1790
(Base—Monthly Average, 1771-1773)

article and its scarcity together, we apprehend the orders for iron cannot possibly be fully executed."[14]

Iron prices had not varied for more than a year and were still quoted at £26 a ton when Drinker explained that his furnace was temporarily out of blast and "as the price for home consumption is £25 to £26 per ton and exchange low it can't be our interest for a while to ship that commodity."[15] Throughout this period when shippers of perishable commodities anticipated an interruption in trade which would lower prices, some iron masters apparently expected the nonimportation measure either to be modified or weakly enforced. "Upon the whole," Drinker confided to Cowper, "we must own that with many of our friends and countrymen we were not settled in our judgment that the Congress would not have abated of the rigour of their resolutions before they had broke up, or that the committees would have carried them into execution with that severity they have hitherto done."[15] Just as the small differential which the iron shippers' agreement attempted to maintain indicates the narrow profit margin upon which the iron industry must have been operating and the sensitivity of the iron masters to seemingly narrow changes in price, so the attempt to stabilize local prices gives a hint of the importance attached to the home market. Obviously, such an agreement could not withstand a severe recession in prices or the loss of export outlets. It did, however, serve to bring the aggressive leaders in the industry together for exchange of opinion and methods of operation, and may well have been a factor in the later pooling of information which was a notable aspect of the first phases of conversion to war uses. Before this stimulus came, iron makers experienced a marked decline in prices already felt to be low.

The contraction in prices in 1775 dropped bar iron to £22 10 shillings, or lower than it had been in the depression of 1769. Pig iron, at the same time, sold for £7 a ton. In an effort to check the decline and keep their vessels at sea, shippers took advantage of the chance to export iron as long as the ports were open. A week before foreign trade was cut off, Drinker was loading his vessel, the *Chalkley,* which regularly plied between Philadelphia and Bristol, with pine and oak boards and staves, a difficult cargo to load without other freight. In accounting for the choice of iron he commented, "By some of your letters we are discour-

[14] November 26, 1774, Reynell and Coates to William Wyer, Newburyport.

[15] February 23, 1775, James and Drinker to Lancelot Cowper & Co., Bristol.

aged from sending further quantities of Atsion piggs, but with the Chalkley's present cargo, iron to mix therewith seemed quite necessary . . . should the non-exportation from North America continue many months, will it not quicken the sale and increase the demand for this article?"[16]

Effect of War on Prices

In the light of the attention given to iron prices on the eve of the Revolution, one might have expected quotations to soar under war conditions. Instead, a comparison of the increase throughout the war indicates that bar iron conformed more closely to the median than did any other commodity in the series. It is true that in January 1776 the price leaped upward £3 10 shillings a ton, but the whole advance of the next seven months increased the average only to the levels set by the stabilizing agreement. Between September and December, prices surged upward until at the close of 1776 bar iron was selling at the unheard of price of £39 15 shillings a ton. Pig iron, at the close of 1776, varied from £10 to £15 a ton.

The importance of a 59 per cent advance in the prices of bar iron between November 1775 and November 1776 lay in the problems created for those who had contracted to manufacture war products. In total, the increase was less than that of any other of the 15 items in the series except wheat, superfine flour, and tar. But as early as October and November 1775 the Committee of Safety was advertising for workmen "willing to contract for the making of firelocks."[17] Such arrangements as were made with artificers for fabricating small arms, and with furnace owners for the casting of cannon, were based on the normal prewar prices of tools and raw materials. When in November 1776 the expenses of the gun factory were reconsidered, it was estimated that prices of steel and iron had increased about 52 and 79 per cent respectively and workmen's wages about 56 per cent.[18] Taking into account the mounting cost of tools, it is manifest that a revision of as much as 50 per cent in the original terms of contracts would barely cover the costs added since they were drawn.

It would be difficult to state the case for renegotiation of contracts

[16] September 2, 1775, the same to the same.

[17] October 23, 1775, *Minutes of the Committee of Safety of Pennsylvania, Colonial Records*, v. 10, p. 380.

[18] November 16, 1776, *Pennsylvania Archives*, 2nd ser., v. 1, p. 690.

more effectively than was done by the Philadelphia gunlock makers in their petition of December 1776 to the Council of Safety of Pennsylvania.

> At the commencement they had materials to procure which were new and uncommon; hands to instruct, who were strangers and unlearned, and even those to purchase at double their value; steel to provide, in which article their loss is manifest to their acquaintances. Still hoping that their perseverance would surmount every difficulty, they continued with labor and assiduity. Notwithstanding which, they now find it impossible to subsist, as their most painful endeavors bear no proportion to the present rate of things. Files are now double what they have been, and some treble; vices, double; steel, scarce any to be found good. Thirty or forty shillings advance on one hundred bushels of coal; journeymen's wages still rising; your petitioners limited, and the enormous price of every other necessary too well known to trouble your honors with a repetition.[19]

Scarce as bar iron seems to have been in Philadelphia markets, it was selling, apparently, at lower prices at the beginning of 1777 than in other seaboard areas. The needs of Boston sent agents scouting in Baltimore and Philadelphia. The explanation given by Cushing was: "No iron is to be had here. The last sold for the enormous price of eighty pounds lawful money per ton. Pray send me fifty tons of bar iron from Baltimore immediately. As many of our northern vessels are there, you may easily prevail with some of them to take a quantity of freight. It will certainly turn out vastly cheaper for the continent; nay I do not see how I can obtain it any other way. You may send some also from Philadelphia."[20] The prices mentioned in Boston were far above any cited in Philadelphia before the summer of 1777. But throughout 1777 Philadelphia prices were rising rapidly and by June bar iron was selling at Charming Forge for more than double the maximum price ever reached in prewar years. Even then quotations were lower in the vicinity of the city than in upstate areas. The gunsmiths of Lancaster, who were bargaining for an increase in the rates paid them for making muskets and bayonets, contended "they were willing to make arms on the same pay the Philadelphians did, provided they could procure mate-

[19] December 1776, Petition of Gunlock Makers, *ibid.*, pp. 718-19.

[20] January 16, 1777, Thomas Cushing, Boston, to John Hancock, *Pennsylvania Magazine of History and Biography*, 1886, v. 10, p. 355.

rials at the same rate, which they were at this time not possessed of."[21]

Bar iron prices continued to mount steadily until by November 1777 they were stabilized for a few months at £150 a ton. A description of the course of the rise from June to November 1777 is hampered by a wide range in the price quotations from different sources—even a spread as wide as £65 to £120 in the price of the same dealer in a single day—in a commodity in which the accounts of many different suppliers normally conformed closely. One can explain the range only by assuming that the lowest quotations indicate the filling of orders contracted for early in the year before the threat of inflation was generally taken into account. Apart from the influence of relatively long-term agreements, the fanning out of prices by the different producers of primary materials represented a lag by some iron masters in adjusting to the speed of currency depreciation. By the end of the year, the various iron works seemed to have corrected their price spread and prices of iron generally surged ahead. It was in December that a correspondent from Easton wrote to President Wharton, "Iron, I learn, may be had at Mayburry's works, the nearest, at £150 per ton."[22]

Difficulties of Transportation and Lack of Manpower

By the time the city of Philadelphia was evacuated by the British in June 1778, bar iron had risen to more than £200 per ton, though the monthly rise in this period was gradual. In October of that year, Mark Bird of East Pennsborough quoted bar iron at £235 a ton. "The above," he wrote, "is the lowest price I can take, and lower than I could deliver at, only I have back loads for the wagons."[23]

Rapid as the advance seems in terms of prewar levels, it was not until June 1778 that the costs of transportation and the pressure for output first lifted the prices of bar iron above the average for all commodities. By December it was exchanging for nearly £280 a ton. It is well known that in these tense war years the colonies were not producing all their

[21] August 14, 1777, Colonel Bartrem Galbraith, Lancaster, to Thomas Wharton, Jr., President of the Supreme Executive Council of Pennsylvania, *Pennsylvania Archives*, 1st ser., v. 5, p. 521.

[22] December 27, 1777, Robert Levers, Easton, to Thomas Wharton, Jr., *ibid.*, 1st ser., v. 6, p. 141.

[23] October 10, 1778, Mark Bird, East Pennsborough, to Colonel John Davis, Deputy Quartermaster General, Carlisle.

own supplies of iron or its products. In the Nantes documents, a student of the commercial relations of the American colonies found 460,700 livres (about 225 tons) of worked iron and bars listed as shipped to the United States.[24]

In the early stages of the war, iron workings had enjoyed some advantages over other industries. Insofar as the indentured servants among their employees had not joined the army, wages were unlikely to increase as rapidly as in other employment. From 1776 to 1778 when farm prices were low in terms of other commodities, the iron industry could offer attractive employment to excess farm labor and thus readily recruit its working forces. Many of the inactive workings, which Henry Drinker described in the late colonial era, could be and frequently were brought back into operation. Notable among these was the Durham Forge and Furnace, which by reason of its volume contributed particularly to the war effort. By 1779, industries as well as the army were feeling the lack of manpower. According to General Washington, there was then "abundant employment in every branch of business; wages, in consequence have become so high, and the value of our money so low, that little temptation is left to men to engage in the army."[25] Even in this situation, the location of furnaces in country areas afforded advantages in obtaining foodstuffs, and owners could often hold employees by using the scarce West India goods as bonuses, though they ultimately resorted to the payment of key occupations in specie.

Uprush of Prices in 1779 and 1780

The most spectacular rise in bar iron prices in the whole war period came in 1779 between January and February when prices, in a single month, increased 111 per cent, followed by a 15 per cent rise in the following month and smaller percentages in each month until May. Country blacksmiths and small tool shops had been willing in this rise to bid higher for iron than city shops, especially as both demand and price seemed to them to be expanding.[26] Bar iron from Pennsylvania by then

[24] Gaston Martin, "Commercial Relations between Nantes and the American Colonies during the War of Independence," *Journal of Economic and Business History*, v. 4, p. 828.

[25] January 15, 1779, General George Washington to Committee of Congress; Jared Sparks, editor, *The Writings of George Washington*, v. 6, p. 161.

[26] March 21, 1779, Robert Levers, Easton, to Timothy Matlack, Secretary of the Commonwealth of Pennsylvania, *Pennsylvania Archives*, 1st ser., v. 7, p. 177.

was not only needed in other areas but was commanding a price above any then current in Boston. Toward the end of April, the agent buying iron in Baltimore was notifying the Massachusetts Board of War, "Am very sorry you have ordered any bar iron as the price of it here now is much higher than what it was in Boston when I left you. You'll be astonished at the immense price of everything here."[27] Bar iron was then quoted by him as high as £800 a ton, though the Philadelphia prices did not reach that level until about June.

Purchasers from other states were not alone in expressing astonishment at the heights reached by prices of primary metal products. For a time, commodities to which little attention had been paid in the various early experiments in controlling prices attracted the attention of local regulatory committees. Careful studies of the markets of April 1779 led them to agree upon £700 per ton as a price for refined bar iron; £500 for bloomery iron; and £1000 for nailrod.[28] It was hoped that, by joint efforts, these terms of sale might be gradually lowered. Instead there was little interruption in the rising tendency. Prices of bar iron advanced above the previous month in every month, except July, from April 1779 to February 1780, as it had done in the nine preceding months. Minor decreases occurred in a few later months before continental notes ceased to circulate. Instead of the £700 which the price control committee hoped to establish, bar iron was selling for £1917 a ton by December 1779; for £2279 in March 1780; and for more than £3000 a ton in December 1780—all prices taken from the accounts of one of the leading dealers in iron products in the period. The maximum and final price quoted in continental currency was £3818, in April 1781, which corresponded with a price of £35 in specie. At this time, prices of pig iron had reached £800 a ton.

Prices in Dual Currencies

The impact of war on prices of iron may be traced at times in the two currencies of most interest to contemporaries. Bar iron was sold in April 1778 at £40 a ton in specie, against £170 in "congress money." Its specie price was no higher than £40 from April to June 1779, when the paper price varied from £755 to £843. Specie prices at the beginning of the last quarter of 1779 were as low as £30 a ton and dropped later to £28—

[27] April 23, 1779, Cumberland Dugan to S. P. Savage.

[28] William B. Reed, *Life and Correspondence of Joseph Reed*, v. 2, p. 144.

a quotation which reappeared in the first half of the following year. As early as October 1780, prices in specie began to advance and by November reached £42 10 shillings, the peak price of the war in any terms that can be contrasted with postwar levels. In continental currency it was then above £3000 a ton, or in the language of the period, paper money was depreciated in the ratio of 71 to one. In the confused months before continental currency was abandoned, the specie price declined as currency ratios gradually increased to about 160 to one.

In specie terms, prices of iron underwent two marked cycles, the first of which reached a peak in mid-1779 about 54 per cent above prewar levels. The second, with a peak in November 1780, was in the stages of slow contraction in the first half of 1781 when the currency standard was altered.

The return to a specie basis in May brought an underlying decline in bar iron prices which lasted until October. The low price of £33 in October 1781 may be regarded as the beginning of a short cycle in iron prices. The peak of this cycle came in November 1782, when bar iron was as high as £47 10 shillings a ton. Products of iron shared in the rise. "Philadelphia steel," Pelatiah Webster wrote, "is risen in price occasioned by the rise of iron."[29] By this time Philadelphia steel, according to him, had attained a quality "equal to any English steel for every purpose and much preferred for edge-tools by our smiths."[30]

Postwar Prices

The downswing was short and lasted from December 1782 to August 1783. It had no sooner begun than some merchants energetically sought markets for Philadelphia products which they formerly exported to London, notably bar and pig iron. Other producers of iron seem to have turned to the manufacture of household products at their own plantations. Drinker explained his need for information and the way in which he avoided having his furnace turned into an arsenal.

> We yet remain proprietors of the Atsion Furnace in the Jersies and, for several years past, have done pretty largely in the casting hollow ware, and that by an air furnace being deterred from setting the blast furnace at work, for a long time, lest it should be taken out of our hands for the making of

[29] June 12, 1782, Pelatiah Webster to John Perit, Norwich, Conn.
[30] June 19, 1782, the same to the same.

cannon and bullets, which evil business we thereby eluded. And now this subject is mentioned we wish for thy information how we could be best supplied with a set of patterns, such as potts, and kettles of various sizes, tea kettles, ovens, round and oval; skillets, etc., etc. Thy advice on this subject sent us per first opportunity where we could most properly apply for an assortment of such patterns, and whether it would be best to have them of brass or iron and what the cost of each would be will much oblige us.[31]

A more enlightening statement of the factors affecting the price of iron at this time was given by a European traveler who visited the iron works in the vicinity of Reading. He wrote, "Bar iron in the cheap times before the war, cost the foundry masters from £22 to £23 a ton; they sold it for £25 cash or £30 at six months credit. At present they cannot produce a ton under from £32 to £37."[32] Iron sold below £37 a ton until November. Even then it was reported to be "very scarce indeed,"[33] an indication that slowness in adjusting costs within the local industry opened the way for part of the competition from imports in the early phases of postwar trade revival.

The second short postwar cycle, with a peak in October 1784, had a longer period of decline than of rise. The scarcity of iron for export in these years was largely attributable to the manufacture of a diversity of articles for domestic use. It was also ascribed by merchants to labor shortage. "There is a great want of workmen in the iron business," Clifford wrote. "Iron is scarce and entirely (the iron masters say) for want of workmen that 'tis worth more than £40 per ton, and lately I heard hardly any to be had at any price." He was willing to bring over workmen, even those who were unable to pay their passage, because "on their arrival here he [Colonel Bird, proprietor of the Hopewell Furnace] engages to pay it for them."[34] The long downward swing in bar iron prices began about the time that failures were reported in England and were felt also in Philadelphia.[35] In March 1786, when bar iron was still declining, Josiah and Samuel Coates cautioned their cor-

31 August 27, 1783, James and Drinker to Peter Price, Bristol.

32 John D. Schoepf, "Travels through Berks County in 1783," *Pennsylvania Magazine*, 1881, v. 5, p. 78.

33 November 5, 1783, Stephen Collins to Willis Hall.

34 August 30, 1784, Thomas Clifford to "Dear Sir."

35 November 7, 1784, William and John Sitgreaves to Arabet, Gautier and Manning, Barcelona.

respondent in Newburyport that it would not be well to hold the iron for a better market as they expected prices would not be higher.[36] They were more right than Drinker, who preferred to "wait sometime longer unless you can make sales at about £32 per ton."[37]

Throughout the spring of 1786, the ironmongers were "pretty well supplied."[38] As usual, the shippers of iron and its products were looking about for markets. Though Drinker knew that the markets in the British dominions were closed to American ships, he sent an inquiry to Nova Scotia in an effort to open an avenue for sales. He wrote,

> It immediately occurred to me that the regulations and restrictions made in England respecting the conduct of commercial matters between the British Dominions and the United States foiled your importing or admitting such articles even if shipped in British bottoms, yet as stoves have several times been purchased of me to go your way, I was led to make the present enquiry whether there is any opening for the introduction of that useful article in your cold country or of the others above mentioned. Pot ware and other hollow castings it is likely you can be supplied with from England on favourable terms.[39]

In July, when prices were at a low, stable level, merchants felt confident enough to assure customers that they would be able to purchase at the quoted price.[40] At the end of the year, Hollingsworth, inquiring about the duty on bar iron to England, commented, "I had it in view to have shipped you a few tons."[41] Apparently the English market proved to be a profitable one for the shippers, and the Coateses, commenting on a slight local rise in the price of bar iron, wrote, "Quantities being shipped to London has raised the price."[42]

The downswing in prices from the end of 1784 was characterized by long stretches of well-maintained prices at levels slightly below the prewar years. In this contraction, quotations as low as £25 10 shillings were maintained for nearly two years. After that, prices of bar iron continued to fluctuate around £26 and £27 a ton, the levels established in the prewar agreements.

36 March 18, 1786, Josiah and Samuel Coates to Samuel Souther, Newburyport.
37 March 25, 1786, Henry Drinker to Embree and Shotwell, New York.
38 April 2, 1786, John Clifford to Thomas Clifford, Jr., Bristol.
39 May 7, 1786, Henry Drinker to Lawrence Hartshorne, Nova Scotia.
40 July 28, 1786, Thomas Clifford to ———.
41 December 30, 1786, Levi Hollingsworth to Thomas Clifford, Jr., Bristol.
42 October 4, 1787, Josiah and Samuel Coates to William Bartlett, Newburyport.

There is evidence that the stability in prices in these years was not as accidental as the comments about markets imply. In their concern to be able to maintain prices, the dealers in iron were said to have effected an organization which assured them sales at the expense of profits. At any rate, a more energetic method of selling was proposed by William and John Sitgreaves.

> It struck us . . . that the mode you have hitherto pursued of vending your iron at a specified price to one of the dealers in that article must subject you to material disadvantage in the sales by allowing a profit to the purchaser more than adequate to the trouble of the sales. As you have now entered into this manufacture upon a large scale, and as we have hitherto had considerable commercial connections together which perhaps might be continued to mutual advantage, we have thought proper to make you the following offer: if you will engage to send us the whole quantity of iron made at your works and sent to this city, we will sell it for you at a commission of 30 shillings per ton, and under that condition will have no objection to allow you a circulating credit of articles in our line to the amount of £500 of which the present debt to be included. The above commission will be esteemed a sufficient compensation for the expense and trouble of selling, weighing, storing and collecting, and for this purpose our situation is as well calculated as any in Philadelphia, being very central and in the neighbourhood of most of the New England houses who are the chief customers in that line . . .[43]

An active demand developed in the spring of 1788 from which the shippers could gain little, owing to bad roads and the small amount of iron coming to market.[44] Bar iron was reported scarce throughout the spring months and prices were stable during the first half of 1789.

In March 1790, iron prices returned to the highest level known in the prewar period. At that time Hollingsworth wrote, "Bar and rod iron are both risen here—bar £28, nail rod £34 to £34 10 shillings per ton nor will they fall in price unless an importation takes place from Europe as the supply from our iron works is not equal to the demand."[45] Prices of iron were then less flexible than those of most other commodities. According to Clifford, the Jersey iron masters, who previously supplied pig iron for export, were holding theirs to a fixed price of £10 per ton.[46] Even toward the end of the year, it was reported to New

[43] March 25, 1788, William and John Sitgreaves to J. and P. Richards, New Hanover.

[44] March 29, 1788, Levi Hollingsworth to Solomon Townsend, New York.

[45] March 20, 1790, the same to the same.

[46] September 25, 1790, John Clifford to Thomas Clifford, Jr., Bristol.

York by a Philadelphia shipper that "bar iron is very scarce here and cannot be had under £28 10 shillings to £29."[47]

SUMMARY

A contrast with prewar price behavior is furnished by long stretches of unvaried prices and the maintenance, even in the trough of the depression of 1786 and 1787, of prices equal to the average of 1771 to 1773 without the recurrence of low months such as marked these years.

During the war, surprisingly few complaints about shortages of iron, despite its many uses, appear in contemporary comment. The location of numerous small iron workings in country areas, beyond the line of march of armies, protected iron masters from the interruptions that were the lot of artificers, gunmakers, smiths, and other users of iron. Some confirmation of the lack of periods of persistent shortage may be drawn from the behavior of iron prices in the period of currency depreciation. By contrast with most other commodities, the rise was not immoderate either in form or extent.

The percentage change in iron prices from April to April shows the steadiness of the yearly advance in the average:

April 1775	to April 1776	4 per cent
1776	1777	87
1777	1778	240
1778	1779	344
1779	1780	200
1780	1781	69

At the height of prices in continental money, in April 1781, the index of bar iron was 14,767. At that time four commodities—wheat, corn, coffee, and tar—were relatively lower, and common flour only slightly higher than iron. October 1778 to August 1779, the longest stretch with prices of iron above the median, may carry an indication of lack of ample supply.

From the movement of prices one may conclude that the postwar readjustment was over by the middle of 1785. The industry, despite complaint about increased costs and changed conditions of sale, had stabilized its prices and, after the middle of 1786, was operating not far from prewar levels.

[47] October 24, 1790, Clement Biddle to Alexander Macomb, New York.

CHAPTER X

NAVAL STORES

PRICES OF THE NAVAL STORES—tar, pitch, and turpentine—were infrequently quoted in the Revolutionary War years. Pitch dropped almost wholly out of the items of trade. The most nearly complete series to represent these important commodities is that of tar, supplemented at strategic dates by small sales of turpentine.

During the colonial period, the prices of tar, pitch, turpentine, and resin, subject to bounties, were much influenced by the London market. Their trend from 1769 was upward. Like grain and its products, prices of tar reached a peak in 1772 and held at relatively high levels until the close of 1774. Once the zenith of the upswing was passed, merchants fearing an abrupt decline in prices of all naval stores shaded their offering bids for tar to their Carolina correspondents slightly below the sale prices then current in Philadelphia.[1] On the other hand, the offers for turpentine, then "very scarce," overtopped the nominal market average. Explaining at this time the scarcity of turpentine, Drinker wrote to the captain of a vessel in port, "We have shipped all the goods ordered, except 10 barrels [of] turpentine, of which there has not been a barrel to be bought in the city for some time past."[2] The vulnerable position of naval stores in the event of an agreement among the colonies to limit trade was pointed out early in the debates of the First Continental Congress when William Hooper, a delegate from South Carolina, said, "Tar, pitch and turpentine we can ship nowhere but to Great Britain."[3] Yet prices of tar adhered to a relatively high level until the close of 1774.

The timing of changes in direction in the Philadelphia market in the seventies contrasts strikingly with the movement of prices of tar at Amsterdam, which reached the maximum of these years between June and August 1771 and declined irregularly in the next two years.[4] An

[1] April 14, 1773, James and Drinker to Samuel Cornell.

[2] June 17, 1773, the same to Captain James Ballaine.

[3] September 26-27, 1774, John Adams, notes on debates, *Letters of Members of the Continental Congress*, v. 1, p. 50.

[4] N. W. Posthumus, *Inquiry into the History of Prices in Holland*, Table 214.

abrupt decline appeared in Philadelphia in January 1775 and continued throughout most of the first half of the year. By the end of April, tar was quoted as low as 12 shillings 6 pence a barrel and turpentine at 26 shillings,[5] and it was not until the last quarter of 1775 that the index of tar mounted as high as it had been in peak months in the previous five years.

War Advance in Prices

The marked upswing in 1776 was accompanied by complaints of scarcity. In April, when the price in Philadelphia had reached 20 shillings a barrel, Hollingsworth was informed by the superintendent of Elk Forge, "We are entirely out of tar and all kinds of grease for the forges. . . . not any to be had in this neighborhood for love or money."[6] The largest purchaser was then the Council of Safety, which acquired 35 barrels of tar in August, 50 in September, and 28 in November[7] at prices far below those found in the scattered accounts on which our price series is based.

The activity of the Committee of Safety in the purchase of naval stores can be attributed to the allocation of authority to various commissions for procurement of material for construction of four frigates ordered by Congress to be built in Philadelphia. In order to relieve the naval constructor of some entrepreneurial duties, separate bodies had been appointed in January to buy and take charge of timber, planks, and other lumber products; other commissioners provided rigging, ship chandlery, and similar supplies as wanted.[8] Equally important was the provision of naval stores for the commercial vessels trading "on account of the continent" with special permits to export produce in return for arms, six of which the Committee of Safety was informed were ready to be dispatched in April 1776.[9]

The concentrated demand, supplemented by official purchases, raised prices of tar between April 1775 and April 1776 as much as 48 per cent, a larger advance than is shown by any other articles in the series except

[5] April 29, 1775, James and Drinker to John Geffrard & Co.

[6] April 2, 1776, Thomas May, Elk Forge, to Thomas Hollingsworth.

[7] August 21, September 2, and November 8, 1776, *Minutes of the Council of Safety of Pennsylvania, Colonial Records*, v. 10, pp. 694, 708, 781.

[8] January 9, 1776, Joshua Humphreys Correspondence. The Committee of Safety, appointed June 30, 1775, was reorganized and enlarged as the Council of Safety on July 23, 1776. The Council served until December 6, 1777.

[9] April 29, 1776, Robert Morris to the Committee of Safety of Pennsylvania.

rum, pepper, and tea. It was unlikely that active local demand would continue, but tar and turpentine were desirable remittances for war equipment expected from Europe. Twice, toward the end of this year, naval stores were mentioned by Silas Deane in his letters from France as an important item to include in shipments. In November he informed the Committee of Secret Correspondence, "Masts, spars, and other naval stores are in demand, and the more so as a war with Great Britain is considered as near at hand."[10] Turpentine seems to have advanced more than tar, and in the closing months of 1776 the Council of Safety paid 37 shillings 6 pence each for the 130 barrels it was able to purchase,[11] or more than double the average prewar price.

Quotations for any article of naval stores in the next two years are infrequent. That they were profitable items of export may be inferred from the account furnished by Michael Gratz for his adventures with Carter Braxton and Robert Morris on the privateer *Shippen*. The book profits on 18 barrels of turpentine and 75 barrels of tar on March 1, 1777, cannot be separated from other items, but that on 48 barrels of tar on August 1 of the same year amounted to a trifle over £38, presumably his third of the total for shipping supplies from southern ports.[12] Tar, especially, was scarce and much needed in Pennsylvania, as much as a substitute for "grease" as for naval and commercial ship supplies. In the spring of 1778, the Board of War was informed, "Since last fall, the continental wagons rub along with their loads without tar. I do not hear of any means used to obtain that article. It is said the axletree of each wagon wears very soon for want of it and that four horses will draw one-fourth less without it than with it."[13] Out of the correspondence came a plan for use of the abundant pine forests of South Mountain as a source for production of tar.

Meantime, the use of tar as a substitute for oils carried its price above that of turpentine. In July 1778, tar sold in Baltimore, from whence the supplies had come during the occupation of Philadelphia, for 25 dol-

[10] November 6, 1776, Silas Deane, Paris, to the Committee of Secret Correspondence; Francis Wharton, editor, *The Revolutionary Diplomatic Correspondence of the United States*, v. 2, p. 191.

[11] November 29, 1776, *Minutes of the Council of Safety of Pennsylvania*, *C.R.*, v. 11, p. 21.

[12] William Vincent Byars, editor, *B. and M. Gratz, Merchants in Philadelphia, 1754-1798*, p. 229.

[13] March 30, 1778, Thomas Armor, York, to Board of War.

lars a barrel, or 187½ shillings. Turpentine, at the same time, was quoted at 20 dollars a barrel.[14]

Important as naval stores were to the colonists and to the British navy, trade in these commodities had not been restricted as it had been in many staple foods. When the soaring prices of foodstuffs and the difficulty of supplying the army with flour forced a discussion of an embargo on the export of provisions, such a measure as was finally adopted was argued on the ground of the advantage to the enemy of procuring foodstuffs in captured vessels. Henry Laurens, fearing the prohibition was too limited, stated, "I am willing to submit articles of which the enemy stand more in need than of either flour or rice, I mean tar, pitch and turpentine, remain unrestrained."[15] This shrewd comment needs no further explanation than that the war had already raised the prices of tar in Great Britain from 7 or 8 shillings a barrel to 30 shillings sterling[16] or to a higher price than it sold for in Pennsylvania before 1778 in inflated currency.

The activity in shipbuilding[17] and the revival in trade, once the population returned to the city, might be expected to heighten the demand for naval stores, but there is no reason to assume that the advance in prices in the closing months of 1778 was peculiar to one state or one locality. In November 1778, a Baltimore merchant wrote to his Philadelphia correspondent, "There is no chance now of doing anything in the speculating way, as goods are full as high here as they are with you."[18] Actually, throughout 1779, tar kept considerably below the median of other commodities as turpentine did in the last months of the previous year, a behavior not at all surprising with shippers marking time while the embargo on exporting foodstuffs lasted. Naval

[14] July 4, 1778, Jesse Hollingsworth, Baltimore, to Levi Hollingsworth.

[15] October 6, 1778, Henry Laurens, President of Congress, to Rawlins Lowndes, President of South Carolina, *Letters*, v. 3, p. 441.

[16] Anderson, *An Historical and Chronological Deduction of the Origin of Commerce*, v. 5, p. 297.

[17] According to the biographer of Colonel Jehu Eyre, he was occupied from July 1, 1778 to March 1779 building ships needed in Philadelphia. "During that time he had four separate sets of ships carpenters at work at different localities under their foremen—one under Captain Jacob Miller at Easton, one under Captain Samuel Clinton at Reading, one under Captain William Bowers at Chester, and one in Philadelphia under Richard Salter." Peter D. Keyser, "Memorials of Colonel Jehu Eyre," *Pennsylvania Magazine of History and Biography*, 1879, v. 3, p. 423.

[18] November 22, 1778, Woolsey and Salmon, Baltimore, to John Pringle.

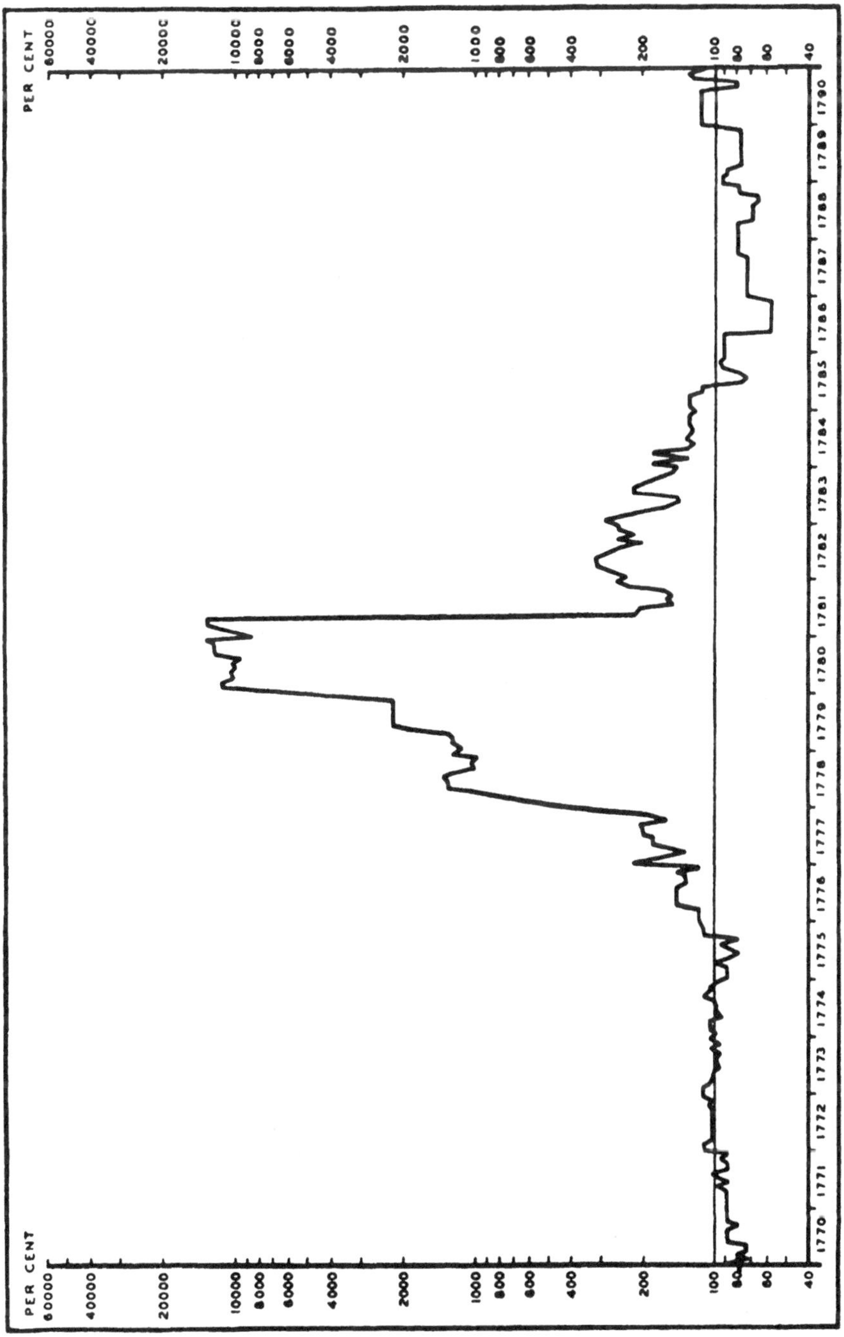

CHART VIII—MONTHLY RELATIVES OF WHOLESALE PRICES OF TAR IN PHILADELPHIA, 1770-1790
(Base—Monthly Average, 1771-1773)

stores, for the remaining years of the war, can be found in the accounts of only a few dealers. The series constructed for index purposes represents sales by Matthew Irwin or the Hollingsworths, one or the other often being the sole source of prices.

Just as experiments had to be undertaken in making tar locally in the course of the war, research in Great Britain revealed a new and, for the future, revolutionary process of supply. As related in Anderson:

> The want of a supply of American tar occasioned, at this time, a discovery of the utmost utility, and which will be a great saving to this country. Some gentlemen of Bristol set up works for extracting the oil from pit-coal, used for making lamp-black; this oil was boiled down to the consistence of tar, which it exactly resembles in colour and quality, and is with difficulty distinguished from real tar. It possesses all the qualities of tar, for half the price, and is found in paying ships bottoms to be an excellent preservative against the worms. The oil is also boiled down to the consistence of pitch, and is found to be an excellent succedaneum for that article. After the oil is extracted from the coal, the residuum is a very good coke.[19]

But it was a discovery that took time to exploit.

Between the close of 1779 and March 1780, prices of tar trebled, then receded slightly only to advance again toward the end of the year. Before continental currency ceased to circulate, tar had reached 1800 shillings a barrel; turpentine and pitch were no longer quoted. The advance, though abrupt, did not raise the index of tar prices, except in a few months in 1780, above the median of the 15 commodities. The peculiarity of its behavior is thus the suddenness of its rise once the war shifted to the southern states and the West Indies. Soon other commodities responded to the same influences. "The news of the enemy landing in your state," Hollingsworth wrote to Carter Braxton in Virginia, "raised the prices of imported goods in a very extraordinary sort and sunk the paper currency in equal proportion."[20]

The course of prices of tar can be traced only in general outline during the period of rapidly changing currency values. Except for responsiveness to intervals of activity in commerce or of ship construction, or to shortage of other lubricants, their rise was not extreme. The index kept above the average of other commodities from October 1775 to June 1776, and again in most of 1778, in January 1779, and for a

[19] Anderson, *op. cit.*, v. 5, p. 346.

[20] November 4, 1780, Levi Hollingsworth to Carter Braxton, Va.

few months in 1780. Except for these relatively short intervals, the longest of which occurred at the beginning of the war, prices of tar followed rather than led other commodities in response to currency depreciation.

In May 1781, when trading for a short period was conducted mainly in specie, tar sold for 30 shillings a barrel, or about 122 per cent above its prewar price. It dropped steadily in the next five months, only to move up briskly about the time of the surrender of Yorktown. At this time, when many factors were operative in heightening the price of some domestic staples and most West India goods, the strong demand for naval stores is especially notable. By December, tar was selling for nearly 36 shillings a barrel and turpentine for as much as 90 shillings. A spurt in shipbuilding would account for some of the demand, but though much of the activity in ship construction arose from orders of Philadelphia shippers, the work was being done elsewhere as "many of our merchants," according to Hollingsworth, were "building vessels to the northward where labor etc. are much cheaper."[21]

Tar, which was quoted at 40 shillings and "in demand"[22] in January 1782, continued to advance until April, when its price exceeded 43 shillings a barrel. Often in these years the strength of the demand for a commodity can be judged more effectively by the terms of trade than by price movements. In the case of naval stores, according to Hollingsworth, the tightening of credit and the price advance corresponded, as he reported in March, "Hemp, tar, pitch, and turpentine will command cash in preference to any other goods."[23] At the peak of the demand in 1782, turpentine reached 120 shillings and pitch 95 shillings. Neither held their high level throughout the year as well as did tar.

Other branches of trade were affected by the war in the Islands, the likelihood of ships' being captured, and the laying up of vessels in safe ports. A general view of the uncertainty of merchants at this time, as given to a merchant in Rhode Island, was, "While our trade was open I could sell almost anything for cash; but the stoppage of the Havanna trade by the English cruisers prevents the best men in the city being punctual."[24]

21 December 10, 1781, the same to Elihu Hall, Mt. Welcome.

22 January 3, 1782, the same to Henry and Thomas Brown, Portsmouth, Va.

23 March 4, 1782, the same to Humphrey Richards.

24 June 5, 1782, Josiah Hewes to Christopher Champlin, Newport, *Commerce of Rhode Island, 1726-1800*, v. 2, p. 160, note.

Prices in Postwar Years

Early in 1783, naval stores reached the beginning of the contraction phase of a long downward movement which was not completed until September 1788, when prices of tar were only two-thirds of the prewar average. At an early stage in the price reversal and before it was certain that final peace would be agreed upon, a merchant house, in an effort to revive former trade connections so as to anticipate the need for a vessel, asked a London correspondent to advise "the price of pig and bar iron, wheat and flour, lumber, tobacco, tar, pitch, and turpentine, these being the chief articles we shall have to load her back with."[25]

From Philadelphia the exports of naval stores were notably high in 1784, but fell in volume in later years, in this respect following the trend of shipbuilding. The number and tonnage of vessels actually built in Philadelphia, in addition to construction to the northward, indicates a burst of activity in 1782 which reached a peak of 44 vessels in 1784, tapered off in 1785, and fell still lower in the two following years.[26]

In the early stages of the downswing, prices of the different items of naval stores diverged widely until the middle of 1786. Tar through May 1785 kept well above the median of other commodities. The closeness of competition in the sale of these goods is shown by the regard for the geographical source of the product. Clifford's prices current to Bristol in April 1784 showed a differential of 3.75 shillings a barrel between tar from North Carolina and that produced in New Jersey.[27] Turpentine was then scarce and pitch relatively high. That there was lack of uniformity in the markets of Great Britain is clear from a letter written by Clifford in midsummer, explaining that, by consulting the Bristol price current, "I find Carolina pitch 10 shillings per hundredweight; the London price current says 8 shillings. I can purchase it at 25 shillings per barrel of 2 hundredweight, 2 quarters," which would be equivalent to 6 shillings per hundred in sterling.[28] In July, Clifford succeeded in loading his vessel, having "put on board about 90 casks of turpentine

[25] April 22, 1783, William and John Sitgreaves to Frederick Pigou, Jr., London.

[26] Edward P. Cheyney, *Commerce, Navigation and Ship-Building on the Delaware River*, p. 74.

[27] April 1, 1784, John Clifford to Thomas Clifford, Jr., Bristol.

[28] July 3, 1784, the same to the same.

which cost 28 shillings per barrel,"[29] a price about 70 per cent above the prewar average.

In the spring of 1785, prices of naval stores sagged markedly. Though the trend was downward, tar kept above the average of our 15 commodities until June. The spring decline seems to have been general along the seaboard. A correspondent, writing from New York to a North Carolina client, urged "that remittances will be more advantageously made to Philadelphia in (I believe) any kind of North Carolina produce than to this place. Trade here is very confined and stagnate. Four or 500 barrels of naval stores will any time reduce the price of them here 25 or more per cent. There will be no difficulty in transferring money from Philadelphia to New York and I think it is pretty certain that markets are generally better at that place than at this."[30]

There was little promise of advantageous sale in the Philadelphia market. At the beginning of 1786 a local merchant, whose business in postwar years was largely conducted in the South, commented, "We are also of opinion that naval stores are too high with you for this market."[31] He was not alone in his estimate of the unprofitable outlook for sales. Four months later Robert Henderson, in an effort to discourage the shipment of naval stores, wrote, "I beg of you neither send tar nor turpentine here; tar sold at public sale for 8 shillings and 9 shillings per barrel. Turpentine 10 shillings and 11 shillings 6 pence, so you see it will not pay a freight."[32]

Prices of tar remained at 8 shillings a barrel until December. Turpentine sold for the low price of 12 shillings a barrel for the next thirteen months. One of the best-informed merchants in the area, at the beginning of these unduly low quotations, summarized the outlook: "Naval stores, pitch, tar, and turpentine, are a great glut here and at any time are dangerous articles to deal in, frequent losses arise in them and none but owners of ships for the benefit of freight should meddle with them."[33]

Clifford, meantime, looked for a market in England through his

[29] July 30, 1784, the same to the same.

[30] April 13, 1785, John Sitgreaves, New York, to John Gray Blount, *Letters*, v. 8, p. 93.

[31] January 28, 1786, Kuhn and Risberg to William Lawrence, Newbern, N. C.

[32] May 11, 1786, Robert Henderson to James Fleming, Wilmington, N. C.

[33] May 23, 1786, Henry Drinker to Delresseline and Williams.

Bristol connection,[34] a choice that must have been dictated by better information about the state of European markets than other shippers possessed. All evidence points to the accuracy of his foresight, since naval stores, as listed in the London prices current, were more than double the domestic quotations.[35] Prices of muscovite tar on the Amsterdam exchange had ended their postwar decline by May 1785, and from then until October 1786 had a marked expansion.[36] Only in May 1785 was there an approach to the highest prewar levels. The extreme stagnation in North American markets must then be attributed to uncertainties of shipping and adverse local factors.

Pessimism about dealing in naval stores was overdone. Whether or not one agrees with Pelatiah Webster that "the effect of the greatest glut is to produce a scarcity in time,"[37] it is certain that when the demand came, orders could not be filled. In October 1786, Clifford informed his Bristol correspondent, "There is no tar come to market. The low price in the spring . . . has stopped their sending it from Carolina."[38] Turpentine, however, forwarded the next spring, netted a discouragingly low price in the local market, though it was then being shipped to London.[39]

Though no reflection appears in the prices, merchants were aware of the lack of incentive to produce tar and the probability of a reversal in its price. Clifford wrote in the spring of 1787, "I think there is a probability of its being high, as but little [has] been made in Carolina owing to the small price it sold for last year."[40] Naval stores were known to be too scarce at Newbern, N. C., to warrant sending a schooner there.[41] For a time, the state of trade in naval stores was as discouraging to producers as to dealers and, when shipments arrived from the Carolinas, there was no likelihood that the consignor would be satisfied with the returns. In answer to a complaint about the sales of tar, Robert

[34] June 3, 1786, John Clifford to Thomas Clifford, Jr., Bristol.

[35] June 27, 1786, Cruger, Lediard and Mullett, London prices for American produce sent to Reed and Forde.

[36] Posthumus, *op. cit.*, Table 214.

[37] May 21, 1787, Pelatiah Webster to Nathaniel Barret, Paris.

[38] October 26, 1786, John Clifford to Thomas Clifford, Jr., Bristol.

[39] April 19, 1787, Reed and Forde to Cruger, Lediard and Mullett, London.

[40] April 23, 1787, John Clifford to Thomas Clifford, Jr., Bristol.

[41] June 5, 1787, Kuhn and Risberg to William French & Co., Fredericksburg.

Henderson, with his usual brusqueness replied, "I got as much as other people were getting at the time. A number stored theirs as the price was low but it is not got better yet nor likely to be. If my advice was to be asked, I would advise you to have as little to do with tar or turpentine as possible, either for this market or Europe. It is low at both places at present."[42]

The counsel was given about three months before the start of an advance in price of all naval stores. Throughout the rest of the period, fluctuations were frequent, prices depending upon the time European vessels chose to crowd or avoid the port. After six months of improved demand at rising prices, North Carolina producers were apprised, "Naval stores have fallen considerably since the European vessels have stopped purchasing. I do not think it will be worth while to send any more stores here for sale before the end of September. Then and till the end of October, I think they will sell to pay a freight."[43] Only in the fact that sales in this period were made "by the quantity" was there a hint of the steep advance found in naval stores in December which lifted prices of tar about 15 per cent above the prewar average.

A period of sustained high prices induced even the most cautious merchants to send cheerful news to North Carolina producers. The unusual openness of the winter had permitted vessels to keep "coming in and going out and there is a considerable demand for every kind of American produce."[44] After quoting the prevailing prices of February 1790, the highest in nearly five years, and much above those previously cited, a Philadelphia informant ventured, "[If] 5 or 600 barrels of naval stores were to arrive here in about a month from this date, I think it would even bring more than I have quoted. . . . From these prices, I think it will be favorable to any person to remit from your state here."[44]

The appraisal included corn, lumber, staves, and other North Carolina products as well as naval stores, and was fully justified by the later course of trade. Reporting again in July, Henderson wrote, "There has been a large quantity of your state produce at our market this spring, but it has kept up very well. Tar is rather dull at present. Turpentine

[42] June 7, 1788, Robert Henderson to John Sheddon, Edenton, N. C.

[43] June 13, 1789, the same to Elisha Norfleet, Edenton, N. C.

[44] February 1, 1790, the same to William Bennet, Edenton, N. C.

will bring 3 dollars very quick; corn still commands 4 shillings 3 pence per bushel, which is still high; pitch and rosin are rather slow sale; tar will do better about the end of September."[45]

The upswing in naval stores was one phase of the improved tone of all business indicators, once the uncertainties of a long transition period had one by one been removed. Merchants then were willing to look ahead in anticipation of the need of future supplies.

[45] June 19, 1790, the same to Elisha Norfleet, Edenton, N. C.

CHAPTER XI

MUSCOVADO AND LOAF SUGAR

THE IMPORTANCE to the Pennsylvania economy of trade to and from the West Indies may be shown indirectly by the number and size of vessels entering its port in the decade before the Revolutionary War. From 1766 through 1774, when the average annual number of entries was 713, over one-third came from the other British colonies on the mainland. Second in importance in terms of number of ships, though first in tonnage except in 1770, 1771, and 1773, was the trade from the British West Indies, the Bahamas, Bermuda, and British Honduras. In the decade before the war, there was no year with less than 160 entries and in three of the years the number of vessels from these areas exceeded 200. During the critical years from 1768 to 1774, the British-owned ports retained a markedly uniform proportion of the total number of vessels entered at the customs house. At the same time fluctuations in the prices of most West India products were extremely mild, although to this trade, and by contrast with it, must be added the steadily growing intercourse with the non-British West Indies. Before the Peace of Paris, the "foreign" islands were a minor source of Philadelphia supply of tropical products. Even in 1766 the 34 vessels registered at the customs house from the non-British islands and Surinam made up less than 5 per cent of the incoming ships. Years of expansion followed until, by 1773, 123 vessels directly from the Spanish, Danish, Dutch, and French islands and South America accounted for 16.4 per cent of the total arrivals at the wharves.[1]

The West Indies not only constituted important markets for Pennsylvania grain and other produce but also were the chief source of supply for sugar, molasses, and rum, their leading staples. Other minor products such as coffee, cocoa, pimento, ginger, indigo, and cotton, which served at first to diversify cargoes, increased in importance, especially during the war years.

[1] Number of ships compiled by Miriam Hussey from a recent discovery of customs records by the Pennsylvania Historical Society.

Muscovado or brown sugar, imported in tierces, hogsheads, barrels, boxes, and bags, was regularly quoted in hundredweights of 112 pounds to retailers and to the local sugar refiners whose processed product was sold by the pound as loaf sugar. Its price, according to an early student of the British sugar trade, depended much upon the prices of molasses and rum, "for as those three commodities are all produced from the sugar-cane, the more money the sugar planters receive for the two latter, the cheaper will they be able to sell the former."[2] Its price in Philadelphia depended upon many other factors, chief of which were quality, of which there was a wide range, lack of local substitutes, importance as a remittance for a cargo sent to the region, and competition among a large number of small mercantile establishments concerned in its sale. Increasing use and the lack of any substitute made sugar an essential import. Valuable as was molasses in the manufacture of rum, spirituous liquors could be and were increasingly produced locally from grain and fruit. Even as a syrup, molasses could be replaced by honey, by maple syrup, and during the war, by the product of admittedly feeble experiments in extracting syrup from green corn stalks. It thus happens that no persistent relations can be traced in the prices of the three leading West India products in the last 25 years of the colonial period.

What was common to the prices of all products of the sugar cane, in the decade of the seventies, was the persistence of gradual enough changes to lead consumers to expect that what they needed could be had on the terms of their former purchases. As West India goods spearheaded the inflationary rise in war years, these customary expectations made their advance a subject of continuous comment. The significance of prewar prices is, thus, the complete contrast with the period which followed.

Even during the nonimportation period of the seventies, merchants felt that the burden was being unequally borne, since trade to the West Indies and southern Europe was not stopped. As a contemporary phrased it, "While the importers of wines, molasses, etc., were pursuing their trade to considerable advantage and paying large sums into the Treasury for revenues raised out of those articles, the importers of British goods were standing still."[3]

[2] Joseph Massie, *A State of the British Sugar Colony Trade*, p. 23.

[3] April 29, 1770, Henry Drinker to Abel James, *Pennsylvania Magazine of History and Biography*, 1890, v. 14, p. 42.

From 1770 to 1773, good muscovado sugar was in steady demand at prices which normally fell between £2 10 shillings and £2 15 shillings a hundredweight. Loaf sugar sold throughout most of 1770 for a shilling a pound, and held slightly below that price until 1774, forcing Philadelphia traders to be selective about the islands from which they purchased their sugars for refining because, as they said, the "sugar boilers cannot get the sort that pleases them."[4]

In 1772, muscovado sugar fluctuated mildly and was sought from Jamaica, though "the ordinary kind" if sent was considered "very unsaleable."[5] Again in the next year, another merchant stressed the fact, "None but the very best, clean, bright muscovado sugars sell here to advantage." There was then a differential of 18 to 20 per cent in the price of bright kinds and the "dark colored and moister sugars."[6] Though market averages show no change in the price of loaf sugar, in 1773 a Philadelphia merchant wrote to New York, "Loaf sugar is in such demand here that our sugar bakers cannot supply the demand."[7] The rise in price came a few months later and both raw and loaf sugar were considered "scarce" in the next months.[8]

The reversal of trend in sugar prices conforms more closely to a marked increase in its rate of importation into England than to happenings in the mainland colonies, whose consumption was at all times only a fraction of the total crop. In 1773, Pennsylvania imports of sugar were less than half their volume of 1771. In the same year, English importation was not only unusually high but was followed by two years of the highest sugar imports of a decade. British cargoes came from many islands; the largest volume originated in Jamaica, Grenada, Barbados, St. Kitts, and Antigua, in the order named. The mainland colonies accounted for only 2.5 per cent of the total sugar exports from Jamaica though they took 33.5 per cent of its rum, 58 per cent of its molasses, 44 per cent of its coffee, and 29 per cent of its pimento.[9]

In 1774, about the time that sugar reached its maximum prewar

[4] February 25, 1771, William Smith to G. G. Beckman.

[5] July 1, 1772, William Pollard to William Plummer, Montego Bay, Jamaica.

[6] September 2, 1773, James and Drinker to Lamolie and B. Lamarque.

[7] October 19, 1773, William Smith to Mercer and Ramsay, New York.

[8] November 22, 1773, the same to Jonathan Worth; December 15, 1773, James and Drinker to Samuel Douglas & Co., Savannah; March 9, 1774, William Pollard to Edward Barrett, Jamaica.

[9] Thomas Southey, *Chronological History of the West Indies*, v. 2, p. 416.

prices, a Philadelphia merchant wrote enthusiastically, "Good clean Barbadoes [sugar] has fetched 60 shillings per hundredweight."[10] Such prices were unlikely to last in a market limited enough to be oversupplied with the arrival of a few ships more than usual, and the year 1774 was no exception. In the month of August alone, the 100 vessels from all areas entered at the customs house might lead one to anticipate such a comment as "Large quantities of sugars having lately arrived has glutted this market, particularly of a very good and dry quality from St. Croix, which at the present keeps the price down."[11] The ample supplies of sugar are reflected in a downward trend of prices until August 1775. Traders could continue to be selective about the quality they purchased. Even in May 1775 a letter to London repeated the preference so commonly felt, "The muscovado sugars most saleable here are the very best, clean and fair grained Barbadoes and Jamaica, of which we have, when their crops prove good, ample supplies in return for our exports to those Islands."[12]

Prices of loaf sugar were insensitive enough in these years to suggest an agreement among the sugar refiners similar to that found in bar iron, especially as the decline in prices of raw sugar is not reflected in those of the local grade of loaf sugar in 1775 or the opening months of the next year. No trace, however, of any joint action has been found.

If an upward trend in prices of muscovado sugar was under way before the events which led to the assembling of the Continental Congress, it was effectively checked by the unexpected increase in the normal supplies of West India produce in Philadelphia "arriving by vessels from New England which are ordered here on account of troubles among them."[13] Prices in April 1775 were only one per cent above the average of 1771 to 1773, and the movement was downward. A year later all the decline of intervening months was wiped out and muscovado sugar was selling nearly 30 per cent above its prewar average. This period begins just as the controversy turned from a political to a military conflict and ends with the abandonment of the early experiments in price control carried on at first on a voluntary basis and later by selective price-fixing by committee action, and therefore raises the question of the

[10] May 24, 1774, James and Drinker to Henry Trotman, Barbados.

[11] August 25, 1774, the same to Edward Welch, West Indies.

[12] May 2, 1775, the same to Pigou and Booth, London.

[13] May 11, 1775, Reynell and Coates to Robert Purviance.

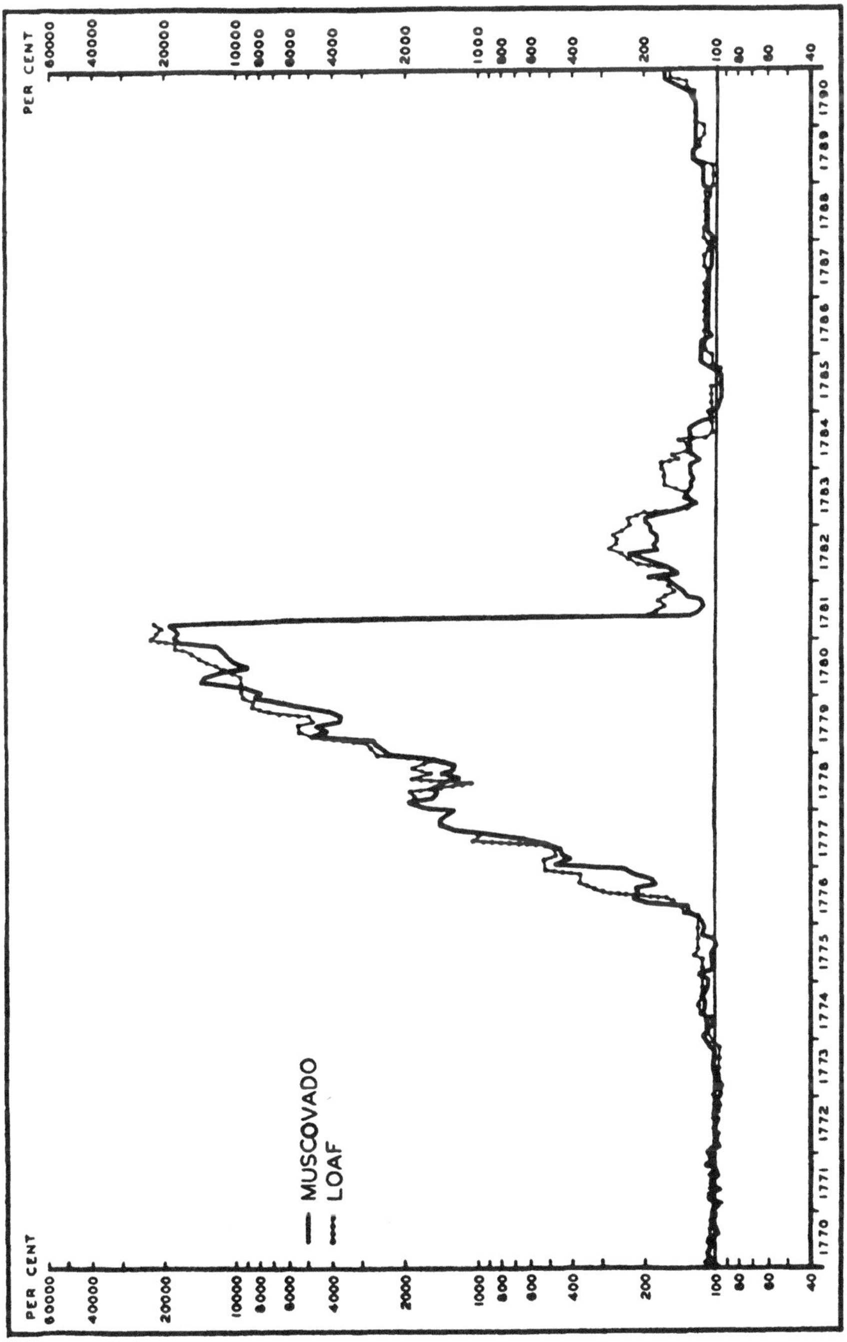

CHART IX—MONTHLY RELATIVES OF WHOLESALE PRICES OF SUGAR IN PHILADELPHIA, 1770-1790
(Base—Monthly Average, 1771-1773)

influence of shortage in initiating the abrupt advance. Adherence to the ideal of the voluntary agreement for maintaining prices at the level of 1774 could create no hardships for dealers while stocks were still large, and until August 1775 previous levels for sugar were adhered to. If the advance in prices of muscovado sugar in the closing months of 1775 were a sign of depletion, it clearly was not so interpreted by officials. Nor is there evidence of shortage in the behavior of prices for the refined product. Loaf sugar held at 13 pence a pound for the last six months of 1775 and even dropped slightly in the opening months of the next year.

Other West India articles, except coffee and chocolate, rose more rapidly than sugar during the early months of 1776 when traders were urged by Congress to "dispose of their goods at such stated reasonable prices, as shall be fixed and ascertained by the commissioners."[14] The local price committee, therefore, concentrated its efforts until April 1776 upon fixing the prices of rum, sugar, molasses, coffee, pepper, salt, cocoa, and chocolate—the commodities first to rise.

First Episode in Sugar Prices

By May 1776, muscovado sugar, which had never been quoted above 68 shillings a hundredweight in colonial years, was approaching 100 shillings. Some merchants were quoting even higher prices. Early in May, Reynell and Coates cited best muscovado sugar at £6 a hundredweight, loaf sugar at 20 pence a pound, and molasses at double the price of five months before. "The Congress," they explained, "having taken off the restriction of prices made by our committee, has produced an amazing alteration . . . in short everything is advanced very high though the scarcity of some West India goods in our opinion is an artificial one."[15] No vessels had lately arrived in the port.[16]

Morris, in the midst of this shortage, wrote to Bingham, "As you are likely to remain some time in the West Indies, it may probably fall in your way to make connections with some good houses that will ship West India produce this way and have in return the produce of these colonies."[17] Sugar was available a trifle lower in the next few months, the decline being connected by Reynell and Coates with ship-

[14] January 27, 1776, *Journals of the Continental Congress*, v. 4, pp. 97-98.

[15] May 3, 1776, Reynell and Coates to Stephen Hooper, Newburyport.

[16] May 4, 1776, the same to William Wyer, Newburyport.

[17] June 3, 1776, Willing and Morris to William Bingham, Martinique.

ping. They reported, "The convoy is also arrived, likewise a prize ship in the river from Grenada to London with upwards of 600 hogsheads sugar and rum, mostly the former"[18] showing how small an importation could lower the level of prices.

The supplies made a temporary halt in prices. Early in September, Coates wrote, "For two days past they have been selling the cargo of a large prize ship. Their best whitish clay sugar sold as high as £5 10 shillings to £6. Other good muscovado sugar sold in general about £4 10 shillings to £5. There is little other prize sugar in port, these articles being chiefly carried among you."[19] A week later, writing to Bingham, Morris commented, "You ask what articles are most in demand here or what are likely to be most so, to which we may safely reply that everything is wanted, it is hardly possible to go amiss."[20] After mentioning the need for woolens, linens, muskets, powder, and medicines, he continued, "West India produce is dear, molasses upwards of 4 shillings per gallon, sugars 60 to 90 shillings per hundredweight, rum 6 to 10 shillings per gallon. In short you may keep shipping us goods as you meet with good conveyances but not too much value at a time, especially in unarmed vessels."[20]

As the first full year of war drew to a close, a wide range developed in the quotations of different merchants for West India goods. Of rum and sugar, one Philadelphia merchant wrote, "It is difficult to ascertain the price though both continue very high and exceed the prices in our last. The latter is the most plenty of these two articles, but people are unwilling to sell. Whether the quantities expected in the winter from your quarter and from the foreign islands may lessen the price much we cannot say, though [we] are inclined to think both rum and sugar will sell high all through the winter as the demand is very great."[21]

The next month, when Morris again found a means of communicating with Bingham, he explained, "You see it is hard to form just opinions concerning adventures in our present situation. When we wrote you in July there seemed little chance of getting anything safe and almost ever since the coast has been quite clear so that the spirit of enterprise has seized most people and they are making or trying to make fortunes.

[18] August 6, 1776, Reynell and Coates to Stephen Hooper, Newburyport.
[19] September 7, 1776, the same to the same.
[20] September 14, 1776, Willing and Morris to William Bingham, Martinique.
[21] September 30, 1776, Reynell and Coates to Stephen Hooper, Newburyport.

Their attempts will probably have the happy effect of procuring us many supplies that we stand much in need of."[22]

At some time in this upswing, the effect of a growing lack of faith in continental notes must be added to factors forcing the rise. As in the previous year, sugar prices soared in the closing months. By November 1776, muscovado sugar was 124 per cent above the average of 1771-1773, more than 15 per cent above the level of six months before, and 99 per cent above the same month of the previous year. Even if a conservative allowance be made for the influence of an unstable currency, the specie price of sugar by November 1776 was at least 71 per cent above prewar levels.

Prices of sugar spurted in December 1776, and opened the next year with a range in merchants' quotations as wide as £6 to £12 per hundredweight. Loaf sugar advanced with the raw material from 3 shillings 6 pence a pound in October to 5 shillings by February. Thus the prospect of halting the mounting prices of West India goods, which had seemed promising the summer before, ended partly because the shorttage was acute and partly because the trade had already attracted the attention of the British navy. "We think it very unsafe to adventure a voyage to this place, there having been many captures of late by a number of frigates and armed vessels that have cruised about the capes for some weeks past."[23] At that time, muscovado sugar was being quoted at £12 per hundredweight, the highest price at which the choicest grade sold in the previous month. Meantime, Morris, with his family and his papers in Baltimore, could not check up promptly on the information he was getting from Bingham in the West Indies. He was especially concerned that the ship *Esperance* should reach the coast laden with molasses. Muscovado sugar was then selling, according to Morris, at £8 to £10 a hundredweight.[24] Only a few days later, when he felt that prices of all West India goods were "enormously dear," Bingham, who earlier chided him on his failure to send remittance in colonial produce, was made aware of the happenings in Philadelphia in the previous months. "You must be sensible," Morris wrote, "that with a river full of ice, our bay full of men of war, and General Howe at our gates

[22] October 20, 1776, Willing, Morris & Co. to William Bingham, Martinique.

[23] February 3, 1777, Reynell and Coates to Stephen Hooper, Newburyport.

[24] February 12, 1777, Robert Morris to William Bingham, Martinique.

would not admit of the usual attention to business or the same facility in doing it; but I now hope to make you a little easier on this subject."[25]

Between February 1777 and the British occupation of the city in September, prices of sugar advanced from £10 to £36 a hundredweight, the sharpest part of the rise being in the two summer months. During the advance, Stephen Girard sought West India goods in Baltimore,[26] and Hollingsworth learned of supplies of brown and loaf sugar in Boston at prices somewhat higher than the market average in Philadelphia.[27] The inquiries, in themselves an indication of scarcities, elicited the comment from a Baltimore correspondent, "No sugars for sale in town."[28]

In February 1778 the first episode in rapidly mounting sugar prices ended with a price of £49 a hundredweight. The movement of dealers out of the city, the scattering and secreting of supplies, and the depreciation of currency had added more than one-third to its price between September 1777 and February of the next year. After this extreme upswing, nine months of recession followed, in which sugar prices immediately eased as much as 200 or more shillings a hundredweight. Apparently the same factors which held prices in check throughout most of 1778 were felt all along the coast, as Simeon Perkins found, "West India goods are said to be cheaper at Halifax than they have been lately."[29] That the decline was felt by merchants is attested by the Bethlehem correspondent of Reed and Forde, who wrote, "The West India goods have fallen near 50 per cent, but the fluctuating prices of these articles are not to be depended on,"[30] and by Chaloner and White, who cheerfully wrote to the Deputy Commissary of Purchases, "It is with great satisfaction that we inform you that all kinds of West India produce is falling."[31]

Refining of sugar, which had to stop before the occupation, was only slowly revived after Philadelphia was repossessed. In July 1778, Chief

[25] February 16, 1777, the same to the same.

[26] June 7, 1777, Benjamin Levy, Baltimore, to Stephen Girard.

[27] July 2, 1777, Samuel Griffin, Boston, to Levi Hollingsworth.

[28] August 9, 1777, Caleb Gough, Baltimore, to J. Hollingsworth.

[29] April 21, 1778, Simeon Perkins Diary, Liverpool, Nova Scotia.

[30] May 5, 1778, Thomas Lawrence, Bethlehem, to John Reed, Boston.

[31] July 30, 1778, Chaloner and White to Colonel Ephraim Blaine, Deputy Commissary of Purchases.

Justice Shippen wrote, "There is no such thing as syrup, the sugar bakers having all dropt the business a long while."[32] Yet prize ships and West India supplies soon reached the port and contributed to the easing of prices during the shipping season. An illustration of the speed of this notable decline may be drawn from Baltimore where, on July 4th, sugar was quoted at £40 and on July 30th at £25 to £32 10 shillings a hundredweight.[33]

This pronounced easing in prices of West India articles corresponds with the beginning of the steepest rise in domestic staples of the war years. It cannot be attributed solely to a temporary appreciation in the value of continental notes, for it lasted until fall. Meantime, General Washington, in countering a suggestion of Gouverneur Morris to pay recruits one-half in solid coin, gave a picture of the soldiers' lack of faith in paper money, writing, "It would have a tendency to depreciate our paper money, which is already of little value . . . The soldiers, seeing the manifest difference in the value between that and paper and that the former would procure at least five or six fold as much as the latter would become dissatisfied."[34]

About the beginning of the next upsurge in sugar and in prices of West India goods generally, Stephen Girard instructed his suppliers in Port-au-Prince to "load the vessel with syrup, salt from Turks Island, sugar and coffee."[35] The prices "in this market" he cited as 33 shillings a gallon for syrup, 108 shillings a bushel for salt, £35 to £40 a hundredweight for sugar, and 8 shillings 5 pence a pound for coffee. With less accuracy he added optimistically, "On these our exchange is 4 for 1, but the paper is gaining favor every day."[35]

Second Episode in Sugar Prices

Though minor declines occurred in monthly prices, the rise at the end of 1778 may be regarded as a turning point from which the second episode in sugar prices began. Its course was speeded by vigorous advertising of West India goods by the merchants who were acting as authorized agents of Congress in the calling in of the emissions of May

[32] July 3, 1778, Chief Justice Shippen to his father at Lancaster; Thomas Balch, *Letters and Papers Relating Chiefly to the Provincial History of Pennsylvania*, p. 266.

[33] July 4 and 30, 1778, Jesse Hollingsworth, Baltimore, to Levi Hollingsworth.

[34] September 5, 1778, General George Washington, White Plains, to Gouverneur Morris; Jared Sparks, editor, *The Writings of George Washington*, v. 6, p. 55.

[35] October 29, 1778, Stephen Girard to Nan & Co., Port-au-Prince.

20, 1777 and April 11, 1778.[36] By February 1779, when Hollingsworth cited prices in specie about 50 per cent above prewar levels, the commissary purchasing supplies for the Pennsylvania line estimated that sugar could not be purchased for less than £75 a hundredweight,[37] a price soon well below the market though only small quantities were being sold.

At the end of March 1779, Chaloner and White reported to Jeremiah Wadsworth, "Price current much as when we wrote you [on March 6] except West India goods which has risen a little, but there is plenty and no demand. The rise is owing to no arrivals. Not three vessels have arrived from sea since you left us."[38] It is a commentary on the way in which high prices after a time are taken for granted that Christopher Marshall could find any cheer in recording in his diary, "News today that sugar [has fallen] in Philadelphia to 15 shillings per pound,"[39] an amount that would have been regarded as absurd even for 28 pounds of sugar only four years before. Civilian committees, then undertaking an experiment in price control for purchases within the city, set the price of muscovado sugar in the schedule of April 1, 1779, at £70 to £95 a hundredweight, to retail at 15 to 16 shillings a pound, a close approximation of the level prevailing in March. Soon the arrival of vessels from the West Indies dropped the price of rum, but in the last week of April muscovado sugar reached £125 a hundredweight and loaf sugar £3 a pound.[40]

There was a slight decline for a few months in 1779 as new "quantities of sugar" arrived in the port,[41] but the end of the year brought a sudden and spectacular advance, once the increased prices, evident first in the accounts of a few merchants, became general. In mid-September, when a Philadelphia importer sent an appraisal of the current price situation to Lancaster, he was able to list sugar at £80 to £120 a hundredweight.[42]

[36] January 2, 1779, and later, *Pennsylvania Packet.*

[37] February 6, 1779, Representation of Lewis Farmer, Commissary for Purchasing Rum, and Jacob S. Howell, Receiver General of Cloathing, to Pennsylvania Assembly, *Pennsylvania Archives,* 1st ser., v. 7, p. 181.

[38] March 31, 1779, Chaloner and White to Colonel Jeremiah Wadsworth, Commissary General of Purchases.

[39] April 21, 1779, Christopher Marshall Diary.

[40] April 27, 1779, Kuhn and Kuhn to Benjamin Joy, Boston.

[41] June 18, 1779, Major Edward Burd to Colonel James Burd, Tinian; Thomas Balch, *op. cit.,* p. 276.

[42] September 13, 1779, Kuhn and Kuhn to Dr. John Lind, Lancaster.

By December the price had risen to a range of £175 to £240 a hundredweight—an unusual spread for a commodity even of as varied grades as raw sugar. Startling as these levels seem, the sugar series in the last months of 1779 kept close to the median and was rising no faster than other commodities.

It would be easy to assume from the progressive depreciation of the next year that the process was one of uniform advance. Instead, a diversity of quotations can be found even in the sales of a single merchant, as is illustrated by a sample from the sugar sales of Hollingsworth during the third episode in sugar in the closing months of 1780 when prices were out of control.

TABLE 6

SALES OF SUGAR TAKEN FROM RECORDS OF LEVI HOLLINGSWORTH
1780

September					October				
		Weight		£			Weight		£
Day	Cwt.	Qr.	Lb.	per cwt.	Day	Cwt.	Qr.	Lb.	per cwt.
2	2	0	25	300	19	2	0	19	317
8	2	1	25	230	21	27	0	25	257
8	9	3	5	285	28	27	3	9	310
11	1	1	18	295					
12	2	1	4	290					
22	1	2	8	300					
23	138	3	12	210					
27	7	2	7	310					

November					December				
		Weight		£			Weight		£
Day	Cwt.	Qr.	Lb.	per cwt.	Day	Cwt.	Qr.	Lb.	per cwt.
7	2	2	17	340	19	2	1	19	450
15	7	0	7	400	23	14	1	2	460
16	4	3	0	430	27	14	2	26	440
28	2	1	21	450					
30	2	1	0	460					

THIRD EPISODE IN SUGAR PRICES

The effort of Congress, in March 1780, to call in the excess paper in circulation was made when sugar was more than three times the price it sold for in the previous September. As in other years, the opening of spring shipping lowered, for a few months, the prices of island produce in general. In May the Board of War was informed, "West India goods within these few days has fallen one-sixth. Sugar that commanded £350 is now dull at £300 and rum that commanded £60 is dull at £45."[43] From the return to rising prices it may be inferred that by August the dullness was over. Girard sought a market for sugar in Baltimore, with the stipulation that hard money be returned in settlement. His agent preferred, in September 1780, to return gold rather than to accept paper at 72 for 1.[44] In explanation of the continued upward drift, Girard was informed, "The delay of the boats from the islands, for which we wait, makes a daily increase in the price of sugar which is in great demand. The best quality has sold at £390 with probable increase. Coffee is also rising."[45] Three days later sugar was being quoted in Philadelphia at £440 in paper currency or £4 10 shillings in specie, and loaf sugar, in continental money, at 168 shillings a pound. Toward the close of the era of "congress money," muscovado sugars fetched above £450 in continental currency and sold at variable quotations even in specie. Hollingsworth, who sold in specie at £6 in March, accepted £3 15 shillings later in the same month. Once the use of specie became general, prices of sugar declined, in response either to the release of stocks or to the desire for specie, to levels lower than could be long maintained.

The series of autonomous cycles characteristic of West India goods during the depreciation period can be illustrated as well in the prices of sugar as in any other. The first spectacular rise from May 1776 to February 1778 amounted to 1400 per cent. In this advance, West India goods led all other commodities and diverged steadily from articles of domestic origin. The upswing was notably broken by the entry of supplies, and prices of sugar even dropped considerably. A second dramatic upswing began at the close of 1778 and lasted eight months, with sugar rising 274 per cent. This time sugar was not following a peculiar course, but was rising along with all other commodities. The third, short episode toward the close of 1780 was a reflection of the spread of war to the Islands, and corresponds in timing with the entry

[43] May 5, 1780, Chaloner and White to the Board of War.

[44] September 1, 1780, Monbos and Latil, Baltimore, to Stephen Girard.

[45] November 14, 1780, the same to the same.

of the Dutch into the war and the danger to shipping lanes to one of the chief sources of West India supplies. Except for response to incidents in the Islands, prices of West India goods in specie equivalents in the later phases of war were declining and offered no such speculative trading advantage as existed in the early years of inflation.

Sugar trading on the Amsterdam market affords an indication of the periods of active rise. Quotations of muscovado, insensitive for the three previous years, began an advance in April 1776 which was not halted until August 1779, when prices were about 67 per cent above their average of 1771 to 1773. A downward trend continued at least through 1780, at which time the prices stood only 44 per cent above their prewar average. Once Holland became involved in war, a marked rising tendency carried prices of sugar in 1781 and 1782 far above any reached on the Amsterdam market during the period of continental money in America.[46]

Prices after Continental Currency Ceased to Circulate

In Pennsylvania there was little rise in sugar prices between December 1780 and April 1781 in continental money, and a downward drift in specie. The further contraction until August could be accounted for by overvaluation of specie, by the arrival of supplies, or by the release of hoarded stocks. It was the timely arrival of vessels "from Hispaniola with sugar and coffee"[47] and several arrivals from Havana that contemporaries noted. Later in the summer, Robert Morris stated, "All our ships have been and continue to be constantly employed in carrying flour to the French and Spanish Islands, our Port is filled in return with West India produce . . ."[48]

The upswing which started in August 1781 was milder in sugar than in either rum or coffee. In the remaining months of the war, prices of sugar kept relatively high, with peaks in May and June 1782 and in the opening months of 1783 which were 100 per cent above prewar levels. Military events in the West Indies and interruptions in shipping contributed to these fluctuations.

Merchant recognition of unusual risks was general. In April 1782, Hollingsworth commented on the uncertainties in the local market,

[46] N. W. Posthumus, *Inquiry into the History of Prices in Holland*, Table 57.

[47] April 21, 1781, Levi Hollingsworth to John Sterrett & Co., Baltimore.

[48] July 2, 1781, Robert Morris to General George Washington, *Collections of the New York Historical Society for the Year 1878*, v. 11, p. 465.

"Our vessels being either taken or absent hath thrown the trade of this port into great stagnation for the present, which hath reduced the price of all exports and raised the value of imports."[49] Another importer was not only uncertain about the course of prices in the Islands to which he traded, but complained, "Embargoes are so common and tedious, that the vessels' expenses run away with all the profits." He continued, "We now have many vessels due from the Havanah since February last."[50] But the fluctuations of these years need not be attributed to local happenings in the light of stirring events in the Islands.

> In the preceding November [1781], the islands of St. Eustatius, St. Martin's, and Saba, were surprised and taken by the French—and, on the third of February 1782, the settlements of Demerary and Issequibo, on the coast of Guiana, were retaken by the same power.
>
> But these successes, though very mortifying to the British nation, were shortly followed by an attempt of much greater importance. The old and valuable island of St. Christopher was doomed to be the next branch that was to be lopped off from the British Empire. . . . The reduction of this island took place on the 13th of February, in the present year [1782]. The islands of Nevis and Montserrat shared the ill-fortune of St. Christophers, so that of all our former numerous possessions in the West Indies, Jamaica, Barbadoes and Antigua now alone remained.[51]

Though sugar was scarce and high at the beginning of 1782, it took the arrival of only a few vessels to lower prices. By the end of June, sugar had "greatly fallen since the arrival of the Havannah fleet of 20 sail"[52] with what was regarded as a large supply of sugar. Actually there were only mild fluctuations in sugar prices until the expectation of peace brought a pronounced drop.

In the last half of 1782, changes in most items were so frequent that as active a merchant as Stephen Collins held, "The markets are now so fluctuating that there is but little dependence even [for] one or two months time."[53] In the beginning of the next year he attributed the "additional damps on trade" to the fresh appearance of talk of peace.[54]

49 April 16, 1782, Levi Hollingsworth to Leeaze and Brumfield, Fredericksburg.

50 April 27, 1782, Chaloner and White to Barnabas, Deane & Co.

51 Anderson, *An Historical and Chronological Deduction of the Origin of Commerce*, v. 6, pp. 555-56.

52 June 26, 1782, Pelatiah Webster to Thad. Perit, New Haven.

53 August 21, 1782, Stephen Collins to ————.

54 January 8, 1783, the same to William Gray, Salem, Mass.

In March, before the continental packet arrived with the preliminary articles of peace, there was "so little business going" that Pelatiah Webster felt "there can scarce be said to be any price that is general."[55]

Postwar Prices

Between February and April 1783, sugar prices dropped. The levels then established persisted until the closing months of the following year. The price decline, especially marked at the close of 1784, continued until August 1785, and established quotations noticeably below prewar and the lowest in postwar years. Under the conditions of regular supplies, Philadelphians were able to revert to their former standards in purchases. In an effort to cater to these, Girard urged, "The sugar should be pale reddish brown, coarse grain, well cleaned and not of a grey color—send no other quality,"[56] thereby implying what is clear in the prices, that the market for loaf sugar again forced sugar refiners to be selective. It seemed futile to hold supplies for a turn in terms of sale, and in July a shipper to the market had to be informed, "I have begun to part with the loaf sugar at 12 pence per pound. I do not think it possible to obtain more for it."[57] Great quantities of French muscovado were on hand at the close of 1784,[58] a year in which importation reached the astounding total of 74,720 hundredweight.[59]

In the ensuing years, the long periods of sustained prices, without any change, offer a complete contrast to prewar and war pricing. Even the period of revival at the close of the decade is marked by months of insensitive prices in a commodity that normally responded speedily to changes in shipping. Loaf sugar prices were even more insensitive than those of its raw material. Merchants' correspondence in these years was concerned mainly with the quantity at market.

In fact, the contrast between the market for sugar in prewar and postwar years cannot be made in terms of prices. A change in habits had greatly increased the consumption. Importation, even in the dullest postwar year for which quantities are available, was more than double, and in 1784 treble, the prewar totals. By contrast, there had been little

[55] March 1, 1783, Pelatiah Webster to Thad. Perit, New Haven.

[56] April 26, 1784, Stephen Girard to John Girard, Cape François.

[57] July 29, 1784, Chaloner and White to Wadsworth and Church.

[58] December 11, 1784, Benjamin Fuller to William Niccolls, Grenada.

[59] Imports into Philadelphia from March 18, 1784 to March 17, 1785, *The American Museum, or, Universal Magazine*, February 1790, v. 7, p. 68.

if any increase in the importation of molasses and a decline in that of rum. Only gradually could such a shift in taste be depended upon, and even when prices were rising, merchants wrote such typical warnings as: "The prices of West India produce is better than they have been for some time past. But what the value of any one article of West India produce may be a month hence, will be quite uncertain. We recommend particular attention to you, in the quality of any goods you send here, as the bad bear no proportion in price to the good."[60] The same caution dominates comment even in 1789 when articles of West India origin were admittedly both scarce and high.[61] Later discussion of the trend of other tropical staples will demonstrate that actions were premised on the previous relation of commodities to each other after their relative importance in consumption had altered.

[60] January 15, 1787, James and John Cox to Thornton, Baillie and Campbell, Grenada.
[61] March and April 1789, correspondence of James and John Cox.

CHAPTER XII

MOLASSES AND RUM

TOWARD THE CLOSE of the colonial period the quantity of molasses consumed annually in Philadelphia and the area dependent on it for supplies, based on the average importation in 1771 and 1773, amounted to 530,000 gallons, a smaller total than was recorded at the customs house in 1768 or 1773. The annual imports of rum from the British and foreign islands varied from 800,000 to 900,000 gallons and after 1783 exceeded the prewar volume only in 1784, an unusual year. Only during colonial wars were the fluctuations in prices of molasses and rum comparable to the considerable variations in annual imports. In fact, prices were held within narrow ranges at relatively low levels by constant vigilance on the part of importers.

An extreme low price of 1 shilling 6 pence per gallon for molasses in February 1765 marked the end of the recession which followed the French and Indian Wars. Prices rose mildly in the next years, reaching 2 shillings in January 1770, a near-maximum quotation for the decade preceding the Revolutionary War. Minor fluctuations on a moderate downward trend until July 1775 carried molasses to little more than its low price of February 1765, ten years earlier.

Unlike molasses, rum, especially the West India product, was subject to frequent and marked variations. It had a two-year rise to a peak in February 1769, then selling for 4 shillings a gallon. In the immediate prewar years, a steady advance from May to December 1771 pushed the price 6 pence above the 1769 high which had been attributed to scant supplies.

Prewar Prices

Imports of molasses and rum were coming to Philadelphia in the spring of 1770 from Barbados[1] and later in the year from St. Christopher.[2] In June of the following year, with prices of rum still advancing,

[1] March 7, 1770, Thomas Clifford to John Martindale, Barbados.
[2] August 20, 1770, the same to William Smith, St. Christopher.

the merchants were disappointed when "three vessels arrived from the Windward Islands with little or no rum on board and as the demand for it is now coming in think it will be up to 3 shillings 2 pence or 3 shillings 3 pence; others think it may rise to 3 shillings 6 pence."[3] It turned out that the merchants had not enough confidence in the market for rum. Their estimates were more than 28 per cent below the prospects of the upswing.

Meantime, the prices of molasses were moving counter to those of rum. Merchants from other parts of the mainland were trying to market their surplus molasses in Philadelphia; according to the comment of one supplier, "We have had great quantities of molasses sent here insomuch the market is quite glutted."[4]

By the end of 1771, both commodities were felt to be overstocked. As prices veered downward, the information sent to the West Indies about the most expensive grade of rum was unduly discouraging, and in August 1772 one merchant at least, regretting his earlier report, informed his correspondent in Jamaica, "I am sorry I mentioned in my last that rum was got down to 3 shillings 8 pence as it has since advanced to 4 shillings 2 pence and is likely to keep up."[5] He was referring to a higher grade of rum than that from Barbados and many of the other islands. In fact, the market for West India supplies was not strong and at the close of the year "rum arrived to a falling market . . . this day we are told the best kind has been bought at 3 shillings 4 pence."[6] Even in the middle of the next year rum consigned to Philadelphia came to a declining market, as may be assumed from an explanation to a New England shipper: "We sold the West India rum at 3 shillings 3 pence which is 2 pence per gallon above the market at this time."[7] Some months later, a New York firm learned that "rum and spirits are very plenty selling at vendue, the former 2 shillings 9 pence to 2 shillings 11 pence, the latter 3 shillings 9 pence and 3 shillings 10 pence."[8]

Rum fell still lower, and in the spring of 1774 Reynell wrote to a

[3] June 8, 1771, William Blyden for Daniel Roberdeau to Purcell and Bruley.
[4] June 17, 1771, Reynell and Coates to John Wood, Newburyport.
[5] August 18, 1772, William Pollard to George W. Lawrence, Montego Bay, Jamaica.
[6] December 11, 1772, James and Drinker to Lamolie and B. Lamarque.
[7] July 9, 1773, Reynell and Coates to John Wood, Newburyport.
[8] August 24, 1773, William Smith to Mercer and Ramsay, New York.

consignor in New England, "Your rum is now dull and believe will not bring more than 2 shillings 2 pence per gallon."[9] At the same time, the stocks of molasses, long in oversupply, must have diminished. Even before any change was reflected in prices, Reynell saw "some prospect of its rising, vessels being arrived from Hispaniola, and brought very far short of expectations."[9] Other merchants commented on the scarcity of good molasses in this year of especially active shipping when 313 ships came from the West Indies, Honduras, Bermuda, and South America—a total of 30 more than in the preceding peak year.

In the closing months of 1774, rum was in "brisker sale"[10] than it had been earlier, but molasses had one of those sudden changes which shows how little the market could absorb and how slight was the margin between shortage and surplus. "Molasses yesterday we believe," Reynell wrote, "would bring 22 pence, if good, today more uncertain, a large brig being this morning arrived with a quantity from Hispaniola."[11]

By the spring of 1775, when prices of both rum and molasses were declining, it was explained that rum "does not bear a price in proportion to molasses which is 23 pence to 2 shillings if very good and our distill houses are supplied which . . . may prevent rum from rising,"[12] a prediction that was not borne out by the movement of prices. The decline in prices of rum ended in the very next month and was followed by a steady though mild advance in the remaining months of 1775. Molasses continued to decline through July, after which it rose less briskly than its product, rum. It was then so plentiful in Philadelphia that whole cargoes were being put in storage.[13] Even in the fall of 1775 a dealer in molasses was "really apprehensive it will not bring more than 22 pence per gallon this fall, if it does that, as a large quantity is still among us and the demand for rum is less. Any person who knew of the vast quantity that kept continually arriving during the course of this summer (so far exceeding our utmost expectation) would not wonder if it was current at 19 pence at this time."[14] The same merchant

[9] April 4, 1774, Reynell and Coates to Little and Greenleafe, Newburyport.

[10] October 10, 1774, James and Drinker to Samuel Welch, West Indies.

[11] November 12, 1774, Reynell and Coates to John Wood, Newburyport.

[12] April 14, 1775, the same to William Teel, Newburyport.

[13] July 4, 1775, the same to Stephen Hooper, Newburyport. The cargoes of molasses brought in by both Captain Whitcomb and Captain Wyer were stored because Reynell and Coates could raise "little or no money" on them.

[14] October 5, 1775, the same to the same.

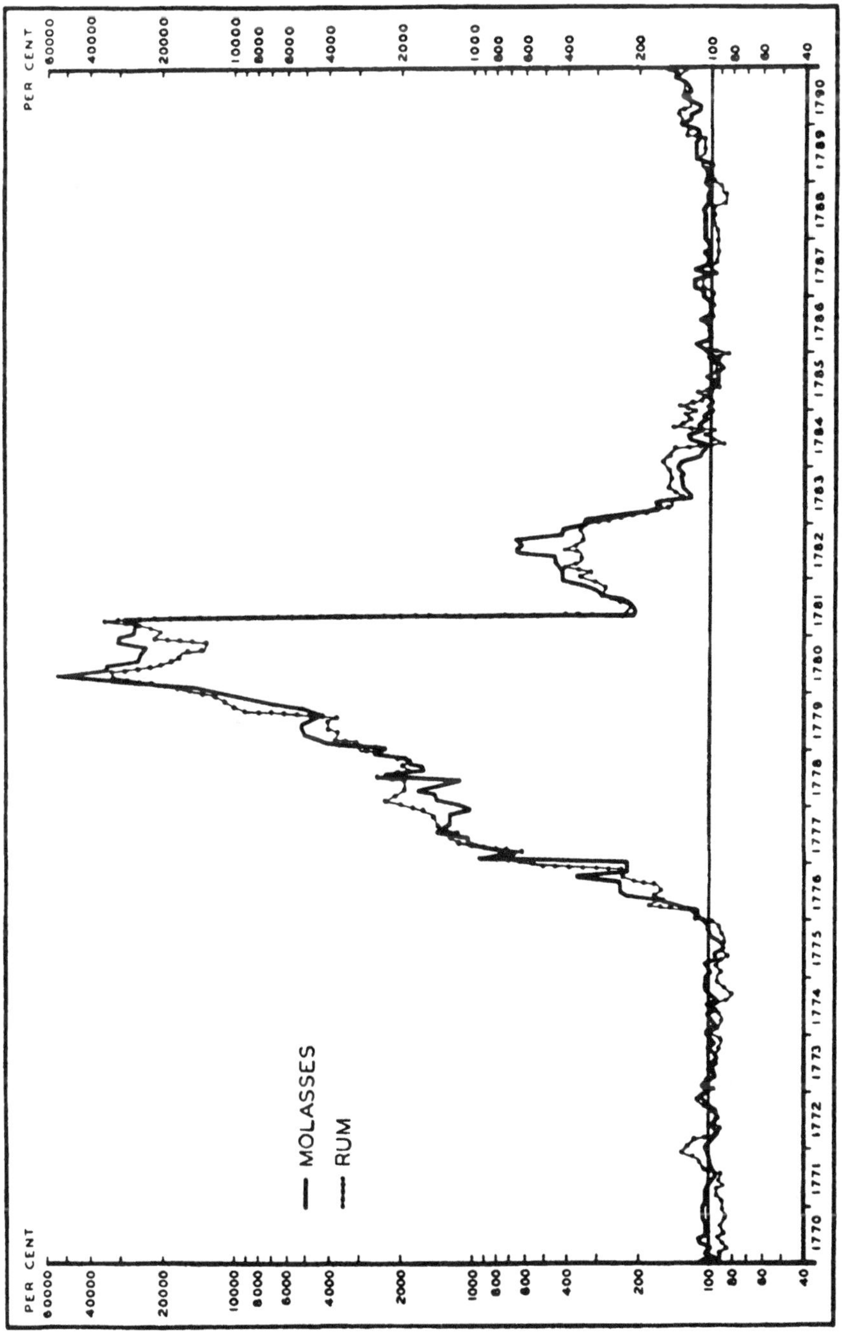

CHART X—MONTHLY RELATIVES OF WHOLESALE PRICES OF MOLASSES AND RUM IN PHILADELPHIA, 1770-1790

(Base—Monthly Average, 1771-1773)

found sales so dull that he resolved to keep molasses "in store unless it will bring 2 shillings per gallon."[15]

Rise in 1776 and 1777

In the light of the actual needs of the next year, the merchants, with unusual stores on hand, had overdiscouraged the shipment of molasses to Philadelphia. The first evidence of a turn came in February 1776 when molasses, in a rising market,[16] began to be sold only for cash and Surinam grades brought 22½ pence or more.[17] The Committee of Safety took this time to peg the price of molasses at a trifle below the prevailing market, a step which led a Philadelphia merchant to apprise a consignor in New England, "Thy molasses sold at the right time as the committee have fixed at 2 shillings,"[18] a price that could be maintained for only a short time. Before the close of the year, the limit set by the committee was doubled. In the course of this rise, characterized by an unusual range in the prices of different merchants, molasses, which was conservatively reported at "upwards of 4 shillings per gallon,"[19] sold only a few weeks later at 5 shillings 6 pence per gallon.[20]

All commodities contributed to the upsurge in prices in the last quarter of 1776. By November the three chief West India imports had deviated so far from the average of other goods that prices of sugar were 33 per cent, molasses 36 per cent, and rum 41 per cent above the median of 15 staples summarized in the index. Such deviations are typical of the fanning out of the price series in early stages of currency depreciation, but the dominant role of West India items in the advance is marked by an increase between November 1775 and November 1776 of 99 per cent in prices of sugar, 123 per cent in molasses, and 160 per cent in rum. No small part of the heightening price levels of imports in these months must be attributed to increased costs and hazards of shipping. In stressing to the Commissioners in Paris the pervasive character of the rise in prices under way at the close of 1776, Robert Morris placed special emphasis upon the impact of costs of shipping: "The value of ships has risen in the same enormous proportion with every-

15 November 11, 1775, the same to the same.

16 February 12, 1776, the same to William Wyer, Newburyport.

17 February 14, 1776, the same to Stephen Hooper, Newburyport.

18 March 10, 1776, the same to the same.

19 September 14, 1776, Willing and Morris to William Bingham, Martinique.

20 September 30, 1776, Reynell and Coates to Stephen Hooper, Newburyport.

thing else, and ships that were deemed worth £1000 twelve months ago, now sell for £3000 or upwards. Every article belonging to them is also excessively dear and hard to be got, and the insolence and difficulty of seamen is beyond bearing."[21]

By the close of 1776, West India rum, like molasses, had doubled the prices of the opening months by a series of mild advances, followed by a leap upward. By the beginning of 1777 the whole character of the market had altered. West India rum, which sold for 8 shillings in November, was quoted at 17 shillings on the second of January and at more than double this price four months later.

Molasses was only a month later than rum in more than doubling its price. In February, when armed frigates made the coasts unsafe for shipping, a firm specializing in the sale of West India produce regretted the non-arrival of a vessel, for "molasses we think would have brought 17 shillings per gallon; continental rum has been sold at 22 shillings 6 pence. The price of West India uncertain though amazingly high." Nor was it only rum and molasses, but "every article of West India goods and dry goods that were in use in common," according to Reynell and Coates, "will bring a great profit."[22] Robert Morris, like other merchants, hailed the clearly marked inflationary rise as an opening for profits. Writing to Bingham he hoped his West India ship would be sent back "laden with molasses. If . . . [she is] and she gets in, the voyage will make a ministerial fortune. That article has been sold for 18 shillings to 20 shillings per gallon; rum 25 shillings to 30 shillings."[23] After citing the prices current of other island products, he added, "You may be sure these prices also make me very desirous that the brig Cornelia and Molly should bring back the molasses ordered by the owners as well as the other things. I long to see her and the ship Betsey return as my design is for them to visit you again."[23]

The price situation in the early months of 1777 was critical. Up to the close of 1776, the rising trend in molasses, rum, and sugar could be accounted for by: (1) the previous overestimate of supplies, which slowed the movement of these items to the port; (2) the resort to new areas of supply; (3) the increased costs of insurance, of ships, and of seamen's wages; (4) the risks and delays of shipping; and (5) a decline

21 December 21, 1776, Robert Morris to Commissioners at Paris; Francis Wharton, editor, *The Revolutionary Diplomatic Correspondence of the United States*, v. 2, p. 237.

22 February 3, 1777, Reynell and Coates to Stephen Hooper, Newburyport.

23 February 12, 1777, Robert Morris to William Bingham, Martinique.

of at least 25 per cent in the purchasing power of government notes. The new type of price response in rum and a few months later in molasses and sugar, though regarded by some importers as an opportunity for profits—especially as domestic staples were still relatively low—marked the beginning of grave uncertainties.

Congress was discussing, without much hope of agreement, the plan for regulating prices adopted in the four New England states. It was claimed that the price regulation of the previous year in Pennsylvania had brought abuses. Benjamin Rush, voicing this sentiment, wrote, "The Committee of Philadelphia limited the price of West India goods about a year ago. But what was the consequence? The merchants it is true sold their rum, sugar and molasses at the price limited by the committee, but they charged a heavy profit upon the barrel, or the paper which contained the rum or the sugar."[24]

The merchants hoped to meet the immediate need by a vigorous effort to bring in supplies. At this time, Robert Morris wrote to Bingham, "If you charter any French vessels to come here, molasses, rum, coffee, sugar, and all West India produce are enormously dear. . . . If you do not send us the molasses by the Cornelia and Molly you ruin us. One hundred hogsheads of that article at this time is worth £10,000."[25] The events of the war were giving a new impetus to privateering, and Morris, who had earlier felt scruples about sending his vessels out as privateers, was now ready to increase his engagements.[26]

That it was not a time when private traders could safely send ships to sea may be inferred from the number idle at the wharfs and the frequent advertising of vessels for sale. In May, the causes of the lull in importation were explained to a Newport merchant who was anxious to sell a vessel in Philadelphia. "Our river," Hewes advised him, "has been [so] long blocked up by men of war that many fine vessels lay idle here, our merchants seem discouraged and knowing that vessels have been sold very cheap in New England won't talk with me at any thing near the price you mention."[27]

The committees of the middle states took no action on the general

[24] February 14, 1777, Benjamin Rush Diary, *Letters of Members of the Continental Congress*, v. 2, p. 250.

[25] February 16, 1777, Robert Morris to William Bingham, Martinique.

[26] April 25, 1777, the same to the same.

[27] May 26, 1777, Josiah Hewes to Christopher Champlin, *Commerce of Rhode Island, 1726-1800*, v. 2, p. 45.

regulation of prices[28] and therefore molasses and rum, which had eased slightly in the spring of 1777, advanced again in the months before the capture of the city. It is not surprising that the combination of impediments to shipping and the movement of provisions out of the city which had been under way since April should be reflected in an accelerated rise in scarce articles. Rum, in August 1777, was fully 10 shillings higher per gallon in Philadelphia than in Baltimore.[29] Prices of other goods were reflecting, according to Henry Laurens, "the total stoppage of imports and the consequent scarceness and dearness of such articles as our real wants cannot, and too many which our luxury will not, forego."[30]

During the nine months of British occupation, molasses was even scarcer than rum, and a price series for either rests upon a few quotations. If any series is to be continuous, prices must be divided into those within the city and those outside. Whichever series is used, prewar quotations for molasses will be found to have more than doubled before the close of 1777, since the hard money price reached 4 shillings 6 pence by December. Early in that month "the commanding general [within the city] issued regulations enumerating certain commodities. No rum or spirits of low quality were to be sold to individuals in quantity more than one hogshead or less than ten gallons, and none without a permit. Not more than one hogshead of molasses could be sold at a time without a license."[31] Actually the only prices found are for smaller quantities.

According to a hitherto unavailable record kept during six months of the British occupation, in conformity to the regulations of the occupying authority molasses sold for 5 shillings a gallon in the prewar currency of Pennsylvania, or about 180 per cent above the prewar price level.[32] A few months after the British evacuated the city, it was selling at about six times the average of the occupation months.

The difficulty in following the trend of rum prices outside the city may be illustrated by the adjustments made in paying for rum taken

28 April 23, 1777, Roger Sherman to Jonathan Trumbull, Governor of Connecticut, *Letters*, v. 2, p. 340.

29 August 9, 1777, Caleb Gough, Baltimore, to J. Hollingsworth.

30 September 10, 1777, Henry Laurens to John Rutledge, President of South Carolina, *Letters*, v. 2, p. 491.

31 Willard O. Mishoff, "Business in Philadelphia during the British Occupation, 1777-1778," *Pennsylvania Magazine of History and Biography*, 1937, v. 61, p. 169.

32 Account book of John and Henry Drinker.

for the use of the army. In October 1777, Blaine instructed that these should be: for good spirits, 60 shillings per gallon; for West India, 52 shillings 6 pence; for French or common rum, 40 shillings "and no more." "The extravagant price of this article," he continued, "is villainous, and the people must not be suffered to have such prices."[33] But it was the price of spirituous liquors distilled from grain and fruit that the Council of Safety, sitting in Lancaster, was interested in controlling.[34]

Irregular Price Movements in 1778

Prices of West India rum exceeded 60 shillings a gallon in continental currency in June 1778, and within the city, when it was reoccupied, there was for a time no settled price. Chaloner and White informed Ephraim Blaine that "the city afforded no supplies of rum." They complained that speculators were "buying cargoes out of our hands at the immoderate prices of 80 and 90 shillings per gallon" and that "the limited prices have . . . secreted a great quantity of goods."[35] Later in the month they sent the deputy commissary the cheerful news, "Since you left us our purchases have been solely confined to the article of rum and of that only a few hogsheads. . . . we hope soon to see the article of rum under 50 shillings."[36] The price of domestic grades of rum in the last quarter of 1778 justified Chaloner and White's short-term policy of refusing to buy at 55 shillings.[37] In October, however, the West India product sold for 62 shillings, while in December a merchant who failed to anticipate the demand had to report, "I have sold the rum, but rather too soon. . . . the best at 70 shillings per gallon, the other at 65 shillings per gallon."[38]

A new era in price behavior was becoming evident. From 1776 to 1778, West India goods were the spearhead of the advance and deviated far from the trend of other commodities. With the rise in grains and other staples under way before the close of 1778, West India goods no longer so far outdistanced other commodities in the general upward

[33] October 23, 1777, Colonel Ephraim Blaine, Deputy Commissary of Purchases, to James White.

[34] November 5 and 7, 1777, *Minutes of the Council of Safety of Pennsylvania*, *Colonial Records*, v. 11, pp. 336, 338.

[35] July 1778, Chaloner and White to Colonel Ephraim Blaine.

[36] July 30, 1778, the same to the same.

[37] November 1, 1778, the same to the same.

[38] December 1, 1778, Samuel Alexander to Colonel John Davis, Deputy Quartermaster General, Carlisle.

movement as they had earlier. The change in impetus cannot be explained wholly by happenings on the mainland. Although the connection between the enhanced price of the West India staples and the demand for them in their areas of origin is obscure, it is notable that the volume of British imports from 1776 to 1778 was uncommonly high. The quantity of molasses imported into England in 1776 was more than treble that of previous years and mounted still higher in 1777 and 1778, reaching in the latter year tenfold the average prewar volume. British imports of molasses shrank to, or below, prewar in 1779 and were negligible from 1780 to 1782.[39] The effect of this shift in demand upon supplies available for the mainland importers cannot be appraised, especially as their stocks should have originated in the foreign islands, but it is certain that the behavior of prices of West India goods, once British demand slackened, diverged less from the trend of other articles in later than in early war years.

Price Behavior in 1779 and 1780

By February 1779, both molasses and rum had advanced to new levels. In this sudden rise, prices of molasses increased more than 150 per cent in less than six months, the bulk of the upswing being in a single month. Rum took a similar rise, though more gradually. At these new high levels, the market stabilized until the closing months of the year, when preparations for the arrival of the French fleet on the coast brought extra pressure upon all supplies. More important was the naval warfare in the West Indies and its disruptive effect upon shipping. The scarcity of molasses in the fall of 1779 is reflected in the lack of any price quotations until December, when it sold for as much as 200 shillings a gallon, or more than 100 times its prewar average. Rum rose even more rapidly than its raw material and, as in other periods of spiraling prices, a wide range developed in the quotations of different merchants.[40]

The characteristic behavior of prices in these years when the underlying movement was upward was a sudden leap in prices in February

39 Anderson, *An Historical and Chronological Deduction of the Origin of Commerce*, v. 6, p. 604.

40 For instance, in November the prices from Hollingsworth's accounts range from 310 shillings to 450 shillings. The averages of two other accounts were 450 shillings, with a third at 350. By the next month the lowest quotation of Hollingsworth was 430 shillings. Other merchants, meantime, had overtopped his maximum.

or March before the normal opening of shipping with the Islands, followed by a moderation or hold in prices until the fall months. The year 1780, like the two previous years, had three months of sudden extreme advance. Prices of rum, which averaged 446 shillings a gallon at the close of 1779, reached 1100 by April 1780. Molasses, in the same period, had a fivefold increase. Both suffered abrupt declines followed by six months of steady recession which, by November, had brought the prices of rum back to those at the close of the previous year, as unusual a case of decline in West India goods as the period affords.

The response of prices was the result of the arrival of many vessels long overdue. Within a few days the new supplies and the release of old ones lowered the quotations of West India imports by about a sixth.[41] By far the largest imports of rum came from St. Eustatius, supplemented by cargoes from Grenada and Martinique. Supplies of molasses arrived from Hispaniola and Martinique as well as from other ports on the mainland, the variation in source often accounting for a lack of conformity in the price behavior of by-products of sugar culture.

Contemporaries, who considered the markets of midsummer 1780 "dull" for all imports, even dry goods, attributed the later extreme rise to further depreciation, to complex quota arrangements in procuring produce, and to shortage of cash while continental bills were being called in. The usual preference for specie may well have been strengthened by the presence of French vessels in port, to which Hollingsworth, at least, laid the drop in value of paper money.[42]

It was in February 1780 that Congress had "called on the several states for specific supplies of provisions and forage." Prices were rising when the action was taken. It was followed by three months of rapid upsurge. Charles Thomson vividly described the situation to John Jay when he wrote, "Everything wanted for the army was, by the month of January, raised to double the nominal price of what it was in the month of October when you left us." Before the specific supplies could be brought in, "such advantage was taken of the public wants, which were wholly supplied by purchase on credit, that the nominal debt of the continent was increased almost beyond calculation. Of this you will easily judge, when you are informed that in the month of March com-

[41] May 5, 1780, Chaloner and White to the Board of War.
[42] July 20, 1780, Levi Hollingsworth to Marsden and Smith, Va.

modities were sold in the market at Philadelphia at four times the price they were in the month of September."[43]

The action of Congress in March in calling in the old currency for a new emission had some deflationary effect, but the marked decline in prices of imported articles, and especially in rum, indicates the artificiality of the previous rise. Toward the end of the decline, when rum was selling for 450 shillings a gallon, Congress was handicapped by lack of funds for its purchase. Blaine wrote at this time, "The want of rum in the army is very great, they have not had one day's allowance this four weeks . . . There are large quantities in the city for sale and in my opinion can be purchased upon exceeding good terms provided means can be adopted to make payment."[44] In other words, the army, the largest customer, was out of the market in the period of price recession. The slowness of sale led Hollingsworth to write, "Rum keeps low and dull with us,"[45] an opinion which is borne out by a steady lowering of prices from May to November 1780.

Though the trend changed suddenly in December, it was April 1781 before rum was as high as it had been in the spring of the previous year. At its peak in April, it was quoted at 1200 shillings in continental currency and about 11 shillings 2 pence in specie. Molasses, for which prices are sparse, sold at the same time for 525 shillings, or well below the maximum prices of the previous spring.

In these inflationary years the major West India products had a diversity of dissimilar movements. The upward trend in sugar prices, under way before the war started, kept its levels relatively above those of molasses and rum until the spring of 1776, or about the end of the first period of price regulation. While continental currency was in use, sugar never again deviated as far from the median as did one or the other of its products—molasses and rum.

From the relation of the three staple products to each other and to the median, the periods of shortage of molasses might be inferred to be: July 1776 to April 1777; October 1778 to July 1779; and February 1780 to February 1781. In these periods, molasses not only departed far

[43] October 12, 1780, Charles Thomson to John Jay, *Letters*, v. 5, pp. 418-19.

[44] October 1, 1780, Colonel Ephraim Blaine, Commissary General of Purchases, to Samuel Adams.

[45] October 31, 1780, Levi Hollingsworth to George Anderson, Richmond.

from the trend of other commodities but usually deviated more than either sugar or rum. The shortage of rum was likely to be most marked in the winter months. It was chronic in the period when Philadelphia was occupied and for three months after its repossession. Another drastic scarcity occurred in the last five months of 1779 when prices of rum soared far above the levels of other West India staples.

The period when exchange of domestic for West India products would seem to have been most favorable to shippers lasted from 1776 to 1778, and was characterized by a wide dispersion in the price level. Once the French capture of one West India island after another began, there doubtless were opportunities for trading in the main specialties of each island, since the first effect of a change in ownership would be to create a demand for mainland staples to replace those formerly supplied by the British. At the same time its loss of the British market would diminish the price of its staples. Shipowners could benefit temporarily from these windfalls which, if passed on to consumers, would be reflected in the lack of a common pattern of price behavior among the products of sugar culture.

Price Behavior after Continental Money Was Abandoned

The first effect of the return to specie was a decline in prices of West India goods which lasted about three months. By August 1781, when the direction of prices had changed, Hollingsworth explained, "Rum and coffee is on the rise, also sugar though not so much as the two former articles."[46] A correspondent of Stephen Girard found prices in Baltimore so like those in Philadelphia that it was difficult to know what to order. Scarcities were then apparent both in sugar and spirits.[47] In Philadelphia, all West India goods were then rising, with molasses especially scarce.[48] Even in March 1782 supplies of molasses had not arrived, and there was "none at market."[49]

The expansion phase of this marked cycle in West India goods lasted through July 1782 in rum and through September in molasses. In May, when cargoes were coming in slowly, it was reported that "West India rum is rising, though the arrival of two or three cargoes knocked it

[46] August 23, 1781, the same to Thomas and Samuel Hollingsworth.

[47] September 8, 1781, G. P. Keeparts, Baltimore, to Stephen Girard.

[48] December 5, 1781, John Wilson to Joseph Pemberton, West River, Md.

[49] March 4, 1782, Levi Hollingsworth to Humphrey Richards.

down lately; 'tis now about 12 shillings."[50] Little could be done to augment supplies while British cruisers kept "very thick and troublesome on our coast."[51]

The recession began in August 1782 in rum and in October in molasses. Summer markets were regarded as uncertain and the arrival of ships doubtful. Molasses was scarce, but the price could be so readily affected by new supplies that the arrival of 50 hogshead might "reduce it one half."[52] Once started, the decline lasted until May 1784, when prices of molasses closely approached those of the prewar period.

The decline from the unusually high prices of the summer of 1782 was attributed to the expectation of peace. By the beginning of 1783, when molasses had dropped from 12 to 6 shillings, and rum from 14 to 9 shillings 6 pence, West India goods were reported to be dull and rum falling: "People here seem to calculate for a peace this winter."[53] The rumors persisted without much documentation. Less than two weeks before the packet arrived from L'Orient with preliminary articles of peace, Webster wrote, "There is nothing certain about a peace, but the rumors of it destroy all business here and reduce the value of goods almost to a peace price."[54] April found "West Indian and European goods at present very unsettled in price."[55]

Postwar Prices

From the beginning of 1785 to 1789, prices of molasses were never long above 2 shillings a gallon. Postwar prices of both it and its product, rum, were fluctuating around prewar levels until 1789. Toward the end of the period, both commodities began a steady rise, the early stages of an expansion which persisted until the middle nineties.

After 1785, the short-run movement of the by-products of sugar cane have little significance. The market for molasses, and more especially rum, was normally fully supplied. Information about prices, imports, and inventories was general and shippers followed their customary practice of controlling supply as a means of steadying prices. The change in underlying trend, which contrasts with the prewar period and affected

50 May 11, 1782, Pelatiah Webster to John Perit, Norwich, Conn.

51 June 19, 1782, the same to the same.

52 August 12, 1782, Stephen Collins to ———.

53 January 8, 1783, the same to Davis and Pitts, Boston.

54 March 1, 1783, Pelatiah Webster to Thad. Perit, New Haven.

55 April 25, 1783, Chaloner and White to [Jeremiah Wadsworth].

the relation of these allied products to each other, even in retrospect is not fully clear and was, at the time, little recognized.

Even before the war, the rate of consumption of sugar seems to have been increasing faster than that of molasses. The later trend in the use of molasses is obscured both by irregularity in annual imports and by lack of evidence of the extent to which syrup, from expanding local sugar refineries, could be substituted for imported molasses. Immediately after the war the quantity of sugar annually imported far exceeded the prewar figures. Even if the heavy inflow of 1784 is disregarded, the entry of more than 2000 tons of sugar in 1787 and 1790 offers a striking contrast not only to the prewar situation but to the absolute decline in the quantity of rum and molasses.

The change in social usage is at first more evident in merchant practices than in their comments. Stephen Girard's failure to explain his heavy emphasis upon trade in sugar and intermittent dealings in rum may be attributed to his ideas of business discretion. To his brother he explained, "I like to keep silence on my affairs for two reasons; if I boast of a good venture, I may make a jealous rival; in the opposite case, I would lose my credit, for they would believe that I was ruined."[56] But, apart from recorded opinion, the import figures cannot be directly related to use in the area because the balance of trade was seldom in favor of the Islands, and West India products, like some Carolina staples, could often be bought for other parts of the mainland and by European traders cheaper in Philadelphia than in the areas of growth.[57]

Rum, in the immediate postwar years, was the least wanted of all island or mainland articles. Its sale was slow and throughout 1786 its suppliers were frequently warned that there was little prospect of a better market. On the other hand, good sugar was usually wanted. Late in the shipping season, a Philadelphia merchant, repeating the information he had frequently given throughout the two previous years, wrote: "Sugar and coffee are the only West India articles that are saleable here."[58] Toward the close of 1786 the same merchants, in summarizing the state of the market for rum, explained, "We do not remember that the market was ever so much glutted with rum, as it has been this last

[56] July 13, 1784, Stephen Girard to John Girard, Cape François.

[57] April 9, 1785, Kuhn and Risberg to Lars Kahra & Co., Gothenberg, Sweden.

[58] October 1, 1786, James and John Cox to Charles Hagart, St. Thomas.

year. We have still a considerable quantity here and the price low. We do not think there will be any demand for rum till spring."[59]

The placing of a tax of 2 pence a gallon on rum did little to cheer Philadelphia traders, especially as it applied to the product of other states. "This measure," Coates informed Moses Brown of Rhode Island, "was unexpectedly adopted, and carried through before we had any previous intimation in time to acquaint our friends. The impolitic step of your legislature in subjecting our loaf sugar to a duty of 2 pence per pound is adduced as an argument to show the propriety of taxing your rum for the encouragement of our own manufacture. To such pernicious restrictions, we are forced to submit, but we hope it will not be long before the people of America will see the impropriety of taxing the industry of each other."[60]

Cargoes of rum arrived soon from Jamaica, Antigua, St. Croix, Tortola, and St. Vincent. These additional supplies, coupled with "a prospect of a very considerable crop in the West Indies this season and a very large quantity of rum expected at the market," led the consignee to dispose promptly of a cargo from Grenada "for the highest price that could be procured for it which has been 3 shillings 2 pence per gallon, payable in sixty and ninety days."[61]

Sugar was slower than rum in responding to the news of a bumper crop. In August a prominent merchant commented to a St. Eustatius supplier that "sugars of the first quality still keep their price, but not so brisk in sale as some time past." At the same time he warned, "Rum is at no fixed price, in short it will not bring money at any rate—a cargo of excellent Antigua has been sold at 3 shillings on a long credit."[62] Another West India importer was unsure enough of the results of his trading to be anxious to settle his accounts in order, as he said, "to ascertain whether we lost or gained anything since we put the brig in the trade of your island of St. Eustatia."[63]

Newburyport rum, long a favored item in Philadelphia trade, now subject to duty, a local importer felt could not compete at the prevailing prices of molasses "which being brought as low as 19 pence by our dis-

59 December 8, 1786, the same to Robert Otway, Grenada.

60 March 24, 1787, Josiah and Samuel Coates to Moses Brown, Providence.

61 April 25, 1787, James and John Cox to Thornton, Baillie and Campbell, Grenada.

62 August 18, 1787, Benjamin Fuller to Henry Ash, St. Eustatius.

63 August 24, 1787, James and John Cox to Charles Hagart & Co., St. Thomas.

tillers enables them to undersell you."[64] But it was thought the two regions might help each other indirectly by efforts to remove the duties. The Philadelphian, accordingly, suggested that influence be used "to have the 1 penny on sugar, which is payable in Massachusetts, taken off, which may contribute much to induce our Assembly to repeal the duty on rum."[64]

Had there been no substitutes for rum, the importation of only 797,000 gallons in 1787 might have improved its prices in the local market. Instead, by autumn the report to the West Indies was, "The consumption of rum will be much lessened this year from the great plenty of grain and fruit which will produce considerable quantity of whisky and cider."[65] At the same time, the Convention of the States had finished drafting a constitution and another fear about future impediments to the trade in rum had to be relayed to the West India suppliers. "It is generally imagined," the Philadelphia wholesalers wrote, "that imported spirituous liquors will be a great object of revenue and it is more than probable that there will be at least 18 pence [a] gallon laid on all imported rum and spirits, and it is conjectured that, for the encouragement of distilleries in the country, molasses will be admitted duty free."[65]

The same merchant who foresaw dull sales for rum was writing to his brother in the very next month, "Sugars are higher than when you went away. I therefore think that the first that arrives in the spring will come to a good market, particularly if they are of the first quality."[66] It was an accurate prediction which could be followed in the spring by the summary, "Good sugars are still in demand though several cargoes have arrived from St. Martins, St. Croix and other places."[67]

Before 1788 few direct statements can be cited which attribute the changed position of sugar by comparison with rum, and at times molasses, in the economy of the area to a change in consumption habits. The general increase in use of sugar, accompanied by a preference for white sugar, kept its prices relatively dependable in as difficult years as were faced in the postwar period. Slowly the growing demand for sugar and coffee turned the attention of the best-informed merchants to steady

[64] September 1, 1787, Josiah and Samuel Coates to Stephen Hooper, Newburyport.

[65] September 26, 1787, James and John Cox to Thornton, Baillie and Campbell, Grenada.

[66] November 17, 1787, James Cox to John Cox, traveling in the West Indies.

[67] March 26, 1788, James and John Cox to Henry Haffey, St. Eustatius.

dependence on these items. Toward the close of 1788 the change in social habits, implicit in the imports and the practice of the period, was noted not alone as a Middle Atlantic phenomenon, but as a trend throughout the country. "From present appearances," Cox averred, "we can give you but little encouragement for the rum of your island at this market. The people of this state as well as every other part of the United States are getting very much out of the use of ardent spirits of every kind. The Quakers who compose about one-quarter of all the inhabitants of this state, have lately made it a part of their religious duty to prohibit the use of it amongst them. Their example will have very, very great effect on every other class of people. This seems to be the age for discouraging slavery and the use of spirituous liquors. We think that unless you can ship your rum and that of a good quality at or under 2 shillings 3 pence per gallon, it will not answer to ship to this market . . . Rum has been so very low all this season that we have not had an opportunity of putting off the small quantity our J. C. [John Cox] received from you unless we had done it at a considerable loss."[68]

Thus, in the period of postwar adjustment, substitutes for rum distilled from molasses and a change in social habits were recognized as forces in affecting the trend of the traditional West India staples.

[68] October 13, 1788, the same to Thornton, Baillie and Campbell, Grenada.

CHAPTER XIII

BEVERAGES

THE ONLY monthly price record heretofore available for beverages in colonial Pennsylvania is a series for bohea tea which was not complete enough to include in the index of 20 commodities for 1720 to 1775 published in *Prices in Colonial Pennsylvania.*[1] Monthly prices for coffee and chocolate, included with tea in this analysis, are thus a supplement to the data already available for the last six years of the colonial era.

Tea was the beverage of the colonial period. Before the seventies, however, coffee was gaining a place as an economical substitute. Chocolate, imported mainly in the form of cocoa beans, was processed locally, part of the product for exportation.

The importance of these items in terms of each other in the war years can be judged only by the allowances set up as standards for army rations. These varied at some stages of the war and often for military personnel of the different states. Though there is no reason to believe that the articles were generally available, the weekly ration to which each Pennsylvania soldier was nominally entitled was set, in March 1779, at one-quarter pound of coffee, one-half pound of chocolate, and one ounce of tea, related to the allowance of one-quarter pound of muscovado sugar.[2]

In international markets during the period of the American Revolution there were no particularly startling changes in the behavior of prices of beverages. From the spring of 1771 to the beginning of 1778, prices of Surinam coffee on the Amsterdam market drifted downward.[3] The uptrend of the next three years raised quotations only slightly before the last quarter of 1780. The sudden elevation of prices in January 1781 erased the effect of the long decline and restored the relatively high levels of the opening month of 1770. San Domingo coffee followed the

[1] Anne Bezanson, Robert D. Gray, Miriam Hussey, *Prices in Colonial Pennsylvania.*

[2] March 1, 1779, *Minutes of the Supreme Executive Council of Pennsylvania, Colonial Records*, v. 11, p. 710.

[3] N. W. Posthumus, *Inquiry into the History of Prices in Holland*, Table 78.

same general trend as Surinam at slightly lower levels. It was in 1781 and 1782 that new high levels were established. Surinam cocoa declined from 1771 to 1778 and rose in 1781 and 1782, but never reached as high levels as it had in 1771. By contrast, Caracas cocoa had a stronger advance in the early eighties than the Surinam variety. Tea at Amsterdam made most of its advance after the war was over, though its trend was upward from 1777 on.

In the light of mild changes in a major European market, one studies the fluctuations of the three beverages, tea, coffee, and chocolate, in a North American mainland area for the effect of internal factors on their movements, considering first the specific changes in each.

Bohea Tea

In the colonial period, prices of tea in Philadelphia were generally higher in the first half of the eighteenth century than they were between 1752 and 1775. At times, even at the low quotations of the late colonial era, and especially when shipping was interrupted, tea, which was sold by numerous mercantile outlets, fluctuated considerably. An illustration is furnished by the events of the early seventies. When the Philadelphia merchants, in March 1769, belatedly joined with those of other colonies in an agreement not to import goods from England, tea was selling for 3 shillings 9 pence per pound. By May 1770 it had advanced to 7 shillings 6 pence a pound and held its high price until September, when shipping was resumed. In August, when New York houses were placing orders, William Strahan of London predicted to his correspondent in Philadelphia that other colonies would soon follow the New York example. "I wish from my heart," he wrote, "yours had yielded first," and added, "I never thought it worth your while to stand out upon the *tea duty* and I always imagined what has now come to pass, that you could not, in the nature of things, hold out long without a free importation; and that, even if you could, for any length of time, all the colonies would never continue long of one mind."[4]

In early September 1770, as prices began to recede, a Philadelphia merchant gave an indication of the source of such tea as was for sale and the dispersion that could develop between coastal ports. Tea by the chest, according to Benjamin Fuller, had been as high as 8 shillings a

[4] August 24, 1770, William Strahan, London, to David Hall, *Pennsylvania Magazine of History and Biography*, 1887, v. 11, pp. 351-52.

pound, but in September he wrote, "It's now 6 shillings and expected to be under, being 4 shillings at New York. The channel of the West Indies has been much used."[5] The agreement to refrain from importation was still in force and both the movement of prices and contemporary opinion indicate that it had been well enforced. In fact, Thomas Clifford wrote to Cowper in Bristol, "If I was not a Pennsylvanian I should almost venture to say no province entered more cautiously into the nonimportation agreement nor any one of them so strictly adhered to it as this hath done."[6]

By the beginning of 1771, tea was selling for 5 shillings 6 pence and as low as 4 shillings from March to August 1772. It was scarce in Philadelphia at the close of the year, and "upon inquiry," Drinker wrote, "we could not find any bohea tea that could be cleared out at our custom house and in any other we will not deal."[7]

As prices began to rise in 1773, a long-standing colonial grievance in the procedure for marketing tea was re-emphasized. It was connected not with the duty but with the inability of merchants from colonies whose staples had no market in England to keep deposits in London for the purpose of buying tea at the "India sales." "They have, therefore, hitherto been constrained, either to purchase their teas from foreigners, or to buy them on exorbitant terms, from the merchants in London."[8]

Toward the middle of this year, stocks were scarce enough to make tea merchants reluctant to sell. Pollard's explanation of the sudden rise in prices of tea was, "The dealers in that article don't incline to sell any large quantity."[9] He later attributed the advance to "the great talk of war [which] altered the prices of several things in our markets and made them fluctuate. Tea got up from 4 shillings 3 pence to 5 shillings per pound in a day or two. Some people do sell this article now for 4 shillings 6 pence per pound by the chest."[10]

The search of London merchants for outlets for tea to be shipped directly to the port of Philadelphia brought the controversial aspects

[5] September 5, 1770, Benjamin Fuller to John Scott, Jr., Armagh, Ireland.

[6] September 6, 1770, Thomas Clifford to Lancelot Cowper, Bristol.

[7] December 8, 1772, James and Drinker to John Clitherall.

[8] Samuel Wharton, "Observations on the Consumption of Teas in North America, 1773," *Pennsylvania Magazine*, 1901, v. 25, pp. 139-40.

[9] June 17, 1773, William Pollard to Samuel Ellit, Boston.

[10] July 16, 1773, the same to Baltus Van Fleek, New York.

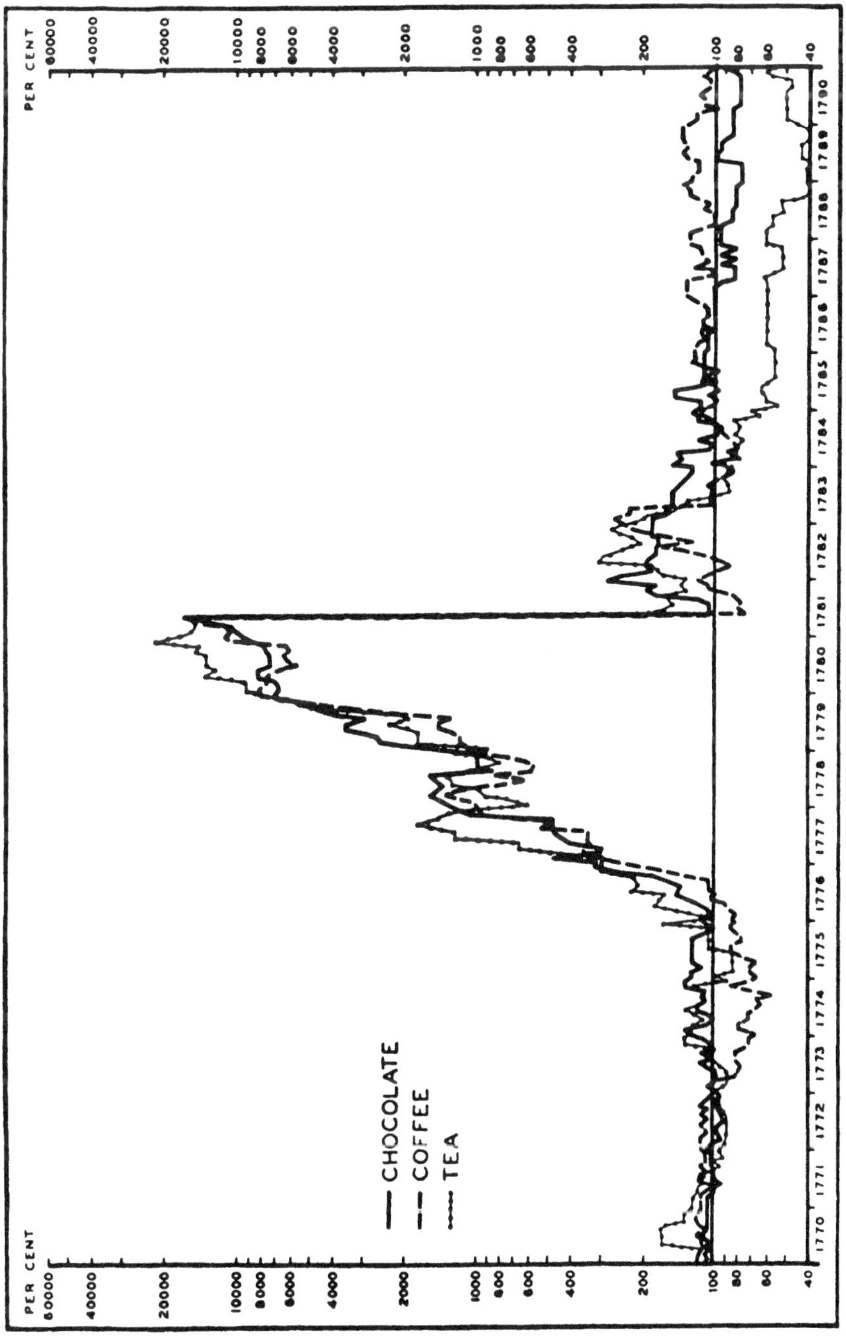

CHART XI—MONTHLY RELATIVES OF WHOLESALE PRICES OF CHOCOLATE, COFFEE, AND TEA IN PHILADELPHIA, 1770-1790

(Base—Monthly Average, 1771-1773)

of a new method of distribution to the fore. In answer to one such inquiry, Drinker wrote to London, "We observe thy expectation that the tea affair will soon take place and that we may probably be appointed one of the agents for the company."[11] Two months later a merchant who was "hourly expecting the tea here" feared its arrival would "make some disturbances as many inhabitants of the city seem disposed to oppose its being landed. I wish the East India Company had kept it at home and I am of the opinion that they will wish so before they receive remittance."[12] Not only would the shipment be opposed but the agents who were to receive it had no agreed-upon alternatives for its handling. Before the tea ship arrived, Drinker wrote to the London agents,

> It would have been a great satisfaction to us to have had an early account from you of the instructions coming out with the tea and of every circumstance respecting the duty to prepare us for its arrival, as this city has been and still continues to be greatly agitated on that account, so that there is very few persons, who if they say anything on the subject, do not speak one general language and that is to oppose its reception, while any duty is to be paid on either side the water for the purposes mentioned in the Revenue Act.[13]

Before the end of 1773, when there was still "no account of the tea ships,"[14] it sold at 6 shillings a pound, a higher price than any after the middle of 1766 except for two months in 1767 and seven months in 1770 when the embargo was in force. Now, too, tea was scarce. In December, a Philadelphia merchant reported to New York, "We have been so bare of tea that all that is come or may be coming will not last above two weeks."[15] Despite the discussion and frequent monthly variation, tea averaged 6.3 shillings a pound in 1770 and 4.5 shillings in the three years 1771 to 1773 used as the base for the computation of index numbers.

In 1774, bohea tea was quoted in the Philadelphia newspapers in only four months. These quotations and the averages from merchants' accounts indicate that prices were weak and generally declining until tea sold during the five months of the next year for less than 4 shillings a pound. Its direct entry being already banned, Thomas Wharton, antici-

[11] September 11, 1773, James and Drinker to Pigou and Booth, London.

[12] November 18, 1773, William Pollard to Benjamin and John Bower, Manchester.

[13] November 20, 1773, James and Drinker to Pigou and Booth, London.

[14] December 18, 1773, Reynell and Coates to Nathaniel Gorham, Charlestown, Mass.

[15] December 18, 1773, William Smith to Mercer and Ramsay, New York.

pating a new danger, wrote, "A disposition is strongly prevalent in most of the colonies that a non-importation from Great Britain shall take place."[16] Thus, before September 22, 1774, when the First Continental Congress, meeting in Philadelphia, decided upon "an absolute and full non-importation agreement from England, Scotland and Ireland to take place the first of December,"[17] merchants had anticipated such an outcome. The resolution of the Association not only covered cargoes direct from Great Britain but read, "Nor will we . . . import any East India tea from any part of the world; nor any molasses, syrups, paneles, coffee, or pimento, from the British Plantations or from Dominica; nor wines from Madeira, or the Western Islands; nor foreign indigo."[18]

As the recommendations became known, importers had to take immediate steps to cancel any orders not already filled.[19] They anticipated scarcity in some items as well as an alteration in the rate of exchange.[20] The effect on prices was hardly a matter of speculation, since the problem was in the hands of the "new chosen committee of sixty persons to act in behalf of this city and suburbs and for the express purpose of carrying into execution the Association entered into and lately published by the Congress . . . one part of which is that importers shall not raise their goods higher than they have been selling them at for the last 12 months."[21]

On the general policy of suspending trade, contemporaries raised the same questions that students of the period still ponder. As Drinker phrased them, they were, "Will not this be much to our injury? is the first question; and the next is, will it produce any desirable good?"[22] Whether goods which arrived after December first could be "stored or sold and the profit (if any) in the latter case given to the town of Boston was the immediate problem."[23] The decision was a matter for the Committee of Sixty, as Drinker discovered when his "unfortunate ship" arrived a few days late. Remembering his early experiences as agent for

[16] August 20, 1774, Thomas Wharton to Thomas Walpole, *Pennsylvania Magazine*, 1909, v. 33, p. 441.

[17] September 23, 1774, the same to his brother in England, *ibid.*, p. 451.

[18] October 20, 1774, "The Association," *Journals of the Continental Congress*, v. 1, pp. 76-77.

[19] October 1, 1774, James and Drinker to Pigou and Booth, London.

[20] October 25, 1774, the same to the same.

[21] November 15, 1774, the same to the same.

[22] November 26, 1774, the same to Jones, Campbell & Co.

[23] December 4, 1774, the same to Robinson and Sandwith, Dublin.

East India tea, but now dealing in gunpowder, Drinker wrote to his backers in London, "*We* think it won't do to expose our invoices to every busybody in office and shall be upon our guard, both in giving a sanction to transactions we have no fellowship or unity with or in submitting the secrets of our trade to others."[24]

Extent of Inflationary Rise

Technically, from September 1775 to April 1776, tea was not on sale in Philadelphia. In the middle of December, Congress was informed that "many persons in Pennsylvania, Maryland and Jersey sell tea and drink tea upon a report that Congress had granted leave so to do."[25] It was not until April 1776 that "Congress gave leave to sell and use what tea was in the country, forbidding any further importation of it."[26] The belated permission to unfreeze funds tied up in idle inventories was accompanied by a resolution that "bohea tea ought not to be sold by retail in the smallest quantities, at a higher price, in any colony, than at the rate of three-fourth parts of a dollar per pound [5 shillings 7½ pence]; and other teas at such a price as shall be regulated by the committees of the town or county where the tea is sold; and that all persons who shall either give or take a greater price for it, ought to be considered as enemies to the American cause, and treated accordingly."[26]

At the time of this resolution, bohea tea was sold at 8 shillings and was as low as a dollar a pound (7 shillings 6 pence) in only one later month of which we have a record. Specie prices of tea in February 1777 reached 9 shillings a pound, a rise of 98 per cent in terms of hard money over the average of 1771-1773. Prices in continental paper were nearly 200 per cent above former levels. Tea advanced in the next two years and was as high as 60 shillings in July 1778 when Benedict Arnold, then in command in the city, was paying £7 10 shillings a pound for green tea.[27] From July 1778 through January 1779, prices of tea declined, only to increase nearly one hundred per cent in the following month. For the rest of the inflation period, tea rose with other commodities. Part of the rise may be attributed to scarcity, since the specie

[24] December 6, 1774, the same to Pigou and Booth, London.

[25] December 13, 1775, Richard Smith Diary, *Letters of Members of the Continental Congress,* v. 1, p. 275.

[26] April 13, 1776, *Journals,* v. 4, p. 278.

[27] July 20, 1778, "Entries in Journal of Benedict Arnold," *Pennsylvania Magazine,* 1900, v. 24, p. 368.

price of bohea tea in the spring and fall of 1779 was 164 per cent above the base period. In June 1780, when it sold for 600 shillings in continental currency, it cost 15 shillings in specie, or 230 per cent more than the average prewar price.

In January 1781 bohea tea was 700 shillings a pound in continental currency, but it suffered a slight decline in February and March. Specie prices began at 7 shillings 6 pence a pound in April when the continental money price was 750 shillings. Thus, contrary to the movement of most commodities, prices of tea did not rise continuously in the last four months of the inflation period.

Prices after Continental Money Was Abandoned

After the currency devaluation, tea gradually declined until it brought little more than 6 shillings a pound, but when prices turned upward early in 1782, contemporaries, noting the lack of ship arrivals, predicted a rise in West India imports, among them coffee and tea.[28] The shortage did not last long. Tea sold at relatively high levels until March 1783. Once a decline started, tea dropped steadily until the fall of 1787, when it was quoted at little more than half the prewar price. Philadelphia was so oversupplied at this time that tea was being reshipped. Trade to the port, according to one merchant, was "overdone from Hispaniola." After the role St. Eustatius had played in expediting shipments to the North American mainland, it is odd to find a Philadelphian asking, "What would choice souchong tea sell for per pound this weight free of all charges? If this article would answer, I could send a few half chests of about 80 pounds each. We are at a loss what returns to order. Every article at your market will sink at this very considerably."[29]

Prices of tea rose only slightly in the next year. The opening of a direct trade to China soon after 1784 focused attention upon the price of oriental goods, but fluctuations in the price of tea were in general mild and a wide choice in grades seems to have been reaching the market. Hyson tea might be "scarce and high" as it was in 1788,[30] but after the close of 1784 bohea tea, which was in most general use, kept below 3 shillings a pound in the whole postwar period. Late in September 1788, when prices were declining, a merchant in the trade to the Orient

[28] May 21, 1782, Chaloner and White to John Jefferies, Hartford.

[29] August 18, 1787, Benjamin Fuller to Henry Ash, St. Eustatius.

[30] July 3, 1788, Levi Hollingsworth to Joseph Byers, Herring Bay.

wrote, "The frigate Alliance is arrived from China, her bohea teas sell at public sale from 22 pence to 2 shillings per pound, hyson from 13 shillings to 15 shillings and souchong from 8 to 9 shillings as in quality. . . . Every kind of business is exceeding dull here."[31] A month later the impact of this dullness was noted by Reed and Forde, who were assembling supplies for the Wilkinson "adventure to Kentucky." Bohea tea could then be bought at public sales in Philadelphia "for 1 shilling 10 pence per pound, very good quality and all that has ever gone to Kentucky has cost 2 shillings 6 pence."[32]

Thus, tea lagged behind many other commodities in the beginning of the upswing that reached a crest in the middle nineties and was heralded only by a slight rise in the very last year of our period.

Coffee

Like those of tea, prices of coffee, which averaged nearly 16 pence a pound in 1770, had a downward trend in the next four years, though most of the contraction came after 1772. At the close of that year, in reporting their sales of a shipment of coffee, James and Drinker wrote, "The coffee was a very good quality and sold at 13½ to 14 pence."[33] These prices were lower than other merchants charged in the winter months. With the arrival of spring shipping, coffee prices receded and by September 1773 Drinker's prices were closely aligned to those of others when he reported, "Choice coffee is worth 10 to 11 pence per pound here."[34] The decline of the next year was still more drastic.

Not only was the supply of these years steady but coffee was frequently exported to other colonies. In 1773, a year of active shipping when 750 vessels entered the port, more than 1600 hundredweight appears in the exports of Philadelphia. Of the arrivals, 154 came from the British islands, 69 from the French, 31 from the Dutch, and 21 from other parts of the West Indies. Of the 816 vessels entered at the customs in 1774, 37.4 per cent had cleared from ports in the West Indies. The regularity of supplies and the increasing use of coffee are also evident in merchants' sales. Few commodities were more continuously quoted. For instance, in the records of a single merchant

[31] September 23, 1788, Benjamin Fuller to Henry Ash, St. Eustatius.

[32] October 10, 1788, Reed and Forde to John Lewis, Fredericksburg.

[33] December 11, 1772, James and Drinker to Lamolie and B. Lamarque.

[34] September 10, 1773, the same to Cadwalader Morris, Kingston, Jamaica.

from 1774 to the close of 1776, only one month was found without sales of coffee.

The effect of both a broader market for coffee in supplying the army and currency depreciation are reflected in the first two years of price advance. Prices rose gradually in the first nine months of 1776 and from July to September were sustained at a uniform average about 5 per cent above the base period. The upswing of the last three months of 1776 raised coffee to 30 pence a pound, double the price it had sold for in September. It is not easy to date the beginning of the inflationary rise, since the upward movement from February 1776 was in part a correction of unusually low prices. Undoubtedly October 1776 may be regarded as the beginning of heretofore unheard-of levels.

Early in February 1777, when shipping was felt to be unsafe and many captures reported "about the Capes," Reynell and Coates found coffee at "upwards of 4 shillings" and the market for most West India goods "amazingly high."[35] A week later Robert Morris, probably anticipating the trend, cited coffee at 4 to 5 shillings a pound.[36] As the advance continued, a spread in the quotations of different merchants developed until by May 1777 coffee was finally stabilized for a few months at 48 pence a pound, or 236 per cent above prewar levels. By then the specie price had reached 16 pence, a trifle above the annual average of 1770 and 12 per cent above the base period—a moderate advance in the light of the risks of shipping.

In the rest of 1777 there was a confusing disparity in the practices of merchants dealing in coffee. Some continued the price of 48 pence, even to September; others, in different months, charged as high as 84 and 90 pence, with two selling at 77 and 77.4 pence.

In 1778 during the British occupation, coffee sold within the city for 30 to 35 pence, Pennsylvania currency.[37] Outside the city, by June 1778, prices were as high as 90 pence, with a wide range in the sales recorded. For instance, after the city was reoccupied and the prevailing price was 120 pence, some merchants were selling coffee at 108 while others were getting as much as 130 pence. Average prices in Baltimore were cited

[35] February 3, 1777, Reynell and Coates to Stephen Hooper, Newburyport.

[36] February 12, 1777, Robert Morris to William Bingham, Martinique.

[37] The accounts of the junior Drinkers, John and Henry, for February, April, May, and June, were given in Pennsylvania currency. They compare with the sterling prices of April and May, when converted at the Pennsylvania ratio of 7 shillings 6 pence to the dollar, instead of 4 shillings 6 pence.

by different informants as 81 pence in June[38] and 111 pence in July.[39] This chaotic period ended in temporarily lowered prices and, during this decline, James White, in his concern about army supplies, mistakenly refused to purchase coffee with the comment, "Coffee though low we do not think will answer at five shillings."[40]

Controls Limit Supplies

The lull gave way to an abrupt leap in December and by April 1779 coffee was quoted in the newspaper at 180 pence. The suddenness of the advance was a matter for comment to John Clifford: "I should [have] gone up to see you, this day in the stage boat, but [I] have some C[ontinental] currency by me which it will [be] necessary to lay out before I go up as everything is rising here: say, tea within this few days from 90 shillings per pound to 140 shillings and coffee from 16 shillings 6 pence to 30 shillings per pound."[41] In May, when the citizens' protest against mounting prices was organized, the published price was 204 pence. The committee attempting to control prices in Philadelphia ruled that the May price should remain until the first of July, when the April level should again become effective. Merchants' ledgers show until August that these regulations were given some weight in their dealings.

During the period of control, the merchants were accused of tied-in sales and of arbitrary practices in the disposal of commodities. A Philadelphian describing his experiences wrote in August,

> I cannot purchase any coffee without taking to one bill a tierce of claret and sour and at £6.8 per gallon. Sugar I may purchase at about the limited price, and that is the only article that can be bought. I have been trying day [after] day, and never could get a grain of coffee, so as to sell it at the limited price these six weeks. It may be bought, but at about 25 shillings per pound. Then it is very dangerous to get it out of town; for the least trifle you must produce your bill and swear that you have given no more, and made no presents; neither that you intend to make any presents after you have a certificate or permit. Some time ago I might have sent wagons out of town and never have been stopped, but that time is over. Should you want sugars, I

[38] June 9, 1778, Thomas McKean, Yorktown, to Sally, his wife.

[39] July 4, 1778, Jesse Hollingsworth, Baltimore, to Levi Hollingsworth.

[40] August 11, 1778, Chaloner and White to William Buchanan, Baltimore.

[41] May 23, 1779, Thomas N. Smith to John Clifford, Rockey Point.

will buy for you; but I think you better wait till this d———d committee is broke. It cannot last long, for we must all very soon shut up stores and starve.[42]

By September, according to Mrs. Galloway, there was hardly any coffee, spirits, salt, or sugar to be bought in town "as the committee has lowered the price and the merchants will not sell at their price nor will they send for more goods."[43] The end of any semblance of order in the rise of prices was over. Although the Philadelphia and New Jersey papers bravely tried to convince their readers that coffee could or should be bought at 270 pence a pound, among the records consulted only one merchant was found selling coffee as low as 300, while others quoted prices within a range of as much as 420 to 630 pence; and even the latter figure was soon overtopped in an alarming rise that was not halted until January 1780, when coffee sold for 1170 pence. Prices continued to mount in the fall months, despite the arrival of more than 30,000 pounds of coffee from Port-au-Prince, St. Thomas, and St. Eustatius.[44]

Imports Break the Upswing in 1780

In 1780 the advance in coffee prices was interrupted. They dropped steadily from February to June with the arrival of vessels from the Caribbean, and then until November kept lower than they had been in November of the previous year, a severe recession for such a general inflationary period. In the light of previous advances, it is not surprising that the enhanced price of beverages should have attracted the attention of shippers. Thus in March 1780 more than 49,000 pounds of coffee was included in the cargoes arriving in Philadelphia from Port-au-Prince, St. Croix, Hispaniola, and St. Eustatius.[45] Other West India Islands appear among the areas from which the 193,300 pounds of coffee arriving between March and December were derived. These imports were supplemented throughout the year by considerable shipments of cocoa from St. Eustatius and tea from Amsterdam and L'Orient, as well as indirectly from French and Dutch islands. According to Girard's informant, the mechanism for trade with St. Eustatius had long been

[42] August 24, 1779, J. Peters, Jr., to Francis Oberlin, Bethlehem, *Pennsylvania Magazine*, 1915, v. 39, p. 231.

[43] September 6, 1779, "Diary of Grace Growden Galloway," *ibid.*, 1934, v. 58, p. 181.

[44] November 18, 1779, *Pennsylvania Packet.*

[45] March 18, 1780, *ibid.*

so well developed that "all the commercial houses" there already had "their business correspondents in Philadelphia."[46]

Toward the close of 1780, prices of coffee advanced sharply and were not again halted until continental currency ceased to circulate. The rapid rise in the autumn affected Baltimore, too, for on the first of September Girard's agents there wrote, "We could . . . sell your coffee at 8½ dollars at 70 for 1 but we did not consent because of its fine quality; we can certainly do much better"[47] and they soon felt they had not "done badly to delay the sale of your coffee for we have succeeded in obtaining 10 dollars."[48]

At no time in the months that followed was there much dispersion in the asking prices of dealers in coffee. Hollingsworth, the most habitual dealer and the one whose records supply most of the data for this series, entered quotations in specie as well as in "congress money." An index computed on the maximum of these specie quotations was 31 per cent above the base period.

In April 1781, the arrival of vessels from Hispaniola and Havana contributed to the spring decline in coffee prices. As much as 312,300 pounds of coffee were imported in the space of a month, to the accompaniment of a weakening of market quotations. Prices, which had fallen to 11.1 pence a pound by July 1781, steadily recovered in the rest of that year and the one following. Toward the end of this long expansion Hollingsworth found "best green [coffee] in demand."[49] The peak of this rise in coffee prices came in January 1783 when it sold for 38 pence a pound or 166 per cent above the prewar level, but in the ensuing contraction coffee fell well below the prewar years.

Another period of irregular expansion beginning in May 1784 marks, in retrospect, the beginning of a stretch of relatively well-sustained prices. Contemporaries regarded these years as full of uncertainties and it is true that all prices became very sensitive to external events. Had the political setting been more stable, merchants dealing in articles in which the quantity demanded was shifting upward might well have been less cautious. Late in March 1785, an external factor was given by Coates as the reason for the lightness of the firm's orders for West India goods.

[46] April 19, 1780, Joseph Baldesqui, St. Eustatius, to Stephen Girard.

[47] September 1, 1780, Monbos and Latil, Baltimore, to the same.

[48] September 23, 1780, the same to the same.

[49] December 2, 1782, Levi Hollingsworth to William Steward, New London.

"Coffee here is 14 pence," he wrote, "and was expected to rise. We intended to encourage thee to send some of thine, but believe it is best not at present as a manoeuvre is attempted which, if it succeeds, we have no doubt will almost immediately reduce the price of every article both of export and consumption and make trade as dull and languid as ever it was in the worst of times. We mean the attack upon our Bank by the present assembly who seem inclined to take away their charter. This step, if carried, will wholly stop the discount of bills, produce bankrupts and other effects not easily forseen." Before the letter was sent, Coates grew less pessimistic and added a postscript which brought his statement more in keeping with the future market: "We have sent a suitable person to enquire the price of coffee and from the account he brings we have no doubt 5 or 6000 weight of green coffee would immediately bring 16 pence per pound and we think it is likely to yield more, but much may depend on the speedy shipment of it from New York in one of the first vessels bound here."[50]

By October 1785, when coffee was selling for 18 pence, Coates wrote to a Newburyport correspondent, "Our price current . . . is somewhat altered; coffee is falling."[51] Actually it fell only half a penny a pound in the next three months and at no time in later years dropped as low as it had been from October 1783 to August 1784, during the first postwar readjustment.

Early in 1786, when some West India products, notably sugar, were "tumbling down very fast,"[52] coffee prices were firm and were expected to keep stable if large quantities did not reach the market.[53] Apparently the profit margin on coffee was narrow enough to make slight variations significant. Even at the close of 1786, when coffee was scarce and prices high, Cox was willing to risk ordering only "eight to ten thousand weight of it"[54] from St. Eustatius, fearing, with merchants like Hollingsworth, that the steady price would attract a large quantity.[55]

Even in a commodity as easy to transport and store as coffee, it was rare in these postwar years for merchants to take a long-term risk. In January, when James Cox wrote to Grenada, he was able to report

50 March 26, 1785, Josiah and Samuel Coates to John Evans.

51 October 16, 1785, the same to William Wyer, Newburyport.

52 March 15, 1786, Benjamin Fuller to Jedidiah Snowden, St. Eustatius.

53 March 21, 1786, the same to the same.

54 November 30, 1786, James Cox to John Cox.

55 December 27, 1786, Levi Hollingsworth to George Douglas, New York.

coffee "in great demand," and "selling by the quantity at 20 pence per pound"; but he cautioned, "What the value of this or any other article of West India produce may be a month hence is altogether a matter of uncertainty."[56] Apparently the fear of a sudden drop in the market was general. To a St. Eustatius shipper Cox explained, "We have endeavoured to put off your coffee by the lump, but can't find a person that will purchase a quantity, merely from the idea that the importation of coffee will be very considerable in the spring."[57] Large quantities did arrive from Hispaniola[58] and prices declined in April, but its sale was dull only for a short time. Before the end of the month, Hollingsworth reported, "It seems to be rather rising,"[59] and by June he found it "scarce."[60] By midsummer, Cox was soliciting both cocoa and coffee from St. Eustatius and in contrast to his previous wariness gave as instructions, "We shall be glad you would send us as much of these articles as you may have money of ours in hand to purchase with,"[61] though he later limited the order for cocoa to eight or ten thousand pounds "as the consumption of that article is not considerable here."[62]

It would not be far-fetched to connect the change in mercantile attitude to faith in the success of the Convention meeting in the city for the purpose of framing a federal constitution. Cox, enclosing an account of the proceedings in a letter to Grenada, wrote, "You will observe that as soon as nine states agree to adopt the government, it is to take effect. There remains little doubt of that being the case very soon."[63] Even a lower price than had earlier been disturbing to merchants was felt to be ample toward the end of 1787, when coffee sold readily "by the quantity."[64]

Domestic produce was low in proportion to prices of West India goods. From a merchant's point of view, it was an ideal setting for profit as long as the market for West India imports was sustained. Taking account of a period of disparate movements in price, a Philadelphia mer-

[56] January 15, 1787, James and John Cox to Robert Otway, Grenada.
[57] February 27, 1787, the same to Henry Haffey, St. Eustatius.
[58] April 5, 1787, the same to the same.
[59] April 24, 1787, Levi Hollingsworth to Hankinson and Barrow, Kingston, Jamaica.
[60] June 7, 1787, the same to the same.
[61] August 18, 1787, James and John Cox to Henry Haffey, St. Eustatius.
[62] September 5, 1787, the same to the same.
[63] September 26, 1787, the same to Thornton, Baillie and Campbell, Grenada.
[64] November 17, 1787, James Cox to John Cox.

chant wrote to St. Eustatius, "Make all the remittance you intend on my account in good coffee provided it does not exceed 11 stivers [18⅓ pence Pennsylvania currency] and that you ship it within a month after you receive this letter."[65]

Prices of coffee in these years had a marked seasonal pattern. It brought its highest prices in the late fall and early winter months, declining with the opening of active spring shipping. The pattern of 1788 followed closely that of previous years. Coffee was too scarce in the spring for a seasonal decline to be prolonged. During a period of dull sales, one merchant preferred to take the risk of storing to selling below his previous price, or as he phrased it, "I intend to keep it for that price except necessity compels me to a sale."[66]

It was a wise decision. Coffee rose even earlier than usual in the fall, and was selling for 18½ pence by September. In October, merchants in Grenada were informed, "Good coffee and the best quality of muscovado sugars are generally in demand here."[67] Only a month later one of the largest dealers in coffee in the area wrote, "Coffee is in very great demand here and will sell for 19 pence, perhaps 20 pence if very good. . . . The duty here on coffee is 1 shilling per 100 pounds and 30 shillings per 100 on value."[68]

The average price of coffee in 1790 was lower than it had been in any year since 1785. Even then it was nearly 11 per cent above the prewar level and it was established as the favorite beverage in daily consumption. The strength and dependability of coffee prices in postwar years offer a striking contrast to the weakness in chocolate and the almost incredible decline in tea prices.

Chocolate

The construction of an index of prices of chocolate, as a beverage, is hampered by the fact that it was imported, in the late colonial period, as cocoa or cocoa beans, priced by the hundredweight, and quoted in merchants' prices current to other mainland colonies in its raw or imported form. After it was processed, it sold by the pound as chocolate. During the war years, prices of the finished product occur more regularly

[65] December 1, 1787, Benjamin Fuller to Henry Ash, St. Eustatius.

[66] March 31, 1788, the same to the same.

[67] October 13, 1788, James and John Cox to Thornton, Baillie and Campbell, Grenada.

[68] November 15, 1788, Levi Hollingsworth to Robert Bowne, New York.

than those of cocoa; thus the article ready for consumption is the only one for which a price series can be constructed.

Between 1770 and 1775, except when stocks in the market were short, prices of chocolate fluctuated mildly. The underlying trend was downward until the summer of 1772 and sharply upward for the rest of the prewar years. Unlike that of the series for tea and coffee, the beginning of the inflationary rise, despite a seasonal dip in 1775, cannot be easily distinguished from the continuation of the rising trend of the three previous years.

The average price for the base years 1771 to 1773 was 15.1 pence a pound. Chocolate was reported to be scarce in part of this period. For instance, in May 1773 a Philadelphia merchant, in sending to New York for a small quantity, explained, "I find there is not a hundredweight of cocoa to be had here and it will fetch by the case 87 shillings 6 pence to 90 shillings per hundredweight, if good. . . . Should there be no cocoa and you can purchase some very good chocolate at 14 pence New York [currency; equal to 13⅛ pence Pennsylvania], you may buy four or five hundredweight as none in town here to be had."[69] Apparently stocks were concentrated in the hands of a few merchants whose accounts carry continuous sales in this and the following years. Cocoa was quoted to clients in other areas in September 1773 and chocolate in December though at considerably higher prices than the May limits of the New York order. The enhancement of prices and such typical information as "we are quite out [of cocoa]"[70] may be cited as evidence of limited stocks.

Chocolate averaged 17.5 pence a pound in 1774, but the year ended with sales of the last two months at 20 pence a pound, a figure that would have been considered unusually high in any preceding year since 1766. Milder prices prevailed in 1775 and processors of cocoa were able to advertise chocolate for sale "manufactured in the best manner."[71] Thus prices during part of the period of the Continental Association were lower than when this more or less voluntary form of price control started, and even the Committee of Safety which undertook to set maximum prices for West India goods from February to April 1776

[69] May 18, 1773, Michael Gratz to Barnard Gratz, New York; William Vincent Byars, editor, *B. and M. Gratz, Merchants in Philadelphia, 1754-1798*, p. 131.

[70] November 21, 1773, William Smith to James Parsons.

[71] February 8, 1775, advertisement of Samuel Garrigues, Jr., *Pennsylvania Gazette.*

had, in the case of chocolate, an easy choice with the high prices of the end of 1774 as a basis.

Since, by some process, the Committee of Safety arrived at a regulated price of 16 pence, the advance in the index of chocolate could be dated from May 1776, or at least from June, when chocolate reached 22 pence a pound. In October, by a sudden upward leap, quotations were lifted more than 78 per cent above the prewar price level. The sales of February, August, and September 1777 were at three times those of September 1776 and nearly five times the prewar average.

Contrary to the behavior of other West India imports, the inflationary rise in chocolate was rarely interrupted. The lacunae in prices in the months when the British held the city obscures part of the process of rise. Only in the months which followed the reoccupation was there an interval when sales were made at an unvarying price. Chocolate was selling at the close of 1778 for 150 pence a pound, or nearly ten times its prewar average. Four months later, after a disturbing rise, the price of chocolate was regulated at 450 pence—a figure which seemed to be well above its former price. At the time, the purchasing power of "congress money" was slipping so drastically that, before the announcement could be circulated, prominent merchants were making sales at rates far above the adopted standard, rendering it out of date almost before it could be announced. In the closing months of 1779, chocolate fetched 12 dollars or 1080 pence a pound.

The advance of the next year was more moderate, and by midsummer prices of chocolate, like those of most imported goods, declined markedly. Such quantities of chocolate as were being sold in 1779 and 1780 originated in St. Eustatius.[72] The small quantities received in the next year, after St. Eustatius was captured by the British, arrived from Grenada and Cape François.[73] The prices upon which the index is based are uninfluenced by divergent policies of traders, being taken from the sales of Shinkle and Graff, the only merchant house among those whose records are available for consultation which had continuous dealings in chocolate from the middle of 1778 to the fall of 1781.

Small imports could not long retard the force of depreciation in the medium of exchange. By November 1780, chocolate was selling for

[72] November 18, 1779, March 18 and June 17, 1780, and January 6, 1781, *Pennsylvania Packet.*

[73] May 19, 1781, *ibid.*

1284 pence in continental currency and 18 pence in specie, exactly the price at which our quotations of 1770 start. In the tumult over currency in the first months of 1781, chocolate was quoted at 22 pence in specie in March, at 30 in April, and at 16 in May when the maximum and final citation in continental currency was 2700 pence.

Once specie became the market standard, the price of 16 pence continued until midsummer, after which prices soared from August to December 1781 to a peak of more than 43 shillings a pound. The recession from this height, which was 188 per cent above the prewar average, was gradual and irregular. Though the decline was speeded by expectations of peace, there was no abrupt break such as occurred in many other commodities.

The severest part of the long recession in chocolate prices came in 1784, when for a few months it sold as low as 15 pence a pound, or slightly below the prewar average. As prices declined, merchants favored the shipment of cocoa, the raw material for the manufacture of chocolate, to Philadelphia. In April 1784, when chocolate sold for 16 pence a pound, Drinker wrote to a correspondent, "Good cocoa, if low with you, may possibly do."[74] Such cargoes as reached Philadelphia in the next four years were brought to a market with an underlying downward drift in prices.

In September 1786, a large quantity of cocoa arrived to a dull market.[75] The next month a Philadelphia merchant wrote to his correspondents in Grenada, "Our market for West India produce, particularly rum and cocoa, has continued to decline since we had the pleasure of writing you last. We have sold a part of the rum at 3 shillings a gallon. The remainder, with the cocoa, we have stored and probably it will be three or four months before we shall be able to close the sales of these articles."[76]

The duty of 4 pence a pound placed by the Assembly in the spring of 1787 disturbed the importers, who held that prices of cocoa were "very low."[77] Supplies were being shipped from St. Eustatius, but correspondents were warned to send "not more than 10,000 weight and not above the last in price and good in quality."[78] In the next month an

[74] April 8, 1784, James and Drinker to Henry Trotman, Barbados.

[75] September 5, 1786, Josiah and Samuel Coates to William Bartlett, Newburyport.

[76] October 13, 1786, James and John Cox to Thornton, Baillie and Campbell, Grenada.

[77] April 28, 1787, James Cox to John Cox.

[78] August 18, 1787, Benjamin Fuller to Henry Ash, St. Eustatius.

agent in Trinidad was warned that cocoa would sell only if it were of the best quality and sent in the best season, "the latter end of summer."[79] Toward the end of 1787 a mild flurry occurred in chocolate prices. Evidently the importers of cocoa had underestimated the demand of chocolate manufacturers, and Benjamin Fuller, after giving a discouraging picture of the dry goods market to his protégé in Trinidad, urged that good cocoa be sent, as "the article is greatly in demand."[80]

Prices of chocolate dropped in the next year, but Fuller was willing to have cocoa sent to him and predicted a demand for it at the prices then prevailing "from this time until Christmas next. Make speculations accordingly."[81] In this he was wrong, so far as the manufactured article was concerned. Chocolate not only declined in July but had dropped to 12 pence by December, the lowest price to which the commodity fell in the period covered by this analysis. Another Philadelphia merchant appraised the situation more accurately when he wrote, "Chocolate is lower than ever known here."[82]

Looked at in retrospect, the dealers in chocolate were faced with a downward trend in prices from December 1781 to the end of the period. After the first months of 1787, prices were continuously below prewar levels and in depressed months even as much as 20 per cent below.

Summary

The three important beverage materials—tea, coffee, and chocolate—differ widely in areas of origin. Chocolate and coffee had always been direct imports; tea, on the other hand, could be brought legally to the colonies only from England. The period of direct trade with China and the tea-producing areas coincided with a drop in prices in terms of pre-Revolutionary levels not evident in any other commodity—it was, in fact, the beginning of a complete change in price structure, even the dangers and delays of a long voyage being insufficient to push prices to their prewar "heights," especially since tea was now no longer the main beverage.

With few exceptions, after October 1784 coffee prices kept well above the average of 1771 to 1773, showing, in the main, only seasonal drops

[79] September 13, 1787, the same to Robert Totten, Trinidad.

[80] October 29, 1787, the same to the same.

[81] July 9, 1788, the same to the same.

[82] October 10, 1788, Reed and Forde to John Lewis, Fredericksburg.

in the spring when supplies began to arrive. Its gain in popularity gave it a fairly well-sustained advance. Chocolate, on the other hand, had not the startling reduction in price shown by tea, but it did display a continuing downward trend for the period here considered.

Of the three commodities chocolate, in the postwar period, would seem to have been the poorest trade risk, since it showed only slight and short-lived lifts in price, while tea, though low, held at a rather stable level until the spring of 1787. Coffee had greater sensitivity than either of the other beverages but in the main fluctuated within fairly well-defined limits, making it a profitable item to those dealers operating with a general knowledge of trade and with facilities for storing.

CHAPTER XIV

PEPPER

EAST INDIA SPICES were quoted infrequently in prices current during the colonial years. Pepper, usually imported by way of Great Britain, was traded all along the seaboard, and sold in small quantities at prices often as low as 2 shillings a pound. From 1765 to 1770, the longest period of relatively high prices before the Revolutionary War, pepper seldom sold below 3 shillings and was sometimes as high as 4 shillings or more.

During the nonimportation agreement, March 1769 to September 1770, pepper was scarce and reached 5 shillings a pound before the agreement was relaxed, when it dropped immediately to about 2 shillings 3 pence.

The prices used for the years 1771 to 1774 come from the accounts of three merchants—Levi Hollingsworth, Thomas Biddle, and William Redwood—though at times these are corroborated by the sales of William Smith, Josiah and Samuel Coates, and Thomas Clifford. In all records, there was little variation from 2 shillings 3 pence a pound until the months when the First Continental Congress was in session. Even then, higher levels lasted only a few months.

The irregularity of the quotations of the earlier years makes it all the more surprising that a series can be found for the war years which, though incomplete, is indicative of the trend of prices of one of the East India spices. Prices in the first eight months of 1775 were only slightly above the average of the three prewar years, 1771 to 1773, which have been used as a base period. The steep rise of later years began in September. Between January and April 1776, pepper sold for 5 shillings a pound, the maximum reached in the peak month of the nonimportation period. It advanced steadily throughout the rest of the year until by March 1777 it was selling at 16 shillings a pound.

No sales of pepper were found outside the city during the months of British occupation; inside, pepper sold, according to the accounts of John and Henry Drinker, for 3 shillings 6 pence a pound, and at a slightly lower price in May, or about 50 per cent above average prewar quotations. The reappearance of pepper sales in merchants' accounts at 18 shillings a pound, soon after the city was repossessed, indicates that in the fifteen months between March 1777 and July 1778 prices advanced only 2 shillings, a slower increase than in the preceding year.

Rarely is there a comment about as minor an article as pepper except in general statements of European or Indian goods. On the other hand, there is little spread in the unit prices of different sources. As prices advanced in 1778 to 30 shillings, Irwin, Webster, Dickinson, and Hollingsworth, when they had sales, approximated closely those which have been used from the accounts of Shinkle and Graff.

In 1779, when pepper was included in the items regulated by civilian committees, its price was fixed at the one current in May, to continue until the first of July, when the quotation of the first of April was to be again effective. Although the April price was published as current in July, the sales price was continuously above the regulated one; however, it was September before there was a complete break from the levels ordained by the price committee. Pepper then sold for 225 shillings a pound, exactly six times the regulated price of July. By the end of 1779, the market stabilized at 300 shillings, which may be regarded as the prevailing price of the first five months of 1780. The irregularity of quotations in later months obscures the process by which the commodity reached 900 shillings in December.

Quotations in February and April 1781 show that pepper declined in the early months but was again on the rise when "congress money" ceased to circulate, a price of 975 shillings per pound being reached in April. Prices in specie rose in the summer months from 9.5 shillings to a peak of 12 shillings in September, with a lull in the next seven months attributed to new supplies which were quickly exhausted.

The last upswing of the war years was under way by June 1782. That it was the result of scarcity may be inferred from a report in the very next month sent by Pelatiah Webster to a client in Connecticut: "Pepper is growing scarce—price 10 shillings."[1] It reached 12 shillings by the beginning of 1783, the price of September 1781 and the highest quoted in these years except in depreciated currency.

During the period of extreme inflation, pepper resembles tea in percentage and timing of advance. Between April 1775 and April 1776,

[1] July 3, 1782, Pelatiah Webster to John Perit, Norwich, Conn.

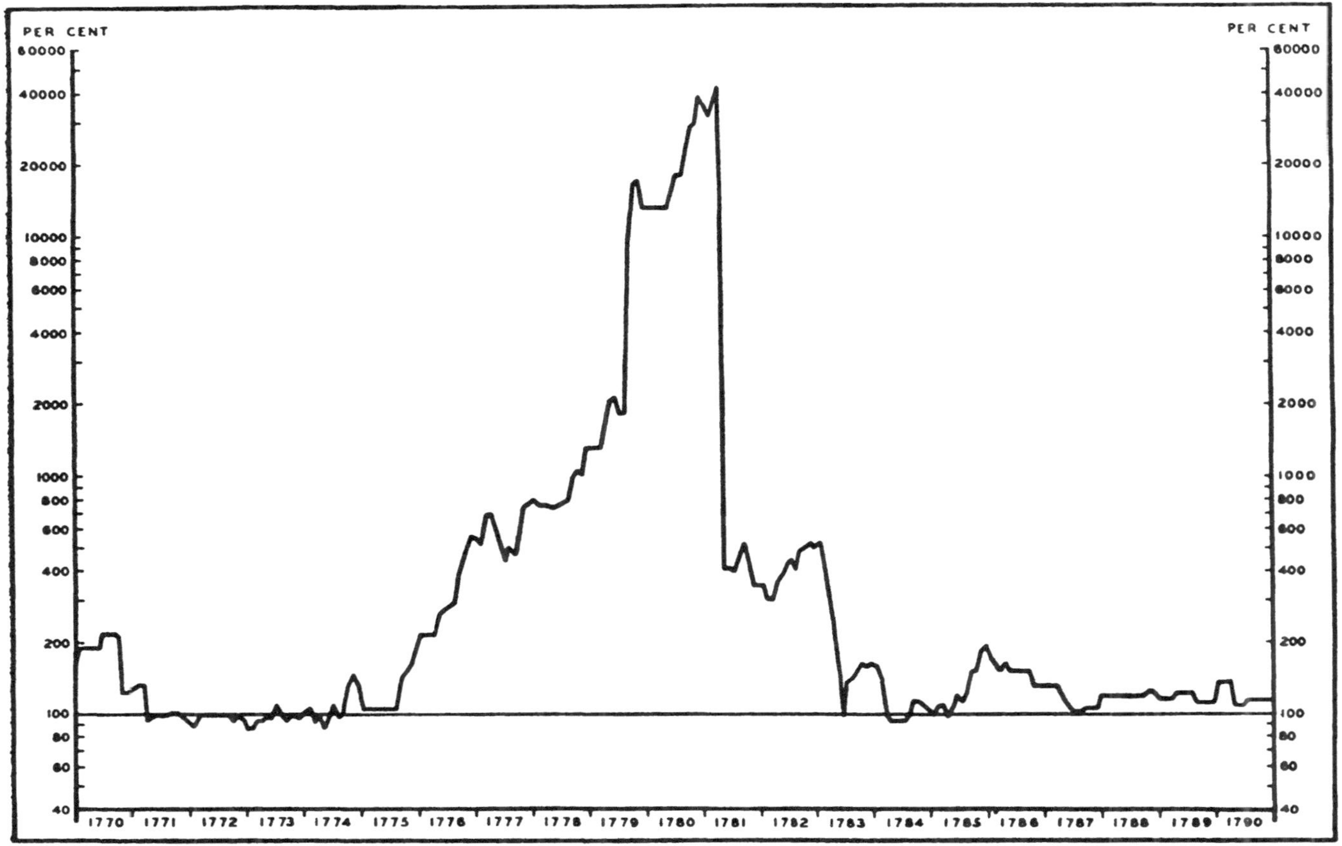

CHART XII—MONTHLY RELATIVES OF WHOLESALE PRICES OF PEPPER IN PHILADELPHIA, 1770-1790
(Base—Monthly Average, 1771-1773)

prices of pepper rose 107 per cent, those of tea 109 per cent. Considering the difference in importance of the two commodities, their advances in the next twelve months conform surprisingly, though in this period tea had the steeper rise. From April 1779 to April 1780, when the value of currency was tumbling rapidly, tea rose 650 per cent, pepper 700 per cent—a likeness of behavior that would seem to be related to the common source of these commodities.

After the medium of exchange was stabilized, there were two complete swings in prices with identical peaks in September 1781 and January 1783, each created by scarcity and followed by quick contraction once new supplies arrived. These reversals in price were mild compared with the collapse which followed the news of peace. The character of this decline is best shown by Pelatiah Webster's own accounts. His price of 12 shillings in January 1783 was lowered to 7 shillings 3 pence in March and to 2 shillings 3 pence in early June. Such a rapid decline could scarcely be expected to last, and prices rebounded in the closing months of the year.

The early postwar years brought more variation than had been usual in prewar prices. Only from April to August 1784 was there a period when pepper prices were lower than their average from 1771 to 1773. The depressed level of these months marked the beginning of a complete cycle with a peak in December 1785 and the end of the contraction twenty months later. Except for the five months in 1784 and three depressed months from June to August 1787 when prices kept only slightly above the prewar average, there was no return in the postwar period to as low levels as had prevailed before the war.

CHAPTER XV

TOBACCO

IN THE LATE COLONIAL PERIOD, Philadelphia played a minor role in the distribution of leaf tobacco from Virginia, Maryland, and other southern areas. Tobacconists in the city furnished a local market for certain grades of manufactured tobacco and snuff. Under the conditions of war, trade in tobacco gained in economic and political importance, though the total exports of the mainland must have dropped to a fraction of what was formerly shipped to Great Britain and later transshipped to the European continent.

Despite incomplete prices for tobacco, the commodity cannot be omitted from a discussion of the problems of trade during the American Revolutionary period. No product shows as clearly as does tobacco the change in merchant organization and the diversion of activity from local trade to dealings in southern products suited to continental European markets. The dependence upon France and Holland for war supplies and the placing of William Bingham in Martinique as a representative of the colonies turned the attention of the limited number of merchants who were licensed to bring in ammunition and other war supplies to trade in tobacco and indigo, the commodities most desired in France. As the British factors withdrew from the tobacco trade, Pennsylvania merchants slowly extended their activities to Virginia and Maryland areas—a change influenced by the openness of shipping. Even before Philadelphia was captured, the safest ports for shipping to the West Indies were in Virginia and along the Pimlico Sound in the Carolinas. As a result, prices of tobacco were often not quoted in Philadelphia and discussion concerned prices in the areas of growth, especially as shipments from 1776 until 1778 were made directly to West India ports.

Once Philadelphia was repossessed and war activity spread southward, an overland trade through Maryland to Philadelphia was carried on, with exports as likely to be shipped directly to French ports as to the Islands. Robert Morris, Peter Kuhn, Levi Hollingsworth, and other local merchants active in this trade had to find reliable agents or establish branches in the tobacco regions. When the war was over and the price of West India goods was shrinking, the trade became a major interest to merchants all along the seaboard, especially those who had good agents in the tobacco areas and business connections in French and Dutch ports.

This trade brought about a far-flung merchant organization. Local agents, if unattached to any other business, were found to be unreliable and it was necessary either to deal with a resident shopkeeper already established or to start a branch in the center of some tobacco region. As a result, some of the Philadelphia merchants in the postwar period for a time made trade in southern products their major line of business. The merchant shipper not only placed a sizable investment in the hands of the local shopkeeper, with whom he kept up a constant correspondence, but also undertook the task of supplying the general information about business conditions which would affect the trade. Current knowledge of the trend of prices was thus the concern of the merchant shipper. The dealer was responsible for knowledge of conditions in his area, activity in purchasing, prompt loading of vessels, keeping accounts, and carrying an assortment of goods which would facilitate his purchases. The problems of merchants who thus converted their organization to deal in a product in which they had little experience are apparent in their correspondence, especially in the years of inflation and in the postwar period in which trade differs vastly from the direct dealings of colonial years.

After the middle of the eighteenth century, prices of leaf tobacco had a mildly upward trend. From 1766 to 1773 it sold in Philadelphia at a comparatively high and stable level averaging, toward the end of the period of rise, as much as 32 shillings. Tobacco suffered a few years of severe depression after the close of 1772, in which its prices ceased to be included in newspaper market reports. Normally in colonial years these weekly price quotations covered a range of all kinds of tobacco without specification of grade or region of origin. During the war, the shipment to neutral countries of leaf tobacco of the growth of Virginia, Maryland, and other southern states, in order to build up credits for needed supplies accentuated the lack of quality specifications in the market information. By the middle of 1780, merchants began to distinguish between the growth of different regions, and later not only applied more minute classification to such areas as James River and Rappahannock River but also differentiated the qualities—best, average, and inferior—under the geographical classes.

The gap in quotations from 1773 to 1775 and the later emphasis upon grading make it as difficult to trace the beginning of the inflationary rise as it is to relate prices of the later war years to any prewar base. The dull market forced merchants to deal in other articles or stimulate sales by a change in the terms of credit. In 1773, when tobacco prices turned downward, Drinker hoped by refusing 30 shillings per 100 pounds for high grade tobacco to get 35 shillings with the offer of a few months' credit[1] for a commodity normally sold on a cash basis. Other merchants sold unspecified grades at 25 shillings or less. Yet, except for the demand from local tobacconists, Philadelphia dealings were too intermittent, dull, and minor to yield a reliable price series from merchants' accounts. All evidence indicates a downward drift in prices once trade was limited to the mainland.

Tobacco as a Means of Payment

Only as the possibilities of exporting tobacco became apparent as one means of financing the war and thus keeping idle vessels employed did Philadelphia merchants begin to divert their activity to the Virginia and Maryland areas. The way was provided by the authorization to the Secret Committee of Congress on October 6, 1775, to export produce in order to purchase arms and ammunition, just as other exceptions to the strict enforcement of the Continental Association had to be made by sending vessels under convoy to procure salt. As letters came in from Guadeloupe, Martinique, and Havana[2] offering to supply powder for tobacco, sentiment grew in Congress for more vigorous activity in shipping. "We have more to expect," Jay stated during the debates, "from the enterprise, activity and industry of private adventurers than from the luke-warmness of assemblies. We want French woollens, Dutch worsteds, duck for tents, German steel, etc."[3] Thus early in the war, a number of items were added to the list of those needed which, to the pacifist group of owners of vessels, had more appeal than the traffic in arms.

Though the main emphasis in this period was on building frigates

[1] March 17, 1773, James and Drinker to Mansell and Corbett.

[2] October 20, 1775, *Journals of the Continental Congress*, v. 3, p. 495.

[3] *Ibid.*, p. 496.

and on manufacturing salt, powder, saltpeter, arms, cannon, and other urgently needed supplies, the receipt of goods by shipping channels was still vital. Early in 1776, Richard Smith recorded, "Foreign goods begin now to come in."[4] From this time, the Dutch islands, as a source of supply and as a market for tobacco throughout the war, cannot be disregarded.

During the period of exportation for defense only, the resolution of October 26, 1775, to export produce "for a certain purpose" was limited to the foreign West Indies. The use of tobacco in this exchange was an offset for supplies which formerly reached the continent from Great Britain and now might be provided by way of the non-British islands. By February 1776, Thomas Hollingsworth was receiving Maryland tobacco in Philadelphia, from Head of Elk by way of Chester Church, at an original cost of 27 shillings 6 pence per hundred and 5 shillings charges.[5] Robert Morris, too, was informed that prices at the plantations were rising and 25 shillings "much more general for crops than it was."[6] By April, when Morris notified the Committee of Safety that six vessels were loaded with Pennsylvania produce "on account of the Continent" and ready to sail under the protection of the "ships of war"[7] the transition from official and licensed trading to general participation was well under way. As private traders speeded their activity, prices of tobacco turned mildly upward, though purchase limits were still closely set. For instance, in September 1776, Samuel Pleasants of Philadelphia, dealing with Robert Pleasants in Virginia, was willing to purchase tobacco at 16 shillings 6 pence in Virginia, using continental money only, and unwilling to pay above 18 shillings to 18 shillings 6 pence.[8]

The incentive to ship tobacco increased as reports from Paris in October quoted it at "the enormous price of seven stivers" per pound in Holland (about 97 shillings in Pennsylvania currency for 100 pounds) "and will soon be as dear in France and Germany and etc."[9]

[4] January 10, 1776, Richard Smith Diary, *Letters of Members of the Continental Congress*, v. 1, p. 306.

[5] February 25, 1776, Caleb Ricketts, Chester Church, to Thomas Hollingsworth.

[6] March 14, 1776, Stephen Steward, Maryland, to Willing and Morris.

[7] April 29, 1776, Robert Morris, Chairman of Secret Committee, to Committee of Safety.

[8] September 3, 1776, Samuel Pleasants to Robert Pleasants & Co., Va.

[9] October 8, 1776, Silas Deane, Paris, to Committee of Secret Correspondence; Francis Wharton, editor, *The Revolutionary Diplomatic Correspondence of the United States*, v. 2, pp. 167-68.

The same correspondent a week later reported tobacco at "8½ pence [a pound] sterling in London."[10]

The advance in prices was international and cannot be explained, as contemporaries tried to do, by blaming Virginians for reluctance to sell at the limits being set by merchants.[11] In Amsterdam, Virginia tobacco which had sold in the first quarter of 1774 for 3.8 stivers a pound averaged 5.2 in 1775. By April 1776 it was being quoted at 5.8, after which there was a lapse of five months until it was quoted again at 8.2 stivers in October on an upswing which carried it to 15.8 by March 1778. In other words, between April 1774 and March 1778, prices of Virginia tobacco on the Amsterdam market more than quadrupled. Lower prices prevailed in the next two years, with Virginia tobacco as low in some months as 9.2 stivers. In 1781 quotations were as high as 15 in April, November, and December, but no month was as high as March 1778, the peak of the war years.[12]

Gradually in the tobacco regions the limits on purchases were raised. Robert Pleasants failed in his attempt to keep the price at 17 shillings 6 pence when purchasing, as "there are many other orders expected," and as "Carter Braxton is foolishly giving 20 shillings [Virginia currency]," adding as an afterthought, " 'Tis strange Robert Morris should form a mercantile connection with such a man."[13] Soon 20 shillings became general as many new purchasers appeared from over the mountains who absorbed the cost of wagonage from the plantations to the inspection house.[14]

Morris, concerned about the number of purchasers in the tobacco trade, confided to Bingham, "We are fearful that the Farmers-General of France will have so many offers for supplying them with tobacco that instead of expecting to pay prices suited to the risque of exporting it, they will begin to think it will be in their power to engross our whole crops on their own terms for you cannot conceive how many proposals made to them have come to our knowledge."[15]

Meanwhile, Deane was urging the Committee of Secret Correspondence to hasten their remittances with the news that "tobacco, rice, indigo,

[10] October 17, 1776, the same to the same, *ibid.*, p. 173.

[11] October 9, 1776, John Harper, Alexandria, to Abel James.

[12] N. W. Posthumus, *Inquiry into the History of Prices in Holland*, Table 86.

[13] October 9, 1776, Robert Pleasants, Va., to Samuel Pleasants.

[14] October 16, 1776, John Harper, Alexandria, to Abel James.

[15] October 20, 1776, Willing, Morris & Co., to William Bingham, Martinique.

wheat, and flour are in great demand and must be so through the year. Tobacco is 9 stivers per pound in Holland,"[16] an estimate which conforms to the summaries of Posthumus. By then, tobacco had risen to 22 shillings 6 pence to 25 shillings in Maryland, and was bringing 27 shillings 6 pence on the Philadelphia market.[17] It was higher in Virginia than in Maryland. "So many orders are lodged with us," Harper wrote, "and so many purchasers appear as will I doubt not raise the price of good tobacco to 25 shillings shortly."[18] But tobacco, even at advanced prices, was still a bonanza item for shippers, as Willing and Morris made clear to Bingham. "We are much disappointed," they wrote, "at your advices respecting the article of tobacco, which ought to continue a good article in all the West India Islands, be the quantity that arrives there more or less, for it is not on the consumption in the West Indias that the value depends; it must be reshipped in French and Dutch bottoms to Europe and will bear well the expense of double freight and charges."[19]

Late in November, Deane estimated that "twenty thousand hogsheads of tobacco are this instant wanted in France, besides the demand in other kingdoms."[20] Meantime, Bingham, in Martinique, was disturbed by the rise in the price of the tobacco being shipped to him by Willing and Morris. "Ours was bought," he was informed, "on as good terms as any at the same time. The quality we are very liable to be imposed on, having no inspection nor in fact any persons here sufficiently judges of it."[21]

All the handicaps of dealing in a product that needed experience had to be met by merchants formerly in other lines. It was, besides, a bulky commodity now being transported in small ships because few large ones were available and small craft, too, could more easily elude capture. Nor were the rules of shipping uniform. Willing and Morris were puzzled that the direct importation of tobacco was not "permitted from Martinico to France as it is from St. Domingo, for we had 150 hogs-

[16] October 25, 1776, Silas Deane, Paris, to Committee of Secret Correspondence; Wharton, *op. cit.*, v. 2, p. 183.

[17] November 5, 1776, John Page, Md., to Thomas Hollingsworth.

[18] November 6, 1776, John Harper, Alexandria, to Abel James.

[19] November 8, 1776, Willing, Morris & Co. to William Bingham, Martinique.

[20] November 29, 1776, Silas Deane, Paris, to Committee of Secret Correspondence; Wharton, *op. cit.*, v. 2, p. 201.

[21] December 6, 1776, Willing, Morris & Co. to William Bingham, Martinique.

heads transshipped from Cape François on our account."[21] Pennsylvania shippers gained experience in the tobacco trade in 1776, though the quantity exported filled but a fraction of European demand. "Our merchants," Robert Morris wrote to Franklin in his summary at the end of 1776, "have been led to purchase much tobacco in Maryland and Virginia, and their ships are employed in the export of this article."[22]

To the surprise of an English observer, the trade was facilitated, after the departure of the Virginia governor, Lord Dunmore, by the failure to guard the Capes of Virginia. "In consequence of this apparent remissness, on the part of the British cruisers," William Eddis found, "a considerable commerce is carried on, with very little interruption, between Virginia and Maryland, and the French and Dutch islands, and even with several ports on the continent of Europe."[23] Extensive as the trade seemed to him, it was discouraging to Robert Morris who, from his post as representative of Congress in Philadelphia, felt that "the quantity of tobacco we should ship to France ought to have no limit and sorry I am that the vigilance of our enemies, the scarcity of ships and seamen, with many other causes keeps us from making the necessary progress, but our difficulties in this respect are almost insurmountable."[24]

Prices Soar in 1777

Though the wide range in quality and the emphasis upon terms of purchase militate against the construction of a price series, all observers in the tobacco areas in 1777 were impressed with the strength of the demand. Thus a Philadelphia participant in the trade was informed in February 1777, "The numerous orders that are continually flowing in upon us from the North and the many hands in which they center has occasioned the price of tobacco to rise . . . and there is reason to believe it will not stop there as the planters begin to think they may get any price they please to ask, and actually talk of 25 and even 30 shillings per hundredweight."[25] Selling prices in Philadelphia reached 40 to 45 shillings in March and frequently 60 in the following months.

As interest in the tobacco trade increased, the feeling grew that its

22 December 21, 1776, Robert Morris to the Commissioners at Paris; Wharton, *op. cit.*, v. 2, p. 237.

23 January 1, 1777, William Eddis, *Letters from America*, p. 345.

24 January 6, 1777, Robert Morris to ——, *Pennsylvania Magazine of History and Biography*, 1946, v. 70, p. 191.

25 February 10, 1777, Robert Pleasants & Co., Va., to Abel James.

lure might be interfering with the war effort. "The advanced price on tobacco may be an advantage to those states that have made that article their staple commodity," an anonymous writer to the *Maryland Journal and Baltimore Advertiser* said, "provided an expectation of the continuance of such a price does not take them off the pursuit of other business, which, while those times continue, will turn infinitely more to their advantage."[26] The essence of concern was that while public money had been provided for establishing manufactures, people in general preferred to "risk their money in a precarious foreign trade (in which if they fail at one time, they are sure to double their profits at another, from the great necessities of the people) than lay it out in erecting or carrying on any other kind of business that may be of any benefit or advantage to the community in general"[26]—a situation more indicative of the unprofitability of managing salt works and weaving cloth than of the certain profits of trade.

Toward the end of April, tobacco in Virginia was "up to 35 shillings per hundredweight and rising."[27] By midsummer, the Council of Safety was informed that the rise in prices of tobacco was "greater than that of flour."[28] It was still in demand in Europe when Deane wrote in September 1777, "Tobacco is the best article at present in the ports of France, or indeed in any part of Europe, and must continue so for a very considerable time yet to come, most probably for twelve months."[29] The part Philadelphians were playing in raising tobacco prices may be illustrated by the cargo of the privateer *Shippen*, which was loading for Martinique with tobacco purchased at 37 shillings 6 pence Virginia currency, when the same commodity was quoted at 60 shillings in Philadelphia, or a differential of about 13 Pennsylvania shillings.[30]

The military reverse which resulted in the capture of Philadelphia caught some dealers with heavy inventories on hand and no means of exporting them. Lovell, on behalf of the Committee of Foreign Affairs, in answer to an inquiry from their commissioner in Martinique, wrote,

[26] April 1, 1777, *Maryland Journal and Baltimore Advertiser.*

[27] April 20, 1777, Robert Pleasants & Co., Va., to Abel James.

[28] Memorandum Book of Council of Safety, *Pennsylvania Archives*, 2nd ser., v. 1, p. 540.

[29] September 3, 1777, Silas Deane, Paris, to Committee on Foreign Affairs; Wharton, *op. cit.*, v. 2, p. 387.

[30] September 30, 1777, William Vincent Byars, editor, *B. and M. Gratz, Merchants in Philadelphia, 1754-1798*, p. 229.

"Your situation must have been very disagreeable, indeed, in consequence of the failure of remittances from hence. Large quantities of tobacco have been long stored; but our bays and coasts are so infested by the enemy's ships of war, that it is impossible for us to conduct [business] agreeably to our earnest wishes."[31]

Continued Rise to May 1781

Once the city was reoccupied, Baltimore and Pennsylvania merchants who began fitting out ships in Virginia to go to St. Eustatius or Martinique were astonished to learn how much the price of tobacco had risen in a few months when, in the meantime, it had "got down to almost nothing in the French and Dutch islands,"[32] a report that was confirmed by a former Philadelphia merchant then resident in St. Eustatius.[33] As prices of West India produce seemed to suffer a decline in continental ports, it was predicted either that tobacco, too, must decline "or else there will soon be an end to all business."[32] Tobacco was then quoted at 110 shillings in Baltimore[34] and about 20 shillings higher in Philadelphia.

From the middle of 1778, monthly price series for two grades of tobacco indicate the merchants' lack of awareness of the factors influencing prices, since their expectation of a decline tallies with the beginning of one of the steepest periods of rise. Toward the middle of November, buyers in Virginia were alarmed at the speedy upswing. "Tobacco our only article of export," an informant from Alexandria wrote, "has been sold from £6 to £6 10 shillings [Virginia currency] and indeed I should not be surprised from the disposition of the country towards our money to see it in the course of three months up to £10 per hundredweight."[35]

31 April 16, 1778, James Lovell, York, to William Bingham, Martinique; Wharton, *op. cit.*, v. 2, p. 554. The round-about way in which tobacco was reaching Philadelphia is indicated by a contract of Levi Hollingsworth's in July 24, 1778, for 46 hogsheads of tobacco to be delivered at Head of Elk and Back Creek at £6 per 100 pounds, to be weighed at Philadelphia under the inspection of Josiah Hewes. Hollingsworth Receipt Book, 1775-78.

32 August 15, 1778, Woolsey and Salmon, Baltimore, to Philip Moore, Boston.

33 August 7, 1778, Elliston Perot, St. Eustatius, to Levi Hollingsworth.

34 August 21, 1778, David Moore, Baltimore, to the same.

35 November 14, 1778, John Harper, Alexandria, to Abel James. Some gold and silver was already in use in the purchase of tobacco as may be inferred from the payment, December 2, 1778, made by Levi Hollingsworth of £533 19 shillings 6 pence in gold and silver to Samuel Howell's tobacco account. Hollingsworth Cash Book, 1777-79.

In the following year, between March and November, prices of tobacco trebled in Philadelphia. The rise was general. In June, the captain of one of Girard's vessels found tobacco quoted in Baltimore at £19, though "They tell me at present they are sure it is worth only £16."[36] He was even less pleased with the prospects in Virginia and concluded, "So I will not buy any tobacco for you."[37] Before the upswing halted, tobacco was selling in Virginia at £20 a hundred, "and everything seems to rise in proportion."[38] In October it was still quoted at £20, with the warning "some ask £25."[39] An unusual number of merchants from Philadelphia, Baltimore, and other mainland cities were then in the West Indies. In addition to John Perot, resident at St. Martin, and Elliston Perot at St. Eustatius, the names of Joseph P. Whitall, Richard Wister, William Shoemaker, Samuel Howell, Mathew Clarkson, and Blair McClenachan appear in memoranda, some concerned with the tobacco trade.[40]

In Philadelphia, prices of tobacco in continental currency soared in the next year, though they had fallen in the Dutch islands. Virginia tobacco, which fetched £100 in March 1780, reached £130 by midsummer and was £150 before the end of the year. The differential over Maryland grades was marked in both the Philadelphia and the St. Eustatius markets.[41] Emphasis on closer estimates of cost appears in the correspondence. George Clymer, engaged in loading a brig with tobacco, answered his partner, "I find you are disappointed as well as myself in the ship's cargo. Nothing is determined with respect to her; two projects has been thought of—the one a voyage to 'Statia, the other to France on freights of tobacco at a certain sum per hogshead. At £10 sterling to the latter she would earn above £6,000 sterling and Fitzsimmons thinks a cargo could be got. The schooner was thought too small to keep running at as great an expense as a vessel of three times her burthen." In arriving at a plan of action, he concluded to "mix Fitzsimmons' decision with Meredith's [his partner] hesitation."[42]

36 June 26, 1779, Captain Mare, Baltimore, to Stephen Girard.

37 July 18, 1779, the same, Leeds, Va., to the same.

38 August 17, 1779, Richard Graham, Dumfries, Va., to Michael Gratz; Byars, *op. cit.*, p. 184.

39 October 28, 1779, Barnard Gratz, Williamsburg, to the same, *ibid.*, p. 188.

40 Richard Vaux Memorandum Book for the year 1779.

41 April 14, 1780, Joseph Baldesqui, St. Eustatius, to Stephen Girard.

42 July 5, 1780, George Clymer to Samuel Meredith.

When the war spread to Virginia, Philadelphia became a main shipping point for tobacco, especially for Maryland grades. Transporting it was not without hazards, and trade suffered early in 1781 from the capture of outward-bound vessels.[43] More serious was the capture of St. Eustatius in February 1781. For a time sales of tobacco were reported to be dull,[44] but its price in paper currency continued to advance until continental money ceased to circulate. In April 1781, Virginia tobacco sold in Philadelphia for £165 per 100 pounds and Maryland for £125. In the next month, Virginia tobacco brought 25 shillings in specie, a lower price than it held once payment in coin became usual. The change in currency in Philadelphia made the wagoners transporting tobacco overland demand their payment in hard money and led to a request that all sales in Virginia for the account of one of the largest traders in tobacco be made in specie.[45]

Prices after Continental Currency Was Abandoned

Some hogsheads of James River tobacco during the summer of 1781 brought as much as 50 shillings a hundred. This advance called forth such an unusual supply that well-informed dealers misjudged the effect. To a Baltimorean, Levi Hollingsworth wrote, "You expect tobacco will rise; I am of contrary opinion, as our city is crowded with it . . . Great quantities more are daily arriving."[46] Virginia merchants were soon informed by the same dealer that great quantities were accumulating in Philadelphia, and finally that "tobacco is without price at this market. I have at least 300 hogshead on hand—no sale for it."[47] There was a flurry in sales in the autumn in which Maryland tobacco led,[48] and it was anticipated that with the fall of Cornwallis and the continuance of French forces in Virginia, there would be an advance in prices in that state.[49]

Confidence began to return as soon as the downward trend ended. In November, Thomas Willing wrote, "There is no vessel offering for Europe and I believe tobacco will sell as well here to the full—its got

[43] January 16, 1781, James Madison to Edmund Pendleton, *Letters*, v. 5, p. 539.

[44] March 16, 1781, Levi Hollingsworth to Bristol Brown.

[45] May 8, 1781, the same to Henry Armistead & Co., Fredericksburg.

[46] July 27, 1781, the same to John Sterrett, Baltimore.

[47] August 21, 1781, the same to Marsden and Smith, Va.

[48] November 5, 1781, the same to Isaac Smith, Fredericksburg.

[49] November 24, 1781, the same to Francis Smyth, Richmond.

to 27 shillings 6 pence [for] Maryland and 37 shillings 6 pence for Virginia. I've bought as much as I want for the cutter before the great advance in the price."[50]

Throughout 1782, prices of tobacco fluctuated uncertainly. The year opened "duller than last year,"[51] but a period of "brisk" demand followed.[52] As James River tobacco rose, Pelatiah Webster explained that it was "made scarce by the vast plunders and destructions of the last year's crop by the enemy in Virginia,"[53] a factor that would be likely to affect future prices more than current ones. The fluctuations seem to have been related to generally cautious trading as rumors of peace circulated, to the uncommonly heavy loss of vessels by capture, and to the piling up of stock in warehouses. "We have no market for tobacco at this port," Hollingsworth wrote to Virginia, "our vessels have been laid up since spring on account of the English ships cruising off our capes."[54] Like that of tobacco, the sale of other goods was "mostly out of the question."[55] In retrospect, the price quotations for tobacco appear surprisingly stable, indicating that the complaint arose from lack of turnover rather than from sacrifice prices.

Postwar Prices

In the spring of 1783, prices of tobacco stiffened and by August Maryland grades were selling for 45 shillings. Virginia tobacco then averaged 55 shillings a hundred. The advance was initially treated with the usual caution of Philadelphia merchants trading on a price upswing. "We designed to make you a larger shipment of tobacco," a Philadelphian explained to his Amsterdam correspondent, "but the very high price of that article and our late discouraging advices from your place for the present prevented us."[56] It was felt that "strangers and adventurers," coming into the merchant group in Philadelphia as trading expanded, introduced incautious methods, while the established houses continued to place emphasis upon quality.[57] In mid-September, Peter

[50] November 13, 1781, Thomas Willing to Samuel Inglis, Baltimore.
[51] February 17, 1782, Levi Hollingsworth to Samuel Galloway, Md.
[52] March 23, 1782, the same to Benjamin Stoddard, Bladensburg, Va.
[53] June 12, 1782, Pelatiah Webster to John Perit, Norwich, Conn.
[54] July 2, 1782, Levi Hollingsworth to D. Periez, Blanchford, Va.
[55] August 21, 1782, Stephen Collins to ———.
[56] October 2, 1783, Kuhn and Kuhn to Duncan Ingraham, Amsterdam.
[57] October 16, 1783, Robert Proud to John Proud, London.

Kuhn wrote to his brother, then engaged in purchasing, "Tobacco of the *very best* quality *only* is in demand here and will bring 50 shillings to 52 shillings 6 pence."[58] That he regarded these as high prices is clear from his statement to a correspondent at L'Orient: "Tobacco still continues high here as well as exchange."[59]

As a British Order in Council had opened the warehouses for the receipt of "tobacco of the growth of the United States of America,"[60] it is not surprising to have a Philadelphia merchant seeking an appraisal of prospects in that market. The result was reassuring "having been informed," he wrote, "that tobacco has taken a very great rise in England I have purchased and shipped . . . for London 24 hogsheads." His invoice shows that the purchase price varied from 48 to 50 shillings.[61] Thus, the postwar period started with many persons interested in dealing in the staples of the southern states which stimulated their trade and widened the market for other products in those areas. Chaloner and White wrote, "Carolina and Virginia take a great deal of specie in payment for rice and tobacco."[62]

Since the readjustment of the postwar period can easily be colored by complaints about the bad state of dry goods sales, it is important to follow the trade in domestic staples in some detail, especially as prices of tobacco were comparatively high in the early postwar years and the fluctuations of 1784 and 1785 were variations from a level well above prewar.

In March 1784, the circular of a French merchant house resident in Philadelphia warned clients that rice and Maryland, York River, and James River tobacco were scarce in the market with prices varying daily.[63] The reasoning of Morris, as sent to his partner in Baltimore, was at variance with that of others:

> The high price which tobacco bore in Europe during the war occasioned a good deal being raised in several of those countries which in part supplied the consumption; the manufacturers mix it with American growths and this lessens by so much the consumption of the latter; so long as the price continues high this practice will exist and then full crops of Maryland and Virginia may

[58] November 18, 1783, Kuhn and Kuhn to Jacob Kuhn.
[59] November 17, 1783, the same to Witt Delmustre & Co., L'Orient.
[60] November 8, 1783, *Gentleman's Magazine and Historical Chronicle*, v. 53, p. 975.
[61] December 1, 1783, Chaloner and White to Wadsworth and Church.
[62] March 21, 1784, the same to the same.
[63] March 20, 1784, Dutilh and Wachsmuth to clients.

be too much. I think also that the Farmers General will go only from hand to mouth in their purchases until Mr. Alexander can buy in this country at suitable prices and that will only happen when the other markets are filled which must soon be the case if France buy sparingly.[64]

The next month, when Willing, Morris and Swanwick summarized the prices and duties on tobacco in London, Amsterdam, Nantes, and Bordeaux, they thought the time "not the most favorable for speculations abroad." Markets, too, were unsettled.[65] The Bank of North America, moreover, faced with a drain on specie, refused to discount, an action which Morris felt would influence prices. In substantiation of the belief, he pointed out that "tobacco was up at 36 shillings to 40 shillings on James River and fell again in three days to 30 to 32 shillings upon the disappointment for want of discounts."[66] Even in the next month he persisted in thinking "the price of tobacco will fall in Virginia; how it may govern in Maryland you can best judge. Money is scarce and tobacco seems plenty."[67] Tilghman, answering his letter, remarked that tobacco showed more tendency to rise than fall. Looking ahead, however, he agreed that "a considerable fall in Virginia will undoubtedly affect this market. Nothing else will, except a fall in Europe. Our planters are in general in good circumstances and always keep an eye to the London prices. They will ship themselves or keep upon land rather than take an under price."[68]

Other well-informed exporters were putting more emphasis on quality than on price. Peter Kuhn, whose agents were purchasing tobacco, gave assurance by reporting Maryland tobacco in "very great demand . . . holding it now at 55 shillings per hundredweight round, which we have some expectation to sell at part cash and part credit. Were it all of the first quality it would bring 60 to 62 shillings 6 pence."[69] When best Virginia tobacco was selling in Philadelphia for 70 shillings and it could be bought in Virginia for 20 shillings less, Clifford concluded, "The difference in price will be a handsome profit."[70] Kuhn intended to make

[64] March 24, 1784, Robert Morris to Tench Tilghman, Baltimore.

[65] April 8, 1784, Willing, Morris and Swanwick to Tench Tilghman & Co., Baltimore.

[66] April 10, 1784, Robert Morris to Tench Tilghman, Baltimore.

[67] May 4, 1784, the same to the same.

[68] May 7, 1784, Tench Tilghman, Baltimore, to Robert Morris.

[69] May 18, 1784, Peter Kuhn to Jacob Kuhn, Fredericksburg.

[70] June 2, 1784, John Clifford to Thomas Clifford, Jr., Bristol.

considerable shipments to France in the fall, or as he explained, "to whatever market in Europe will be the most encouraging."[71]

Activity in the local market, insofar as it was induced by the demand for loading "our European vessels,"[72] could not be expected to last. Once these sailed, merchants became aware of some of the factors which influenced Morris in concluding, "Tobacco is quite too high for Mr. Alexander of the firm of Alexander and Williams [purchasing in Virginia at limits set by the Farmers-General], so that I doubt if he can do much before next crop."[73] Morris did not cease purchasing but advised his partner in Baltimore to "buy with ready money such parcels as you can meet with of the fine bright tobacco such as is really fine and fit for London and Amsterdam markets because I think you will always make money on such purchases if laid in reasonably."[74] Meantime, the news of the state of foreign markets led others to trade warily. In August, the changed sentiment appears in Kuhn's comment, "Tobacco in Europe is fast on the lowering price; shall therefore wait for further advices from thence before we determine upon any shipments."[75] A comparable decline in the domestic market would have pleased Morris, as he was anxious to furnish tobacco at limits set by the French agent: prices of tobacco and wheat were not "reasonable" to Morris in that sense. He therefore wrote to his Baltimore partner, "You must try hard to keep down prices and then you will have much business."[76] A week later he wrote, "I am glad that wheat is likely to fall and wish the same of tobacco."[77] Morris was nourishing a false hope, since a ship waiting for a cargo was "not likely to get a freight before the new crop comes in, tobacco being very scarce."[78] Others had continued to purchase in Virginia.

Nor did the estimates of Baltimore merchants tally with future trends. Early in September a wholesaler in Baltimore wrote to a New England correspondent:

71 June 14, 1784, Peter Kuhn to Witt Delmustre & Co., L'Orient.
72 June 22, 1784, the same to Jacob Kuhn.
73 July 17, 1784, Robert Morris to Tench Tilghman, Baltimore.
74 July 20, 1784, the same to the same.
75 August 10, 1784, Peter Kuhn to James Finlay, Port Royal, Va.
76 August 16, 1784, Robert Morris to Tench Tilghman, Baltimore.
77 August 24, 1784, the same to the same.
78 September 3, 1784, Chaloner and White to Wadsworth and Church.

The late accounts of the decline of tobacco in England and Holland and the favorable appearance of abundant crops have had some effect on the price here and I am persuaded in the course of two months it will be considerably lower. The crop of wheat has also been very plenty and it is expected the price will be about 6 shillings or 6 shillings 6 pence per bushel.[79]

Reverting to a wartime purchasing device, Peter Kuhn sent a cargo of salt to his agent in Virginia to "facilitate the procuring of tobacco which we wish you particularly to attend to and secure every hogshead in your power of good quality,"[80] for a cargo he hoped to send to Europe. Toward the end of the year, the active trade and rising market in tobacco, which continued to be "exceeding scarce and difficult to obtain,"[81] were in striking contrast to the lack of sales of dry goods, the fear of failures abroad, and the slow remittances from domestic sales. In these months it was found that little tobacco had been purchased and little offered. An Alexandria merchant wrote in November, "Since peace took place, tobacco has been a cash article and I have found it impossible to purchase on any credit without giving 2 or 3 shillings per hundredweight more than the current price, even for two months."[82] Professor Nussbaum points out that in 1784 "the Farm got no tobacco."[83] The price of wheat and tobacco continued high, the one from an unusual scarcity in Spain and Portugal,[84] the other from the diversity of markets in northern Europe.

The result of the search for profitable cargoes was the geographical spreading of merchant organizations. Just as the merchant shippers found occasion to question the judgment of the local factors purchasing for their account, so their actions became a cause of criticism by the growers of tobacco. The situation was complicated by an arrangement which left all the judgment about general market activity and price changes to master shippers and all the knowledge of quality and the state of supplies to factors resident in the tobacco areas.

Since all experience pointed to the need for a dependable local pur-

[79] September 7, 1784, Mark Pringle, Baltimore, to Christopher Champlin, *Commerce of Rhode Island, 1726-1800*, v. 2, p. 228.

[80] September 26, 1784, Kuhn and Kuhn to James Finlay, Port Royal, Va.

[81] November 5, 1784, Chaloner and White to William Macarty.

[82] November 31, 1784, Josiah Watson, Alexandria, to Christopher Champlin, *Commerce of Rhode Island, 1726-1800*, v. 2, p. 234.

[83] Frederick L. Nussbaum, "American Tobacco and French Politics, 1783-1789," *Political Science Quarterly*, 1925, v. 40, p. 501.

[84] January 8, 1785, Thomas and John Clifford to Amos Hillicar & Son, Bristol.

chaser, the organization of the main initiator spread as the tobacco area expanded. As Morris disliked the character of prices in the older tobacco states, he began to look further south. Already he had supplied the Farmers-General with a range of samples of the various grades of tobacco. With this review of the sources of supply in mind, he confided late in January 1785 to his partner in Baltimore, "I expect the price of tobacco will fall both in Virginia and Maryland. The large crop in Virginia, the quantity now made in Georgia and South Carolina, the falling prices in Europe and the scarcity of money in America all point to a decline of price."[85] For once, Kuhn's information made him, too, expect lower prices "shortly."[86] Neither prediction fitted the reality. After a mild decline in March, prices of James River tobacco held without a change and at a high rate until November, when contraction started.

Morris, anxious to load a cargo at a price that would suit the representative of the Farmers-General, asked Tilghman to "keep down and lower the price."[87] If he could get the ship away, he was resolved to "wait for that decline of price, which the advices from the other side of the Atlantic and the scarcity of money on this side cannot fail to produce."[88] Neither trade conditions nor the "cursed large shipment"[89] of specie to London, which inclined the managers of the Bank to stop discounts, seemed to exert any pressure on tobacco prices. Morris, who signed a contract in April 1785 to supply 60,000 hogsheads to the Farmers-General between then and the close of 1787, was concerned with events on both sides of the Atlantic when he wrote, "I am sorry tobacco should look up. Nothing can justify it. No prices in Europe will and money is too hard to be got, I think, to admit people to sport with it carelessly";[89] and a week later he concluded, "You must lay yourself out for purchasing all the tobacco you possibly can at 35 shillings and under."[90]

With the stopping of discounts, Willing, Morris and Swanwick found themselves in "some difficulties respecting payments," and had to decide to trade only on the basis of detailed information. They wanted

[85] January 29, 1785, Robert Morris to Tench Tilghman, Baltimore.
[86] February 1, 1785, Kuhn and Kuhn to James Finlay, Port Royal, Va.
[87] March 10, 1785, Robert Morris to Tench Tilghman & Co., Baltimore.
[88] March 16, 1785, the same to the same.
[89] March 22, 1785, the same to the same.
[90] March 29, 1785, the same to the same.

to know not only the purchase terms of different qualities of tobacco, the amount ready to ship, the charges, and the quantities available for market but the amount already shipped.[91]

Tobacco vessels had to be cleared from southern ports. It was not a trade that distant merchants could attend to directly. Though rice could be kept in warehouses in Philadelphia for later shipment, vessels transporting tobacco did better, according to Kuhn, to "proceed to Virginia which has induced the principal merchants here to provide themselves there with good agents."[92]

The attack on the Bank, and the evidence of hoarding of specie in anticipation of a state issue of paper currency, made Morris positive that "the price of tobacco must come down. I think four dollars [30 shillings Pennsylvania currency or 24 shillings Virginia currency] is a good price for the planters and the merchants might live at that rate";[93] but finding that several ships were waiting for Virginia tobacco with the likelihood that prices would rise still further, he had to offer 37 shillings 6 pence for what was in storage.[94]

As a long-run method of affecting prices, Morris attempted to lower the price of exchange "so as to prevent remitters from thinking themselves under a necessity to adventure in shipments of tobacco particularly, or produce generally." His reasoning was that the price of tobacco had "been maintained by a number of raw adventurers who have engaged in the purchase in the hope of making better remittances than the course of exchange admitted."[94]

Even when the Assembly of Pennsylvania was taking steps to issue £150,000 in paper currency, Morris was convinced "that not only tobacco, but all produce of the country must fall," which he believed would be for the public good.[95] He hoped Alexander would "get the field to himself and fix the price at 30 shillings [Virginia] which certainly is high enough; 20 to 25 shillings were formerly high prices and will be so again. Georgia and South Carolina now supply above 10,000 hogheads per annum and North Carolina a very large quantity so that the European markets cannot hold up and shippers at high prices must

[91] April 2, 1785, Willing, Morris and Swanwick to the same.

[92] April 9, 1785, Kuhn and Risberg to Lars Kahra & Co., Gothenberg, Sweden.

[93] April 14, 1785, Robert Morris to Tench Tilghman, Baltimore.

[94] April 19, 1785, the same to the same.

[95] May 9, 1785, the same to the same.

suffer."[96] Once the three ships then loading were ready to sail, Morris decided to cease all purchases of tobacco as "the advices from England and Holland are discouraging for adventures to those markets."[97] All markets had to be carefully watched. For a time, prices remained firm in Maryland when they were falling in Virginia, and a withdrawal from dealings in Maryland was suggested with the provision that "if tobacco comes down to 30 shillings or under you may continue the purchase as fast as you can."[98] This, again, was a plan that could not be carried out in the light of the stable price level in the summer of 1785, and a maximum of 32 shillings 6 pence at Baltimore and 30 shillings on the Eastern Shore was determined upon with the injunction "try to bring these to be the credit prices."[99]

In mid-September, Kuhn sent a Swedish correspondent a new prices current for Philadelphia with the information that prices of some commodities suitable for shipment to him had declined and that tobacco was 20 per cent below previous quotations furnished to him.[100] Morris was still concerned that his partner in Baltimore found a reduction of price impracticable, as he felt sure shippers would incur a loss.[101]

Both Virginia and Maryland tobacco dropped in the Philadelphia market in November 1785 and declined still further until August of the following year. It had lowered earlier in the areas of growth and the Swedish buyer was told that "tobacco can now be had in Virginia at 30 to 35 shillings our currency per 100 pounds, which is near the price it commanded before the war."[102] The drop was cheering to Morris, who set his maximum for the purchase of Maryland tobacco at 25 shillings because prices had already receded in England and begun to lower in France.[103] It was this decline in prices that precipitated a "lively protest" by the French merchants at Philadelphia against the Morris contract because of its effect upon commerce.[104]

Had the state of markets been the only factor to be anticipated, the

96 May 31, 1785, the same to the same.

97 June 7, 1785, the same to the same.

98 June 14, 1785, the same to the same.

99 July 21, 1785, the same to the same.

100 September 16, 1785, Kuhn and Risberg to Schon & Co., Stockholm.

101 September 27, 1785, Robert Morris to Tench Tilghman, Baltimore.

102 October 20, 1785, Kuhn and Risberg to Schon & Co., Stockholm.

103 November 7, 1785, Robert Morris to Tench Tilghman, Baltimore.

104 Nussbaum, *op. cit.*, p. 503.

drop of quotations for tobacco might have been more severe than it was. As it turned out, the prices of April to October 1786 were as low as any recorded before the latter part of 1789. By April 1786, a wide range was given in the tobacco prices reported to the Bristol market.[105] Morris temporarily declined shipping tobacco to Holland, partly as a result of unfavorable accounts he had received from there and partly because of the derangement of his business by the death of his trusted partner at Baltimore.[106] But no one with an expanded organization could long follow a waiting policy, especially in the trough of a depression when debts, if collected at all, were paid in produce. It was necessity that induced Morris's purchases of 1786 in Maryland and Virginia. "I am . . . ," he wrote, "in the way of buying there a larger quantity than I want for this year, owing to the present state of the European markets, which are such as to deter even the Scotch factors (formerly the great exporters of tobacco) from shipping and many of them are now selling to my agents the tobacco they receive in payment of debts for goods and charter their ships to carry it. This state of things, however, convinces me that the state of North Carolina or the United States must suffer very greatly by any shipments made to Europe."[107] Advances for these purchases were so heavy that even Morris felt he could not continue unless the quantities on hand could be dispatched promptly.[108] Doubtful as the outlook was, other merchants had to conclude that good tobacco was the only southern "produce that will pay freight."[109]

By autumn, the market for farm produce of Pennsylvania became "very brisk"[110] at the same time that the demand improved for some West India products. Tobacco offered a puzzling situation, but Kuhn decided to purchase two thousand dollars' worth rather than have "so large a sum remain inactive."[111] He was, however, closing some of his outlets in the tobacco areas and preparing for a time when trade would "become in a more fixed and regular channel."[112] There was no lack of

[105] April 2, 1786, John Clifford to Thomas Clifford, Jr., Bristol.

[106] April 20, 1786, Robert Morris to William Hunter, Jr., Alexandria.

[107] May 18, 1786, the same to Samuel Osgood, Walter Livingstone, and Arthur Lee.

[108] June 4, 1786, the same to Thomas Tilghman, Baltimore.

[109] June 17, 1786, Robert Henderson to James Fleming, Wilmington, N. C.

[110] October 21, 1786, James and John Cox to Archibald Campbell, Baltimore.

[111] November 11 and 19, 1786, Kuhn and Risberg to William French & Co., Fredericksburg.

[112] December 5, 1786, the same to the same.

faith in the salability of tobacco in these plans, for in the midst of them he wrote, "We have no doubt of almost always getting a ready sale for the real mountain tobacco of *first* quality,"[113] though he would not encourage an immediate shipment to Europe "as the markets are very discouraging and very few persons have made a saving remittance in that article."[114]

Tobacco averaged a trifle higher in 1787 than in the previous year. Its rise was noted in Virginia as soon as shipping began.[115] Dealings were cautious. A few hogsheads of choice tobacco, an agent was advised, "sent round occasionally we think would make a good remittance for the use of our own tobacconists here."[116] It was quoted in a diversity of grades from choice to inferior, new and old, according to trading areas, as it was still one of the few southern items which would "pay any kind of freight."[117] The best the Philadelphia market had was at a stable, low price and "dull sale."[118]

Only by awareness of the geographical area of purchase is it possible to reconcile merchant comment with the somewhat nominal range of prices carried in newspaper reports. The distrust of state paper currency, also, made for variation. For instance, in midsummer a merchant was quoting Carolina tobacco at 33 shillings in "cash and 35 shillings 6 pence in paper."[119]

There was little variation in the price of tobacco in Philadelphia from 1787 to the close of 1790. Best Virginia averaged about 47½ shillings. The better kinds of Carolina "for the Irish market"[120] varied around an average of 40 shillings in early 1788, and even Hollingsworth, in the early postwar years a regular dealer in Maryland and James River tobacco, did not expect a rise.[121] As the season advanced, he risked the prediction "rice is likely to be brisker sale than tobacco though at present both are dull."[122] Certainly no part of the dullness could be attributed to the quality of the product from new tobacco-

113 December 21, 1786, the same to the same.

114 January 9, 1787, the same to William Lawrence, Newbern, N. C.

115 February 27, 1787, the same to William French & Co., Fredericksburg.

116 March 13, 1787, the same to Jacob Kuhn.

117 April 12, 1787, Robert Henderson to James Fleming, Wilmington, N. C.

118 April 19, 1787, Kuhn and Risberg to William French & Co., Fredericksburg.

119 July 11, 1787, Robert Henderson to David Lamb, Charleston, S. C.

120 February 22, 1788, the same to John Shedden, Edenton, N. C.

121 February 27, 1788, Levi Hollingsworth to Weston Clark, Savannah.

122 April 4, 1788, the same to the same.

growing areas. "Tobacco . . . [of] the Augusta inspection," Hollingsworth attested, "is . . . the best I ever saw from Georgia and not inferior to James River."[123] In the autumn, when not much old James River tobacco was "at market," Pelatiah Webster gave a key to the unwillingness of merchants to deal in large parcels when the demand was "not great nor any probability that it will rise," since tobacco, normally a cash item, had to be "sold at 60 days credit at least";[124] yet with little change in prices, small quantities could safely be stored.

Merchant interest had already changed to the flour trade and to other cargoes suited to trade with southern Europe or with India and China. The inactive market in tobacco was attributed to "the price in Europe being low."[125] Obviously, the Virginia grades suffered in local trade from the competition with new areas. "Tobaccoes from Savannah and Charleston come so much lower"[126] was an explanation given in this period to a correspondent in the preferred Richmond area, although a few months later the cheerful news was sent, "James River tobacco has taken a little start; at present the shippers have offered 35 shillings . . . good tobacco will always bring near its value here unless there is an over quantity at market."[127] The bulk of the demand, however, was still among local manufacturers.[128]

Summary

Comparisons of the levels of prices of tobacco before and after the Revolutionary War are hampered by the lack of specifications in the grades sold in colonial years. Between 1764 and 1771, tobacco made its steepest prewar rise. If the 31 shillings for the grades sold in Philadelphia can be taken as a typical prewar price for Virginia tobacco, then only inferior grades of James River tobacco were as low after the war as before. York River tobacco fell below 31 shillings in June 1789, and Maryland averaged less than that from November 1787 onward.

The importance of tobacco in American commercial policy during and after the war, especially in arranging for trade between the United

[123] April 22, 1788, the same to the same.

[124] October 31, 1788, Pelatiah Webster to John Red[man].

[125] April 3, 1789, Levi Hollingsworth to Joseph Byers & Co., Herring Bay.

[126] August 9, 1790, Robert Henderson to Patrick Hart, Richmond.

[127] October 18, 1790, the same to the same.

[128] November 5, 1790, the same to the same; November 12, 1790, the same to William Galt, Richmond.

States and France, adds interest to a comparison of the course of its European price. The published tables of Posthumus indicate that the peak price of Virginia tobacco on the Amsterdam market occurred between November 1781 and January 1782. After a lapse in price data from March 1782 to April 1784, quotations were resumed at double the average prewar price. An irregular decline followed which slowly reduced tobacco prices at Amsterdam until between August and November 1786 they were at the average of 1771. At the end of 1786 the market rebounded and held at high levels for the next two years.

If the contraction in tobacco prices in the United States after the war is to be attributed to manipulation of the market by Morris and the Farmers-General, which undoubtedly was attempted, it is well to consider the way in which the activity of other merchants upset the plans, and the lack of any close relation between the price behavior and the dates when the controversial contract was in effect. In the light of the expansion of areas of growth, the firmness of the postwar tobacco prices and the deferred date of severe decline are worthy of emphasis.

CHAPTER XVI

COTTON

THE PREFERRED AREA for the supply of cotton for the Philadelphia market in the late colonial period, was the British island of Tortola. Small quantities could be imported at times from many other islands as the interest in diversification of semi-tropical areas spread the culture of cotton to most of the West Indies as well as to the French mainland possessions along the Mississippi. According to a student of southern agriculture, "Just before the Revolution cotton had come to be raised extensively in the various Colonies for domestic use, and there was a further increase in its use during the Revolution, even in Maryland."[1] Thus the cotton for which prices can be obtained in the war years may have been grown in many of the foreign West Indies, the captured British islands, Virginia, Maryland, or other southern parts of the North American mainland.

Trade in cotton was especially sensitive to war conditions. During colonial wars, prices of cotton fluctuated extremely and were notably slow in readjusting once peace was restored. One of the longest periods of postwar contraction, that following the Seven Years' War in which the price of cotton dropped from 2 shillings 10 pence to 14 pence a pound, lasted more than seven years. The early months of 1770 marked the end of this long decline, but cotton kept at low levels until after the first quarter of 1773, varying in the main from 14 to 16 pence.

Imports of cotton fiber were relatively large in the early seventies by comparison with former years, and merchants' quotations frequently overtopped the average prices given in weekly newspaper summaries. For instance, in 1772 when the market average never exceeded 16 pence, a prominent merchant quoted 17 to 18 pence in answer to a New England inquirer.[2] Later that year, another importer wrote, "The cot-

[1] Lewis Cecil Gray, *History of Agriculture in the Southern United States to 1860*, v. 1, p. 183.

[2] July 3, 1772, Reynell and Coates to John Moffat, Portsmouth, N. H.

ton we expect to sell from 17 pence to 18 pence per pound,"[3] and in the next month adopted the higher figure of 18 pence[4] as the most likely future price. Obviously these merchants, on the basis of supplies in the market, were anticipating the coming spring trade. They were dealing in a commodity in which a variation of a few pence a pound would have been risky had not demand recently been expanding. If forwarded in small quantities, it could at this time safely be included in a cargo, as may be inferred from such a typical comment as "We should think good coffee and cotton would be likely to answer in the spring as also strong proof rum.[5]

In the spring of 1773, prices of cotton advanced. A merchant anxious to replenish his supplies urged that four or five bales of cotton be sent to him. "It will fetch," he wrote, "18½ to 20 pence by the bale, if good and clean of seeds."[6] Such prices held for a few months only; before the close of the year cotton was again selling for 15 pence. In September 1774 and again in December, raw cotton reached the high price of 22 pence. In this brisk advance, it was raised to a level equaled in colonial years only in unsettled periods, and one that turned out to be the lowest quotation before September 1790, the bottom of a major cycle in its price.

Cotton was selling slightly above 2 shillings a pound when Christopher Marshall quit his "state of retirement" to become one of the managers in the Philadelphia Manufactory of woolen, cotton, and linen goods which then had only 158 women spinners and "a number of men such as hemp and flax dressers, wool combers, weavers, etc., etc."[7]

Textile weaving undertakings during the war were doubtless facilitated by previous interest in improving bleaching and finishing operations. Early in January 1772, the *Philadelphia Gazette* hailed the news that an experienced cloth printer was migrating to the area by carrying an item from a letter received in Baltimore.

> We learn that a person who has for many years been a master in several large manufactories for linen, cotton, and calico printing, likewise cutting and stamping of copper plates for same, intends some time this month to leave

[3] November 30, 1772, James and Drinker to Lamolie and B. Lamarque.

[4] December 8, 1772, the same to John Clitherall.

[5] December 11, 1772, the same to Lamolie and B. Lamarque.

[6] May 18, 1773, Michael Gratz to Barnard Gratz; William Vincent Byars, editor, *B. and M. Gratz, Merchants in Philadelphia, 1754-1798*, p. 131.

[7] June 24, 1775, Christopher Marshall to Peter Barker, London.

England for America with six journeymen and all machinery for carrying on the same business, which unknown to the English manufacturers, has been shipped.[8]

John Hewson (the "person") arrived in Philadelphia in September 1773, set up his bleach works, and soon was able to advertise his readiness to bleach and also to print materials brought to him "by merchants and others."[8] Thus a basis for the expansion of fabric manufacture was laid by the development of necessary subsidiary processes before the supply of British dry goods was cut off.

With the attempt to expand fabric production as a war measure, a dependable supply of textile fibers became measurably more urgent than formerly. The flax crop might fail in a poor year, as it did in 1774[9] and again in the middle of the war. The price of cotton provides as much of a measure as can be recreated of the mounting costs of raw material faced by these new ventures. That they played a useful part may be inferred from the restoration of the calico printing works in 1779 and from the award as late as 1789 to its manager of a premium "for the best specimen of calico printing done within this state."[8]

At this date a complete series of textile fiber prices for all the war years cannot be assembled. Only a few merchants among those whose records have survived had dealings in cotton and such prices as can be obtained after April 1775 are pieced together from a limited number of transactions. They agree sufficiently to make it clear that in May 1776 cotton prices rose suddenly to about double the average of the previous year. Since the record is fragmentary, the rise may be traced by information from one of the dealers. On February 12, 1776, Reynell and Coates, who were impressed by the lack of an advance in some West India products, quoted cotton to a New England correspondent at 2 shillings 3 pence a pound.[10] Two days later they quoted "best cotton" to another Newburyport client at 2 shillings 4 pence with the explanation, "Some sell at 2 shillings 2 pence, but [we] believe ours to be 4 pence a pound better."[11] Evidently the stock on hand was fast being depleted, for the next month no statement of price was ventured,

[8] Harrold E. Gillingham, "Calico and Linen Printing in Philadelphia," *Pennsylvania Magazine of History and Biography*, 1928, v. 52, p. 98.

[9] January 18, 1775, James and Drinker to Pigou and Booth, London.

[10] February 12, 1776, Reynell and Coates to William Wyer, Newburyport.

[11] February 14, 1776, the same to Stephen Hooper, Newburyport.

merely the brief comments, "Cotton—scarcely any (or none that is good to be had),"[12] and "not to be had."[13] Before Reynell and Coates again furnished a prices current, Congress had lifted the restrictions on price laid by the Committee of Safety, thereby producing immediately, according to Reynell, "an amazing alteration."[14] Thus, early in May 1776 cotton was priced at 4 shillings 3 pence a pound.[14] It had advanced no higher by July, when a New England merchant was furnished with a long prices current and a general statement of the condition and prospects of trade.[15] No insurance was then to be had on ships, "it being thought scarcely possible for a vessel to go and come safely."[15]

Before another comment about cotton appears in the merchant correspondence, all commodities were involved in a rapid upswing. "Good cotton," according to Reynell late in September 1776, "would bring 5 shillings per pound, if the quantity was small. We are inclined to think that 200 bales would reduce the value of that article a great deal and therefore think it not so safe to speculate in as some others"[16]—an opinion which shows both the limited quantity the market could absorb and the belief of the merchant that scarcity up to this time was a more dominant factor in the advance of cotton fiber prices than was depreciation of currency. As he acted upon his own caution, his records provide no further dealings in cotton in the war years. Nor do those of other importers supply the lack. The price of cotton was cited in February 1777 in a letter of Robert Morris to William Bingham in Martinique. By then an uncommonly wide range prevailed in a commodity in which merchants' quotations formerly varied little. The range in cotton as reported to Bingham was 4 to 7 shillings 6 pence per pound.[17] The period of gradual but orderly advance was over and by June 1777 cotton had reached 10 shillings a pound.

Looked at in terms of the preceding years, the upward trend in cotton prices must be dated from the last quarter of 1774. Although the rise throughout 1775 and the first four months of 1776 was gradual, the net effect was an increase of 70 per cent above the average of 1771-1773, which marked the early stage of recovery from severe depression.

[12] March 6, 1776, the same to the same.

[13] March 9, 1776, the same to Thomas Thomas.

[14] May 3, 1776, the same to Stephen Hooper, Newburyport.

[15] July 1, 1776, Reynell and Coates to William Teel, Newburyport.

[16] September 30, 1776, the same to Stephen Hooper, Newburyport.

[17] February 12, 1777, Robert Morris to William Bingham, Martinique.

The sharp spurt in April 1776 brought the average to 222 per cent above prewar. If the range given in February 1777 were averaged, a price more than 300 per cent above prewar years might be established. On this showing, cotton began to advance before the general movement of most other commodities.

Initially the advance in Philadelphia conformed to what was happening elsewhere. Surinam cotton, one of the three grades then quoted on the Amsterdam market, began an upward drift in the last half of 1772. The rise at Amsterdam, though gradual, carried the price by the end of 1774 nearly 35 per cent above the average of the three previous years. By the close of 1775, when the expansion ended, Surinam cotton was 72 per cent above the average of 1771-1773—an increase parallel to that shown by the Philadelphia cotton series. Contrary to the trend in the Philadelphia area, cotton prices in Amsterdam receded from the beginning of 1776 and continued downward until the spring of 1780, though in no month was there a return to such low levels as were quoted in the early seventies.[18]

Price Fluctuations, 1777 to 1781

From 1777 until July 1779, only intermittent sales can be found in the records of four merchants. These serve merely to mark stages in the upswing. In 1778 cotton sold for 15 to 18 shillings a pound in different parts of the year. In the summer, when it was being quoted at 15 shillings in Philadelphia, Elliston Perot informed his Philadelphia correspondent that the price in St. Eustatius was 18 pence.[19] There is no evidence that any reached Philadelphia until prices were well above 50 shillings a pound.

In 1779, when sales became frequent enough to furnish data for a price series, the supplies of cotton known to have come from Port-au-Prince, the French port of Hispaniola, amounted to 33 bags. If these are rated at 300 pounds a bag, the weight used in Anderson's *Origin of Commerce* in reporting the produce of the French part of Hispaniola in 1770, when the total crop of cotton was given as 8000 bags,[20] the amount entered at Philadelphia in the last quarter of 1779 would be

[18] N. W. Posthumus, *Inquiry into the History of Prices in Holland*, Table 121.

[19] August 7, 1778, Elliston Perot, St. Eustatius, to Levi Hollingsworth.

[20] Anderson, *An Historical and Chronological Deduction of the Origin of Commerce*, v. 5, p. 181.

9900 pounds,[21] about an eighth of the annual importation in the early seventies.

Imports of cotton sold for 55 to 58 shillings a pound before September; those sold in the last quarter of 1779 were priced at 120 shillings, less than one-half the quotation of three months later. Cotton in these months was higher relatively than other West India goods, a behavior which might be attributable to diverse sources of supply. Areas no longer accessible were credited with a considerable growth of cotton. For instance, a writer in the *Pennsylvania Packet*, commenting on British possessions in the West Indies, rated the island of Grenada as "by far the most valuable colony which Great Britain possesses" except Jamaica. Besides its exports of sugar and rum, he held it produced coffee and cotton in greater abundance than all other British islands taken together.[22]

The small supply of cotton known to have entered directly at the port of Philadelphia in the first half of 1780 came from Port-au-Prince[23] and amounted to about 18,000 pounds. Apparently the shipments were not enough to satisfy the demand fully as, in midsummer, Hollingsworth advised his correspondent in Baltimore, "Cotton is rather late at market but is worth 28 dollars [210 shillings] per pound by the bag,"[24] a comment which confirms other evidence that some part of the supply of cotton was of domestic growth. The large quantities of dry goods listed in the cargoes of this year made reliance upon domestic textiles less than it had been in the opening years of the war. In November, cotton was bringing about what it had in midsummer, with the specie price at 3 shillings a pound, nearly two and a quarter times prewar. By the next month it had increased to 4 shillings 7 pence, the highest specie price for cotton in the war years. Shinkle and Graff, the merchants making these sales, converted the totals to continental currency at 75 to one.

The speed with which a leap in prices could come about is illustrated by the records of this same merchant house which on October 30, 1780, sold cotton for 32 dollars (240 shillings) a pound and on March 16, 1781, for 60 dollars (450 shillings) a pound.[25] Early in the next month

21 November 18, 1779, *Pennsylvania Packet.*

22 January 8, 1780, *ibid.*

23 March 8, 1780, 25 bags on Brigantine *Delaware*, and June 4, 1780, 35 bags on Ship *Flora*; *Pennsylvania Packet*, March 18 and June 17, respectively.

24 July 25, 1780, Levi Hollingsworth to John Sterrett, Baltimore.

25 Shinkle and Graff accounts.

the specie price at which Shinkle and Graff sold was 3 shillings 2 pence to 3 shillings 4 pence a pound, a figure which conforms closely to that of other dealers. A rapid decline occurred between April and May 1781 as continental currency, which played little part in the cotton trade after October 1780, ceased to be current. The last opportunity for comparing the relation of prices of cotton in the two currencies is furnished by Levi Hollingsworth, who made sales in May 1781 at 2 shillings 6 pence in hard money and at 445 shillings in continental, or at a ratio of currency to specie of 178 to one. By this time, continental money was "dead" or "not heard of in any place here."

As might be expected from its behavior in colonial years, cotton was one of the most sensitive commodities in the Revolutionary War period in its response to war and inflation. It rose relatively more than most other commodities, and was exceeded at times only by pepper, molasses, and rum.

Mild Swings in Prices

The end of the first decline in cotton prices after dealings were put on a specie or state paper basis came in midsummer 1781. From then, two mild cycles may be described: the first lasting from August 1781 to June 1784, the second from June 1784 to October 1790. On the upswing of the first cycle, to a peak at the end of 1782 and the beginning of 1783, buying seems to have been selective. In the spring of 1782, Hollingsworth found "no sale nor price" for Virginia cotton.[26] The West India islands had so changed hands as the war progressed as to interfere with customary channels for their products. The British complained that the capture of Tobago "was of the greatest consequence to this nation; its cotton was the finest we got from the W. Indies; and by the loss of Tobago that article had risen from 1 shilling or 1 shilling 8 pence to 3 shillings and 3 shillings 9 pence."[27] Those prices in sterling were given by a complainant in England who held that "20,000 people in Lancashire got their bread by the manufacture of cotton."[27] But it was the loss of vessels and the "infesting" of the coast by enemy shipping which accounted for an upswing in West India goods in Philadelphia.[28] Undoubtedly, as the British rightly surmised, continental

[26] March 4, 1782, Levi Hollingsworth to Humphrey Richards.

[27] April 1782, *Gentleman's Magazine and Historical Chronicle*, v. 52, p. 157.

[28] April 15, 1782, Pelatiah Webster to W. Charles Miller, Boston.

ship supplies and dry goods were affected by the loss of St. Eustatius.[29]

The summer of 1782, with rumors of peace circulating, found a slowing down of sales and all merchants waiting for "further advices from Europe."[30] In an effort to revive trade, merchants began to circulate long price lists[31] in which cotton was quoted, even in January 1783, as high as 3 shillings 3 pence a pound.

Postwar Trade

News of peace, which was accompanied by a drastic revision in prices of many imports, brought no abrupt decline in cotton. The explanation for the relative firmness might be that given by Collins: "There is scarce any cotton at this market and what is here [is] very ordinary at 2 shillings 4 pence per [pound]."[32] By June 1784, prices of cotton had gradually sunk to 2 shillings a pound, only to rebound to 2 shillings 6 pence before the close of the year. Its peak price of 3 shillings 3 pence in the expansion phase of this upswing, reached in August 1786, was followed by thirteen months of insensitive prices. Newspapers, in these months, published an average slightly above that cited by merchants for imported cotton. When the papers persistently listed 3 shillings, a merchant house seeking cotton at St. Thomas in the West Indies wrote, "Good clean cotton is worth from 2 shillings to 2 shillings 6 pence per pound."[33] Obviously sales were "slow" and all quotations nominal, as may be inferred from a comment of the same merchants: "We have still four bales of your cotton on hand. We have kept it up at 3 shillings per pound, but have not been able to sell any more than one bale and a packet."[34]

As the season advanced, merchants lowered slightly both their purchase price and the quantities they were willing to order. "If very good cotton," Benjamin Fuller wrote in August 1787, "can be had at 2 shillings 4 pence your money or under you may send three or four bags; but we particularly recommend your not having anything to do with this article except you can procure it of the first quality."[35] Another cor-

[29] May 14, 1782, Debates in the House of Lords; *Gentleman's Magazine*, October 1782, v. 52, p. 465.

[30] August 21, 1782, Stephen Collins to ———.

[31] September 11, 1782, the same to William Gray, Salem, Mass.

[32] September 24, 1783, the same to John and John Brown.

[33] October 1, 1786, James and John Cox to Charles Hagart & Co., St. Thomas.

[34] May 31, 1787, the same to Henry Haffey, St. Eustatius.

[35] August 18, 1787, Benjamin Fuller to Henry Ash, St. Eustatius.

respondent was assured that "the cotton is good and when it can be sold will bring 2 shillings 6 pence to 3 shillings per pound."[36]

Merchants were at a loss to know what to order by way of remittance for the cargoes they were shipping to the various islands. Commerce with Trinidad was handicapped by the lack of regular voyages between it and Philadelphia. Trade sentiment, too, was unsettled. When many were complaining of uncertainty in business, Fuller described the outlook, "The dry goods business is greatly changed. Few can obtain credit in Europe and those that can are loath to part with their goods on time, government being in a very fluctuating state." In specific terms he added, "No demand at present for cotton but expect it will mend in a little time."[37] As prices eased, the hope of dealers was to find an export market for trade in cotton. With this in mind, an inquiry about laws, surcharges, prices, and seasons of trade was sent to Ireland to see whether "cotton of the growth of the West Indies can be shipped from hence to Ireland with perfect safety."[38] The query, made at the end of a long period of trade under the authority of annual acts of Parliament, could scarcely have received an answer before it was proposed in Parliament to put the "commercial intercourse between the subjects of His Majesty's Dominions, and the inhabitants of the countries belonging to the United States of America, and of the foreign islands in the West Indies" on a more permanent basis.[39]

What is surprising in a commodity grown in part in southerly states is the wide area from which supplies were being drawn. In the spring of 1788, when cotton prices were receding mildly, "a large quantity of cotton, imported from the neighborhood of Carthagena, sold at 2 shillings 6 pence per pound."[40]

In the absence of a commercial treaty with Great Britain, American merchants were still in doubt about the basis on which products not the growth of the United States could be entered in British ports—a pressing question if a diversified trade were to be undertaken. In his search for exact knowledge about the regulations affecting trading, Fuller ventured the explanation, "Many here are at a great loss respecting these matters. Indigo, cotton, cocoa, hides, deer skins, furs and several

[36] September 13, 1787, the same to Robert Totten, Trinidad.

[37] October 6, 1787, the same to the same.

[38] December 1, 1787, the same to Doyle and Rowe, Dublin.

[39] Anderson, *op. cit.*, v. 6, p. 901.

[40] March 25, 1788, Benjamin Fuller to Robert Totten, Trinidad.

articles of medicine as gums, balsams, barks, etc., are frequently brought here from the Spanish Main. Can they or any of them be imported into Great Britain from thence in American bottoms or in British?"[41] Being in doubt, he shipped his best indigo to Holland; a later lot went to Liverpool. No cheer was to be found in the state of European markets or the terms of trade, and in midsummer Fuller's protégé in Trinidad was cautioned, "I would not advise your shipping cotton to Europe this season or crop. You may depend the ball is up there and it is probable may affect the price here and in Ireland. . . . Depend the account of failures is actually true."[42]

In serving as distributors for cotton assembled from points on the South American mainland, a number of the islands of the West Indies, and the domestic areas of its culture, Philadelphia merchants were troubled both by variation in quality and in methods of preparation. Prices seemed to be more predictable than quality in the summer of 1788 when Fuller reported that he had sold cotton on a very long credit, "otherwise could not have obtained the price I did owing to its being very foul and full of seeds (which the foreigners that purchase abhor). This article will generally answer if you can ship it so as to be sold here from 2 shillings 6 pence to 2 shillings 9 pence or perhaps 3 shillings."[42] The price trend was then mildly downward. In September, when Fuller believed that cotton "would not bring more than 2 shillings 3 pence," he reported that "all exportation of that article to Europe is at a stand and will continue so until more favorable accounts come from thence."[43]

International factors were held to be exerting a depressive influence on prices, especially upon products sold in northern Europe. Fuller kept his adventurous supplier in Trinidad warned as fully as he could. "You will perceive," he wrote toward the end of September, "that even we at this distance have not escaped the consequence of the many and great failures in Britain. Depend, this has been the cause of the fall of indigo and it will greatly affect cotton."[44] Other merchants, too, expected a lowering of the already "much reduced" price of cotton.[45] Henderson, who was dealing in Carolina cotton, stressed the importance

[41] April 18, 1788, the same to Warder Dearman & Co., London.

[42] July 7, 1788, the same to Robert Totten, Trinidad.

[43] September 10, 1788, the same to the same.

[44] September 24, 1788, the same to the same.

[45] October 4, 1788, James and John Cox to Charles Hagart, St. Thomas.

of quality. "Even if it is very good," he advised, "it will not bring above 2 shillings to 2 shillings 2 pence this money at present."[46]

Merchants were searching not only for ways of by-passing limitations on trading with the British and their islands but also for means of acquiring accurate information from them. It was certain that if anyone took a part interest in a vessel, the merchant's name "must be kept out of sight being an American subject, the British nation not suffering any joint concerns of the kind under strict penalty of confiscation."[47] Information, which depended upon the alertness of correspondents, seems to have lagged in all the early postwar years. "I wish you had given me your opinion on cotton as I could now purchase at about 2 shillings this money. But as there has been a very considerable convulsion in that branch both in England and Ireland, am at a loss to form a judgment."[48] Sales became so discouraging toward the close of the year that cotton was "a great drug—much at market and no sale"; it would then "not bring more than 2 shillings on a credit." The explanation was still, "Cotton in Europe is very low owing to many bankruptcies in that branch."[49]

A new note appeared in correspondence toward the close of 1788 as inquiries for cotton began to reach the dealers. Before the season for shipping closed, a correspondent at St. Thomas could be advised, "We are happy to find that your cotton shipments are likely to turn out better than you or your friends expected."[50] The change in sentiment must have reflected the prospect of a settled new government more than a change in the direction of prices or favorable news from Europe. A discouraging picture of the Liverpool market, written early in February, arrived with the spring vessels. Cotton, it revealed, was "as low as 14 pence to 15 pence [sterling, equal to a little more than 2 shillings in Pennsylvania currency]. Several parcels having arrived last month from France and Portugal, there is an overstock of cotton at this market (not less than 27,000 bags) and the manufacturers have not yet recovered the shock occasioned by the many failures last summer."[51] Later

[46] October 24, 1788, Robert Henderson to David Lamb, Charleston.

[47] October 25, 1788, Benjamin Fuller to John Mitchell, Kingston, Jamaica.

[48] October 27, 1788, the same to Doyle and Rowe, Dublin.

[49] December 10, 1788, the same to Abraham Tuckness, Demerara.

[50] December 10, 1788, James and John Cox to Charles Hagart, St. Thomas.

[51] April 12, 1789, quoted by Benjamin Fuller to Robert Totten, Trinidad.

in the year, when the French and United States governments were expected to remove uncertainties—the one by opening ports on the south side of Hispaniola[52] and the other by completing its impost and tonnage laws—cotton was "very plenty" in the Philadelphia market.[53]

With the changed political outlook, merchants dropped some of their concern about the price level. Fuller wrote optimistically, "I am full of opinion cotton will rather mend in price than otherwise. You need not be afraid to ship a few bales at any time so as to be sold here at 19 pence or under."[54] He was writing before the British act which "prohibited every article from the United States but what are of the growth thereof,"[55] leaving the continental dealers with an assortment of island and South American products of which local consumption was small. He was disregarding, too, the hurry to get goods of all kinds to the port in anticipation of the duties.

In August, when supplies of cotton from the French island of Guadeloupe were still on hand, the consignee wrote, "Several parcels have arrived lately which has made that article rather dull sale and the consumption is not very considerable but we have no doubt but we shall sell it in a short time. We could sell it at present but we do not wish to do it under its value."[56]

Toward the end of 1790, in the very month when cotton prices began to recover, Fuller was complaining, "The cotton will not sell at any price in reason owing to more than a twelve months stock on hand and parcels pouring in daily to save the approaching duty."[57] Although a major upswing in cotton prices, which reached its peak in November 1792, was under way, there was nothing in the behavior of prices to herald it, and complaints about the low quotations appeared even at the close of the year.[58]

An overreliance upon contemporary comment would give an unduly dreary account of the postwar trade in cotton. Opinion was colored by uncertain trade regulations and lack of full information about European

52 June 22, 1789, Josiah and Samuel Coates to Moses Brown, Providence.

53 June 3, 1789, the same to James Clayton White, England.

54 March 15, 1790, Benjamin Fuller to Robert Totten, Trinidad.

55 July 14, 1790, the same to the same.

56 August 25, 1790, James and John Cox to Laurent Pedemonte, Guadeloupe.

57 November 15, 1790, Benjamin Fuller to Robert Totten, Trinidad.

58 December 8, 1790, Robert Henderson to William Barclay, Baltimore.

markets. Actually, from January 1786 until August 1788, prices of cotton were more than 100 per cent above prewar averages, and the trade in it, even in 1789 when prices were lower, was vastly above prewar.[59] At no time in the lowest months of 1790 was the price of cotton less than 20 per cent above the prewar base period.

[59] Exports from Philadelphia, August 7 to December 31, 1789, *The American Museum, or, Universal Magazine*, January 1790, v. 7, p. 12.

CHAPTER XVII

TEXTILES

THROUGHOUT THE COLONIAL PERIOD, years of great activity in the sale of textile fabrics and other British goods were followed by others in which the market was overstocked, payments slow, and bankruptcies frequent. Trade in the last decade was so affected by nonimportation measures, accompanied by attempts to stimulate local manufacture, that it is difficult to find a year in which imports conform to the usual needs of the community.

From March 1769 to September 1770, when dry goods merchants sacrificed heavily by continuing their nonimportation agreement,[1] some on both sides of the ocean hoped to benefit from the disposal of slow-moving stocks on hand, or even stressed the opportunity created for those who owed money in Britain to discharge their debts at more than "20 per cent discount, by the fall of bills of exchange," in this way making a temporary lull in trade "hurtful to neither side of the water."[2]

Early in 1770, coarse woolen goods, checks, osnaburgs, and calicoes were either out of stock or limited enough to give a general impression of scarcity. In some cases hand-loom products could be used as substitutes. Lancaster, Pennsylvania, boasted that, in the year ending May 1770, "fifty looms and seven hundred spinning wheels were in constant use" and produced "over thirty thousand yards of home-spun linens and woolens."[3]

Obviously the encouragement a partial embargo would afford to home manufactures depended upon the ease of importing supplies from other areas than Britain. Woolens especially were needed when Benjamin Fuller wrote to his brother in Ireland, "As long as ever the English government keep the duty act on tea in force, woolen goods of most

[1] April 29, 1770, Henry Drinker to Abel James, London, *Pennsylvania Magazine of History and Biography*, 1890, v. 14, p. 43.

[2] January 11, 1770, William Strahan, London, to David Hall, *ibid.*, 1887, v. 11, p. 223.

[3] R. L. Brunhouse, "Effect of the Townshend Acts in Pennsylvania," *ibid.*, 1930, v. 54, p. 369.

kinds, in the fall season, from your place, would bring a very great profit."[4] By agreement of the merchants, duck for use of ships was permitted to enter because it was held to be scarce.

While he was in England, the opportunity to ship ravens duck attracted the attention of Abel James, the partner of Henry Drinker, who arranged with Pigou and Booth, their supplier in London, to forward a relatively large quantity. Had other shippers been uninformed, doubtless a period of profitable sales could have been realized, for ravens duck was then selling in Philadelphia at 2 shillings 6 pence a yard. But the state of supplies was well known, and James wrote hastily to his partner,

> Neate, who knows nothing of what P & B [Pigou and Booth] and I have done, is determined to send about 50 pieces of an extra quality and about the same quantity of heavy duck, very good—all which I mention that thee may hasten off what Booth took with him either at public or private sale as thee may judge best, for I have reason to believe that that article will go out very low for some time, lower perhaps than I thought when I wrote thee about the cheapness of what we had bought which is said to be occasioned by the great Russian merchants sending it here on their own account to be sold for the money to supply the Empress with to carry on her war.[5]

As soon as New York withdrew from the agreement, the London merchants trading there hurriedly filled orders, as one of them wrote, "shipping large quantities of all sorts of our manufactures; those for woolen goods, in particular, are so extensive that there are not enough in the market, I am well assured, to supply them."[6]

Before nonimportation ended in Pennsylvania, orders for linens for spring shipment were reaching Ireland.[7] Prices, especially unpredictable with stocks unknown, were already declining in New York. A merchant, in placing an order in Ireland, explained that linen had "readily brought all this year from 100 to 110 per cent on the genuine Irish invoice (being substituted in the lieu of checks, always a capital article) and I am of opinion will continue so, until a general importation takes place,

[4] June 6, 1770, Benjamin Fuller to Joseph Fuller, Cork.

[5] July 31, 1770, Abel James, London, to Henry Drinker.

[6] August 24, 1770, William Strahan, London, to David Hall, *Pennsylvania Magazine*, 1887, v. 11, p. 351.

[7] September 3, 1770, Thomas Greer, Dungannon, Ireland, invoice for Reynell and Coates.

which will not be till next spring as most of the traders are against ordering goods before November next."[8]

Whether fabrics came by "the road of the Indies" or found their way from New York or even more directly or, with the threat of unhindered importation, were brought out of hiding, cautious merchants, even before the ban on imports ended, were warning suppliers, "Our shops are not quite so bare as one might expect."[9] Later, when the importation of all except taxed items became general, merchants called for goods ordered nine or ten months previously.[10] Little evidence of bare shelves greeted Abel James when he arrived in New York and found it "exceedingly glutted with goods."[11] Philadelphia, too, seemed to offer a poor market for "many sorts, such quantities being admitted from New York, Maryland, etc."[11] In writing to his British correspondent, James specifically stated, "Irish linens are very plenty at present and therefore we could not wish any great quantity to arrive before spring."[11]

Domestically manufactured tow cloth or tow linen forms the basis of an appraisal of the prewar and war price behavior of country-made textiles which are important because of their contribution to fabric supplies in the war years. During the months of nonimportation, the price of tow cloth rose, fluctuating afterwards as foreign textiles became plentiful. It had reached 2 shillings 6 pence a yard by the beginning of 1771, a higher price than it was again sold for before the spring of 1776. Osnaburgs, an imported fabric of which there were many varieties, declined as soon as it was certain that the agreement would be modified and, after the heavy importations of 1771, dropped sharply. The prices of Russian sheeting and ravens and other duck fabrics, reflecting influences outside the colonies as much as within them, seem to have declined.

The quantity of dry goods imported in the spring of 1771 was so "amazingly great"[12] that even the sales of a fabric known to be scarce might be influenced by substitution. Clifford felt that "the great import of ravens duck for some time past may have occasioned oznabrigs to be so remarkable dull."[13] He noted the sacrifice of goods at vendue at

[8] September 5, 1770, Benjamin Fuller to John Scott, Jr., Armagh, Ireland.
[9] September 15, 1770, Thomas Clifford to Lancelot Cowper, Bristol.
[10] September 22, 1770, Reynell and Coates to Samuel Elam, Leeds.
[11] November 24, 1770, Abel James to Lancelot Cowper, Bristol.
[12] May 22, 1771, Benjamin Fuller to John Scott, Jr., Armagh, Ireland.
[13] October 16, 1771, Thomas Clifford to Thomas Clifford, Jr., Bristol.

"manifest loss"[14] and finally summarized the outlook at the close of 1771 by reference to the slowness of payment. "Our sale for European goods is not encouraging nor can we get paid for what we do sell in proper season. It therefore appears to me our imports will be less another year."[15] The total importation in 1772, though slightly lower than that of the previous year, continued at a high rate. To merchants who felt the trade in dry goods was "being much overdone"[16] it seemed likely that quantities would long be on hand.

Depression, heralded by an abrupt drop in prices, came earlier in Europe than across the Atlantic.[17] The series of bankruptcies which followed the failure of the banking house of Neal, Fordyce, James and Downs was said to be so far-reaching in its effect that "no event for 50 years past has been remembered to have given so fatal a blow both to trade and public credit."[18]

Meantime, prominent dry goods merchants kept warning that imported fabrics were selling in Philadelphia at "the different vendues for much less than they cost."[19] Not all the surplus stocks were the result of faulty anticipation, for Henry Drinker wrote tartly, when his ship *Chalkley* arrived, "We were greatly concerned to find the quantity and value of goods on board on speculation, at a time we are so glutted and overdone with almost every article usually imported from England; what can be done with the goods mentioned in the twenty invoices on thy own account we are at a loss to know."[20] Resistance to purchasing when supplies were known to be abundant, requirement of credit on items normally bought for cash, and refusal to buy from new or unknown shippers were all part of a two-years buyers' market brought about by false estimates on both sides of the ocean during the nonimportation period. If one could assume that the local merchants were well informed, the dull sales of imported linen goods could be attributed in part to "constant improvement in manufacturing low priced linen

[14] October 17, 1771, the same to David and John Barclay, London.

[15] December 20, 1771, the same to Thomas Frank, Bristol.

[16] May 16, 1772, the same to David and John Barclay, London.

[17] Coal which sold in London on April 8, 1772, for four guineas a chaldron had dropped by the 16th to 31 shillings, according to *Gentleman's Magazine and Historical Chronicle*, v. 52, p. 197.

[18] June 22, 1772, *ibid.*, pp. 292-93.

[19] July 1, 1772, William Pollard to John Woolmer, Halifax and Yorkshire.

[20] August 4, 1772, Henry Drinker to Lancelot Cowper, Bristol.

among ourselves,"[21] as contemporaries claimed; but at this time woolens sold no better than linens.[22]

Prospects for dry goods remained discouraging even at the close of 1772, when outgoing vessels should have carried the merchants' orders for the next season, and even in the late spring of 1773 local merchants were urging their suppliers to charge their "goods as low as possible"[23] and fumbling to find items of dry goods which would stimulate sales. Russian-type fabrics seemed to offer such a possibility. "In these excessive bad times," Drinker wrote, "we hope to gain some advantages from the Russia sheetings and ravens duck . . . The object of profit seems in our present and late sales to be very much out of the question; after that is given up the greater difficulty remains of selling at *any rate* and where the money can be depended on in any reasonable time."[24]

Toward the middle of 1773, a change of sentiment in the plans of dry goods dealers made it likely that orders for the year, though small, would be "tolerable."[25] Drinker pictured the discouragement of this gloomy period in the sales of dry goods, which had a later parallel in the excessive importations of the first years after the war. In both periods, prices of grains and grain products were high and part of the economy enjoyed a degree of prosperity, but the over-all tone was set by the articulate dealers in dry goods. In midsummer, just as an upswing not yet evident to contemporaries was starting, Drinker wrote, "We can with truth assure you that since the commencement of our partnership now near 20 years since, our trade has not been in so disagreeable and discouraging a state as for 12 or 18 months back, which has prevented our continuing to order the usual and seasonable supplies, as we don't see the propriety of following trade for the mere name without the benefits which have formerly followed our care and industry."[26] It was not merely that the spring goods sold slowly but that such items as calicoes, imported at lower prices than formerly, were being offered at "15 to 17½ per cent less than the exchange and charge attending the importing."[27] The dullness was pervasive and interna-

[21] September 21, 1772, James and Drinker to Walker, Dawson & Co.

[22] October 3, 1772, William Pollard to Peter Holme, Liverpool.

[23] April 28, 1773, the same to Benjamin and John Bowers, Manchester.

[24] April 30, 1773, James and Drinker to Pigou and Booth, London.

[25] June 8, 1773, William Pollard to Benjamin and John Bowers, Manchester.

[26] July 3, 1773, James and Drinker to Peach and Pierce.

[27] July 5, 1773, the same to Walker, Dawson & Co.

tional. "The many failures in England and Holland have much affected the West Indies, South Carolina, Virginia and Maryland drawers [of bills of exchange] from whence we have our most considerable supply of bills and, indeed, we have in this place felt its consequences so much that we hardly know how to lay out our money in bills with safety."[27]

Although the record of sales is not continuous, it is clear that duck and sheetings advanced in price from the middle of 1773 to the close of 1774. They were then the most hopeful items of the dry goods trade, and in the fall of 1773 the satisfactory report was sent to London that "All our brown 7/8 ravens duck and 9/8 sheetings are sold and shall have room for more of them when they can be bought to your mind."[28] Other merchants found the improvement general enough to venture the opinion, "Goods will fetch a better price this fall."[29]

By April 1774 importers were freely admitting that the market for fabrics was "getting into a better situation."[30] Then, low-priced Irish linens were in "great demand" and were expected to yield a "good profit."[31] A brisk revival of sales started before all old stock was worked off and with country and city stores said to be still in debt for some of their last purchases.[32]

Sentiment veered and a note of urgency appeared in merchants' correspondence as it became evident that "most kinds of European and India goods" were "very scarce."[33] Linens were in demand with "the town . . . empty of most sorts and our crops of flax likely to fail this year."[34] Should an agreement banning imports result from the agitation in the market and the meeting of the deputies from the other colonies, it would find the area with little raw material for the manufacture of coarse linens, a general call for them, and a still more urgent demand for muslins and calicoes "which are the chief articles consumed."[35] Explaining in detail the urgent need for prompt importation Drinker wrote, "We don't remember a time (except during the last non-importation agreement) when our city has been so bare of European and India

[28] September 11, 1773, the same to Pigou and Booth, London.
[29] September 27, 1773, William Pollard to Benjamin and John Bowers, Manchester.
[30] March 16, 1774, the same to James Buck, Leeds.
[31] April 4, 1774, the same to William Crosby, Jr., & Co., Liverpool.
[32] May 16, 1774, the same to Benjamin Bowers, Manchester.
[33] May 31, 1774, James and Drinker to John Clitherall.
[34] June 11, 1774, the same to Pigou and Booth, London.
[35] June 29, 1774, the same to the same.

goods in general, especially of all kinds of coarse linens, but it seems likely that a supply may arrive in a few weeks, by the fall ships."[36]

While merchants were still guessing the time of the expected embargo on importation, finally set for December 1, 1774, they enjoyed a period of profitable sales. Pigou and Booth in London could be told that the brown Russian sheetings they had shipped in such quantities in July were "mostly sold at 77 shillings 6 pence, . . . most of white at an equal profit. The Irish linen is sold at 22 pence per yard. . . . Some of the muslins, calicoes, napkining diaper and ravens duck are sold to a handsome profit."[37] By November, Stephen Collins was selling brown sheeting at 10 shillings above the price Drinker felt to be handsome and white sheeting for 100 shillings a piece, but by then anyone receiving goods long in passage might be forced to store them "or to submit them to a public sale and give up the profits for Boston."[38]

Apart from the effect on the attitude of the group of merchants most closely allied to British trade, the succession of active and dull years preceding the war affected the supplies on hand at its start. The nonimportation measure went into effect at a time of pressing demand for coarse linens and a "knowledge of the general failure of flax last season."[39] Though goods were still being offered at vendue[40] by those preparing to return to England, the assortment of stock was so unbalanced that it might well be expected that prices of dry goods would lead all except military goods in the later upswing.

From the point of view of apparel, imports doubtless bulked larger than supplies expected from the efforts to start manufacture; yet the minutes of the manufactory of wool in 1775[41] illustrate the importance attached to local production by the way in which workers in wool, flax, hemp, and cotton were being recruited as a result of the realization that the nonimportation measure might not be "so transitory a thing as some have supposed."[42]

36 August 29, 1774, the same to Jones, Campbell & Co.

37 September 17, 1774, the same to Pigou and Booth, London.

38 December 6, 1774, the same to the same.

39 January 18, 1775, the same to the same.

40 February 8, 1775, *Pennsylvania Gazette,* advertisement of William Sitgreaves.

41 March 25, April 25, July 6, 1775, Minutes of the United Company of Philadelphia for Promoting American Manufactures.

42 March 16, 1775, Speech delivered in Carpenter's Hall, *Pennsylvania Packet,* March 27, 1775.

Scarcity of Textile Fabrics Felt Early in War

The best sailcloth was scarce enough in the spring of 1775 to make it wise for ships to equip with spare foresails and topsails in England as "the sailcloth is not to be had here."[43] Two months later, when an order for duck was placed from Massachusetts, there was not enough in Philadelphia to be worth sending.[44] Soon Congress found it necessary to order a "diligent enquiry" into the quantity of "duck, russian sheeting, tow cloth, oznaburgs, and ticklenburgs" in the city,[45] and finally to buy a quantity of such fabrics as were obtainable.[46] Immediately the cost of repairing sails rose as the price of sailcloth and Russian duck, the principal items in sailmakers' accounts, was much advanced.[47]

As plans progressed for building and equipping a naval armament, canvas took a place second only to gunpowder as a necessary item of import. At the close of 1775 the Marine Committee of Congress estimated that 7500 pieces of canvas were needed for this purpose alone.[48] Only quantities in excess of those normally imported could have supplied such a sudden demand. With trade cut off, these fabrics started the first marked price advance of the war. By the beginning of 1776 even osnaburgs had doubled their normal prewar prices.

From occasional indirect references, one gets a hint of the keen interest in the cloth-making undertakings within the city. For example, a January 1776 item in Richard Smith's diary reads: "Dr. Franklin shewed me today a pattern paper containing 6 or 8 sorts of cloths lately manufactured at one or both of the company manufactories of Philadelphia."[49] Only two days later John Hart advertised a long list of textiles for sale for cash only.[50] More indicative of the future source of textile supplies was the significant entry in Smith's diary during the second week of January, "I bought some linnen from St. Eustatia at

[43] April 11, 1775, James and Drinker to Captain Edward Spain, sailing for Bristol.

[44] June 18, 1775, John Hancock to Elbridge Gerry, *Letters of Members of the Continental Congress*, v. 1, p. 135.

[45] July 19, 1775, *Journals of the Continental Congress*, v. 2, p. 190.

[46] September 21, 1775, *ibid.*, v. 3, p. 258.

[47] October 5, 1775, Reynell and Coates to Stephen Hooper, Newburyport.

[48] December 13, 1775, *Journals*, v. 3, p. 426.

[49] January 6, 1776, Richard Smith Diary, *Letters*, v. 1, p. 300.

[50] January 8, 1776, *Pennsylvania Packet*.

4 shillings per yard,"[51] a relatively high price for any grade of linen then on sale.

Calculations being made of the cost of home-manufactured linens assumed the cost of flax at 7 pence a pound, an annual use of 157 pounds of flax per spinner, and an annual product of 1096 yards of linen per weaver, which it was estimated would be worth 3 shillings per yard.[52] Four months later all estimates had to be revised and the wages for spinners advanced to 1 shilling per dozen skeins of linen yarn, a sum more nearly "equal to or sufficient for the maintenance of people so employed."[53]

A more speedy prospect was to purchase "some linens or other European manufactures," for which Willing and Morris were ready to be half concerned with Bingham in Martinique.[54] Yet the local manufactory was producing and offering its cloth. In June 1776, when "linens and jeans" were advertised "to be sold at the manufactory in Union Street," weavers were encouraged to apply at the factory, but an unexpected element of cost was making itself felt in the rise in the price of flax to 14 pence a pound[55] instead of the 7 pence taken as current in the February calculations.

The problem of procuring raw material, combined with that of keeping skilled workmen, soon led to a preference for small private undertakings rather than further public ones. In answer to an inquiry for a weaver, Joseph Hewes wrote in July:

> The manager of the linen manufactory in this city informs me that it is his opinion that small manufactories set up by private persons in their own families would be much more profitable both to the adventurers and to the community in general than large ones established by the public or by companies. He seems to be a sensible fellow and well acquainted with the business and I think his observations are very just. The more I converse with him on the subject the less inclination I feel to be concerned in any thing of the kind; so many people in these colonies are going into it, that I despair of getting a weaver for you on any terms. Those that are good for anything are chiefly

[51] January 10, 1776, Richard Smith Diary, *Letters,* v. 1, p. 306.
[52] February 24, 1776, *Pennsylvania Evening Post.*
[53] June 25, 1776, *ibid.*
[54] June 3, 1776, Willing and Morris to William Bingham, Martinique.
[55] July 4, 1776, *Pennsylvania Evening Post.*

engaged, and the Army and Navy pick up all the rascally artificers of every kind.[56]

Linen for making tents was so scarce in the city that the Marine Committee was directed to release all "the light sailcloth in their hands" for the use of the Clothier General.[57] A lack of many other fabrics may be inferred from the leeway given by Robert Morris to Bingham in the choice of textiles according to the season of their arrival. "If they can be shipped from France so as to be out with you in all the month of December and January we would wish nearly the whole amount to consist of woolen goods fit for winter wear, blankets, cloths, chiefly coarse coatings, flannels, worsted and yarn kerseys, some good silk stockings, threads, pins, needles, sewing silk, mohair, twist and buttons. But if they are to arrive later you must order an assortment of sailcloth, coarse and fine linens, sheetings, etc."[58] Among these goods, woolens were expected to "yield the greatest profit." Linens were "in full demand notwithstanding a most glorious crop of flax was gathered the last season, but we have not weavers and manufacturers to work it up fast enough."[58]

Before the British occupied the city, prices of tow cloth in continental money had doubled and osnaburgs nearly trebled their average prewar prices. Russian sheeting and ravens duck sold from four to five times their prewar average. As no series for woolens can be computed, the rise in prices can be established only indirectly. In March 1777, when Congress was buying woolens and coarse linens at auction, it paid one dollar in currency (7 shillings 6 pence) for what cost one shilling sterling. Irish linen that cost 2 shillings 8 pence per yard sterling sold for 24 shillings a yard currency. On the other hand, coarse linens, bought at 4 shillings 6 pence, were only a few pence above the price of tow cloth in the third quarter of 1776.[59]

Manufacturing in Maryland, encouraged by "large sums of the public money," was not answering the intended end because "some people have charged nearly as much for weaving, in particular, as cloth was worth

[56] July 24, 1776, Joseph Hewes to Samuel Johnston, *Pennsylvania Magazine*, 1919, v. 43, p. 263.

[57] September 4, 1776, *Journals*, v. 5, p. 735.

[58] September 14, 1776, Willing and Morris to William Bingham, Martinique.

[59] March 12, 1777, Francis Lewis, Baltimore, to the New York Convention, *Letters*, v. 2, p. 298.

when done."[60] At the Philadelphia manufactory, Samuel Wetherill had encountered such a rise in wool and workmanship that cloth promised to the Board of War for 20 shillings a yard "cannot now be made for less than 27 shillings 6 pence."[61] His problems multiplied in the next two months when he explained, "Some who had engaged to let me have wool at 7 shillings 6 pence per pound, now part with it with reluctance, and think they sold it too cheap; such are the extravagant ideas of some people; my spinners and weavers have double their wages, and labour in every branch nearly so, so that upon the whole cloth cannot be made but at an exceeding high price indeed."[62]

Some idea of the increase in fabric prices by November 1777 may be gained from the allowance of 8 shillings a yard for "good tow linen" by the Council of Safety for goods collected for the use of the army from the inhabitants who had aided the enemy or had failed to take the oath of allegiance.[63] Tow cloth, which never sold in the five prewar years above 2 shillings 6 pence a yard, reached 3 shillings 6 pence in specie in that month, from which it is clear that there was a price increase of about a shilling a yard and that the depreciation was close to 2⅓ for one.

During the British control of the city, the army purchasers had to seek linen of country manufacture. In April 1778 an informant at York wrote Colonel John Davis: "Coarse linen is scarce. All I have purchased has been taken from me as fast as I got it."[64] Some doubt about the price to be paid for it induced the definite statement, "I understood you did not exceed 10 shillings for coarse cloth."[65] Soon the York agent was able to relieve part of the needs of the army. He wrote: "I have just received a quantity of sail duck to make valises for to carry officers baggage. Please to send down all the sail-makers that is in Carlisle. Colonel Cox wants them made with the utmost expedition."[66] But there was no halt in the rise of the price of tow cloth. According to Colonel Davis,

60 April 1, 1777, *Maryland Journal and Baltimore Advertiser.*

61 May 16, 1777, Samuel Wetherill, Jr., to Board of War for Pennsylvania, *Pennsylvania Archives*, 1st ser., v. 5, p. 342.

62 June 5, 1777, *ibid.*, p. 355.

63 November 8, 1777, *Minutes of the Council of Safety of Pennsylvania, Colonial Records*, v. 11, p. 339.

64 April 16, 1778, W. Nichols, York, to Colonel John Davis, Deputy Quartermaster General, Carlisle.

65 April 20, 1778, Colonel David Grier to the same.

66 April 21, 1778, W. Nichols, York, to the same.

it was "much higher than I expected." Ten to 12 shillings had then to be paid for it at Carlisle.[67]

Dry goods in midsummer of 1778 were "very high" in Baltimore,[68] and in Philadelphia, according to Chaloner and White, had "become very precarious and differ very widely in their value: coarse linen, russia duck, dowlas, etc. are high. Fine goods not so, but on an average may be safely estimated one with the other from 12-1500 per cent on the sterling cost purchased as in the last importation from England,"[69] a rise not in excess of that of other articles.

Prices in 1779

Though no prices can be established for coarse linen except tow cloth, in January 1779 Russian linens and ravens duck were being advertised for sale.[70] Prices of dry goods, with trade routes "infested with the British privateers,"[71] were known to be "cheaper in Boston than any place on the continent, but the distance being great, considerable alterations might happen before they could be brought here."[72]

Toward the close of April 1779, a merchant, in sending out a prices current, reported "several arrivals from the West Indies and one large ship from France with wines, tea, salt and some dry goods." His list contained the information that dry goods were then 3000 per cent on sterling cost.[73] Prices of domestic cloths at this time are irreconcilable. For instance, one agent at York reported buying "a quantity of coarse tow cloth at 25 shillings per yard"[74] when it was very scarce and selling for 45 to 52 shillings per yard in Philadelphia. Instructions accordingly went out to "get all you can."[75]

In September, when merchants were purchasing fabrics in the Dutch islands, the price of homespun tow cloth in Doylestown was set at 37 shillings 6 pence, flax at 15 shillings a pound, and spinners' wages

[67] April 24, 1778, Colonel John Davis, Canidoguinet, to General Green.

[68] July 4, 1778, Jesse Hollingsworth, Baltimore, to Levi Hollingsworth.

[69] August 11, 1778, Chaloner and White to William Buchanan, Baltimore.

[70] January 2, 1779, *Pennsylvania Packet.*

[71] March 6, 1779, Chaloner and White to Colonel Jeremiah Wadsworth, Commissary General of Purchases.

[72] March 10, 1779, Matthew McConnell to Colonel John Davis, Carlisle.

[73] April 27, 1779, Kuhn and Kuhn to Benjamin Joy, Boston.

[74] May 11, 1779, William McClure, York County, to Colonel John Davis, Carlisle.

[75] May 16, 1779, Colonel John Mitchell, Deputy Quartermaster General, to the same.

at 15 times the 1774 rates.[76] Dry goods and a list of hardware were being advertised in November as "just imported in the last vessels from France."[77] Once imports could be obtained at less expense than home products, it was explained that the United Company of Philadelphia for Promoting American Manufactures "hath been some time dissolved and a final dividend settled."[78] The other cloth manufactory, directed by Samuel Wetherill, Jr., was still advertising "a variety of goods suited to every season of the year, viz., jeans, sagathies, everlastings, shalloons, coatings, etc." To reassure the home workers, the phrase "spinners employed as usual" was included in the publicity.[79]

Imports Relieve Shortage

Contemporaries believed, in the summer of 1780, that the urgent demand for fabrics had passed, as one may infer from such a comment as "Dry goods rather dull,"[80] and from the fact that osnaburgs, which sold for 150 shillings a yard in January, could be bought for 120 shillings by midsummer. If there was no urgency about civilian supplies, certainly a lack of sailcloth of all types remained. Before the war, ravens duck sold regularly for about 60 shillings a piece of some 25 yards. In August, Colonel John Mitchell reported enthusiastically, "This morning [I] have an offer of forty-five pieces of very good raven duck at £500 per piece."[81] If the quotation were adjusted for the 70 for one average depreciation of that time, the price would be a trifle more than two and a third times the prewar level. In the fall, Russian sheetings, low-priced linen handkerchiefs, and woolen hose were stressed among the goods ordered from St. Eustatius.[82]

Supplies of essential fabrics reaching St. Eustatius may have been affected by the failure of "one of the first mercantile houses in Amsterdam,"[83] but the rise in prices of imported goods in general was attributed

[76] September 14, 1779, *Pennsylvania Packet.*

[77] November 10, 1779, *Pennsylvania Journal and Weekly Advertiser.*

[78] January 18, 1780, *Pennsylvania Packet.*

[79] May 27 and July 20, 1780, *ibid.*

[80] July 20, 1780, Levi Hollingsworth to Marsden and Smith, Va.

[81] August 11, 1780, Colonel John Mitchell to Joseph Reed, President of the Supreme Executive Council of Pennsylvania, *Pennsylvania Archives,* 1st ser., v. 8, p. 501.

[82] September 19, 1780, Kuhn and Kuhn to William French, en route to St. Eustatius.

[83] October 30, 1780, *Gentleman's Magazine,* v. 50, p. 537.

to the landing of British troops in Virginia.[84] Hollingsworth was then reporting "all dry goods very high."[85] Osnaburgs, selling for 33 pence a yard in specie or about double prewar prices, were 1980 pence in continental currency. Russian duck was relatively higher despite the "bundles" of dry goods listed in the ships entered in this and the previous year.

About this time John Adams, writing from Amsterdam, encouraged the opening of direct trade between Russia and North America on the ground that "there is at present such a demand in America, especially in Philadelphia and Boston, for hemp and duck, etc., that they cannot be sent to any market upon earth that will give one half so much for them."[86] Prices in paper currency climbed steadily and Russian duck, which sold in August for £500 a piece, brought £750 in January 1781 and £1000 in the following month.

The capture of St. Eustatius on February 3, 1781, considering the role it played in trade, seemed a major loss to shippers. Curiously, Lord Shelbourne deplored its capture by the British. He believed that the surrender of Lord Cornwallis at Yorktown was due to the taking of St. Eustatius because "the stores that were found there, were purchased by those who sold them to the Americans, who could no[t] otherwise have been so well supplied."[87] As far as dry goods were involved, he might well have given thought to the leakage from New York, where a Scottish merchant found that "people knows goods so well here that if they are not laid in on the lowest terms, we can have no quick sales."[88]

The opposite opinion was held by Hollingsworth who, in the spring of 1781, found "all dry goods much higher than last fall,"[89] in part an illusion related to the fluctuating character of continental currency in the last month of its acceptance. Adams' correspondence reveals the origin of the ample dry goods which merchants' stocks confirm: "British Manufactures are going in vast quantities to America from Holland, the

[84] November 4, 1780, Levi Hollingsworth to Carter Braxton, Va.

[85] November 17, 1780, the same to Andrew Leiper, Richmond.

[86] December 6, 1780, John Adams, Amsterdam, to Stephen Sayre, St. Petersburg, *Correspondence of the Late President Adams*, p. 290.

[87] Minutes of what passed in Parliament on the first day of the second Parliament; *Gentleman's Magazine*, Supplement, 1781, v. 51, p. 607.

[88] February 17, 1781, Robert Henderson, New York, to Coventry and Henderson, Glasgow.

[89] March 2, 1781, Levi Hollingsworth to James Leatch, Lyons Creek.

Austrian Flanders, France and Sweden as well as by the way of New York and Charleston, etc. Whether it is possible to check it (this clandestine traffic) much less to put a stop to it, I know not; and whether it would be good policy to put an end to it, if that were practicable, is made a question by many."[90] Even before the capture of Yorktown, New York seemed to be "overstocked with every kind of goods,"[91] and "the very best English goods," according to Robert Henderson, "can be bought at what they cost at home," so many were "selling off their stock . . . at first cost."[92] Not satisfied that he had made the difficulties of sale fully clear, Henderson again reported from New York, "You can buy goods 15 per cent cheaper in this place at present than you can purchase them in England."[93] His impression of sales in the fall of 1781 tallied with that of Philadelphia merchants.

At the end of November 1781, Hollingsworth found that "all imported European goods are dull; all country produce in demand."[94] Two days later he reported "dry goods plenty and rather falling."[95] At the close of 1781 a mild advance in European goods was attributed by Josiah Hewes to the non-arrival of vessels from Holland in the fall, and by Hollingsworth to captures of some vessels and the diversion of shipping to ports safer than Philadelphia then was. In detail Hewes explained that European goods were "rather on the rise . . . owing to several vessels from France lately lost and some gone into other ports, and not one of the Gottenburg or Amsterdam vessels arrived."[96] Congress took this time to act upon the unauthorized trade in British goods by a resolution that "all merchandise of the growth or manufacture of Great Britain are forfeit after March 1 next."[97]

There is no indication of change in the prices of osnaburgs and tow cloth, though the scattered quotations in the summer of 1781 and the beginning of 1782 show a decline for Holland or Russian duck. Short-run fluctuations in 1782 were primarily attributable to risks of

[90] June 26, 1781, John Adams, Amsterdam, to Congress, *op. cit.*, p. 526.

[91] June 6, 1781, Robert Henderson, New York, to James Muir, Glasgow.

[92] August 14, 1781, the same to Alexander Glen, Glasgow.

[93] November 5, 1781, the same to Coventry and Henderson, Glasgow.

[94] November 26, 1781, Levi Hollingsworth to George Anderson, Richmond.

[95] November 28, 1781, the same to H. and T. Brown, Portsmouth, Va.

[96] December 24, 1781, Josiah Hewes to Aaron Lopez, *Commerce of Rhode Island, 1726-1800*, v. 2, p. 157.

[97] December 25, 1781, Levi Hollingsworth to James Boyce, St. Thomas.

shipping. In May, Pelatiah Webster wrote, "No certain news of anything, but the continual capture of our vessels . . . which must make imported articles of great consumption scarce here."[98] Calicoes, in June, brought the highest price that had "been obtained for any goods imported this spring."[99] Dry goods in September were still "rather on the rise."[100]

The "thundergust" of news of peace, according to Stephen Collins, was the force which "totally stunned trade for the present . . . I can assure you there now is no more sale for goods here than there is for Bibles and warming pans in the West Indies." In the picture he gave to his correspondent, he found "people that have got goods do little else at present than stare at each other."[101]

With rumors of peace, additional leakage of supplies from New York might be expected. British reports declared "the communication between New York and the country is now so open that boats from Philadelphia, Boston and the other provinces pass and repass with flags of truce, and buy and sell goods without molestation."[102]

Prices of dry goods eased until sheeting sold at 3 shillings a yard and merchants, anticipating as early as September 1782 that the departure of the British from New York would have "an amazing effect on the price of goods as great quantities will be left there,"[103] began to revise prices of fabrics and discourage their entry from other areas. Later, two brigs arrived "in our bay from France loaded with dry goods,"[104] and before the end of the year, sheetings were selling "for 2 shillings 6 pence a yard and they will not sell quick at that."[105]

Postwar Years

Since conditions in the closing months of the war and in early postwar years have often been described as chaotic, it is necessary to dwell upon the items of trade that gave rise to the impression. Actually, flour, iron, and, in some years, tobacco, rice, and other mainland products were in

[98] May 11, 1782, Pelatiah Webster to John Perit, Norwich, Conn.

[99] June 10, 1782, Chaloner and White to Oliver Phelps.

[100] September 17, 1782, Levi Hollingsworth to Thomas Ridgate, Port Tobacco, Va.

[101] August 14, 1782, Stephen Collins to Jenks and Forrester.

[102] September 11, 1782, *Gentleman's Magazine*, v. 52, p. 451.

[103] September 18, 1782, Stephen Collins to William Gray, Salem, Mass.

[104] September 25, 1782, the same to the same.

[105] December 3, 1782, the same to Jenks and Forrester.

demand at high prices. Dry goods felt the full impact of large unknown inventories in New York and Virginia, early ordering of goods from English merchants while peace negotiations dragged on, belated delivery of fabrics ordered on the continent during the war, and the influx of inexperienced merchants into mercantile pursuits once the hope of stable currency seemed to have been realized. In its over-all aspects, the situation was not unlike that experienced in 1771 to 1773 when heavy imports depressed the prices and sale of dry goods while domestic staples were rising. Dry goods merchants felt the slowness of sales even before the rumors of peace reached them.

By the summer of 1783 ravens duck was selling at prewar levels. Early that year, contemporaries in England reported "that very large orders had been sent to the manufacturing towns for goods to be sent to America."[106] In March 1783, definite inquiries went from Philadelphia to Pigou and Booth, John Roberts & Son, and Daniel Roberts in London; to Robert and Nathan Hyde Company in Manchester; to Lancelot Cowper in Bristol; and to merchants in Leeds and Liverpool as well as L'Orient in France.[107] The goods listed were requested "by the first opportunity."[108] Importers in April found "West India and European goods at present very unsettled in price."[109] As spring advanced, the need for caution found general expression. For instance, Robert Proud, in a letter to his brother in Hull, pointed out: "It is apprehended that divers adventurers here from Europe with merchandise the ensuing summer will be considerable losers as some have been already. I have lately seen some kinds of manufactures bought here lower than they could possibly be afforded where they were made, though the British and Irish are mostly preferred and pouring into this place in large quantities at present as well as from France, Holland, etc."[110] Not all agreed. Despite uncertainties, as cautious an importer as Clifford believed Bristol goods were much wanted.[111]

Henry Drinker, looking further ahead, deplored "a disposition for entering eagerly into business,"[112] which he anticipated might turn out

[106] February 28, 1783, Debates in House, *Gentleman's Magazine*, v. 53, p. 477.
[107] March 19, 1783, William Sitgreaves to Pigou and Booth, et al., London, etc.
[108] March 20, 1783, the same to Frederick Pigou, Jr., London.
[109] April 25, 1783, Chaloner and White to [Jeremiah Wadsworth].
[110] May 26, 1783, Robert Proud to William Proud, Hull.
[111] May 29, 1783, John Clifford to Thomas Clifford, Jr., Bristol.
[112] May 29, 1783, Henry Drinker to John Pemberton, Liverpool.

to be unprofitable. Such warnings were timely. By June, one of the earliest inquirers for imports found that "goods in general are very plenty, and about the old peace price, a hundred sail of vessels having arrived in the month of May, and more continually coming."[113]

Sailcloth, Russian duck, osnaburgs, and even domestic tow cloth declined in the last half of 1783 in an adjustment which was not unexpected. In giving full recognition to the public benefits of peace, Hazard wrote to Boston in June: "Our merchants will suffer much, for foreign speculators seem to shove them out of business, but goods are so low now (the market being overstocked) that trade will not answer their expectations. In a year's time it will become regular and our folks, I mean our old merchants, will come into play again. Till then, mushrooms will wither."[114] In the confused price movements of this year, some dry goods, notably Russian sheeting, continued "very dear,"[115] while others were uncommonly cheap. Caution and the balancing of orders such as characterized prewar trade was for a time abandoned. Stephen Collins wrote in much the same terms as Hazard: "The peculiar circumstances attending trade at this time and the amazing influx of goods from almost every part of the world, which I clearly foresaw would immediately follow the cessation of hostilities by numberless speculators in Europe under an idea of the country's being in great want of goods, when in fact, the country was full at the conclusion of the war. The arrival of vessels and goods here for two months past is beyond credibility. This will evidently cause an amazing stagnation and low ebb in trade for a while."[116] But the necessity for caution arose as much from lack of experienced merchants as from excess of supplies. Some of the old houses were "ruined" and others "standing aside." The opportunity for revival of the latter could come from the strong demand for flour at a time when crops were good, meat prices high, and farmer-buying likely to provide a market for well-selected imports, always assuming that the "foreigners" who were held to "have run the market down to nothing"[117] could be discouraged. Dutch cordage, ravens duck, and other well-assorted ship supplies were offered in many places.[118] By July,

[113] June 4, 1783, William and John Sitgreaves to William Little, Lebanon, Conn.

[114] June 13, 1783, Ebenezer Hazard to the Reverand John Eliot, Boston.

[115] June 14, 1783, Chaloner and White to Archibald Stewart, Hacketts Town.

[116] June 17, 1783, Stephen Collins to Harrison and Ansley, London.

[117] June 25, 1783, the same to John and John Brown, Boston.

[118] June 25, 1783, the same to Taylor and Rogers.

English sail cloth, "Scotch oznabrigs," and many good grades of cordage were selling below prewar levels.

It was a period when informed merchants kept warning, "We are constantly receiving quantities of goods from divers new channels never open to us before," or "Be careful in giving credit to the people here; their circumstances are greatly altered and many in trade have no principles." Already the artificers were "mortified at the great importation of ready made goods from the nations of Europe who greatly undersell them, and throw them out of their living." They proposed either an embargo on imports or such a "duty on the articles they make as will disable strangers from underselling them."[119]

What weight should be given to statements such as that of Robert Proud—"Trade is now very much in strange and new hands, mostly of strangers and adventurers, who have raised the rents of stores and houses higher than ever was in this place before, while many of the old hands refrain from a fear of consequences"[120]—it is difficult to say. As far-sighted a merchant as Peter Kuhn was using the new channels of direct trade as a means of diversifying his assortment of goods and filling a small unsatisfied demand for certain German manufactures in the farm areas of Pennsylvania[121] without neglecting the extension of his commercial connections in England.[122] It was to the withholding of discounts at the bank that he attributed the difficulties "which has in no small degree deranged us and [we] have solemnly protested against putting ourselves in future into their power as we will rather be content with one-half the business than be subject to so much anxiety."[123] He was not disappointed in his predictions about the strength of the market for goods in up-state areas and late in the month was able to increase his order to Bristol—"the demands from our friends in the country for supplies having exceeded our expectations."[124]

Flour, beef and pork, bar iron, and tobacco sold in 1784 at relatively high levels. Spices, tea, and other East India goods were high enough to surround the initiation of direct trade to Canton in China with a measure of optimism. Trade in other directions had at times such com-

119 July 14, 1783, Reynell and Coates to Thomas Rutter, Bristol.

120 October 16, 1783, Robert Proud to John Proud, London.

121 October 2, 1783, Kuhn and Risberg to Duncan Ingraham, Amsterdam.

122 October 19, 1783, the same to Cruger, Lediard and Mullet, Bristol.

123 November 18, 1783, the same to Jacob Kuhn.

124 November 30, 1783, the same to Cruger, Lediard and Mullet, Bristol.

pulsion as Cadwalader Morris noted when he wrote, "I must endeavor to bring up the losses of the last year of the war, which you know the merchants of Philadelphia were very sensible of and we were not without our share."[125] On the other hand, there was no assured market for textiles, for, though Russian sheetings were being shipped from Holland 8 or 12 shillings a piece lower than from London, they would not sell, "as many Flanders and Dutch linens come much better for the money."[126]

Effect of Heavy Inventories

Nor was the problem wholly a local one. Markets abroad showed signs of unsettlement. As a result, merchants were limiting their spring orders to Manchester and Bristol for fall delivery.[127] Still worse, it was known that as prominent a British merchant as "Jonathan Nesbitt had made such shipments of goods to this country just before the cessation of hostilities on account of his own house and others as have put him under embarrassments which he cannot surmount in a short time."[128]

Problems of payment were complicated by the high price of domestic staples, a high rate for bills of exchange, and a resulting export of specie. Problems of sale were in no way eased by the desire of foreign merchants to lighten their inventories of slow-moving merchandise or by their substitution of items other than those ordered. A typical protest, in August 1784, reads: "We are much surprised at the very frequent and great deviations from our order in the goods you sent us, both in kind and number—many omitted that were particularly wrote for and others shipped us that we did not mention a syllable of. . . . The muslin, crape lawn, French net and patent net, with a few of other kinds are entirely superfluous, and were not even named by us; exclusive of these exceptions, we must observe that they all appeared to be old shopkeepers, many of them having yellow stained edges, and all of them having lost their colors, therefore unmerchantable."[129]

All the difficulties of readjustment are evident in the complaints. Inexperienced merchants were being discouraged by failures, others

[125] January 5, 1784, Cadwalader Morris to William Bingham, *Letters*, v. 7, p. 408.

[126] January 27, 1784, Stephen Collins to Harrison, Ansley & Co., London.

[127] May 14, 1784, William and John Sitgreaves to Joseph Smith, Bristol; June 8, 1784, the same to Samuel Greg, Manchester.

[128] June 8, 1784, Robert Morris to Tench Tilghman, Baltimore.

[129] August 2, 1784, William and John Sitgreaves to William Stuart, Paisley.

were contracting their lines, and, as excess stocks were worked off, business seemed to be gravitating to more experienced hands. There were dangers for the future in the long terms of credit that accompanied the reduction in stocks. Awareness of these dangers led Kuhn to write to his suppliers, "From prudential motives and a desire to have our outstanding debts more collected, we have reduced our orders for the spring very considerably in order fully to discharge our present engagements before the time for our fall orders come round, which we hope to make more considerable."[130] Bills of exchange on London in October 1784 at "£176½ this money for £100 sterling"[131] would discourage payment of accounts—a concern on both sides of the Atlantic. Late in the fall, the precarious condition of trade was vividly stated by Kuhn, who wrote, "The late failures in England has put the American houses there in a very distressing situation and thereby occasioned pressing solicitations to their friends here for relief."[132]

Well-informed merchants were looking ahead, even at the risk of doing little immediate business. In this mood, Benjamin Fuller did not hesitate to write John Donaldson, then traveling in Ireland and England, "Trade of every kind is much overdone here, and I would advise your having little to do, in the purchase way, particularly *dry goods*—a year or two will bring forth, not wonders, for it requires no very great foresight to discover there must and will be many failures."[133] The same month, when failures were multiplying, Coates cited the case of Lazarus Barnet who owed "upwards of £30,000" when he was forced to close, adding, "We should suppose he was not entitled to a credit even of £500, for he was a stranger without any apparent property or respectable connection here to entitle him to credit; but having some address, he successfully claimed the attention of some inconsiderate people who are (some of them) injured and others are ruined by trusting him." In more general terms he deplored "the imprudence of some English merchants in sending large quantities of goods to unprincipled men here on credit who have immediately sent them to vendue to raise money [which] has more than anything else contributed to hurt the fair trader and in the end will prove of little benefit to themselves and

130 October 30, 1784, Kuhn and Risberg to Oxley and Hancock.

131 October 30, 1784, Robert Henderson to ———.

132 November 17, 1784, Kuhn and Risberg to Holmes and Kelso, Norfolk, England.

133 November 17, 1784, Benjamin Fuller to John Donaldson.

we live under the constant dread of paper money being made with an expectation of its depreciation at the same [time] it will be declared lawful tender in the payment of debts."[134]

Prices of textiles were lower in 1784 than in the next year and a half. There was little sale for linens, and even domestic tow cloth dropped as low as it sold for in the more generally depressed year of 1786.

Bills of exchange, which normally dropped in the fall months when merchants were exporting the produce of the country, held at high levels in 1784, to the disappointment of those who had delayed sending their remittances.[135] The explanation is found in the disparity in the prices of certain exportable commodities.[136]

Failures Accompany Recession

In the early phases of the developing depression, two Philadelphia houses—Reed and Forde and Clement Biddle—were known to be in financial difficulties.[137] Robert Morris felt that the state of commerce was as "bad as it well can be" when he reported the failure of Kenyon in Liverpool and the alarm of the British firm of Strahan and Company at the American failures.[138] More serious was the form which remittances had taken. To his partner in Baltimore, Morris wrote, "There has been such a cursed large shipment of money by a brigantine just gone for London that the managers of the Bank are grown sore and seem inclined to stop discounts."[139] The stoppage of discounts in Boston, New York, and Philadelphia was expected to have an adverse effect upon the price of domestic commodities, in no way eased by the opposition of the country members of the Assembly to the Bank itself.[140]

[134] November 29, 1784, Josiah and Samuel Coates to Thomas Rutter, Bristol.

[135] January 1, 1785, Edmond Physick to Lord Dartney, London.

[136] Contrary to the usual relation, the price of superfine flour, for a time, was so near to common flour that it was shipped to New England to fill orders for ordinary grades. As soon as demand from Lisbon and other parts of southern Europe developed, a differential between the two grades reappeared. Early in 1785, a New England correspondent received no superfine in his shipment because "the common [flour] now is only 39 shillings 2 pence and superfine cannot be had good under 48 shillings 3 pence per barrel—before there was only 2 shillings or 2 shillings 6 pence per barrel difference," a sure indication of an active export market. February 22, 1785, Josiah and Samuel Coates to William Teel, Newburyport.

[137] March 2, 1785, Christopher Marshall Diary.

[138] March 28, 1785, Robert Morris to Tench Tilghman, Baltimore.

[139] March 22, 1785, the same to the same.

[140] March 25, 1785, Josiah and Samuel Coates to Benjamin Ellery.

Among other matters plaguing the traders was an action of the Pennsylvania Assembly to emit £150,000 in paper money, which would "induce those who are possessed of a little specie to keep it carefully in their own pockets."[141]

Merchants had taken lower prices for textiles previously than they complained of in this second year of peace, but then the laws were not so favorable to debtors, exchange was not as high as £180 for £100 sterling, nor were a multiplicity of other factors so variable. The type of uncertainties were described by the far-sighted merchant house of Josiah and Samuel Coates, in June 1785:

> Our new paper emission is just coming into circulation; some depreciation has already taken place which as an opinion is like to continue. Large quantities of goods are yet on hand but not so much imported as the last year. . . . The rigorous execution of your Navigation Act, the exclusive benefits you allow your remaining colonies in America, the few privileges of other foreigners, or, rather, let us say their interdictions, added to the dread of the Algerian cruisers, do grievously operate to ruin our trade. Unless we can open a commercial intercourse with European nations and exchange our staples for their produce and manufactures we are like to remain poor.[142]

Other merchant houses were developing such connections as they could with the continent. To this end Peter Kuhn and his partner, trading to Sweden, listed the sizes and types of iron and copper products they could use and other goods, especially "good Russian hemp," which might be included in a cargo. Among these "Russian sheeting, ravens duck and drilling would answer well." Payment would have to be "remitted to your correspondent in London as no bills can be had direct on Sweden."[143]

Trade with New England figured prominently in the activity of Philadelphia merchants. Coates regularly informed Caldwell Fletcher & Co., William Teel, William Bartlett, and William Wyer, all of Newburyport, Moses Brown of Providence, and Samuel Souther of Haverhill, of the prices current of a long list of items important in their trade. That a way had been found to circumvent some of the "exclusive benefits" to the areas still belonging to the British may be inferred from their

141 April 11, 1785, Edmond Physick to [Robert] Bremner.

142 June 4, 1785, Josiah and Samuel Coates to Thomas Rutter, Bristol.

143 September 16, 1785, Kuhn and Risberg to Schon & Co., Sweden.

question to Moses Brown, "What signifies your heavy impost law if British goods are so easily smuggled from Nova Scotia?"[144]

Despite the existence of a good market for wheat in Lisbon and Barcelona at the beginning of 1786,[145] cautious exporters were anticipating that "the scarcity of money will become much greater."[146] The evidence of strain appeared in a shift from wholesaling to retailing with the hope of payment in cash or, at least, barter, the closing of some of the outlets that Philadelphia merchants had opened in the tobacco areas, a drop in the market for pine lumber and later for staves, a search for outlets for iron products, and a diffusion of merchants' dealings into unaccustomed directions in which extension of credit could be avoided. All were signs of deepening depression or, as Henry Drinker phrased it, "the face of things have rapidly and progressively changed from bad to worse."[147] Dry goods were less affected in this decline than were more perishable items, but English shippers were out of touch with the change in fashion that had come from the use of continental fabrics. Cambrics and Irish sheeting were coming in not only high priced but "uncommonly narrow." Muslins were "not fine enough for the market; inferior kinds will not do."[148]

Signs of Recovery in Mid-'87

Prices of dry goods held in 1787, and the tone of the last part of the year was distinctly more cheerful than at its start. In April, Levi Hollingsworth, ordering Russian hemp, noted, "Business in general is dull here though I have not cause to complain."[149] A merchant aware of the Pennsylvania duty on linen goods advised his Manchester shipper "to term the whole *Cotton* in your invoice, and those really so also upon each piece—leaving the linen goods unmarked—as the latter kind pay a double duty at our custom house which is ascertained by the invoice."[150]

A turn in the market appeared in commitments as well as in sentiment. Pelatiah Webster, ordering goods from France, admitted: "Though

[144] December 31, 1785, Josiah and Samuel Coates to Moses Brown, Providence.
[145] January 3, 1786, Robert Morris to Tench Tilghman & Co., Baltimore.
[146] April 2, 1786, Kuhn and Risberg to William Taylor & Co., Alexandria.
[147] April 5, 1786, Henry Drinker to Dorcas Montgomery, Paris.
[148] October 31, 1786, William and John Sitgreaves to Harrison, Ansley & Co., London.
[149] April 14, 1787, Levi Hollingsworth to Murray and Sansom, New York.
[150] April 20, 1787, William and John Sitgreaves to Charles Wood & Co., Manchester.

the European trade has been greatly overdone in America, yet the goods grow scarce here. (You know the effect of the greatest glut is to produce a scarcity in time.) . . . every article should be good in its kind for there is not a worse market on earth for bad goods than this."[151] Encouraged by the accomplishments of the Convention which had been meeting in the city for the purpose of framing a federal constitution, Benjamin Fuller, who had refrained from dealing in dry goods in the early postwar years, decided to re-enter the lines he had followed in colonial time. By November he was ready to order "Lang's" linens and "any kind of coarse tow stuff" from Ireland.[152] A month later he was "desirous of knowing every article which can be introduced into your Island from this country."[153]

Though fluctuations in rates of sterling exchange can never be directly related to the trade in British goods, the height of the rates on London was a matter of concern throughout the early postwar years. Bills on London, which kept close to the par of £166⅔ Pennsylvania for £100 sterling in the first eight months of 1783, rose to £173 in September and increased in the ensuing months. Between January 1785 and June 1788, exchange on London was below 175 only in two spring months. Though the rate of appreciation of Pennsylvania currency was gradual from August 1788 to December 1789, sterling exchange varied only from 170 to 172½ and finally dropped to par or below in the first half of the following year.[154] This lower level of exchange in the middle of 1788 improved the conditions under which textiles could be imported.

Though selective for types of goods, the tone of comment in 1788 was not all "dull." "Russian duck," Levi Hollingsworth commented, "will sell readily at 85 to 90 shillings per piece, if of the best quality"[155] —a condition that was less likely after the spring shipping brought quantities of sail cloth from England and Holland and some Russian duck. A surprising trade in domestic goods grew up with New England, which is notable mainly because it was formerly a specialty of the Pennsylvania countryside. When produce was dull "some pretty good tow cloth" sent from New England, "charged at 1 shilling lawful money

[151] May 21, 1787, Pelatiah Webster to Nathaniel Barret, Paris.
[152] November 15, 1787, Benjamin Fuller to Doyle and Rowe, Dublin.
[153] December 1, 1787, the same to the same.
[154] For rates of sterling exchange 1780-1790 see Appendix Table 6.
[155] March 29, 1788, Levi Hollingsworth to Solomon Townsend, New York.

[of Rhode Island] . . . sold . . . to a good profit. Some of that article at that price we think would answer."[156] It was then selling at 18 pence and "some at 20 pence per yard."[157] Trade with Great Britain was bedeviled by the uncertainty of the regulations as to what could be exported "not of the growth of the United States"[158] and under what ownership of vessels.

Levi Hollingsworth, who had already pointed out that America was not in the state of confusion that Europeans assumed, felt early in 1788 that the "commerce of this city seems to revive a little this spring,"[159] stimulated by the "large shipments of wheat to Lisbon and flour to Spain"[160] which brought with them the logical consequence of a decline in the rate of exchange.

New England tow cloth in 1788 was selling only slightly lower than in the year before, but it was unbleached and narrower than was preferred. The instructions then were: "Try to get some of your tow cloth whitened and if you can get it wove 1 yard and ⅛ wide 'tis best for sheets. Some of the yard wide may do."[161] The great differences in the quality of New England tow cloth were frequently complained of to Moses Brown and other shippers. The interchange of domestic manufactured goods at this time was felt to be significant by contemporaries. A general statement covering conditions in the United States sent to England by Thomas Clifford particularly stressed the extent of linen manufacture in New York and New Jersey,[162] but the width specifications still troubled Philadelphia merchants.[163]

Along with the development of a strong market for the sale of domestic fabrics came a renewed interest in the sale of imported dry goods. The Philadelphia market was poorly supplied with woolens when Peter Kuhn wrote, "We do not believe that in *this* city there are 12 pieces coatings for sale and almost *all* woolens equally scarce; the demand has been so great on account of the small importations that the chief sales have been made *for cash.*"[164]

156 March 29, 1788, Josiah and Samuel Coates to William Bartlett, Newburyport.

157 March 29, 1788, the same to Jonathan Gage.

158 April 18, 1788, Benjamin Fuller to Warder, Dearman & Co., London.

159 April 21, 1788, Levi Hollingsworth to Mark Pragers, London.

160 May 20, 1788, James and John Cox to Charles Hagart, St. Thomas.

161 June 2, 1788, Josiah and Samuel Coates to John Osgood.

162 August 1, 1788, Thomas Clifford, Jr., New York, to his wife in England.

163 August 8, 1788, Josiah and Samuel Coates to Moses Brown, Providence.

164 November 17, 1788, Kuhn and Risberg to William French & Co., Fredericksburg.

With the market bare of carried-over goods and an active demand in France, Spain, and Portugal for wheat and its products, the heavy imports of 1789 were not likely to derange the market. Exchange, which had been declining, reached par before the year ended. The uncertainties of the amount of imposts to be laid by Congress and the possibility of a duty on foreign bottoms, which would be less advantageous to the southern than to the northern and middle states, speeded shipping.[165] When the duties were finally announced, some were lower than had been expected. Textile duties were not so regarded, but could they be minimized by shipping practices? In September 1789, Benjamin Fuller disclosed a possible method to his London supplier when he wrote:

> Our new government has fixed on a permanent revenue which will be collected with strictness. On prints it will be 5 per cent on the invoiced price with an addition thereto of 10 per cent, which sum will be made currency at 66⅔ per cent and then the 5 per cent paid on said sum. Formerly it was on the sum the goods sold for here. This will make a very considerable difference in the duty, as the prints will not bring near one-half the invoiced price, but should you incline to pursue this business with Mr. Hubley, I would recommend your sending him with the goods a bill of lading and invoice rated at about *one-third* what you usually rate them at. He will enter them accordingly. By these means they will pay but a duty of about 5 per cent on what they will net here which is, in my opinion, about what the general run of goods will pay. The genuine invoice you may forward to me without mentioning anything of the affair to Mr. Hubley.[166]

Henderson, with his usually pessimistic outlook, expected an extreme inflow of goods which would make them "as plenty here as they were in [the] fall [of] '84—a very great importation both here and at New York."[167] But he failed to give due weight to the basic difference in underlying conditions and to the resourcefulness of the experienced group who had gained confidence in the future of the dry goods trade.

In prewar years, the difficulty of estimating the amount and kind of fabrics necessary to keep in stock for community demand was maximized by interruptions to shipping and nonimportation measures. Surpluses then were marketed normally in other colonial mainland ports. During the extraordinary demand of the war, notably for linens, even domestic

[165] April 22, 1789, Josiah and Samuel Coates to Stephen Hooper, Newburyport.
[166] September 19, 1789, Benjamin Fuller to John Boydell, London.
[167] October 7, 1789, Robert Henderson to David Lamb, Charleston.

manufacture was hampered by years of light crops of flax and continuous shortage of domestic raw wool. The acuteness of these shortages and the devious methods evolved for procuring British-made textiles, especially woolens, account for the speedy return after the war to the British market and trading in dry goods. As in colonial years, some of the excess might have been relieved by clearing surpluses to other mainland ports, but some of the states were placing tariffs on goods which were not the growth or manufacture of the area shipping it. Besides, the awareness of dependence upon other countries for staples of clothing had awakened all states to their need for developing manufactures of their own.

CHAPTER XVIII

COMMUNITY ADJUSTMENTS TO INFLATION

CONTEMPORARY OPINION, cited throughout the discussion of commodities, gives many a hint of the way various sectors of the economy adjusted to meet the impact of inflation or to participate in the efforts to revive trade after the peace. During the war, the merchants' opinions, often limited to dealings in particular commodities, give a clue to the way channels were kept open for the flow of goods from the different parts of the continent. The commissaries' opinions often reveal the point of view of farmers as well as the impediments to assembling supplies for the army—some connected with difficulties of procurement, some with problems of transportation. The letters of delegates to Congress at times provide an over-all view of the efforts made by public authorities to cope with inflation and, at times, reveal the measures statesmen were devising to meet practical difficulties.

The adjustment of less articulate groups must be inferred from many small happenings in a period in which a succession of swift price movements was continually changing the relation of sectors of the economy to each other. In the inflationary period there was no long-term price policy, no control over profits, and no general procedure for wage adjustment. To be sure, there were experiments in controlling prices, in allocating scarce items, in unfreezing stocks of goods, and in limiting shipments. Even these were piecemeal measures, invoked to meet immediate practical difficulties. On the other hand, a considerable part of the community was largely self-sufficient and the rest engaged in mercantile or artisan pursuits with marked ability to effect adjustments.

The striking characteristic of the period is the way in which individuals assumed leadership and the amount of independent action that could be taken by local groups. This initiative, often crucial in the conduct of the war, gave opportunities for speculation and often the means by which some of the risks of inflation were minimized and part of its costs diffused among groups in the community.

If one looks upon the prices of individual commodities as symptomatic of the way the war affected sectors of the economy, it can be said that no one group held an advantage throughout the period. All searched for means of shifting part of the impact of inflation. Just as merchants resorted to accounting formulae to relate paper currency prices to specie prices, so other groups, to adjust to the mounting inflation, adopted measures of which some had a temporary effect while others created problems for postwar readjustment. The captains and seamen who suffered from unemployment in the early stages of the war, as they had in the nonimportation periods which preceded it, found a way of supplementing their compensation when shipping was open by insisting that all articles they carried be consigned to them or they would "not go the voyages."[1] Thereby they started a practice which plagued Philadelphia trade long after the war and delayed a prompt revival of the prewar marketing organization with its dependence, especially in the flour trade, upon agents resident in the trading areas. While the war lasted, the departure from a means of providing regular agents with an inducement to assemble materials for a return cargo may have been only a minor disadvantage, since the connections in the British islands were broken anyway, and those exporting staples in order to bring back military supplies met no problem in procuring such a return cargo. It proved to be a signal handicap after the war, when all countries were searching for export markets.

Like merchants, some sea captains in various parts of the continent turned to purchases of tangible goods when continental money accumulated in their hands. One Remembrance Simmons of Newport, in the spring of 1778, sent £194 "conti" to be invested by a Philadelphia merchant for him. The possible avenues for such investment being limited to land, joint shares in vessels, and a few nonperishable articles, the merchant thought he "did for the best" by investing in hard dollars, though a similar remittance from a merchant was used to purchase bar iron "which remains in my hands."[2]

Adjustments in workers' income were not all made in terms of goods. As prices rose, part of the accommodation took the form of piecemeal wage increases. In October 1776 the Council of Safety had to grant pilots, "in addition to their pay from the state . . . 5 shillings per foot

[1] September 14, 1776, Willing and Morris to William Bingham, Martinique.

[2] April 1778, Joseph Anthony Ledger A.

for every vessel" they conducted to and from Chester.[3] As journeymen in rural areas were absorbed in war activities, wages were often raised in conformity with past practice by taking account of the advance in the prices of grain and its products. The evidence contained in petitions of wagoners, butchers, gunsmiths, carpenters, coopers, and even seamen, along with the fact that grain prices were sluggish in the first phases of inflation, is sufficient indication that only those who found multiple employment, as many did, received allowances in conformity with the rise in price level. Had adjustments been general or continued on the basis of previous customs, the lag in time would have been overcome, but citizens and officials confronted with unprecedented price changes could not well be expected to think in anything but immediate terms. In fact, many of the problems could scarcely have been met on a long-term basis.

The critical problem of procuring wagoners may be cited as one of the most serious bottlenecks of the war. Payment for wagon service in New Jersey was put on a contract basis which varied according to the supplementary allowances permitted in the way of supplies, forage, clothing, repairs, and other expenses. Pennsylvania, after a series of early experiences, set a price of £4 10 shillings a day in September 1778, which was increased by 10 shillings in July of the next year. The following October, after commodity prices had increased at least tenfold over prewar, the wagoners' rate had to be reconsidered. It was known then that the price "between man and man" had reached £25 a day. A committee on behalf of the state, disregarding both the prevailing private rate and the New Jersey contract arrangements, arrived at £12 a day, which it hoped would be "fully satisfactory and produce the desired number of teams."[4]

If the work of teamsters is looked upon as their sole employment, then the compromise took account of only part of the increased costs of providing transportation. If it is looked upon as a supplementary source of income for farmers who had to maintain teams, the compromise may be said to illustrate the way in which part of the cost of inflation was being distributed among various groups in the community.

Supplementary payments in kind, such as New Jersey made to wagoners, were common in colonial years. Their use was expanded in war

[3] October 8, 1776, *Minutes of the Council of Safety, Colonial Records*, v. 10, p. 745.

[4] October 15, 1779, Joseph Reed, President of the Supreme Executive Council of Pennsylvania, to Jenifer and Root, *Pennsylvania Archives*, 1st ser., v. 7, p. 750.

years. They took many forms, from rations of rum to full subsistence rations for shipbuilders and many others. As the war progressed, scarce items, such as bacon, molasses, or sugar, often could be used as inducements to keep a force of workers. The initiative in procuring these concessions was more often taken by a contractor or the operator of a manufacturing establishment than by the workers. These "fringe" payments in kind interfere with the compilation of any quantitative series of wages. An illustration of the combination of increase in wage rates and minor concessions in kind may be cited from the experience of a contractor who was having difficulty in filling his agreement to pack meat for the army. At the start of his contract, he explained, "I got laborers for 6 shillings per day. Now I must give from 20 shillings to 3 dollars [22 shillings 6 pence] at that work, besides the cooper that is to pack." The difficulty was finally adjusted by his agreeing to pack the rest of the pork, "You finding me 6 rations of rum for my laborers each day."[5] In other cases, the manager of an iron works might inform the owner or even the Board of War that unless he was provided with a barrel of sugar he would be forced to close down the furnace. Even the quartermasters found payment in kind useful in purchasing supplies. In the autumn of 1779, Jeremiah Wadsworth, Commissary General of Purchases, was supplied with sugar to use as an inducement "to enable you to fulfill your engagements for flour."[6] Salt was widely used in the same way and was preferred even to payment in specie.

Craftsmen, who enjoyed a measure of prosperity during the war, could hedge against a small part of the rise by purchasing some of their raw material in advance. Such foresight was limited both by their small capital and by the quantity of the raw material for sale. They were less likely to be charged with "engrossing" than were the merchants who were in a position to hold goods for future sale. But complaints of engrossing were made against many groups, especially in periods when shortages developed. Even the corders and carters of wood to the public market were charged with engrossing the wood "so as to accumulate the price."[7]

Had the impact of inflation upon prices of commodities been uniform,

[5] October 17, 1778, Joseph Cowperthwaite to Chaloner and White.

[6] October 6, 1779, Committee of Congress to Colonel Jeremiah Wadsworth, Commissary General of Purchases, *Letters of Members of the Continental Congress*, v. 4, p. 475.

[7] December 4, 1779, *Minutes of the Supreme Executive Council*, *C.R.*, v. 12, p. 190.

fewer compensatory devices would have been tried. Had wage adjustments been guided by any general policy, the problem of estimating costs in a period when price policy was closely related to costs would have been eased. As it was, the price of one article provided no guide to the level of another. The unevenness of the inflationary rise was characteristic of all regions. For instance, in February 1778, Samuel Ogden of New Jersey, in his calculations of the cost of slitting iron, found that though coal cost "six times as much as formerly, carting hath cost me eight times as much, my workmen's wages about five times as much, provisions about four times, rum about twenty times as much as formerly."[8]

Many similar illustrations of the disparities created by the inflationary rise may be found in the comparisons of contemporaries who frequently cited prices of "former times" with those prevailing at some later date. Six months after Ogden made his careful estimates of the impact of the war upon the cost of slitting iron, the clerk of the Radnor Meeting found that saddles had increased fivefold, leather breeches nearly tenfold, blankets threefold, and cloth by the yard less than twofold. The particular comparisons, or even the extent of the rise in the price level, are less important than the clue they give to the way inflation was probably changing the relative status of groups in the community. Some of the disparities were the result of scarcities, some of dependence upon distant instead of local supply, some of methods of marketing or a slowness of the functioning of the market machinery, and some of the sheer desirability of some commodities for immediate use.

All groups resorted, at times, to barter on one basis or another. In some direct exchanges of commodity for commodity, an arbitrary price of one item seems to have been set to determine the quantity of it to be exchanged for another. Strangely, no one commodity became the yardstick for these measurements as bar iron did for a time in Maryland. A quantity of bar iron, when exchanged in Philadelphia in the spring of 1779 for 8¾ bushels of wheat, was valued at £40 to £50 a ton. A similar exchange of rye for iron was made by rating the iron at £50 a ton. The barter of butter for sole leather or sole leather for shoes rested upon an agreement on the price of the sole leather at the time of the exchange. But these and many others which might be cited are not the typical form of commodity exchange developed by the inflation of the Revolutionary

[8] February 4, 1778, Samuel Ogden, Boonton, N. J., to Robert Morris.

period. Nor would such exchanges have met the needs of a metropolis with a high proportion of its 30,000 inhabitants engaged in mercantile pursuits, serving a large agricultural area, with more to sell than they needed to buy.

The First Continental Congress, in its effort to avoid a general mark-up of prices once the ports were closed to foreign trade, had really set up the belief that the relation between the prices of different commodities and even the wages of various occupations which prevailed in 1774 was the desirable standard to be maintained. As the individual prices fanned out and the former relation of prices became hopelessly distorted, all groups tended to hark back to the prewar basis, finding in some cases by its use a means of living and transacting business outside the pecuniary system. One of the complications in determining the prevailing prices in early phases of the inflationary period grows out of these private arrangements for stabilizing prices at customary levels. The bases for these contracts were the wages and prices in the period preceding the war, always referred to as the "rate they used to be." The start of such dealings can scarcely be dated, since in the early stages of inflation prices differed only slightly whether stated in specie, continental or state money, or determined by agreement. Substantial illustrations of the use of the practice throughout the whole war have been preserved in the records of a community group living outside the city limits and maintaining farms and workshops. The accounts of Thomas Evans, a dealer in leather, may be taken as typical of the method of paying for work and exchanging with other workshops on the basis for which leather sold before the war, in return for wages and commodities at the prewar rate. Thus, throughout the inflationary period, the payment for a day's mowing was 2 shillings 6 pence, except for an entry here and there when some particularly hard assignment was stepped up a shilling or more. Cider, butter, and staple grains were exchanged at the old rate, just as the weaving of cloth—both cotton and linen—was paid for "all at old price." Settlements with workmen who did ploughing, mowing, and other farm and shop chores were rarely for large balances.

The importance of such transactions is that they furnish an illustration of the devices by which neighborhood groups carried on, through an inflation that would have bankrupted a modern economy, without much dependence upon paper money or specie and without any substantial purchases of imported items except salt. Obviously, in these nonpecuniary dealings no advantage was taken of the opportunity to profit by the high prices of farm produce nor was note taken of changes in the rate of wages that were doubling and trebling in other parts of the community. It is important, however, that such arrangements prevented the normal flow of goods to market and kept up the demand for some scarce commodities by permitting consumers to continue their normal use.

Similar use of the level of prices prevailing before the war can be found in many adjustments of the period made by Congress, by landlords in rental arrangements, and even between states in the determination of the cost of specific supplies. No such devices would have taken care of a large part of the agricultural population with surplus grain to dispose of. Though they had profited from high prices in the early 70's, they were subjected to a declining price level from 1774 to the last quarter of 1776, and their products lagged behind others in the rise until the middle of 1778. Thus other groups enjoyed some advantage from the delayed rise in farm products in the early phases of inflation. For instance, in the months of export for defense, the small number of shippers licensed to trade domestic staples for ammunition gained by the decline in the price of grain. Consumers of breadstuffs and dealers in it, when prices of grain were responding slowly to the upswing in other parts of the economy, had an advantage which farmers could offset only insofar as they could profit from the active market for derivative farm products such as beef, pork, and butter, forgo the use of imported commodities, which were out of line with their products, or follow subsidiary employments such as lumbering, teaming, road repair, and many others which the war opened.

From the level of prices, there is no reason to think that farmers were in a disadvantageous position in the last half of the war. All contemporary opinion confirms the belief that the discrepancy between groups narrowed as the war progressed. The complaint of the farmer in this period arose from payment in quartermaster certificates or in the currency which he could neither afford to keep nor spend advantageously.

CHAPTER XIX

CONCLUSIONS

THE PRIMARY AIM of this detailed study of the eventful transition years from 1770 to 1790 is to make generally available a continuous record of prices for a period hitherto neglected. It will have served its main function if it aids in viewing the evolution of the era as a connected whole.

Merchants' comments, used throughout the study as a check upon the typical character of the data drawn from, at most, a limited number of accounts, reveal many of the short-run factors affecting the supply and interchange of goods as seen by those who lived through these stirring events, often as active participants. Prices, in a period of extreme inflation, however verified, would provide only a dramatic record of limited analytical use if a basis had not been found for comparing the movement of prices during the period of inflationary rise with those before and after it. For this purpose, the purchasing power of competing currencies in use in local trade had to be studied in exasperating detail. Specie, valued before the war as a means of payment for essential imports or as a substitute for bills of exchange in foreign remittances, early in the inflation went to a premium and later became the surest means of drawing out scarce resources.

Besides the difference in the amount, source, and worth of the currency media in circulation, the twenty-one years included in this study span three periods which differ vastly in mercantile organization, in areas of trade, and in occasions for interchange of products with other parts of the mainland. Most obvious of the differences in a study oriented around prices is the contrast of the periods in the uncertainties faced by producers and all those performing the function of finding markets for the expanding surplus of the region or anticipating the demand for a diversity of imported essential and luxury products.

Uncertainties, always attendant upon the importation of goods in an era when communication was slow, were multiplied by purchase on long terms of credit. In colonial years, fluctuations in the amount paid for bills of exchange were severe enough to keep merchants continually alert to the difference in the value of money between the time of contracting and paying a debt. These considerations were inherent in any form of external trade. Within the colony, the local issues of paper money could be anticipated and their short-term impact on prices foreseen, though a persistently rising secular trend in late colonial years may indicate that their effect was cumulative.

In local trade before the war, Pennsylvania bills of credit passed on a par with specie. In all dealings between colonies, calculations had to be made for the different ratings given to the Spanish milled dollar in each,[1] but these were primarily accounting procedures in which no change was made by the issue of congressional currency that passed freely among them.

During the war years, the changing value of money warped all aspects of local trade. Part of the uncertainties stemmed from the circulation of two and, at times, three currencies side by side. Even within a region, the value of money could not for long be taken for granted, to say nothing of the difference in timing and extent of variations between localities. It is true that before its recall, commonwealth paper of Pennsylvania, though hoarded by pacifist groups and exchanged in rare cases at a premium over continental money, normally passed on a parity with continental. Certainly no persistent differential can be found in merchants' accounts and, if tendered in payments, both were accepted on the same basis. But a particularly acute problem in values arose from the circulation of dual currencies—specie and paper—the one at a substantial and increasing premium over the other.

A preference for specie complicated all wartime bargaining. That a considerable amount of hard money was on hand at the time war started and was later carefully hoarded can be inferred from the conflict over its use in lieu of the old paper of the colony within the city during the British occupation—a difference which was compromised by another dual currency arrangement between commonwealth paper and sterling (the one at its old rating of 7 shillings 6 pence to the dollar, the other at its British rating).

Occasional reliance upon specie in making contracts throughout the

[1] On the basis of those ratings, prices in Pennsylvania, New Jersey, Maryland, and Delaware were 25 per cent above those in New England and Virginia; and 6.25 per cent below New York and North Carolina.

whole period has been made clear in the correspondence cited in detailed sections of this study. Its regular, though guarded, use by certain merchants is evident in ledgers and in the cash transactions assembled for the specie and commodity ratios given in Chapter IV. Besides, when shipping was open, small quantities of specie reached the port with most incoming vessels, as often in the hands of seamen as in the balances of captains and merchants. As the war spread, hard money, disbursed in the proximity of the British army and later for some of the supplies of the French fleet and army, reached the farm areas as it occasionally did at other times for the purchase of especially scarce items. The persistent collection of some rentals in specie is a phase of the economy of the period as yet too unexplored. At any rate, Girard's purchase of his house at Mt. Holly and the regular payment of the rental of his store in specie can be matched by many other instances in which the prewar level of prices persisted if payment could be made in specie or its equivalent in goods.

The possibility of depreciation because of the addition of continental paper to the already expanded state issues was early foreseen. Even before the "congress bills" went into general circulation, the danger of inflation and the need for supporting the continental credit was anticipated in Congress.[2] Merchants were more prone than others to apprehend the likely effect of a marked increase in the money of account. In 1775 some merchants, especially those changing to new lines of activity, called in such payments on past indebtedness as they could before the significance of the protection thus gained for themselves could have been wholly foreseen or fully understood. Besides, though the stoppage of trade in 1775 greatly interfered with the usual sources upon which merchants depended for their supply of sterling bills, the rate of exchange was watched throughout 1776 as in the past. Whatever conclusions were drawn from the comparisons of sterling equivalents, it is certain that from 1776 to 1790 the value of money was seldom absent from the mind of anyone, whether grower, merchant, or consumer, and was the dominant consideration of all citizens from 1776 to 1781. The fantastic prices of the period of extreme inflation may be summarized

[2] An illustration is contained in the comment, "The Mississippi scheme, in France, and the South Sea scheme, in England, were written for our learning." October 12, 1775, *Journals of the Continental Congress*, v. 3, p. 491.

in terms of the shrinking value of currency in the purchase of certain staple commodities, free from the influence of price relations in the base period, by the amount of each that could be purchased with £100 in April of each year.

TABLE 7

QUANTITY OF CERTAIN STAPLES THAT COULD BE PURCHASED FOR £100 IN PAPER CURRENCY

April	Flour cwt.	Sugar cwt.	Iron cwt.	Beef bbl.
1774	105.9	36.4	76.9	36.4
1775	133.3	39.5	77.9	33.3
1776	143.3	30.8	74.8	26.7
1777	83.8	8.89	40.0	10.5
1778	63.2	2.75	11.8	9.78
1779	6.67	0.84	2.65	1.82
1780	1.15	0.30	0.88	0.22
1781	0.71	0.21	0.52	0.11

cwt. = 112 lbs.; bbl. = 225 lbs.

As a result of all factors involved in pulling prices upward, it is clear that an amount of £100 which in April 1776 would buy 143 hundredweight of flour, or 31 hundredweight of sugar, or 75 hundredweight of iron, or 54 hundredweight of beef, would purchase in the same month five years later only 80 pounds of flour, or 24 pounds of sugar, or 58 pounds of iron, or less than 25 pounds of beef. Nor had the effect upon prices of commodities been uniform in extent or synchronous in timing. In 1777, as a result of the drastic rise in prices of these articles, the worth of £100 of continental currency in the purchase of sugar and beef contrasts strikingly with its worth in flour or iron. Congress could take some action in the case of the rapid rise in beef, as it did by placing an embargo on the shipment of it except for the use of the ship's crew. Less control could be exercised in the case of many articles freely traded in, though the dissimilar rise among them provided opportunities for speculation between commodities and a mounting degree of friction and discontent in which anyone who made provision for the future became in his own way a speculator.

Any summary of the war years must consider both the advances and the dispersion of prices. The percentage changes in prices of individual commodities from April to April of each year and the level reached in the final month of the circulation of continental currency indicate how varied was the impact of inflation upon goods of different origin.

TABLE 8

ANNUAL PERCENTAGE CHANGES IN PRICES OF FIFTEEN COMMODITIES
APRIL OF ONE YEAR FROM APRIL OF PRECEDING YEAR

	April							Relatives*
Commodity	1775	1776	1777	1778	1779	1780	1781	Apr. 1781
Beef	9	25	153	8	438	718	100	33113
Chocolate	23	−4	153	400	100	180	93	16067
Coffee	−6	33	271	262	6	490	84	13648
Corn	18	−15	116	26	1255	119	57	10126
Flour								
Common	−21	−7	71	33	847	482	62	14979
Superfine	−4	−27	94	116	466	425	99	16840
Iron, Bar	−1	4	87	240	344	200	69	14767
Molasses	6	40	505	94	203	1001	−48	29915
Pepper	8	107	220	8	117	700	225	42895
Pork	−12	31	192	−15	550	813	81	24451
Rum, W. I.	3	95	396	123	88	780	9	35598
Sugar, Musc.	−8	28	246	223	226	180	43	18987
Tar	−4	48	7	578	23	678	29	13327
Tea, Bohea	−23	109	275	47	81	650	25	16502
Wheat	−21	−22	64	57	692	321	164	14438
Median	−5	24	153	156	131	489	59	16502

* Average of 1771–1773 = 100.

On the basis of the changes between April 1775 and April 1776, the 15 products included in the index fell into three groups: chocolate, corn, common and superfine flour, and wheat continued their decline; beef, coffee, bar iron, molasses, pork, sugar, and tar rose mildly; rum, pepper, and tea spread away from the group by rising 95 to more than 100 per cent.

A comparison of the percentage of change six months later reveals all products rising. Between November 1775 and November 1776 the commodities which rose 100 per cent or more were mainly West India goods and pork, which latter had lagged in the early months of the advance.

Between April 1776 and April 1777, prices not only again fanned out but widened the spread between domestic and imported commodities. Molasses, rum, tea, coffee, and sugar advanced from 246 to 505 per cent above the level of the year before. The sluggish movement in the prices of grain and breadstuffs kept down the rise in the cost of living, but in the high percentage changes from April 1778 to 1779 domestic staples began to displace the West India goods. Corn, flour, pork, beef, and wheat, and even bar iron, tower above the West India goods in percentage advance in an interval in which only four commodities rose less than 100 per cent.

The November 1778 to November 1779 comparison reflects the alarming depreciation of the close of 1779. Beef, common flour, pork, and pepper rose from 1100 to more than 1900 per cent above the price of the same month the year before. Only one of the other commodities rose less than 341 per cent. It was this advance, particularly vigorous in domestic staples, which focused attention on the necessity of reducing drastically the amount of bills of credit in circulation in addition to stopping their issue—a measure which had been determined upon earlier.

In the percentage rise from April 1779 to 1780, some West India goods, notably molasses and rum, rose briskly, as did pork, but their behavior was only slightly more extreme than the mounting percentage climb of other domestic items like beef and tar. The milder percentage increases of the months from April 1780 to April 1781 are as much a reflection of the height the price level had attained as they are of a calmer market in commodities.

Though monetary factors were the dominant influence in the extravagant rise in prices, the part played by shortages cannot be overlooked in accounting for disparities between commodities. Apart from monetary inflation, shortage of goods and increased costs raised prices in specie terms 50 to 100 per cent. These shortages developed now in one sector of the economy, now in another. That they were not persistent, except in the case of salt and specialized military equipment, because the channels were kept open for the flow of goods, must be rated as one of the crowning achievements of the period.

At the beginning of the war, stocks of textiles, notably sailcloth and duck, were uncommonly low as the result of a long period of dull sales, unwillingness of merchants to take the risk of placing large orders, and the movement out of the trade of some houses specializing in dry goods. As a result, prices of dry goods soared early in the war. By the close of

1778, the combination of home weaving and importation built up stocks, diversified the choice of fabrics, and eased prices. Similarly, the early and rapid advance in imported goods before the ports were opened to foreign trade was chiefly brought about by consumption and shipment of stocks. The ensuing shortage of sugar was fully overcome by 1779 and the movement of prices in later stages of inflation cannot be attributed to lack of supply.

Grains were abundant until after the generally poor harvest of 1778. A combination of unusual demand, poor crops, and an unfavorable reaping season started an alarming and rapid climb in prices all the more serious because the grain on hand had to be used as fodder as well as for breadstuffs. From 1779 on, only a slight part of the rise in breadstuffs can be attributed to shortage of farm products, though in these years it is fairly clear that the heightening prices of meats can be accounted for by previous heavy slaughter of farm animals. A shortage of meat, and primarily beef, persisted even in postwar years, indicating the long interval involved in building up farm stocks.

The sudden changes in tempo of price movement which gave the period the appearance of a succession of autonomous cycles can be accounted for by temporary shortages in one sector of the economy after another. In the same way, the piecemeal price controls must be viewed as practical measures directed at particular points of strain. One baffling result of the disparate rise was that in some cases it affected the basis upon which commodities from one sector of the economy interchanged with others. Before the war, farmers knew the price their wheat should bring as soon as they learned what flour was selling for. Similar general conformities could be assumed between the prices of beef and pork or even rum and molasses. During the war, prices of commodities that had formerly varied from each other within narrow limits over long periods no longer furnished a guide to either buyer or seller.

The shortages may well have been intensified by frequent resort to barter and still more ingenious private arrangements for stabilizing prices at customary levels and maintaining those prices by personal agreement, since all such arrangements kept up the demand for scarce goods and prevented the normal flow of commodities to market. These practices, common to all inflationary periods, must in these years be attributed primarily to the obvious lack of equivalence between the money of account and specie.

Depreciation of State Issues

Monetary uncertainties did not end with the reduction of the volume of currency in circulation. State paper fluctuated in value in all the postwar years. Its first decline is connected with the effort of Congress early in 1780 to find a new basis for financing the continuance of the war. The act of March 18, 1780, passed by Congress, was intended to effect the calling in of continental currency and the emission of new bills with a security in state funds. On the 25th of the same month, the Pennsylvania Assembly authorized the issue of £100,000 of state money (the first state issue since 1777) valued on a par with specie and secured by property owned by the state. Both this issue and the 1,250,000 dollars of the new joint emission were to be interest-bearing and redeemable in six years.

Congress had expected that, through taxation and exchange, the old bills would quickly go out of circulation. Had the states been in a position to collect the necessary taxes, the calling in of the old and the emission of new currency might have been effected reasonably promptly. Instead, the "old continental" continued to circulate and to depreciate along with the state issue which had been put forth with high hopes for its circulation on a par with specie. It was an effort to bolster the state issues that accounted for the act of the Assembly of December 23, 1780, making them "legal tender." The attempt in practice in the following months to rate state money to continental and both to specie so tried the patience of the hard-pressed public that soon paper money of every sort was refused. It was a likely outcome, since hard money was known to be plentiful from the sums being expended by the British army for its supplies, from the large amounts remitted by the French for the purchases of their army and navy, and from importation of specie from Havana and other places. The delegates to Congress and the purchasers for the government, state and federal, were those most affected by the inability to purchase anything with continental money. The Maryland delegates saw no other means of paying their expenses than the shipment to them of flour which they could sell for hard money,[3] and the Virginia delegates explained that they were "reduced to extremities for want of money—the state paper passes under great depreciation and not

[3] May 15, 1781, Daniel of St. Thomas Jenifer to John Hall, *Letters of Members of the Continental Congress*, v. 6, p. 88.

willingly received by the people; specie appears to be the money chiefly in circulation."[4]

In August 1781, the state's new emission of March 18 of the year before was the only paper in general circulation and exchanged for specie at 2.5 for one. It later depreciated further and was not rated above 3 to one in 1782 and even as late as January 1783. State paper began to appreciate in February 1783 and was not more than 20 to 25 per cent "worse" than specie until another emission which was under discussion in the last half of 1784 began to be feared.

The immediate effect of the issues is obscured by months of lacunae in the record, but for at least two months—September and October 1785—state paper fell to 2.5 to 3 for one in exchange for specie, a more disadvantageous rating than it ever again had in the period of the Confederation. In 1786 Pennsylvania currency appreciated and throughout the year was at a discount of not more than 5 to 11 per cent. In the next three years it was subject to disturbing monthly variations and discounted at somewhat poorer rates than in 1786.

The fluctuating value of state currency shown in Appendix Table 4 during these years must be considered in comparing the level of prewar and postwar prices. No attempt is made to adjust the index, nor would such an adjustment be in conformity with practice. Business was being carried on "not so much by credit as formerly."[5] Even in transactions between merchants the depreciation was frequently disregarded, as it was customarily in payments to workers. In December 1786 Hollingsworth explained, "Our paper is at 10 to 12 per cent discount, though in small quantities—payments to tradesmen and laborers—it passes at full value."[6] Among merchants, discounts for depreciation were intermittent. In the spring of 1789 James Cox explained, "The very fluctuating state that our paper money has always been in, makes it difficult to ascertain the value of it at different periods and more particularly to me as I have had so little to do with it that I have never kept any depreciation account."[7]

Other sorts of losses were frequently noted in these years from having

[4] May 22, 1781, Virginia Delegates to Thomas Jefferson, Governor of Virginia, *ibid.*, p. 97.

[5] August 9, 1786, Stephen Mix Mitchell, Wethersfield, to William Samuel Johnson, *ibid.*, v. 8, p. 418.

[6] December 27, 1786, Levi Hollingsworth to George Douglas, New York.

[7] April 27, 1789, James and John Cox to Aaron Burr, New York.

retained old commonwealth or continental money until it became of little value. For instance, John Penn was apprised in April 1783 of the retention of a sum of £130 of continental money received in 1776 "and which now may be considered of no worth."[8] In the same way Henry Drinker held old commonwealth paper, to pay a note for goods purchased before the Revolution, until it "became totally useless,"[9] and as late as May 1789 Clement Biddle inquired, "Is there any demand for old continental money with you? I have about 30,000 dollars which I should be glad to get 3 dollars per thousand for."[10] These are less typical of general practice than was the hasty passing on of depreciated currency even at the risk of having funds in unliquid form, notably in land and town lots. Losses from the decline in the value of land, suffered by those who needed quick assets if they were to participate in the revival of trade, must have scaled down materially some of the profits from war trading, especially as it is known that between 1783 and 1789 the value of some farm land in Montgomery County dropped to about one-half of its earlier value.[11] These fluctuations and the necessity of scaling down the interest on certain old indebtedness by reckoning it to January 1776 and then "taking it up again at May 1, 1783"[12] and similar arrangements kept a discussion of the value of money continually before a community which had lived through years of extreme inflation followed by sudden and drastic currency devaluation.

It would be as one-sided to ignore these evidences of strain as to overlook considerable areas of strength. Many other studies have stressed the steady return of trade to prewar volume. By the level of prices of domestic staples shown in this analysis it is possible to appraise the extent to which prices were higher after the Revolution than before it. Despite an underlying contraction in the average of all commodities, produce of Pennsylvania origin sold at relatively high levels after the war. For instance corn prices were continuously above prewar until November 1786, common flour until September 1787 except for two months in 1786, and superfine flour until August 1787; pork, except in March and April 1786 and February 1787, was above prewar until December 1787 and beef never dropped below its prewar level until

[8] April 11, 1783, Edmond Physick to John Penn, England.
[9] February 20, 1784, Henry Drinker and Sons to Hoare and Potts, Jamaica.
[10] May 8, 1789, Clement Biddle to Adam Gilchrist, Charleston.
[11] January 24, 1789, Joseph Price Diary.
[12] June 4, 1785, Stephen Collins to Smithson and Greaves.

May 1788. Only wheat, among the basic exports, fluctuated around and often below the prices at which it sold before the war. Comparisons made, in most cases, with the peak prices of colonial years indicate that the agricultural part of the economy was far from stagnant. Shippers of these staples complained as frequently about extravagant prices as Robert Morris did about the prices of tobacco, which he attempted unsuccessfully to lower, if not to regulate, by influencing both the rate of exchange and the conditions of export.

The wholly chaotic area in postwar years, which contemporaries explained only in short-run terms, was in the dry goods trade. Trade was open enough in the late years of the war to provide a reasonable and in some cases an abundant supply of dry goods. The news of peace caught some merchants with considerable stock. Besides, it required no great astuteness to anticipate that goods in the hands of merchants in New York would be sacrificed rather than returned to their original shippers. More important, bills of exchange before 1783 were extremely low and kept at or close to par during the first eight months of that year. It was a situation that could not fail to encourage the placing of orders which had to be paid for after exchange turned sharply upward. In addition, goods purchased in Europe before dry goods prices declined had to compete with later importations acquired at lower prices. Since foreign exchange was above par from 1783 to January 1790, it is not surprising that complaints were continuous about the shipment of specie out of the country.

Some branches of the dry goods trade were early singled out as especially unprofitable. For instance, in March 1784 when sterling exchange was about 172, Collins, in a general summary of the prospects for the sale of various grades of Russian sheetings for which the war had earlier greatly increased the demand, commented, "There has been at least half a guinea dead loss on every piece of sheeting imported from England, since the peace."[13] But it was the methods adopted in the consignment and in the sale of consigned goods that seemed to cautious, experienced merchants to be violating all recognized safe practices. These factors contributing to the uncertain state of the dry goods market were stressed by Collins to his London correspondent. He wrote,

> Trade is much more overdone here, than I believe the merchants in England have any conception of and it is in a great many very indifferent hands.

[13] March 31, 1784, the same to Harrison, Ansley & Co., London.

Are the British merchants quite mad in shipping out so freely, and so very indiscriminately, as some seem to do? They must soon bite the bit off the bridle or I will not guess again. Between ourselves Champion and Dickason have shipped with very little prudence, caution or judgment. I much doubt if they could get their debts insured here, on the arrival of the goods, for 20 per cent, though they have some good hands.[14]

Throughout 1784 and 1785, comment about the shipment of specie as a result of the high price or scarcity of sterling bills of exchange was general—typically, "Hard money is going out of sight very fast,"[15] and "Times in this country now are extremely difficult, worse than thee ever saw them before the war and wise is he who can steer himself safely through them."[16] Experienced merchants for a time were barely, if at all, covering the duties and charges of the merchandise shipped to them. Ultimately, they were not superseded by the new drapers, but for a short period after the war they were added to and competed with by new merchants, some of whom came with the hope of collecting old accounts while selling dry goods as a side line or of disposing of stocks of goods that would seem to have been accumulating in British merchant houses. Some of them, operating on commission, adopted methods bound to be disapproved by the old merchant group and in local opinion upsetting to the whole stability of business in the area. The drop in dry goods prices, the slowness of sales and payment, and the bankruptcies eliminated many of the least wary, and in the case of others added a few new merchants as dependable as the community ever had. At the very time that the depreciation of Pennsylvania currency was being reflected in the amount of foreign exchange it would buy, shippers in Philadelphia and Baltimore believed that the high price of middle Atlantic products made them unsuitable for export to some foreign markets.[17]

Part of the accumulation of state and public securities by creditors may be traced to the difficulties of collecting payments in any form and the resultant willingness to accept any tangible evidence of acknowledgment of the debt. The practice soon acquired other characteristics. Before the close of 1785, it was reported from Boston that "there are paper

[14] June 12, 1784, the same to the same.

[15] July 16, 1785, Robert Henderson to William Gardner, Glasgow.

[16] October 29, 1785, John Clifford to Thomas Clifford, Jr., Bristol.

[17] Homer Bast, "Tench Tilghman—Maryland Patriot," *Maryland Historical Magazine,* 1947, v. 42, p. 91.

speculators dispersed over every part of the United States. They keep up a constant and accurate communication. The information flies from one to another in every direction like an electric shock."[18] Though comment about the price of public securities was continuous between New York and Philadelphia, and less frequent between Baltimore and Philadelphia, the activity has little significance for the record of prices of these years, since no spectacular rise occurred in state issues until the latter part of 1789.

The opportunities for speculation which were the concern of a small group were of little interest to the well-established houses, busy with the problem of reviving trade in more normal ways. In the spring of 1790, Cox summarized the many factors that together seemed to be favorable to those interested in profits. He noted:

> Flour and grain of all kinds have risen to a most enormous price. Bills of exchange a mere drug, they are selling from 25 to 50 per cent, and a-begging. Superfine flour has been sold at 60 shillings per barrel. Wheat at 11 shillings 3 pence, Indian corn at 5 shillings and certificates rising. You'll surely say these are glorious times. I am sorry to tell you that under all these favorable circumstances, I have received no immediate benefit, for I had not faith enough to speculate in certificates, and my funds are so appropriated at present I can't take advantage of the low exchange.[19]

The drop in exchange was directly connected with the rise in the price of wheat and flour—the purchasers of the latter, according to Fuller, "in order to procure money have been obliged to sell their bills."[20] Exchange was then 13 per cent below par and likely to be encouraging to importers of British goods, and it was soon noted that the influx of dry goods in the spring of 1790 resembled the well-remembered situation in 1784 to 1785 when goods were sacrificed at auction.[21] Equilibrium was restored when high prices of flour stopped its export to Europe, with a resulting rise in bills of exchange.

The memory of price fluctuations beyond anything the community had hitherto encountered colored all postwar currency discussions. The experience with an over-issue of continental money set up a desire to

[18] December 17, 1785, Royal Flint, Boston, to Constable Rucker & Co.

[19] March 3, 1790, James and John Cox to Peter Wikoffe, Charles Town.

[20] March 9, 1790, Benjamin Fuller to George Ellcock, Barbados.

[21] May 22, 1790, Robert Henderson to Miller and Gardner, Glasgow.

avoid as much as possible any issues of paper currency and strengthened a general tendency of the period to define within narrow limits the role of the state in relation to the money system. Against this background should be judged the considerable readjustment achieved in the postwar period and the ultimate full appreciation of state currency.

Appendix Table 1

Average Monthly Wholesale Prices of Commodities in Philadelphia

1770

Commodity	Unit	Jan.	Feb.	Mar.	Apr.	May	June	July	Aug.	Sept.	Oct.	Nov.	Dec.
Beef	£-bbl	2.50	2.75	2.58	2.50	2.50	2.75	2.50	2.75	2.50	2.50	2.50	2.50
Chocolate	d-lb	*18.0*	18.0	18.0	17.0	16.0	16.0	17.0	16.0	16.0	16.1	16.0	16.0
Coffee	d-lb	15.5	15.0	15.5	14.7	15.7	15.8	16.5	15.5	16.4	16.7	16.2	16.0
Corn	s-bu	3.00	2.75	2.92	3.13	3.47	3.75	3.75	4.29	4.50	4.54	4.04	3.00
Flour, Com.	s-cwt	14.5	14.6	14.8	14.7	14.8	15.5	16.0	17.0	16.5	15.9	17.0	17.2
Sup.	s-cwt	17.5	17.5	17.4	17.8	*18.5*	19.2	19.5	20.0	20.3	21.0	21.2	20.8
Iron, Bar	£-ton	23.0	23.0	23.0	23.0	23.0	23.0	23.0	24.0	23.0	23.0	23.0	24.0
Molasses	s-gal	2.00	1.67	1.83	1.76	1.92	1.96	1.83	1.83	1.83	1.88	1.88	1.88
Pepper	s-lb	*3.75*	4.33	4.33	*4.33*	*4.33*	*4.33*	*5.00*	*5.00*	5.00	4.93	*2.83*	2.83
Pork	£-bbl	3.75	3.75	3.81	4.00	4.00	3.94	4.00	4.12	3.92	3.71	3.65	3.58
Rum, W. I.	s-gal	3.38	3.08	3.06	2.83	2.96	3.04	2.92	3.00	3.00	2.96	2.91	2.98
Sugar, Mus.	£-cwt	2.75	2.56	2.62	2.70	2.69	2.70	2.65	2.44	2.46	2.51	2.51	2.48
Tar	s-bbl	12.0	10.0	11.0	10.0	10.0	12.0	12.0	12.0	11.0	12.0	12.0	12.0
Tea, Bohea	s-lb	5.30	5.25	5.25	5.00	7.50	7.50	7.50	7.50	7.25	6.00	6.00	5.88
Wheat	s-bu	5.50	5.50	5.71	5.56	5.67	5.88	6.00	6.13	6.08	6.11	6.38	6.50
Bread, Ship	s-cwt	13.0	13.0	13.2	13.2	13.3	13.5	13.5	14.5	15.1	15.2	15.6	16.1
Cotton	s-lb	1.17	1.25	1.25	1.21	1.33	1.50	1.33	1.33	1.42	1.33	1.33	1.33
Flour, Mid.	s-cwt	15.0	14.0	13.4	14.0	13.9	13.8	15.0	15.9	16.1	15.8	16.4	16.4
Indigo	s-lb				11.5	11.5			10.0	10.0	*10.0*	*10.0*	*10.0*
Leather, sole	s-lb	1.33	1.33	*1.33*	1.33	1.33	1.33	*1.33*	*1.33*	1.33	1.33	1.33	1.33
Rice	s-cwt	18.0	17.5	17.5	17.0	16.5	16.0	15.0	15.0	15.2	16.0	15.7	16.0
Sugar, Loaf	s-lb	0.92	1.04	1.00	1.02	1.01	1.00	1.00	1.00	1.00	1.00	0.99	0.98
Tobacco	s-cwt	24.8	31.2	31.2	31.2	31.2	31.2	20.0	20.0	26.2	32.5	32.5	32.5
Turpentine	s-bbl	15.0	15.0	15.0	12.0	12.0	14.0	14.0	14.0	13.0	14.0	14.0	14.0
Wine	£ pipe	45.0	50.0	50.0	50.0	50.0	50.0	50.0	50.0	50.0	50.0	50.0	50.0

Sources—Thomas Evans; Hollingsworth Collection; Matthew Irwin (L of C); Pennsylvania Chronicle and Universal Advertiser; Pennsylvania Gazette; Pennsylvania Journal; Philadelphia Merchant, unknown, AM3081; Wharton Papers; John Wilson.

1771

Commodity	Unit	Jan.	Feb.	Mar.	Apr.	May	June	July	Aug.	Sept.	Oct.	Nov.	Dec.
Beef	£-bbl	2.58	2.62	2.62	2.50	2.54	2.58	2.58	2.50	2.54	2.50	2.50	2.81
Chocolate	d-lb	*16.0*	*16.0*	16.0	15.0	14.8	14.0	15.0	15.0	15.0	15.5	15.3	15.1
Coffee	d-lb	*16.0*	16.0	16.0	15.0	14.0	15.9	16.0	15.0	16.0	15.5	15.5	15.6
Corn	s-bu	3.00	2.95	3.33	3.42	3.31	3.42	3.69	3.78	4.00	3.67	3.77	3.63
Flour, Com.	s-cwt	16.3	16.6	17.0	17.1	17.6	17.8	17.4	17.0	17.7	17.8	18.7	19.0
Sup.	s-cwt	*20.4*	20.0	20.5	20.4	20.7	22.3	21.9	21.2	21.6	21.5	21.4	21.2
Iron, Bar	£-ton	23.5	24.0	24.0	24.0	24.0	24.0	24.0	24.0	24.0	24.0	24.3	25.0
Molasses	s-gal	1.89	1.83	1.83	1.83	1.78	1.73	1.67	1.69	1.72	1.75	1.78	1.79
Pepper	s-lb	*2.92*	3.00	3.00	2.17	2.20	2.25	2.25	2.25	2.31	2.31	2.25	2.17
Pork	£-bbl	3.62	3.62	3.88	4.00	4.00	4.00	4.00	4.10	4.46	4.50	4.00	4.00
Rum, W. I.	s-gal	2.97	3.00	3.17	3.17	2.97	3.07	3.04	3.28	3.56	3.67	3.85	4.50
Sugar, Mus.	£-cwt	2.56	2.38	2.65	2.65	2.38	2.58	2.59	2.42	2.47	2.75	2.54	2.56
Tar	s-bbl	12.0	12.0	12.0	12.0	13.2	12.0	13.0	14.0	12.0	12.0	12.7	12.0
Tea, Bohea	s-lb	5.50	5.50	5.50	5.38	5.25	5.08	5.00	4.75	4.33	4.50	4.17	4.25
Wheat	s-bu	6.33	6.13	6.75	6.88	7.00	7.20	7.00	6.38	6.67	7.00	7.06	7.00
Bread, Ship	s-cwt	15.0	15.0	15.0	15.0	16.0	16.5	16.4	15.7	15.8	15.5	15.9	16.2
Cotton	s-lb	1.25	1.17	1.33	1.25	1.42	1.25	1.25	1.25	1.25	1.17	1.17	1.17
Flour, Mid.	s-cwt	15.4	17.0	17.0	17.0	16.9	17.9	18.0	18.0	18.0	18.0	18.0	18.0
Indigo	s-lb	*10.0*	10.0	*9.25*	8.50	10.3	10.5	*11.0*	11.5	*11.3*	11.1	10.8	11.5
Leather, sole	s-lb	1.33	1.33	1.33	1.33	1.33	1.33	1.33	1.33	1.33	*1.33*	1.33	1.33
Rice	s-cwt	16.0	16.0	16.0	16.0	15.0	16.3	17.5	17.0	17.5	17.5	18.0	19.5
Sugar, Loaf	s-lb	0.97	0.96	0.96	0.96	1.00	0.98	0.97	1.00	0.99	0.96	0.98	0.96
Tobacco	s-cwt	32.5	32.5	32.5	32.5	32.5	32.5	32.5	32.5	32.5	32.5	32.5	32.5
Turpentine	s-bbl	14.0	14.0	14.0	14.0	14.0	14.0	15.0	16.0	14.0	14.0	14.7	14.0
Wine	£-pipe	50.0	50.0	50.0	50.0	50.0	50.0	50.0	50.0	50.0	50.0	50.0	50.0

Sources—Thomas A. Biddle Business Records and Correspondence; Miers, Thomas, and Samuel Fisher; Hollingsworth Collection; Pennsylvania Gazette; Pennsylvania Journal; Philadelphia Merchant, unknown, AM3081 William Smith; Wharton Papers.

Appendix Table 1—(*Continued*)

Average Monthly Wholesale Prices of Commodities in Philadelphia

1772

Commodity	Unit	Jan.	Feb.	Mar.	Apr.	May	June	July	Aug.	Sept.	Oct.	Nov.	Dec.
Beef	£-bbl	2.62	2.50	2.69	2.75	2.83	3.00	3.50	3.00	3.00	2.75	2.67	2.92
Chocolate	d-lb	15.0	15.4	14.0	14.3	14.5	14.4	13.7	14.0	14.5	14.7	15.0	14.0
Coffee	d-lb	16.0	16.0	16.0	15.0	15.4	15.9	15.0	16.0	15.2	16.0	15.1	14.8
Corn	s-bu	3.50	3.50	3.56	3.72	3.96	3.98	3.83	3.78	3.63	3.83	3.58	3.40
Flour, Com.	s-cwt	19.0	19.0	19.2	19.1	19.9	20.6	21.4	21.2	21.2	21.0	21.0	20.4
Sup.	s-cwt	21.8	22.2	22.8	23.0	23.2	23.8	23.5	23.5	23.4	23.5	23.4	23.2
Iron, Bar	£-ton	25.0	26.0	26.0	26.0	26.5	28.0	28.0	28.0	28.0	28.0	28.0	27.3
Molasses	s-gal	1.83	1.75	1.71	1.61	1.69	1.75	1.68	1.67	1.67	1.80	1.86	1.95
Pepper	s-lb	2.08	2.00	2.25	2.25	*2.25*	2.25	2.25	2.25	2.25	2.17	2.25	2.17
Pork	£-bbl	4.00	4.00	4.22	4.50	4.69	4.94	5.05	5.00	5.10	5.04	4.97	4.56
Rum, W. I.	s-gal	4.25	4.10	3.79	3.15	3.04	3.18	3.12	3.19	3.32	3.61	3.78	3.62
Sugar, Mus.	£-cwt	2.65	2.38	2.44	2.49	2.51	2.45	2.45	2.42	2.52	2.47	2.41	2.45
Tar	s-bbl	15.0	15.0	14.0	14.0	14.0	14.0	14.0	14.0	14.0	14.5	14.0	15.3
Tea, Bohea	s-lb	4.25	4.08	4.00	4.00	4.00	4.00	4.00	4.00	4.17	4.25	4.25	4.25
Wheat	s-bu	7.50	7.75	7.69	7.60	7.88	8.02	8.04	7.92	8.00	7.83	7.53	7.17
Bread, Ship	s-cwt	16.5	17.0	17.0	17.3	21.0	22.7	22.5	20.8	21.2	21.2	21.4	20.8
Cotton	s-lb	1.17	1.17	1.17	1.17	1.33	1.33	1.28	1.33	1.33	1.33	1.33	1.33
Flour, Mid.	s-cwt	17.9	18.5	19.3	20.0	20.0	21.0	21.8	21.8	21.6	21.1	21.2	20.5
Indigo	s-lb	*11.8*	12.0	12.0	*11.2*	10.3	10.2	11.0	10.7	11.0	11.5	11.5	*12.0*
Leather, sole	s-lb	1.33	1.33	*1.33*	1.25	1.30	1.33	1.33	1.33	1.38	1.33	1.37	1.33
Rice	s-cwt	20.0	20.0	21.0	23.0	25.0	24.0	26.3	27.0	24.0	24.0	24.0	22.3
Sugar, Loaf	s-lb	0.96	0.96	0.95	0.94	0.94	0.95	0.94	0.95	0.94	0.93	0.95	0.94
Tobacco	s-cwt	32.5	32.5	32.5	32.5	32.5	32.5	32.5	32.5	32.5	36.2	*33.1*	30.0
Turpentine	s-bbl	15.0	15.0	16.0	16.0	16.0	16.0	17.8	18.0	17.7	17.5	17.5	17.8
Wine	£-pipe	50.0	50.0	50.0	50.0	50.0	50.0	50.8	60.0	60.0	57.5	60.0	60.0

Sources—Thomas A. Biddle Business Records and Correspondence; Coates and Reynell Papers; Thomas Evans Hollingsworth Collection; Pennsylvania Gazette; Pennsylvania Journal; Philadelphia Merchant, unknown, AM3081; William Pollard Letterbook.

1773

Commodity	Unit	Jan.	Feb.	Mar.	Apr.	May	June	July	Aug.	Sept.	Oct.	Nov.	Dec.
Beef	£-bbl	2.75	2.75	2.75	2.75	2.75	2.75	2.75	2.75	*2.75*	2.75	2.50	2.75
Chocolate	d-lb	15.0	16.0	15.0	14.5	14.9	16.2	17.0	15.0	17.0	14.8	15.5	16.6
Coffee	d-lb	14.0	15.2	13.7	11.5	11.3	11.0	11.5	11.5	11.4	10.3	10.0	10.0
Corn	s-bu	3.75	3.92	3.47	3.11	3.04	3.00	3.06	3.06	3.00	2.94	2.67	2.71
Flour, Com.	s-cwt	20.0	20.0	20.0	19.2	18.4	17.7	18.4	19.4	18.5	18.4	18.5	18.5
Sup.	s-cwt	23.5	23.0	22.5	22.2	22.0	21.0	21.2	21.6	22.9	22.8	23.9	22.0
Iron, Bar	£-ton	*28.0*	27.0	27.0	26.0	26.0	25.8	25.4	26.0	26.0	27.0	27.0	26.0
Molasses	s-gal	1.83	1.92	1.78	1.67	1.71	1.72	1.72	1.65	1.71	1.78	1.69	1.75
Pepper	s-lb	2.00	*2.00*	*2.17*	2.17	2.21	2.18	2.50	2.25	2.17	2.25	2.22	2.21
Pork	£-bbl	4.25	4.50	4.50	4.50	4.52	4.42	4.28	4.30	4.25	3.71	3.71	3.44
Rum, W. I.	s-gal	3.33	3.50	3.42	3.25	3.33	3.30	3.19	3.19	3.13	3.14	3.08	3.08
Sugar, Mus.	£-cwt	2.38	2.40	2.32	2.50	2.44	2.56	2.50	2.51	2.50	2.50	2.65	2.75
Tar	s-bbl	15.0	15.0	14.3	14.0	13.7	13.0	13.1	13.4	13.0	14.0	13.0	14.0
Tea, Bohea	s-lb	4.37	4.17	4.00	4.00	4.00	4.25	4.50	4.75	4.63	4.50	6.00	6.00
Wheat	s-bu	7.50	7.50	7.95	8.00	7.63	7.00	7.17	7.29	7.50	7.33	7.06	7.13
Bread, Ship	s-cwt	20.0	19.0	18.2	18.2	18.0	16.7	17.0	16.5	16.2	16.3	15.7	15.8
Cotton	s-lb	1.33	1.33	1.28	1.63	1.50	1.58	1.58	1.50	1.46	1.50	1.33	1.25
Flour, Mid.	s-cwt	20.0	19.7	19.6	19.8	18.4	18.0	17.9	19.2	19.9	19.2	19.0	18.0
Indigo	s-lb	12.5	*11.2*	10.0	10.0	10.0	10.0	10.0	9.91	10.1	10.0	10.0	10.0
Leather, sole	s-lb	1.37	1.42	1.33	1.42	1.42	1.42	1.42	1.42	1.42	1.42	1.42	1.42
Rice	s-cwt	19.0	18.0	18.0	17.5	18.0	18.2	19.0	18.0	18.2	18.5	18.5	19.0
Sugar, Loaf	s-lb	0.96	0.92	0.92	0.92	0.92	0.92	0.92	0.92	0.92	0.92	0.92	0.96
Tobacco	s-cwt												
Turpentine	s-bbl	17.5	18.0	17.3	17.5	20.0	19.0	*17.0*	17.2	18.0	20.0	20.0	18.0
Wine	£-pipe	60.0	55.0	57.5	55.0	55.0	55.0	55.0	55.0	55.0	62.5	62.5	53.5

Sources—Thomas Evans; Hollingsworth Collection; Pennsylvania Gazette; Pennsylvania Journal; Philadelphia Merchant, unknown, AM3081; William Pollard Letterbook; William Smith; Wochentliche Pennsylvanische Staatsbote; Wharton Papers.

Appendix Table 1—(*Continued*)

Average Monthly Wholesale Prices of Commodities in Philadelphia

1774

Commodity	Unit	Jan.	Feb.	Mar.	Apr.	May	June	July	Aug.	Sept.	Oct.	Nov.	Dec.
Beef	£-bbl	2.75	*2.75*	2.75	2.75	2.75	2.75	2.75	2.50	2.75	2.75	2.83	3.00
Chocolate	d-lb	19.0	20.0	16.0	15.0	16.0	17.7	17.8	16.0	17.0	16.0	20.0	20.0
Coffee	d-lb	9.63	11.1	11.0	10.1	10.1	9.37	9.00	9.33	8.50	9.79	12.0	10.1
Corn	s-bu	*2.75*	*2.75*	2.75	2.75	2.67	2.54	2.58	3.08	2.71	3.21	3.10	3.08
Flour, Com.	s-cwt	19.0	*18.8*	18.8	18.9	18.5	18.5	18.8	17.5	17.9	17.1	17.2	17.8
Sup.	s-cwt	21.5	21.5	21.6	21.5	21.6	21.4	21.7	22.5	22.5	21.7	21.3	21.0
Iron, Bar	£-ton	25.0	28.0	26.0	26.0	26.0	26.0	26.4	26.0	26.0	26.0	26.0	26.0
Molasses	s-gal	1.83	1.79	1.67	1.72	1.83	1.67	1.83	1.67	1.75	1.83	1.85	1.83
Pepper	s-lb	2.33	2.43	2.17	2.25	2.00	2.25	2.50	2.25	2.29	3.06	3.40	3.00
Pork	£-bbl	*3.38*	*3.50*	3.50	3.42	4.25	3.32	3.29	3.38	3.62	3.58	3.42	3.04
Rum, W. I.	s-gal	3.33	3.17	3.08	3.00	3.08	3.25	3.25	2.83	2.71	2.83	3.00	3.14
Sugar, Mus.	£-cwt	2.80	*2.75*	2.75	2.75	2.75	2.88	2.80	2.79	2.85	2.80	2.75	2.72
Tar	s-bbl	13.5	*14.0*	14.0	14.0	13.0	13.2	*13.4*	13.5	15.0	*14.5*	14.0	13.0
Tea, Bohea	s-lb	5.76	5.65	5.50	5.00	5.50	6.00	5.33	5.00	5.00	5.00	5.50	4.00
Wheat	s-bu	7.50	*7.50*	7.50	7.58	7.75	7.00	7.00	6.50	6.75	5.75	6.50	6.83
Bread, Ship	s-cwt	*15.5*	*15.0*	15.0	15.0	15.0	15.0	14.5	14.5	13.8	14.0	14.0	13.6
Cotton	s-lb	*1.25*	1.58	1.33	1.33	1.33	1.58	1.67	1.75	1.83	*1.58*	1.33	1.83
Flour, Mid.	s-cwt	18.5	18.5	18.3	18.1	18.0	18.1	18.4	18.7	18.0	17.1	16.9	17.6
Indigo	s-lb	12.0	*11.1*	10.2	10.0	10.0	9.88	9.50	9.00	9.00	10.4	10.0	10.0
Leather, sole	s-lb	1.42	1.42	1.42	1.42	1.42	1.42	1.42	1.42	1.42	1.44	1.42	1.42
Rice	s-cwt	18.4	22.0	17.5	17.5	17.0	17.2	16.5	17.9	*17.0*	*16.0*	16.0	16.0
Sugar, Loaf	s-lb	1.00	1.04	1.00	1.00	1.00	1.12	1.12	1.12	1.08	1.08	1.08	1.08
Tobacco	s-cwt												
Turpentine	s-bbl	*18.0*	*20.0*	20.0	20.0	18.0	*18.0*	*18.4*	*18.8*	*19.2*	*19.6*	20.0	20.0
Wine	£-pipe	56.0	*53.5*	53.5	53.5	62.5	56.0	48.0	*50.2*	52.5	*56.2*	60.0	60.0

Sources—Henry Drinker Papers; Thomas Evans; Hollingsworth Collection; Morris and Miercken; Pennsylvania Gazette; Pennsylvania Journal; Pennsylvania Packet; Philadelphia Merchant, unknown, AM3081; Pine Forge, Samuel Hazard Letterbook (Princeton University Library); William Redwood; William Smith; Richard Sweetman ; Wharton Papers.

1775

Commodity	Unit	Jan.	Feb.	Mar.	Apr.	May	June	July	Aug.	Sept.	Oct.	Nov.	Dec.
Beef	£-bbl	2.62	2.75	2.70	3.00	2.75	3.12	2.88	2.88	2.88	2.81	2.81	2.81
Chocolate	d-lb	18.5	18.8	17.0	18.5	*18.5*	18.5	18.5	18.5	18.5	*16.8*	15.0	*16.0*
Coffee	d-lb	9.50	10.1	10.0	9.50	10.5	12.0	12.0	11.0	11.0	11.6	12.0	11.5
Corn	s-bu	3.00	3.25	2.92	3.25	2.75	2.63	3.10	3.25	2.92	2.58	2.67	2.50
Flour, Com.	s-cwt	17.5	16.8	15.2	15.0	13.5	14.0	16.2	15.2	15.2	13.0	12.5	12.5
Sup.	s-cwt	21.5	21.5	21.5	20.8	18.5	18.5	18.5	18.5	18.5	18.0	18.0	18.0
Iron, Bar	£-ton	26.0	26.0	26.0	25.7	23.9	23.9	24.3	24.2	23.2	24.0	22.5	22.5
Molasses	s-gal	1.83	1.75	1.80	1.83	1.67	1.68	1.56	1.58	1.75	1.75	1.79	1.79
Pepper	s-lb	2.42	2.42	2.42	2.42	2.42	2.42	2.42	2.42	3.25	*3.50*	3.75	4.50
Pork	£-bbl	3.00	3.00	3.06	3.00	3.00	3.09	3.27	3.94	4.25	4.00	2.88	2.88
Rum, W. I.	s-gal	3.17	3.08	3.13	3.08	2.83	2.99	2.97	2.96	2.92	3.08	3.08	3.25
Sugar, Mus.	£-cwt	2.70	2.90	2.52	2.53	2.57	2.56	2.54	2.47	2.51	2.85	2.81	2.81
Tar	s-bbl	12.0	12.0	12.0	13.5	11.8	10.8	11.8	12.5	11.0	15.0	15.0	*15.5*
Tea, Bohea	s-lb	4.50	3.83	3.83	3.83	3.83	3.83	*4.75*	4.75	4.75	*4.75*	*4.75*	7.50
Wheat	s-bu	6.75	7.00	6.38	6.00	5.75	5.69	5.88	5.56	4.88	4.50	4.75	4.75
Bread, Ship	s-cwt	13.5	13.0	13.0	13.0	13.0	12.9	13.9	15.0	13 9	*13.3*	12.8	*12.9*
Cotton	s-lb	1.83	1.83	1.92	2.00	*2.05*	2.09	2.17	2.25	*2.22*	*2.20*	2.17	*2.17*
Flour, Mid.	s-cwt	17.0	17.0	17.0	15.5	15.5	15.5	15.5	15.5	15.5	15.0	15.0	15.0
Indigo	s-lb	*9.83*	*9.67*	9.50	*9.55*	9.60	11.7	11.5	11.0	11.0	10.0	11.8	12.0
Leather, sole	s-lb	1.38	1.36	1.42	1.50	1.42	1.42	1.42	1.42	1.42	1.50	1.50	1.50
Rice	s-cwt	16.0	16.0	15.5	14.5	14.2	15.0	17.1	17.8	20.0	*20.5*	21.0	21.0
Sugar, Loaf	s-lb	1.08	1.08	1.08	1.08	1.08	1.17	1.13	1.13	1.13	1.13	1.13	1.13
Tobacco	s-cwt												
Turpentine	s-bbl	20.0	21.5	25.0	27.5	25.0	25.0	28.0	26.5	25.0	*25.0*		
Wine	£-pipe	50.0	60.0	60.0	60.0	66.2	65.0	65.0	66.2	67.5	*68.8*	70.0	70.0

Sources—Berkshire Furnace; Charming Forge; John and Peter Chevalier; Coates and Reynell Papers; Henry Drinker Papers; Thomas Evans; Hollingsworth Collection; Morris and Miercken; Pennsylvania Chronicle and Universa lAdvertiser; Pennsylvania Gazette; Pennsylvania Journal; Pennsylvania Magazine or Monthly Museum; Pennsylvania Magazine of History and Biography; Pennsylvania Mercury; Pennsylvania Packet; Philadelphia Merchant, unknown, AM3081; Pine Forge, Samuel Hazard Letterbook (Princeton University Library); William Redwood; Nathan Sharples; Richard Sweetman; John Wilson.

Appendix Table 1—(*Continued*)

Average Monthly Wholesale Prices of Commodities in Philadelphia

1776

Commodity	Unit	Jan.	Feb.	Mar.	Apr.	May	June	July	Aug.	Sept.	Oct.	Nov.	Dec.
Beef	£-bbl	2.81	2.81	3.25	3.75	3.75	7.50	5.41	*5.52*	5.62	4.69	4.69	6.64
Chocolate	d-lb	17.0	15.5	16.0	*17.8*	19.5	22.0	*21.5*	21.0	*24.0*	27.0	*37.5*	*48.0*
Coffee	d-lb	11.9	11.5	12.3	12.7	14.9	14.0	15.0	15.0	15.0	19.5	24.0	30.0
Corn	s-bu	2.67	2.79	2.63	2.75	2.81	3.00	2.82	3.25	2.82	4.57	4.92	5.42
Flour, Com.	s-cwt	14.8	13.5	14.8	14.0	11.3	11.5	12.0	12.9	13.8	16.5	20.0	22.0
Sup.	s-cwt	18.0	17.8	17.0	15.1	14.5	14.0	13.4	13.9	18.5	21.8	22.5	22.9
Iron, Bar	£-ton	26.0	26.5	26.6	26.8	26.0	28.0	26.2	28.8	30.4	30.4	35.8	39.8
Molasses	s-gal	1.93	2.00	2.00	2.56	3.00	4.00	4.25	4.25	4.25	6.50	4.00	4.00
Pepper	s-lb	5.00	5.00	5.00	5.00	6.00	*6.25*	6.50	6.70	9.00	*10.3*	*11.7*	13.0
Pork	£-bbl	2.97	3.00	3.50	3.93	5.25	6.00	7.50	*7.50*	*7.03*	6.56	6.69	5.54
Rum, W. I.	s-gal	3.88	3.95	4.50	6.00	5.31	5.81	5.44	5.50	7.00	8.00	8.00	17.0
Sugar, Mus.	£-cwt	2.87	3.02	3.25	3.25	4.83	5.57	5.38	5.50	4.50	4.65	5.60	6.06
Tar	s-bbl	16.0	16.0	*16.0*	*20.0*	20.0	20.0	20.0	20.0	18.0	18.0	20.0	16.0
Tea, Bohea	s-lb	4.69	5.50	7.00	8.00	*7.75*	7.50	10.0	9.71	*9.86*	10.0	*13.5*	*13.5*
Wheat	s-bu	4.50	5.00	4.92	4.67	4.06	4.26	4.00	4.12	5.50	5.50	5.92	7.47
Bread, Ship	s-cwt	13.0	*13.0*	13.0	13.0						12.5	17.8	*17.4*
Cotton	s-lb	2.25	2.25	2.25	*3.25*	4.25	*4.25*	4.25	*4.62*	5.00			
Flour, Mid.	s-cwt	15.8	15.0	15.0	13.2	13.0	12.0	10.9	10.8	14.8	16.4	17.0	16.9
Indigo	s-lb	12.0	12.0	14.0	14.8	16.2	17.5	18.0	12.5	*13.2*	14.0	*13.2*	
Leather, sole	s-lb	1.50	1.50	1.50	1.59	1.53	1.50	1.64	1.94	2.25	*2.62*	3.0	3.25
Rice	s-cwt	16.5			37.3						37.5		
Sugar, Loaf	s-lb	1.12	1.12	1.26	1.31	1.42	1.50	2.63	*3.07*	3.50	3.50	*3.50*	*5.00*
Tobacco	s-cwt												
Turpentine	s-bbl								35.0			37.5	37.5
Wine	£-pipe	65.0	69.0			67.5	72.0			62.5	60.0	59.0	

Sources—William Barrell, Stephen Collins Papers (L of C); Berkshire Furnace; John Brown; Charming Forge; John and Peter Chevalier; Clarkson and Morrison, Gratz Collections; Coates and Reynell Papers; Stephen Collins, Etting Collection; Minutes of the Council of Safety of Pennsylvania, Colonial Records, v. 11; John Davis Papers (L of C); Thomas Evans; Hewes and Anthony (John Carter Brown Library): Hollingsworth Collection; Matthew Irwin (L of C); Meredith Papers; Morris and Miercken; Owen Jones Papers; Pemberton Papers; Pennsylvania Gazette; Pennsylvania Packet; Philadelphia Merchant, unknown, AM3081; Potts Grove; William Redwood; Scharf and Westcott, History of Philadelphia, 1609-1884; William Smith; Thompson Collection; Wharton Papers; John Wilson.

1777

Commodity	Unit	Jan.	Feb.	Mar.	Apr.	May	June	July	Aug.	Sept.	Oct.	Nov.	Dec.
Beef	£-bbl	6.96	6.75	6.95	9.50	8.13	9.38	11.2	*11.2*	11.2	9.00	9.00	9.38
Chocolate	d-lb	48.0	72.0	45.5	45.0	61.2	66.6	70.8	72.0	72.0	*72.0*	162.0	*181.5*
Coffee	d-lb	37.5	48.0	50.7	47.0	48.0	*48.0*	48.0	77.0	69.0	*102.0*	135.0	*139.5*
Corn	s-bu	7.50	6.00	5.75	5.94	6.87	8.00	*8.92*	9.83	9.82	6.50	6.50	10.0
Flour, Com.	s-cwt	*23.0*	24.0	24.2	23.9	23.8	22.5	27.5	22.5	23.2	23.0	24.8	25.2
Sup.	s-cwt	28.0	28.4	29.8	29.3	28.2	30.0	27.8	25.4	23.4	*23.1*	*24.9*	*25.4*
Iron, Bar	£-ton	44.1	49.2	54.5	50.0	55.0	70.0	90.0	100.0	120.0	115.0	150.0	150.0
Molasses	s-gal	4.00	17.0	12.5	*15.5*	18.5	18.5	24.8	24.5	22.5	*22.5*	*22.5*	18.0
Pepper	s-lb	*12.5*	12.0	16.0	16.0	*14.0*	12.0	*10.0*	*11.5*	*10.9*	*13.5*	*17.3*	*17.7*
Pork	£-bbl	6.34	6.79	8.90	11.5	11.0	14.0	12.0	13.0	13.1	13.6	14.0	9.96
Rum, W. I.	s-gal	18.0	27.5	21.4	*29.8*	38.2	40.8	40.0	46.7	50.0	50.0	50.0	*58.4*
Sugar, Mus.	£-cwt	12.0	10.0	11.2	11.2	12.4	16.0	22.5	32.2	36.0	*36.0*	33.6	32.0
Tar	s-bbl	30.0	*24.0*	18.0	*21.5*	25.0	*24.8*	*27.3*	*27.3*	*27.6*	*22.0*	26.0	*42.9*
Tea, Bohea	s-lb	*13.5*	13.5	22.5	30.0	30.0	*55.0*	55.0	*67.5*	80.0	*66.4*	*59.6*	*50.6*
Wheat	s-bu	8.00	7.50	7.83	*7.66*	7.50	7.50	7.50	7.50	7.50	10.0	12.0	*12.0*
Bread, Ship	s-cwt	17.0	*21.0*	25.0	30.0			40.0	40.0				
Cotton	s-lb		5.75				10.0						
Flour, Mid.	s-cwt	20.0	20.4	20.8	20.4	22.5	22.5	16.2	22.5	20.0	15.0		
Indigo	s-lb								20.0	18.0			
Leather, sole	s-lb	4.0	4.0	4.0	3.99	4.08				3.0	2.5	2.5	3.33
Rice	s-cwt			35.0	35.0		38.0	45.0					
Sugar, Loaf	s-lb	5.00	5.00	4.50	4.50	5.00	10.0	9.38					
Tobacco	s-cwt			42.5	47.5	60.0	69.0	55.0	62.0	60.0			
Turpentine	s-bbl	40.0			33.8	28.3							
Wine	£-pipe			140.0	200.0		124.0						

Sources—John Brown; Chaloner and White Papers; Charming Forge; John and Peter Chevalier; Coates and Reynell Papers; Stephen Collins, Etting Collection; Minutes of the Council of Safety of Pennsylvania, Colonial Records, v. 11; Henry Drinker Papers; Michael Gratz, Etting Collection; Hollingsworth Collection; Charles Humphrey; Jacobs Papers; Christopher and Charles Marshall Ledger, Daniel Parker Papers; Meredith Papers; Morris and Miercken; Robert Morris, Dreer Collection; Norris Papers; Pennsylvania Archives; Pennsylvania Gazette; Pennsylvania Magazine of History and Biography; Pennsylvania Salt Works Account Book; Philadelphia Merchant, unknown, AM3081; Pine Forge, Samuel Hazard Letterbook (Princeton University Library); Potts Grove; William Redwood; John Ross; William Smith; Thompson Collection; Wharton Papers; John Wilson.

Appendix Table 1—(*Continued*)

Average Monthly Wholesale Prices of Commodities in Philadelphia

1778

Commodity	Unit	Jan.	Feb.	Mar.	Apr.	May	June	July	Aug.	Sept.	Oct.	Nov.	Dec.
Beef	£-bbl	10.1	9.74	10.4	10.2	10.5	12.0	10.1	10.7	11.2	11.2	10.7	18.8
Chocolate	s-lb	*16.8*	*18.4*	20.0	*18.8*	17.5	*18.7*	20.0	10.9	12.5	12.5	12.5	12.5
Coffee	s-lb	12.0	14.0	16.0	14.2	10.6	7.50	10.0	7.00	6.86	7.50	8.66	12.5
Corn	£-bu	*0.48*	0.45	0.38	*0.38*	0.38	*0.38*	0.71	0.67	0.78	1.11	1.24	1.54
Flour, Com.	£-cwt	1.31	1.34	1.49	1.58	1.49	1.60	2.48	2.32	3.63	4.69	4.50	7.56
Sup.	£-cwt	1.65	3.50	3.25	3.17	*3.08*	3.00	3.01	2.94	4.45	4.93	6.34	8.05
Iron, Bar	£-ton	154.9	150.0	150.0	170.0	198.2	205.9	201.5	211.7	221.9	228.3	256.5	279.8
Molasses	£-gal	1.03	1.27	1.29	1.50	1.25	1.00	2.00	1.48	1.46	1.66	1.73	2.29
Pepper	£-lb	*0.92*	0.88	*0.88*	*0.87*	0.86	*0.88*	0.90	0.92	1.12	1.21	1.18	1.50
Pork	£-bbl	9.31	9.50	9.78	9.78	9.75	9.78	10.9	13.6	10.9	10.9	19.4	24.0
Rum, W. I.	£-gal	3.34	4.00	*3.66*	3.32	3.24	3.25	4.33	3.20	3.32	3.09	3.68	4.30
Sugar, Mus.	£-cwt	*40.5*	49.0	38.3	36.4	40.0	*35.0*	30.0	36.1	32.2	31.2	38.5	58.6
Tar	£-bbl	*3.27*	*4.47*	*5.69*	*7.29*	*8.96*	*8.99*	9.38	*8.76*	7.00	7.00	*6.84*	*8.55*
Tea, Bohea	£-lb	1.40	1.69	2.08	2.20	2.88	2.88	3.00	2.63	2.00	1.85	2.00	2.75
Wheat	£-bu	0.60	0.60	0.60	0.60	0.60	0.60	0.64	0.75	0.90	1.25	1.58	1.84
Bread, Ship	£-cwt							2.50		2.50		6.75	7.45
Cotton	£-lb		0.90		0.90			0.75	0.75				
Flour, Mid.	£-cwt							1.58	2.20	3.33	4.01	5.08	7.30
Indigo	£-lb								1.25	1.12	1.19	1.21	1.25
Leather, sole	s-lb	2.50				2.25				10.5	10.0	10.0	
Rice	£-cwt	2.25				4.00	4.00	4.00	4.50	4.50	4.89	6.00	6.50
Sugar, Loaf	£-lb	0.78	0.91	0.88	0.90	0.74	0.50	0.90	0.75	0.90	0.83	0.70	1.25
Tobacco	£-cwt						5.00	6.50		7.50		9.50	10.2
Turpentine	£-bbl						7.50	7.50	8.25	6.38	6.45	6.75	5.63
Wine	£-pipe							500.0	500.0	*500.0*	*500.0*	500.0	

Sources—William Armstrong; William Barrell, Stephen Collins Papers (L of C); Chaloner and White Papers; Coates and Reynell Papers; Stephen Collins, Etting Collection; John and Henry Drinker (IRD); Hollingsworth Collection; Charles Humphrey; Matthew Irwin (L of C); Frederick Kuhl; William R. McBay; Meredith Papers; Pennsylvania Archives; Pennsylvania Magazine of History and Biography; Pennsylvania Salt Works Account Book; Pine Forge, Samuel Hazard Letterbook (Princeton University Library); Reed and Forde Papers; Shinkle and Graff (IRD); Pelatiah Webster; Wharton Papers.

1779

Commodity	Unit	Jan.	Feb.	Mar.	Apr.	May	June	July	Aug.	Sept.	Oct.	Nov.	Dec.
Beef	£-bbl	16.5	50.0	50.3	55.0	75.0	84.4	98.4	125.2	77.3	84.8	220.0	242.5
Chocolate	s-lb	*22.2*	32.0	32.5	37.5	45.0	45.0	37.5	*48.8*	60.0	60.0	84.4	90.0
Coffee	s-lb	13.0	14.0	13.9	15.0	17.0	17.0	15.0	25.0	42.5	60.0	77.2	97.7
Corn	£-bu	1.94	1.75	2.75	5.08	5.75	6.00	*6.00*	*6.00*	7.00	6.75	7.88	8.83
Flour, Com.	£-cwt	9.79	11.0	10.5	15.0	18.0	18.0	18.0	18.0	28.6	*48.4*	70.0	83.4
Sup.	£-cwt	10.2	13.1	16.0	17.9	23.8	20.0	20.0	20.0	*31.8*	46.9	67.8	87.8
Iron, Bar	£-ton	294.7	623.6	719.0	754.9	778.3	843.0	765.0	782.7	800.0	1038.3	1424.6	1917.1
Molasses	£-gal	2.12	3.70	4.00	4.54	4.62	4.62	4.29	3.80	*4.50*	*6.25*	*7.89*	10.0
Pepper	£-lb	*1.50*	*1.50*	1.50	1.88	2.38	2.42	2.12	2.12	11.2	18.8	19.5	15.0
Pork	£-bbl	38.0	*44.0*	50.0	63.5	80.0	80.0	70.0	*75.0*	80.0	*80.0*	245.0	300.0
Rum, W. I.	£-gal	5.02	5.20	6.35	6.25	6.75	6.75	6.25	8.00	15.8	17.5	19.0	22.3
Sugar, Mus.	£-cwt	61.0	67.0	67.5	118.8	105.0	117.0	93.2	92.5	105.0	140.0	170.0	207.5
Tar	£-bbl	8.00	8.50	8.50	9.00	13.1	15.0	15.0	15.0	*15.0*	15.0	15.0	22.5
Tea, Bohea	£-lb	2.06	4.00	*4.00*	4.00	4.50	5.25	4.50	4.75	10.0	12.5	13.5	15.5
Wheat	£-bu	2.07	2.25	4.25	4.75	7.50	6.00	6.00	9.00	7.00	7.50	15.0	18.8
Bread, Ship	£-cwt		11.2	16.0	16.0	22.6	22.5	23.5	28.0	60.0		60.0	108.5
Cotton	£-lb				2.62			2.92	2.75	6.00	6.00	6.00	
Flour, Mid.	£-cwt	8.50	11.2	13.8	15.7	18.0	15.0	15.0		30.0	46.0	53.0	62.5
Indigo	£-lb	1.50	1.50	2.25	3.60	3.56					15.0	15.0	
Leather, sole	s-lb	15.0		10.0	16.0			16.0					
Rice	£-cwt	*7.50*	9.00		16.8	16.8	16.8	16.8	*53.2*	89.6	89.6	70.0	72.5
Sugar, Loaf	£-lb	1.30	1.35	1.50	2.31	2.62	2.62	2.31	2.36	3.38	4.00	4.00	4.50
Tobacco	£-cwt	15.0	14.5	15.0	22.5	22.5	25.0	25.0	25.0	36.2	46.2	50.0	60.0
Turpentine	£-bbl	7.21	7.21	15.0	15.0							30.0	
Wine	£-pipe	770.0	*835.0*	900.0	950.0	1650.0		1320.0		2475.0	3300.0	3080.0	4125.0

Sources—Richard Backhouse (Bucks Co. HS); William Barrell, Stephen Collins Papers (L of C); Berkshire Furnace; Chaloner and White Papers; Clifford Papers; Stephen Girard (Girard College Library); John Holker Collection (L of C); Hollingsworth Collection; Matthew Irwin (L of C); William R. McBay; Meredith Papers; Norris Papers; Pemberton Papers; Pennsylvania Archives; Pennsylvania Gazette; Philadelphia Merchant, unknown, AM3081; Potts Grove; Reed and Forde Papers; William B. Reed, Life and Correspondence of Joseph Reed, v. 2; Shinkle and Graff (IRD); William Smith; George Wall, Jr. (Bucks Co. HS); Wharton Papers.

Appendix Table 1—(*Continued*)

Average Monthly Wholesale Prices of Commodities in Philadelphia

1780

Commodity	Unit	Jan.	Feb.	Mar.	Apr.	May	June	July	Aug.	Sept.	Oct.	Nov.	Dec.
Beef	£-bbl	178.1	253.1	450.0	450.0	456.7	550.0	675.0	*675.0*	*506.2*	506.2	650.0	600.0
Chocolate	s-lb	86.2	*86.2*	90.0	105.0	105.0	93.7	93.7	93.7	97.5	97.5	107.0	120.0
Coffee	s-lb	97.5	90.0	90.0	88.5	79.5	67.5	74.9	76.9	73.1	75.0	125.9	132.5
Corn	£-bu	7.50	9.00	8.75	11.1	13.0	15.5	16.2	15.7	16.9	16.0	17.6	17.5
Flour, Com.	£-cwt	64.6	85.0	90.7	87.3	85.8	84.0	87.3	90.8	97.7	92.9	104.8	109.4
Sup.	£-cwt	81.2	90.0	96.5	94.1	97.9	96.2	98.9	110.0	114.6	106.5	112.9	129.7
Iron, Bar	£-ton	2032.4	2001.8	2279.1	2264.0	2482.4	2628.1	2839.5	3079.3	2743.8	2844.8	3015.6	3003.5
Molasses	£-gal	12.0	*16.8*	*28.8*	50.0	30.0	30.0	22.5	*22.1*	*21.3*	*20.9*	*27.1*	*26.7*
Pepper	£-lb	*15.0*	*15.0*	*15.0*	*15.0*	15.0	18.8	20.6	*20.6*	*26.7*	32.7	34.0	45.0
Pork	£-bbl	242.5	244.4	400.0	580.0	580.0	500.0	587.5	562.5	550.0	575.0	*662.5*	*750.0*
Rum, W. I.	£-gal	26.0	31.8	46.2	55.0	55.0	35.9	33.4	28.9	28.0	22.5	22.2	35.5
Sugar, Mus.	£-cwt	200.0	235.9	350.0	332.0	286.7	224.8	255.2	268.3	277.5	294.7	416.0	450.0
Tar	£-bbl	*51.2*	80.0	80.0	70.0	72.5	69.5	70.0	65.0	82.5	85.0	85.0	90.0
Tea, Bohea	£-lb	21.0	21.0	23.2	30.0	28.1	30.0	30.0	30.0	33.0	32.2	50.0	40.0
Wheat	£-bu	*18.8*	19.0	20.0	20.0	23.6	23.1	23.0	24.5	36.0	26.2	28.2	29.9
Bread, Ship	£-cwt			184.1	120.6		104.3		110.0	105.0			
Cotton	£-lb			12.8	12.9	11.2	9.00	11.2	9.98	10.1	11.4	11.2	17.2
Flour, Mid.	£-cwt	60.0	70.0	81.9	58.3	76.7	73.2	81.7	82.0	76.7	81.2	93.5	109.6
Indigo	£-lb			11.2	16.9	16.9	*15.9*	15.0	18.4	20.0	22.5	22.5	
Leather, sole	s-lb						97.5						
Rice	£-cwt	66.8	*103.4*	140.0	140.0	*162.5*	185.0	180.0	180.0	168.0	180.0	200.0	*210.0*
Sugar, Loaf	£-lb	4.50	4.50	4.50	4.50	*5.06*	5.62	6.45	*6.98*	7.50	8.50	8.40	10.9
Tobacco	£-cwt		80.0	105.0	110.0	110.0	120.0	125.0	132.5	135.0	132.5	135.0	150.0
Turpentine	£-bbl				92.2								
Wine	£-pipe	5500.0		5000.0	4228.1			6600.0				9900.0	

Sources—Richard Backhouse (Bucks Co. HS); Chaloner and White Papers; Coates and Reynell Papers; Thomas Evans; Stephen Girard (Girard College Library); Hewes and Anthony (John Carter Brown Library); John Holker Collection (L of C); Hollingsworth Papers; Hughes Papers; Matthew Irwin (L of C); John Marshall; William R. McBay; George Nelson Diary; Pennsylvania Archives; Pennsylvania Assembly; Reed and Forde Papers; Royal Gazette; Shinkle and Graff (IRD); James Strawbridge Correspondence; Richard Sweetman; Wharton Papers.

1781

Commodity	Unit	Jan.	Feb.	Mar.	Apr.	Unit	May	June	July	Aug.	Sept.	Oct.	Nov.	Dec.
Beef	£-bbl	650.0	600.0	550.0	900.0	£-bbl	5.00	4.22	4.23	4.27	3.73	3.33	3.86	3.28
Chocolate	s-lb	*127.5*	135.0	*168.8*	202.5	d-lb	16.0	16.0	16.0	18.0	27.0	30.0	27.0	43.5
Coffee	s-lb	130.0	135.0	162.5	162.5	d-lb	10.6	11.4	11.1	11.5	12.0	15.0	15.4	17.0
Corn	£-bu	15.0	18.0	15.5	17.4	s-bu	3.67	2.67	3.75	3.50	3.75	3.00	3.75	3.78
Flour, Com.	£-cwt	119.8	143.8	142.9	141.5	s-cwt	20.8	19.7	17.6	16.7	15.6	18.0	18.9	20.4
Sup.	£-cwt	136.9	157.9	170.4	186.9	s-cwt	24.1	23.6	21.2	18.6	19.5	21.4	22.2	24.8
Iron, Bar	£-ton	2970.1	3376.3	3274.7	3818.0	£-ton	34.1	34.4	33.9	34.4	33.5	33.0	34.5	42.5
Molasses	£-gal	23.5	23.2	22.5	26.2	s-gal	*3.82*	*3.73*	*3.80*	*4.08*	*4.99*	*5.39*	6.00	7.50
Pepper	£-lb	*40.9*	36.8	*42.8*	48.8	s-lb	*9.50*	9.50	9.17	10.5	12.0	10.0	8.00	8.00
Pork	£-bbl	750.0	*825.0*	900.0	1246.7	£-bbl	8.33	8.33	8.75	9.00	8.75	8.00	8.75	8.25
Rum, W. I.	£-gal	35.0	37.5	43.5	60.0	s-gal	8.00	7.51	7.36	8.56	9.50	9.33	9.33	10.7
Sugar, Mus.	£-cwt	438.5	440.0	450.5	475.5	£-cwt	3.23	2.96	2.83	2.88	3.33	3.42	3.62	4.03
Tar	£-bbl	60.0	*75.0*	90.0	*90.0*	s-bbl	30.0	28.5	20.4	21.8	20.8	22.5	31.2	35.6
Tea, Bohea	£-lb	35.0	33.8	33.8	37.5	s-lb	8.17	7.50	7.00	7.13	7.50	6.13	6.25	6.13
Wheat	£-bu	30.0	50.3	65.0	52.8	s-bu	6.00	6.00	*6.00*	6.00	*6.25*	6.25	6.00	6.50
Bread, Ship	£-cwt	100.0			95.0	s-cwt	30.0	17.5	16.4	15.0		21.2	20.0	20.0
Cotton	£-lb	*18.9*	*20.6*	22.5	22.2	s-lb	2.50	2.50	2.25	2.25	*2.38*	2.50	2.29	2.42
Flour, Mid.	£-cwt	103.8	134.4	133.6	150.4	s-cwt	20.0	15.5	12.9	13.2	14.0	13.9	14.4	17.5
Indigo	£-lb			30.0	41.2	s-lb		7.25	9.00	8.17	7.50	*7.50*	7.50	7.50
Leather, sole	s-lb					s-lb		1.58	*1.58*	*1.62*	*1.67*	1.67	1.71	1.50
Rice	£-cwt	*220.0*	220.0			s-cwt		43.5	43.5					30.0
Sugar, Loaf	£-lb	10.2	9.94	10.4		s-lb	1.83	1.72	1.56	1.67	1.56	1.42	1.50	1.50
Tobacco	£-cwt	165.3	160.0	180.0	165.0	s-cwt	60.0	50.0	40.0	28.5	30.0	30.0	32.5	34.5
Turpentine	£-bbl					s-bbl								90.0
Wine	£-pipe				12375.0	£-pipe		137.5		110.0				95.6

Sources—Charming Forge; Thomas Evans; Freeman's Journal; Stephen Girard (Girard College Library); Hewes and Anthony (John Carter Brown Library); Hollingsworth Collection; Hughes Papers; Matthew Irwin (L of C); Jacobs Papers; Peter Kuhn (Bucks Co. HS); William R. McBay; Pemberton Papers; Pennsylvania Archives; Philadelphia Merchant, unknown, AM3081; John Pringle (L of C); Thomas Roberts III; Nathan Sharples; Shinkle and Graff (IRD); Wetmore Papers (Boston HS); Wharton Papers.

Appendix Table 1—(*Continued*)

Average Monthly Wholesale Prices of Commodities in Philadelphia

1782

Commodity	Unit	Jan.	Feb.	Mar.	Apr.	May	June	July	Aug.	Sept.	Oct.	Nov.	Dec.
Beef	£-bbl	3.55	3.28	4.22	3.05	3.75	4.23	4.41	3.75	*3.52*	3.28	3.28	3.75
Chocolate	d-lb	39.0	28.0	30.0	30.0	*28.5*	27.0	27.0	26.5	26.5	28.0	28.0	*28.0*
Coffee	d-lb	15.5	13.5	12.6	13.9	15.5	19.7	24.0	18.0	22.0	28.0	32.5	34.5
Corn	s-bu	4.03	4.70	4.70	3.55	2.75	2.75	*3.73*	4.71	5.50	5.00	5.00	7.50
Flour, Com.	s-cwt	18.4	19.1	18.4	14.9	12.0	12.0	12.8	16.5	18.0	18.0	17.0	15.5
Sup.	s-cwt	22.6	22.3	22.5	20.5	17.2	17.0	15.5	20.0	20.0	21.2	20.0	21.3
Iron, Bar	£-ton	43.5	43.8	45.0	44.6	46.3	45.0	45.0	45.0	45.0	45.6	47.5	45.0
Molasses	s-gal	7.50	*7.50*	*7.75*	*8.00*	8.00	11.5	11.5	11.0	12.0	7.50	7.50	6.00
Pepper	s-lb	*8.00*	*7.00*	7.00	8.31	8.94	10.0	10.2	9.50	11.2	11.7	12.0	11.7
Pork	£-bbl	7.25	6.80	5.50	5.36	5.10	5.50	5.63	6.00	6.00	6.00	6.00	5.50
Rum, W. I.	s-gal	11.9	10.8	14.0	12.0	11.8	11.8	14.0	12.0	11.7	11.8	11.9	11.5
Sugar, Mus.	£-cwt	4.45	3.62	3.79	4.30	5.00	5.83	4.50	4.62	4.50	4.50	4.76	4.75
Tar	s-bbl	32.5	37.5	42.8	43.1	43.0	38.8	35.0	27.5	35.0	30.0	35.0	35.0
Tea, Bohea	s-lb	7.50	7.92	8.44	14.0	13.5	11.8	10.9	9.67	10.2	11.5	12.1	11.2
Wheat	s-bu	6.25	6.25	7.00	6.25	6.25	6.25	8.17	6.25	6.25	7.50	6.00	*6.00*
Bread, Ship	s-cwt	18.0	*18.0*	*16.0*	16.0	16.0	*18.0*	*18.0*	*18.0*	*18.0*	18.0	18.0	*18.0*
Cotton	s-lb	2.50	2.50	2.50	*2.50*	*2.50*	2.50	2.33	2.62	3.08	3.25	3.25	3.13
Flour, Mid.	s-cwt	16.1	15.7	14.8	15.2	11.2	11.0	14.0	*13.1*	12.2	15.5	14.5	15.0
Indigo	s-lb	7.50				6.50	7.50	7.50	6.00	6.00	6.00	6.50	7.50
Leather, sole	s-lb	1.50	*1.58*	1.67	1.67	1.67	1.67	1.67	1.67	1.67	1.67	1.67	1.67
Rice	s-cwt					60.0	70.0				36.8	37.5	37.5
Sugar, Loaf	s-lb	1.83	1.42	1.46	2.00	2.25	2.38	2.75	2.50	2.50	2.56	2.38	2.25
Tobacco	s-cwt	37.5	40.0	35.0	40.0	37.5	35.0	35.0	35.0	35.0	40.0	37.5	37.5
Turpentine	s-bbl	90.0	80.0	76.2	120.0	100.0	90.0	80.0	55.0	50.0	50.0	40.0	*37.5*
Wine	£-pipe	110.0	110.0	74.2	111.4	111.4	98.7	103.1	84.3	82.5	93.5	103.1	

Sources—Charming Forge; Stephen Collins, Etting Collection; Coates and Reynell Papers; Gilbert Cope Historical and Genealogical Collection; Durham Furnace (Bucks Co. HS); Thomas Evans; Hewes and Anthony (John Carter Brown Library); Hollingsworth Collection; Hughes Papers; Jacobs Papers; Norris Papers; Philadelphia Merchant, unknown, AM3081; Potts Grove; Nathan Sharples; Pelatiah Webster; Wetmore Papers (Massachusetts HS); Wharton Papers; Woolsey and Salmon (L of C).

1783

Commodity	Unit	Jan.	Feb.	Mar.	Apr.	May	June	July	Aug.	Sept.	Oct.	Nov.	Dec.
Beef	£-bbl	3.75	3.75	3.94	*4.47*	5.00	5.00	5.00	3.75	4.11	4.13	4.00	4.00
Chocolate	d-lb	28.0	*24.3*	*24.3*	*23.0*	*23.0*	*23.0*	23.0	*22.0*	21.0	*20.0*	19.0	19.0
Coffee	d-lb	38.0	33.0	33.0	14.5	15.0	15.0	14.5	15.2	14.1	12.9	12.2	12.3
Corn	s-bu	5.50	*5.12*	4.75	4.50	6.00	5.51	6.25	5.50	4.71	5.06	4.50	4.42
Flour, Com.	s-cwt	15.0	17.0	*18.5*	20.0	22.1	23.0	26.1	23.7	23.7	24.3	21.9	22.3
Sup.	s-cwt	23.5	21.9	22.9	25.7	25.8	26.2	27.5	27.8	28.6	28.2	28.5	27.2
Iron, Bar	£-ton	45.0	42.5	42.0	39.7	40.0	35.9	30.6	30.0	33.9	33.6	37.0	*37.0*
Molasses	s-gal	6.00	5.00	3.25	2.88	3.00	2.12	2.25	2.33	2.36	2.39	2.35	2.46
Pepper	s-lb	12.0	9.50	7.25	*5.50*	3.75	2.25	3.17	3.20	3.52	3.75	3.67	3.75
Pork	£-bbl	5.50	5.00	5.00	3.88	5.63	5.40	5.19	5.33	5.50	5.25	4.88	5.00
Rum, W. I.	s-gal	9.50	8.00	5.75	5.00	5.00	4.38	4.75	5.00	5.00	5.00	5.00	5.06
Sugar, Mus.	£-cwt	5.00	5.00	*4.16*	3.31	3.11	3.46	3.33	3.15	3.18	3.12	3.25	3.25
Tar	s-bbl	39.4	*33.1*	26.8	21.9	19.4	20.0	30.0	30.0	27.0	24.2	20.8	20.0
Tea, Bohea	s-lb	9.50	9.00	6.75	6.38	6.00	4.75	4.00	4.08	4.00	4.25	4.07	4.00
Wheat	s-bu	6.00	6.25	6.13	5.39	7.69	8.00	8.32	6.73	6.98	6.83	6.78	6.39
Bread, Ship	s-cwt	*18.0*	18.0	18.0	*19.8*	21.6	22.0	20.0	*22.0*	24.0	23.5	23.5	22.0
Cotton	s-lb	3.25	3.00	*3.00*	*2.50*	2.50	*2.50*	*2.42*	*2.33*	2.33	*2.33*	*2.50*	2.50
Flour, Mid.	s-cwt	*15.0*	*16.0*	16.0	16.5	17.7	18.7	21.8	20.3	19.5	19.4	17.3	17.8
Indigo	s-lb	*6.62*	5.75	5.75	7.00	7.00	7.00	*7.00*	*8.00*	8.00	8.00	*7.75*	7.50
Leather, sole	s-lb	1.67	1.67	1.67	1.67	1.67	1.67	1.67	*1.67*	1.67	1.67	1.67	1.67
Rice	s-cwt				21.2	20.2		33.0		56.0		31.2	32.5
Sugar, Loaf	s-lb	2.25	2.25	1.88	1.25	1.17	1.25	1.25	1.42	1.58	1.57	1.58	1.60
Tobacco	s-cwt	32.5	30.0	40.0	45.0	48.8	47.5	50.5	55.0	52.5	51.2	47.5	48.8
Turpentine	s-bbl	35.0				22.5	20.0						
Wine	£-pipe	137.5				75.0	55.0	50.0					55.0

Sources—Anderson, An Historical and Chronological Deduction of the Origin of Commerce; Thomas A. Biddle Business Records and Correspondence; Chaloner and White Papers; Charming Forge; Coates and Reynell Papers; Stephen Collins, Etting Collection; Thomas Evans; Stephen Girard (Girard College Library); Hollingsworth Collection; Jacobs Papers; Owen Jones Papers; Meredith Papers; Morris and Miercken; Norris Papers; Philadelphia Merchant, unknown, AM3081; John Ross; Pelatiah Webster; Wharton Papers.

APPENDIX TABLE 1—(*Continued*)

AVERAGE MONTHLY WHOLESALE PRICES OF COMMODITIES IN PHILADELPHIA

1784

Commodity	Unit	Jan.	Feb.	Mar.	Apr.	May	June	July	Aug.	Sept.	Oct.	Nov.	Dec.
Beef	£-bbl	4.00	4.00	3.00	3.00	3.38	3.75	4.58	4.00	4.00	4.00	4.50	3.50
Chocolate	d-lb	23.0	21.0	22.0	16.0	15.8	18.0	15.0	15.0	15.0	18.0	18.0	20.5
Coffee	d-lb	13.7	11.8	12.8	11.5	12.0	12.5	13.2	13.5	14.1	15.0	16.8	16.3
Corn	s-bu	5.50	3.75	3.50	4.00	5.75	4.79	5.14	5.17	5.33	6.00	4.67	4.50
Flour, Com.	s-cwt	22.6	22.6	22.5	21.4	21.4	24.3	24.0	23.4	24.0	24.6	24.6	22.3
Sup.	s-cwt	28.1	27.1	29.0	26.3	26.7	28.9	28.7	28.6	27.4	26.3	28.6	27.1
Iron, Bar	£-ton	*37.5*	37.5	37.5	37.5	38.8	40.0	41.5	40.0	41.0	42.0	40.5	39.0
Molasses	s-gal	2.40	2.25	1.94	1.90	1.88	2.17	2.25	1.92	2.00	1.88	1.92	1.75
Pepper	s-lb	3.67	3.33	2.28	2.17	2.15	2.18	2.17	2.25	2.62	2.58	2.50	2.42
Pork	£-bbl	4.36	4.75	4.50	4.56	4.47	5.46	6.82	6.75	6.25	7.50	6.00	5.00
Rum, W. I.	s-gal	5.25	5.17	5.00	4.88	3.00	3.29	3.42	3.33	4.88	4.17	4.33	3.95
Sugar, Mus.	£-cwt	3.25	3.00	3.25	3.25	3.25	3.25	3.25	3.25	3.25	3.01	2.62	2.75
Tar	s-bbl	25.0	17.5	25.0	18.0	17.0	18.0	*17.5*	17.0	17.5	17.5	17.5	16.8
Tea, Bohea	s-lb	4.75	3.63	3.75	3.67	3.69	3.50	3.75	3.67	3.67	3.75	3.00	3.17
Wheat	s-bu	6.50	6.75	6.50	6.86	7.05	6.81	7.76	8.00	8.00	8.00	8.50	8.75
Bread, Ship	s-cwt	*20.0*	20.0	23.5	18.7	18.5	25.0	24.2	24.0	23.5	23.0	24.0	22.0
Cotton	s-lb	2.50	2.13	2.17	*2.15*	2.13	2.00	*2.03*	*2.07*	*2.10*	2.13	2.50	*2.50*
Flour, Mid.	s-cwt	17.5	13.5	14.1	13.4	15.5	20.4	21.8	20.0	20.0	21.1	21.4	20.0
Indigo	s-lb	7.50	8.25	6.92	6.92	9.00	*9.00*	*11.2*	11.2	*12.0*	12.0	10.0	9.00
Leather, sole	s-lb	1.67	1.63	1.67	1.67	1.67	1.67	1.58	1.67	1.67	*1.62*	1.58	1.50
Rice	s-cwt	*31.2*	31.2	35.0	35.0	29.0	32.5	33.5	32.5	35.0	32.5	32.5	32.5
Sugar, Loaf	s-lb	1.60	1.42	1.44	1.24	1.27	1.39	1.05	1.00	1.00	1.00	1.00	1.00
Tobacco	s-cwt	60.0	60.0	61.2	58.8	62.5	70.0	70.0	65.0	57.5	62.5	57.5	57.5
Turpentine	s-bbl	*30.7*	30.0	30.0	30.0	32.5	*30.2*	28.0	28.0	30.0	30.0	30.0	27.0
Wine	£-pipe	56.0	62.5	66.0	68.8	75.0	61.9	*67.5*	67.5	65.0	65.0	70.0	70.0

SOURCES—Thomas A. Biddle Business Records and Correspondence; Chaloner and White Papers; Clifford Papers; Coates and Reynell Papers; Gilbert Cope Historical and Genealogical Collection; Dutilh and Wachsmuth (L of C); Thomas Evans; Stephen Girard (Girard College Library); Hollingsworth Collection; Owen Jones Papers; Frederick Kuhl; Peter Kuhn (Bucks Co. HS); McPherson's Philadelphia Price Current; Morris and Miercken; Pennsylvania Mercury; Philadelphia Merchant, unknown, AM3081; Wetmore Papers (Boston HS); Wharton Papers; Wynkoop and Sieman.

1785

Commodity	Unit	Jan.	Feb.	Mar.	Apr.	May	June	July	Aug.	Sept.	Oct.	Nov.	Dec.
Beef	£-bbl	3.50	3.50	3.00	3.00	3.00	3.00	3.00	3.50	3.75	3.75	3.75	3.75
Chocolate	d-lb	19.0	19.0	22.5	22.5	*18.8*	15.0	17.0	17.0	17.0	17.0	17.0	17.0
Coffee	d-lb	14.5	14.0	15.5	14.0	14.5	16.5	15.8	14.0	16.0	18.0	17.5	17.5
Corn	s-bu	3.50	3.50	3.75	3.83	3.75	3.83	3.83	3.88	4.42	4.50	4.71	4.71
Flour, Com.	s-cwt	22.6	22.3	21.7	21.7	20.0	21.4	21.4	21.4	23.1	21.7	22.0	22.0
Sup.	s-cwt	25.7	25.7	25.7	24.6	25.7	25.7	25.1	25.1	24.9	24.9	24.6	24.0
Iron, Bar	£-ton	37.5	37.5	36.0	34.0	33.0	30.0	30.0	28.0	29.0	29.0	29.0	29.0
Molasses	s-gal	1.83	1.75	1.83	1.75	1.75	1.67	1.67	1.67	1.58	1.67	1.67	1.75
Pepper	s-lb	2.25	2.50	2.50	2.25	2.50	2.75	2.58	2.88	3.50	3.50	4.25	4.50
Pork	£-bbl	5.25	5.00	5.25	5.00	5.25	5.50	6.00	6.00	6.38	5.75	5.75	4.38
Rum, W. I.	s-gal	4.58	3.75	3.67	3.80	3.17	3.25	3.50	3.17	3.17	3.25	3.38	2.88
Sugar, Mus.	£-cwt	2.48	2.48	2.41	2.41	2.41	2.40	2.40	2.40	2.52	2.81	2.94	2.94
Tar	s-bbl	17.5	17.5	17.5	15.5	15.5	10.5	10.0	11.0	12.5	13.0	12.5	12.5
Tea, Bohea	s-lb	2.50	2.83	2.83	2.92	2.92	2.75	2.58	2.58	2.58	2.58	2.58	2.58
Wheat	s-bu	8.42	8.50	8.50	8.00	8.00	8.00	7.96	7.25	7.38	7.75	7.88	7.92
Bread, Ship	s-cwt	22.0	22.0	20.0	22.0	24.0	24.0	23.5	23.5	23.0	22.5	23.2	23.2
Cotton	s-lb	2.50	2.50	*2.47*	*2.44*	*2.42*	*2.39*	*2.36*	2.33	*2.33*	2.33	*2.42*	2.50
Flour, Mid.	s-cwt	21.4	21.4	20.0	20.0	19.4	20.0	19.3	19.3	19.6	20.0	18.6	18.6
Indigo	s-lb	8.92	8.92				6.75	6.75	6.75	6.75	6.75	6.75	6.75
Leather, sole	s-lb	1.58	1.58	1.25	1.50	1.54	1.54	*1.58*	1.62	1.62	1.71	1.77	1.69
Rice	s-cwt	32.5	30.0	27.0	27.0	26.0	27.5	26.0	26.0	25.0	26.0	27.5	27.5
Sugar, Loaf	s-lb	1.00	1.00	1.00	1.00	1.00	0.92	0.92	0.92	0.92	1.00	1.00	1.00
Tobacco	s-cwt	57.5	57.5	55.0	55.0	55.0	55.0	55.0	55.0	55.0	55.0	50.0	50.0
Turpentine	s-bbl	27.5	27.0	27.0	26.0	25.0	18.0	17.5	17.5	19.0	18.0	18.0	18.0
Wine	£-pipe	70.0	70.0	80.0	80.0	70.0	70.0	65.0	65.0	60.0	60.0	60.0	60.0

SOURCES—Coates and Reynell Papers; Stephen Girard (Girard College Library); Hollingsworth Collection; Owen Jones Papers; Pennsylvania Evening Herald; Pennsylvania Mercury; Philadelphia Commercial List and Price Current; Wharton Papers.

Appendix Table 1—(*Continued*)

Average Monthly Wholesale Prices of Commodities in Philadelphia

1786

Commodity	Unit	Jan.	Feb.	Mar.	Apr.	May	June	July	Aug.	Sept.	Oct.	Nov.	Dec.
Beef	£-bbl	3.75	3.75	3.75	3.50	4.00	4.00	4.00	4.00	4.00	4.00	4.00	4.00
Chocolate	d-lb	16.5	16.5	16.5	16.5	15.5	15.5	15.5	15.5	15.5	15.5	15.5	15.5
Coffee	d-lb	17.5	17.0	16.0	16.5	15.0	16.0	16.0	15.5	15.5	16.0	18.0	19.0
Corn	s-bu	3.63	3.88	4.50	4.04	4.00	5.00	5.63	5.92	5.50	4.50	3.13	3.04
Flour, Com.	s-cwt	18.9	20.3	20.3	18.6	19.4	21.4	21.7	20.0	22.6	21.1	21.4	20.6
Sup.	s-cwt	*24.0*	24.0	23.7	23.1	22.9	24.6	24.6	24.6	24.3	24.3	24.0	22.9
Iron, Bar	£-ton	29.0	29.0	27.5	27.5	26.5	25.5	25.5	25.5	25.5	25.5	25.5	25.5
Molasses	s-gal	1.92	2.08	1.75	1.75	1.75	1.79	1.96	1.75	1.75	1.75	1.79	1.92
Pepper	s-lb	4.00	3.75	3.50	3.75	3.50	*3.50*	3.50	3.50	3.50	3.00	3.00	3.00
Pork	£-bbl	4.38	4.50	3.75	4.25	5.00	5.00	5.00	5.00	5.25	5.25	6.00	4.50
Rum, W. I.	s-gal	3.38	3.38	3.38	3.38	3.38	3.38	3.38	3.33	3.33	3.33	3.33	3.33
Sugar, Mus.	£-cwt	2.94	2.94	2.94	2.69	2.75	2.75	2.75	2.75	2.75	2.75	2.75	2.75
Tar	s-bbl	12.5	12.5	12.5	12.5	8.00	8.00	8.00	8.00	8.00	8.00	8.00	10.0
Tea, Bohea	s-lb	2.63	2.75	2.75	2.79	2.75	2.75	2.75	2.75	2.75	2.75	2.75	2.75
Wheat	s-bu	7.75	7.50	7.50	6.88	6.88	7.75	8.00	7.25	7.88	7.13	7.25	7.50
Bread, Ship	s-cwt	21.0	20.0	18.5	19.2	19.2	19.2	19.2	19.2	19.2	19.2	19.2	19.2
Cotton	s-lb	2.75	2.75	2.75	2.75	3.13	3.13	3.13	3.25	3.00	3.00	3.00	3.00
Flour, Mid.	s-cwt	18.3	17.7	17.7	18.6	19.4	20.3	18.6	19.7	18.6	17.1	17.9	16.3
Indigo	s-lb	6.75	6.75	6.75	6.75	6.75	6.75	6.75	6.75	6.75	6.75	6.75	6.75
Leather, sole	s-lb	1.58	1.54	1.58	1.50	1.42	1.42	1.42	1.42	1.50	1.62	1.50	*1.50*
Rice	s-cwt	27.5	27.5	23.0	22.5	21.5	22.5	27.5	27.5	26.0	26.0	26.0	26.0
Sugar, Loaf	s-lb	1.08	1.08	1.08	1.08	1.08	1.08	1.08	1.08	1.08	1.08	1.08	1.08
Tobacco	s-cwt	45.0	43.0	43.0	35.0	35.0	35.0	35.0	35.0	37.5	37.5	40.0	40.0
Turpentine	s-bbl	17.5	17.5	17.5	17.0	12.0	12.0	12.0	12.0	12.0	12.0	12.0	12.0
Wine	£-pipe	60.0	60.0	60.0	60.0	60.0	60.0	60.0	60.0	60.0	60.0	60.0	60.0

Sources—Coates and Reynell Papers; Complete Counting House Companion; Pennsylvania Mercury; Philadelphia Commercial List and Price Current.

1787

Commodity	Unit	Jan.	Feb.	Mar.	Apr.	May	June	July	Aug.	Sept.	Oct.	Nov.	Dec.
Beef	£-bbl	4.00	4.00	4.00	3.88	3.88	3.88	3.88	3.88	3.88	3.88	3.13	3.00
Chocolate	d-lb	15.5	15.5	14.5	12.5	12.5	12.5	14.5	12.5	14.5	12.5	14.5	14.5
Coffee	d-lb	19.0	19.0	19.0	14.8	15.0	17.5	15.5	16.0	16.2	16.8	18.5	18.5
Corn	s-bu	2.88	3.00	3.00	3.13	3.50	3.00	3.92	3.29	3.29	3.29	3.17	2.75
Flour, Com.	s-cwt	21.1	20.6	20.0	19.7	20.0	20.3	21.4	19.4	17.4	17.4	16.9	16.3
Sup.	s-cwt	22.9	22.9	22.9	22.9	22.9	24.3	24.3	20.9	18.9	18.9	18.0	17.6
Iron, Bar	£-ton	25.5	25.5	25.5	25.5	25.5	25.5	25.5	25.0	25.0	25.0	25.5	25.5
Molasses	s-gal	1.92	2.08	2.08	2.08	1.75	2.08	1.83	1.83	1.92	1.79	1.79	1.88
Pepper	s-lb	3.00	3.00	3.00	2.67	2.50	2.33	2.33	2.33	2.42	2.42	2.42	2.75
Pork	£-bbl	4.50	4.25	4.50	4.50	4.50	4.50	4.50	4.62	4.75	4.75	4.50	4.00
Rum, W. I.	s-gal	3.33	3.63	3.63	3.63	3.25	3.38	3.25	3.17	3.17	3.17	3.17	3.17
Sugar, Mus.	£-cwt	2.75	2.75	2.75	2.75	2.75	2.75	2.62	2.62	2.62	2.62	2.62	2.62
Tar	s-bbl	10.0	10.0	10.0	10.0	10.0	10.0	10.0	10.0	11.0	11.0	11.0	11.0
Tea, Bohea	s-lb	2.75	2.75	2.75	2.88	2.63	2.42	2.42	2.42	2.42	2.42	2.75	2.75
Wheat	s-bu	7.50	7.50	7.25	6.75	6.75	8.25	7.25	6.50	5.75	5.75	5.75	5.25
Bread, Ship	s-cwt	19.2	19.2	19.2	19.2	19.2	19.2	19.2	18.0	17.5	17.5	17.0	15.0
Cotton	s-lb	3.00	3.00	3.00	3.00	3.00	3.00	3.00	3.00	3.00	2.92	2.92	2.92
Flour, Mid.	s-cwt	16.3	14.9	14.9	15.4	14.3	16.3	17.0	15.1	14.0	14.0	13.7	13.3
Indigo	s-lb	6.75	6.75	6.75	6.50	5.25	5.25	5.75	5.75	5.75	6.25	6.75	6.75
Leather, sole	s-lb	1.50	1.63	1.54	1.54	1.33	1.33	1.33	1.33	1.33	1.33	1.33	1.33
Rice	s-cwt	26.0	26.0	25.5	25.5	25.5	25.5	26.0	25.0	25.0	23.5	23.5	23.5
Sugar, Loaf	s-lb	1.08	1.08	1.08	1.04	1.04	1.08	1.08	1.08	1.08	1.03	1.03	1.08
Tobacco	s-cwt	40.0	40.0	40.0	40.0	41.2	40.0	37.5	40.0	42.0	42.0	42.0	42.0
Turpentine	s-bbl	12.0	12.0	12.0	12.0	12.0	12.0	10.0	10.0	10.0	10.0	10.0	10.0
Wine	£-pipe	60.0	60.0	60.0	60.0	60.0	60.0	60.0	60.0	60.0	60.0	60.0	60.0

Sources—Coates and Reynell Papers; Complete Counting House Companion; Pennsylvania Mercury; Philadelphia Commercial List and Price Current.

Appendix Table 1—(*Continued*)

Average Monthly Wholesale Prices of Commodities in Philadelphia

1788

Commodity	Unit	Jan.	Feb.	Mar.	Apr.	May	June	July	Aug.	Sept.	Oct.	Nov.	Dec.
Beef	£-bbl	2.88	2.88	2.88	2.88	2.63	*2.61*	2.58	2.58	2.58	2.58	2.58	2.58
Chocolate	d-lb	14.5	14.5	14.5	13.0	13.0	13.0	12.5	12.5	12.5	12.5	12.5	12.0
Coffee	d-lb	18.5	16.5	14.5	14.5	14.5	16.0	15.5	16.2	18.5	18.5	19.5	18.5
Corn	s-bu	2.58	2.50	2.29	2.58	2.75	2.83	2.88	2.75	2.67	2.92	2.75	2.22
Flour, Com.	s-cwt	15.6	15.4	15.3	15.7	18.7	17.9	17.7	18.7	18.0	18.3	17.7	18.3
Sup.	s-cwt	17.4	17.4	20.0	20.6	21.1	21.1	20.0	20.0	20.0	19.7	19.4	20.0
Iron, Bar	£-ton	25.5	25.5	26.0	26.0	26.0	27.0	27.0	26.8	26.5	26.0	26.0	25.5
Molasses	s-gal	1.88	1.88	1.88	1.88	1.88	1.92	1.88	1.81	1.81	1.77	1.77	1.88
Pepper	s-lb	2.75	2.75	2.75	2.75	2.75	*2.75*	2.75	2.75	2.75	2.88	2.88	2.71
Pork	£-bbl	4.00	4.00	3.44	3.62	3.68	3.68	3.68	3.81	3.81	3.81	3.81	3.75
Rum, W. I.	s-gal	3.17	3.17	3.25	3.25	3.25	3.25	3.25	2.92	2.92	3.00	3.00	3.21
Sugar, Mus.	£-cwt	2.62	2.75	2.75	2.75	2.75	*2.75*	2.75	2.75	2.75	2.69	2.69	2.88
Tar	s-bbl	11.0	11.0	11.0	9.50	9.50	*9.50*	9.50	9.00	9.00	10.6	10.6	12.5
Tea, Bohea	s-lb	2.75	2.75	2.67	2.63	2.63	2.38	2.42	2.42	2.00	1.83	1.83	1.88
Wheat	s-bu	5.25	5.25	6.00	6.00	6.75	6.75	6.25	5.50	5.50	6.00	5.88	6.13
Bread, Ship	s-cwt	16.0	16.5	16.0	*15.2*	14.5	14.5	*14.5*	14.0	14.0	13.5	13.5	13.5
Cotton	s-lb	2.92	2.92	2.92	2.75	2.75	2.75	2.75	2.75	2.50	2.50	2.50	2.25
Flour, Mid.	s-cwt	12.0	12.1	12.1	12.1	14.3	15.3	14.3	14.9	14.3	14.3	13.7	13.9
Indigo	s-lb	6.75	6.75	6.00	6.00	6.00	*6.00*	6.00	6.00	5.38	7.25	7.25	5.75
Leather, sole	s-lb	*1.25*	1.17	1.33	1.25	1.25	1.25	1.21	1.19	1.19	1.42	1.42	1.42
Rice	s-cwt	23.5	23.5	22.8	22.8	21.2	*22.2*	23.2	22.5	22.5	22.8	24.0	24.5
Sugar, Loaf	s-lb	1.08	1.08	1.08	1.06	1.06	*1.06*	1.06	1.06	1.06	1.06	1.06	0.98
Tobacco	s-cwt	42.0	42.0	41.0	41.0	41.0	*41.0*	41.0	41.0	41.0	40.0	35.0	35.0
Turpentine	s-bbl	12.0	12.0	12.0	12.0	12.0	*12.0*	12.0	12.0	12.0	12.5	12.5	13.8
Wine	£-pipe	60.0	60.0	60.0	60.0	60.0	*60.0*	60.0	60.0	60.0	60.0	60.0	60.0

Sources—Clifford Papers; Coates and Reynell Papers; Columbian Magazine; Federal Gazette; Benjamin Fuller; Hollingsworth Collection; Pennsylvania Mercury; Pennsylvania Packet; Philadelphia Commercial List and Price Current; Wharton Papers.

1789

Commodity	Unit	Jan.	Feb.	Mar.	Apr.	May	June	July	Aug.	Sept.	Oct.	Nov.	Dec.
Beef	£-bbl	2.58	2.58	2.40	2.40	2.40	2.40	2.40	2.40	2.40	2.40	2.68	2.45
Chocolate	d-lb	12.0	12.0	12.0	12.0	15.0	15.0	14.5	14.5	14.0	13.0	13.0	13.0
Coffee	d-lb	18.0	17.0	17.0	17.0	19.0	20.0	19.0	19.5	20.0	20.0	20.0	18.5
Corn	s-bu	2.36	2.38	2.13	2.08	3.00	3.50	3.33	3.63	3.67	3.75	4.00	3.42
Flour, Com.	s-cwt	16.9	17.1	17.1	17.4	19.7	21.3	20.0	21.1	21.6	21.9	20.9	24.0
Sup.	s-cwt	20.0	19.4	20.0	20.0	22.9	24.3	22.1	23.4	24.3	24.3	22.9	24.3
Iron, Bar	£-ton	26.0	26.0	26.0	26.0	26.0	26.0	26.0	27.0	27.0	27.0	27.0	27.5
Molasses	s-gal	1.81	1.81	1.81	1.73	2.08	2.08	2.08	2.08	2.00	2.02	2.02	2.33
Pepper	s-lb	2.71	2.71	2.71	2.83	2.83	2.83	2.83	2.58	2.58	2.58	2.58	2.58
Pork	£-bbl	3.75	3.75	3.53	3.53	3.53	3.67	3.67	3.53	3.53	3.53	3.53	3.53
Rum, W. I.	s-gal	3.50	3.50	3.63	3.63	3.75	3.63	3.63	3.63	3.63	4.13	4.13	4.50
Sugar, Mus.	£-cwt	2.88	2.88	2.88	2.88	3.19	3.19	3.19	3.06	3.06	3.06	3.06	3.06
Tar	s-bbl	12.5	12.0	12.0	10.5	10.5	10.5	10.5	10.5	10.5	10.5	10.5	15.5
Tea, Bohea	s-lb	1.88	1.88	1.88	1.81	2.00	2.00	2.00	2.00	1.88	1.88	1.88	2.00
Wheat	s-bu	6.00	5.75	5.75	6.25	7.13	7.25	7.50	6.75	6.75	7.50	7.50	8.42
Bread, Ship	s-cwt	13.5	13.5	13.5	13.0	13.0	14.0	16.0	15.5	15.5	15.5	15.5	18.0
Cotton	s-lb	2.25	2.25	2.25	2.06	2.06	2.06	2.06	2.06	2.06	2.06	2.06	2.06
Flour, Mid.	s-cwt	13.6	13.6	13.6	13.6	16.3	16.6	16.6	16.6	17.7	16.9	17.1	19.3
Indigo	s-lb	5.75	5.75	5.75	5.75	5.75	5.75	5.75	5.75	5.75	5.75	5.75	5.75
Leather, sole	s-lb	1.42	1.42	1.17	1.17	1.17	1.17	1.42	1.42	1.42	1.42	1.42	1.42
Rice	s-cwt	24.5	24.0	24.0	20.0	20.0	19.0	19.0	19.0	19.0	19.5	19.5	22.5
Sugar, Loaf	s-lb	0.98	0.98	0.98	0.98	1.17	1.17	1.17	1.13	1.13	1.08	1.08	1.08
Tobacco	s-cwt	35.0	35.0	35.0	35.0	35.0	35.0	35.0	35.0	35.0	32.5	32.5	32.5
Turpentine	s-bbl	13.8	13.8	13.8	12.5	12.5	12.5	12.5	12.5	12.5	12.5	12.5	17.5
Wine	£-pipe	60.0	60.0	60.0	60.0	60.0	60.0	60.0	60.0	60.0	60.0	60.0	60.0

Sources—Federal Gazette; Pennsylvania Mercury; Philadelphia Commercial List and Price Current.

Appendix Table 1—(*Concluded*)

Average Monthly Wholesale Prices of Commodities in Philadelphia

1790

Commodity	Unit	Jan.	Feb.	Mar.	Apr.	May	June	July	Aug.	Sept.	Oct.	Nov.	Dec.
Beef	£-bbl	2.45	2.45	2.45	2.45	2.45	2.45	2.74	2.74	2.74	2.74	2.53	2.53
Chocolate	d-lb	13.0	13.0	13.0	12.0	12.0	12.0	12.0	12.0	12.0	12.0	12.5	14.0
Coffee	d-lb	17.5	17.5	14.0	16.0	16.0	16.5	15.5	15.5	15.5	16.2	15.5	14.5
Corn	s-bu	3.25	3.75	5.00	5.25	5.00	4.50	3.88	3.75	3.88	3.08	4.00	3.50
Flour, Com.	s-cwt	24.3	26.4	30.0	32.0	34.3	31.7	29.1	28.9	22.9	23.7	25.1	24.3
Sup.	s-cwt	25.4	28.7	32.1	33.3	35.7	33.1	31.1	30.6	25.7	24.7	26.3	26.3
Iron, Bar	£-ton	27.5	27.5	28.0	28.0	28.0	28.0	28.0	28.0	28.0	28.0	30.0	30.0
Molasses	s-gal	2.17	2.17	2.00	1.94	2.17	2.33	2.13	2.21	2.29	2.54	2.50	2.75
Pepper	s-lb	3.17	3.17	3.17	2.50	2.50	2.50	2.67	2.67	2.67	2.67	2.67	2.67
Pork	£-bbl	3.53	3.53	3.53	3.53	3.53	3.53	3.94	4.75	4.75	5.02	4.89	4.21
Rum, W. I.	s-gal	4.50	4.63	4.63	4.13	4.13	4.13	4.38	4.38	4.38	4.63	4.50	4.33
Sugar, Mus.	£-cwt	3.06	3.06	3.06	3.06	3.06	3.19	3.25	3.50	3.75	4.12	4.12	4.12
Tar	s-bbl	15.5	15.5	15.5	15.5	15.5	15.5	15.5	10.9	10.9	16.5	17.5	15.0
Tea, Bohea	s-lb	2.33	2.33	2.33	2.33	2.33	2.33	2.33	2.21	2.21	2.67	2.75	2.58
Wheat	s-bu	9.00	10.2	11.3	12.8	13.2	11.2	10.2	9.50	8.25	8.00	8.75	8.42
Bread, Ship	s-cwt	18.0	18.0	23.5	25.0	25.0	28.0	27.0	26.0	19.0	17.5	18.0	19.0
Cotton	s-lb	1.88	1.88	1.88	1.88	1.88	2.08	1.88	1.88	1.58	1.58	1.67	1.67
Flour, Mid.	s-cwt	19.4	20.7	27.1	25.7	27.9	26.6	22.3	22.4	21.4	18.6	18.6	21.4
Indigo	s-lb	5.75	5.75	5.75	5.75	5.75	5.75	5.75	5.75	5.75	5.75	5.25	5.25
Leather, sole	s-lb	1.42	1.42	1.42	1.42	1.42	1.42	1.42	1.42	1.42	1.42	1.42	1.42
Rice	s-cwt	22.5	22.5	22.5	22.5	22.5	22.5	24.0	24.0	23.0	23.0	20.0	22.8
Sugar, Loaf	s-lb	1.17	1.17	1.17	1.17	1.17	1.17	1.17	1.25	1.25	1.50	1.50	1.50
Tobacco	s-cwt	32.5	32.5	32.5	32.5	32.5	32.5	32.5	32.5	32.5	32.5	38.8	38.8
Turpentine	s-bbl	17.5	17.5	17.5	17.5	17.5	17.5	17.5	17.5	17.5	18.0	20.0	20.0
Wine	£-pipe	60.0	60.0	60.0	60.0	60.0	60.0	60.0	60.0	60.0	60.0	61.2	61.2

Sources—Federal Gazette; Pennsylvania Mercury; Philadelphia Commercial List and Price Current.

Appendix Table 2

Median of Price Relatives of Fifteen Commodities and Average Deviation as a Percentage of the Median

1770-1790

Year	Jan.	Feb.	Mar.	Apr.	May	June	July	Aug.	Sept.	Oct.	Nov.	Dec.
						Median of Relatives						
1770	92.0	91.4	90.8	92.0	93.1	101.2	93.1	97.6	92.0	94.6	95.7	92.8
1771	91.8	92.8	96.4	94.0	95.7	98.4	96.3	96.5	98.0	99.7	98.9	100.0
1772	101.6	100.6	100.6	101.1	103.7	107.0	105.0	105.9	105.4	107.0	103.9	104.6
1773	101.2	104.4	101.4	99.8	98.3	96.3	98.0	99.2	98.9	99.0	96.5	99.3
1774	100.6	102.0	99.2	99.2	98.9	97.9	99.6	95.2	100.6	100.6	100.6	94.7
1775	96.4	95.7	92.9	94.4	84.3	84.3	88.9	92.6	89.9	93.1	91.4	96.4
1776	103.2	102.5	105.8	117.4	128.9	145.5	148.1	148.1	158.7	152.8	168.0	210.0
1777	227.9	248.3	255.7	297.5	299.1	335.9	348.1	413.9	464.1	444.8	580.2	580.2
1778	599.1	661.4	769.9	761.1	766.7	772.1	791.9	813.9	858.2	814.1	880.1	1049.8
1779	1127.8	1319.8	1597.0	1760.2	2145.5	2310.2	2221.2	2460.4	3569.4	4760.7	6482.7	7916.8
1780	7589.3	8998.0	9602.5	10365.8	10736.0	10165.0	10365.8	10712.3	11080.3	11765.7	12587.0	13327.4
1781	12676.7	14851.5	15354.8	16501.7	132.0	133.0	131.0	133.0	137.2	134.9	142.0	161.0
1782	168.3	158.3	155.3	171.7	178.9	174.1	174.1	174.1	174.1	179.7	185.1	189.7
1783	185.1	164.4	160.7	140.4	143.5	125.7	132.9	125.7	131.2	130.0	129.8	128.3
1784	136.8	122.3	110.5	110.4	107.1	127.1	128.2	124.0	127.0	120.3	128.4	118.0
1785	115.8	115.8	110.4	110.7	109.3	110.4	110.4	108.3	112.0	112.3	112.4	112.2
1786	108.1	109.1	106.8	104.3	102.8	109.8	110.7	105.9	108.5	109.4	102.5	103.0
1787	103.0	103.0	104.8	103.2	101.6	104.8	104.3	96.7	95.9	95.5	95.9	94.0
1788	94.0	94.0	95.9	92.7	96.4	95.2	93.7	90.1	90.1	89.0	89.0	94.9
1789	92.6	90.7	90.1	90.1	100.6	101.6	100.6	105.4	106.6	108.9	104.4	113.5
1790	114.8	122.3	114.8	112.0	114.8	115.5	114.8	110.6	112.7	113.7	117.5	115.1
						Average Deviation as a Percentage of the Median						
1770												
1771	11.7	11.2	9.4	6.0	3.8	5.2	5.2	4.8	4.4	5.6	5.3	6.5
1772	6.4	6.5	4.6	4.1	5.3	6.4	8.1	6.8	5.4	5.0	4.6	5.1
1773	4.8	4.5	3.9	5.3	4.4	5.0	4.6	3.7	5.0	5.5	9.5	9.7
1774	10.3	10.3	8.6	7.8	8.7	11.0	10.7	9.7	10.6	10.5	13.7	13.1
1775	10.1	11.0	11.0	12.5	13.2	13.9	10.5	10.0	15.9	17.6	19.7	26.5
1776	22.2	23.5	26.5	32.2	33.7	39.9	40.0	39.4	39.6	45.3	41.5	48.4
1777	46.2	74.2	66.8	69.5	77.8	80.5	87.7	89.6	84.2	91.7	77.6	74.8
1778	75.0	79.4	67.9	68.2	66.4	62.4	72.9	55.3	47.4	46.8	45.1	45.8
1779	42.8	56.0	47.4	54.1	40.0	41.5	39.8	38.0	44.8	47.4	33.2	25.4
1780	28.9	33.1	51.4	67.6	48.2	47.5	44.1	40.2	34.7	36.1	43.4	46.2
1781	45.8	31.6	32.1	44.0	47.3	45.3	42.1	48.3	52.7	49.0	45.1	50.1
1782	46.4	45.4	53.3	57.5	57.0	64.2	59.7	52.6	57.8	47.1	50.5	44.9
1783	45.1	39.6	24.9	20.7	14.8	14.5	18.2	16.3	13.9	14.4	13.8	14.5
1784	16.6	15.0	19.6	13.9	17.3	13.6	16.7	16.3	14.2	15.9	12.6	10.1
1785	13.3	11.3	11.3	10.5	9.4	10.8	10.7	13.9	16.0	14.0	16.4	17.1
1786	13.6	12.6	13.7	13.0	15.1	16.4	16.3	18.9	18.2	15.2	17.4	14.3
1787	14.8	15.0	15.0	13.0	11.8	14.3	11.4	13.4	14.2	14.9	12.8	15.2
1788	15.6	15.2	14.1	13.9	11.6	12.3	13.4	15.6	17.3	15.7	16.0	15.6
1789	16.2	16.4	17.3	18.1	16.3	16.1	15.4	14.6	15.1	15.7	15.9	15.2
1790	15.6	15.9	21.6	22.2	23.4	20.1	16.3	18.0	14.2	15.9	14.2	16.0

Appendix Table 3

Weighted and Unweighted Arithmetic Averages of Price Relatives of Fifteen Commodities

1770-1790

Year	Jan.	Feb.	Mar.	Apr.	May	June	July	Aug.	Sept.	Oct.	Nov.	Dec.
						Weighted Average						
1770	89.2	87.5	88.5	88.2	91.5	94.8	94.5	97.9	96.4	95.8	95.2	92.9
1771	92.0	91.4	95.4	95.1	94.3	97.0	96.9	95.5	98.6	99.2	98.9	101.3
1772	101.6	100.8	101.8	101.5	104.2	107.3	109.1	107.0	107.3	107.4	106.0	104.3
1773	103.1	104.2	102.2	99.7	98.4	96.3	96.9	98.2	98.2	96.8	96.3	95.8
1774	96.5	97.4	96.1	95.6	97.7	94.9	95.3	93.2	94.5	95.6	95.3	94.5
1775	92.6	93.4	89.8	90.4	84.0	86.1	89.2	89.6	88.7	86.8	83.8	85.2
1776	89.3	90.1	95.6	101.8	105.9	127.3	122.2	126.1	131.0	142.6	151.2	183.0
1777	219.4	256.9	251.8	291.1	314.4	360.3	401.4	456.2	480.5	466.8	486.4	492.8
1778	541.1	633.7	601.9	597.0	604.3	584.2	683.1	628.0	661.1	704.6	812.6	1076.5
1779	1221.9	1630.8	1859.4	2303.1	2653.5	2683.7	2570.2	2838.1	3530.6	4482.7	6608.5	7989.1
1780	7542.0	8897.7	11623.0	13129.7	12581.4	11864.8	12477.2	12540.0	12309.8	11804.7	13819.2	14800.0
1781	14803.0	16313.0	17035.6	19888.3	142.6	134.0	131.9	133.6	136.9	135.4	144.9	155.9
1782	155.5	150.7	160.5	148.9	146.7	156.9	162.7	159.6	165.0	159.0	159.4	161.1
1783	154.9	145.1	134.0	124.5	137.3	132.8	137.8	128.4	130.0	129.5	125.8	125.2
1784	129.0	122.2	119.3	116.5	118.6	125.4	134.1	130.3	133.2	135.6	131.8	121.6
1785	118.2	115.7	114.3	111.4	109.5	111.0	112.0	110.6	116.3	115.9	117.2	112.8
1786	108.8	110.7	108.9	105.1	107.8	113.7	116.0	113.9	116.1	111.8	111.0	106.9
1787	106.9	107.1	106.9	105.0	104.7	107.6	108.1	101.9	98.9	98.7	94.8	91.1
1788	89.6	89.2	89.8	91.3	94.5	94.5	92.9	92.1	91.6	92.7	91.7	92.4
1789	92.1	91.4	90.3	90.6	99.8	103.5	100.7	102.1	103.0	105.3	105.1	109.4
1790	110.4	117.1	125.5	129.1	132.9	126.5	122.8	123.0	114.8	116.4	120.9	116.6
						Unweighted Average						
1770	100.5	98.8	100.5	98.7	104.2	107.3	109.1	110.5	109.2	107.9	101.0	98.9
1771	98.4	97.9	101.0	97.7	96.5	98.0	98.6	97.6	99.1	100.1	99.5	101.0
1772	102.6	100.9	100.9	99.9	102.0	104.3	104.5	103.6	104.0	105.0	104.1	102.9
1773	101.5	103.2	100.5	97.5	96.9	96.2	98.0	97.4	97.8	96.3	96.9	97.9
1774	99.6	101.3	97.4	96.1	97.8	97.4	97.8	94.3	96.0	99.4	103.0	98.5
1775	95.0	95.2	91.9	93.7	88.8	90.3	93.3	93.7	95.0	96.1	94.4	101.1
1776	103.2	104.7	111.0	121.5	130.7	149.8	150.3	153.1	162.7	183.5	197.4	233.0
1777	269.3	341.8	332.8	380.8	413.8	475.5	521.8	600.1	627.0	617.0	681.5	685.4
1778	729.0	841.6	843.6	847.9	850.8	815.9	966.7	824.7	827.1	865.4	958.5	1239.8
1779	1358.9	1784.4	2014.2	2431.9	2770.2	2844.2	2644.3	2930.1	4216.6	5428.6	7136.8	8146.4
1780	8390.2	9756.8	12517.1	14923.9	13426.5	12830.9	12963.7	12870.4	13224.5	13164.5	15626.1	16893.5
1781	16075.5	16976.4	18225.0	21348.3	166.8	159.0	154.0	162.4	176.3	171.0	176.0	197.2
1782	196.7	186.8	199.6	202.8	203.4	220.3	224.6	210.3	226.0	213.4	219.2	215.8
1783	211.3	187.7	161.6	138.5	141.6	130.3	139.0	132.8	132.5	131.3	126.6	123.3
1784	134.0	121.6	119.4	112.1	112.7	118.3	123.9	120.6	125.2	127.8	123.8	117.5
1785	113.2	111.8	113.1	109.2	107.0	105.1	105.7	105.0	111.7	113.1	116.0	113.8
1786	110.4	111.2	108.3	106.6	104.9	109.2	111.4	109.5	110.5	106.1	105.9	104.9
1787	104.8	105.6	105.1	100.9	99.0	101.8	101.4	97.1	97.4	96.2	95.6	94.2
1788	93.3	92.5	91.9	91.6	93.3	93.8	92.4	91.2	91.2	92.8	92.5	93.0
1789	92.9	91.9	91.0	90.7	99.9	102.4	100.5	100.4	100.4	102.0	102.4	107.1
1790	108.9	113.0	116.5	116.6	119.0	115.7	113.4	111.9	108.4	113.3	116.7	113.4

Appendix Table 4

Ratios of Pennsylvania State Currency to Specie

1780-1789

Year	Jan.	Feb.	Mar.	Apr.	May	June	July	Aug.	Sept.	Oct.	Nov.	Dec.
1780											3.00	
1781	1.33		1.73	1.99	4.09	4.38	5.00		2.25			2.50
1782	3.00	3.00						4.00				
1783	3.00	1.25	1.25			1.25	1.33					
1784												
1785									2.50	3.00	1.75	1.12
1786		1.11			1.05	1.08	1.11		1.12			1.12
1787			1.10		1.75	1.16	1.22	1.30	1.38	1.58		
1788		1.43				1.56						
1789		1.33	1.43	1.33	1.28						1.13	

Appendix Table 5

Median of Price Relatives of Fifteen Commodities in Amsterdam, Holland

1770-1789

Year	Jan.	Feb.	Mar.	Apr.	May	June	July	Aug.	Sept.	Oct.	Nov.	Dec.
1770	88.3	88.3	86.2	85.1	86.3	87.8	89.4	91.0	92.5	94.1	95.6	96.5
1771	96.5	98.8	98.8	100.0	102.4	97.1	100.0	100.0	101.8	101.8	106.9	109.9
1772	100.1	105.0	104.9	103.5	100.1	100.8	100.0	100.0	100.0	100.0	100.0	100.1
1773	100.1	100.0	98.4	92.9	94.4	94.4	94.4	94.4	94.4	94.4	94.4	92.5
1774	94.4	93.0	93.0	91.2	86.8	89.0	88.6	88.6	90.4	90.4	90.4	90.4
1775	94.4	94.4	94.4	94.4	94.1	94.4	97.4	94.9	94.9	93.6	93.6	92.3
1776	89.9	89.6	92.0	92.9	90.7	88.5	86.3	85.9	89.7	88.2	87.7	84.8
1777	84.8	85.7	96.5	87.7	85.7	102.3	102.3	102.3	107.1	108.2	86.8	86.8
1778	88.1	89.3	90.6	103.9	93.0	93.0	93.0	96.1	102.3	102.3	100.8	100.8
1779	96.3	96.3	96.3	96.3	103.0	103.0	103.5	104.3	105.3	106.1	105.4	105.4
1780	105.4	105.4	105.1	104.8	104.9	105.2	105.5	103.6	103.3	103.0	102.7	102.3
1781	107.0	107.0	107.0	108.4	109.3	109.3	109.3	116.1	117.4	118.2	117.7	117.7
1782	116.3	116.3	116.3									
1783												
1784				94.4	94.7	94.4	93.5	95.9	95.3	105.0	105.1	97.4
1785	97.8	101.3	99.2	97.4	97.2	97.2	92.6	90.5	92.3	89.6	88.3	89.6
1786	88.5	88.5	88.5	97.4	89.6	91.6	95.5	99.4	105.0	105.0	109.6	113.6
1787	105.2	107.6	105.6	105.6	105.6	105.6	111.1	114.5	114.5	115.8	116.7	114.5
1788	114.5	114.5	114.5	114.5	114.5	114.5	114.5	114.5	114.5	117.7	117.7	117.7
1789	117.7	117.7	117.7	117.7	115.4							

Appendix Table 6

Monthly Rates of Exchange on London
Pennsylvania Currency for £100 Sterling
1780-1790

Year	Jan.	Feb.	Mar.	Apr.	May	June	July	Aug.	Sept.	Oct.	Nov.	Dec.
1780											150.0	
1781											147.5	
1782			156.7	161.2				161.5				
1783			166.7			166.7	168.3	166.7	173.3		174.2	172.6
1784	174.2	172.5	171.9	169.9	170.6	172.2	171.2	175.8	176.2	177.0	178.5	176.5
1785	176.5		166.7	177.2		180.0	175.0	177.5	176.5	179.0	179.2	
1786		172.0	180.0	178.3	178.5	177.5		178.9	177.4	177.5	177.0	
1787	177.6	176.2	175.5	175.5	175.8	175.6	175.6	176.9	175.7	176.1	174.8	175.0
1788	175.5	176.2	176.0	175.2	175.0	175.3	174.2	172.5		171.7	171.8	172.0
1789	172.2	172.2	172.4	171.2	170.6	171.6	172.9	172.4	172.4	170.9	171.8	170.4
1790	165.0	153.0	146.6	145.9	155.0	166.3	171.2	173.3	170.3	169.5	174.0	172.5

BIBLIOGRAPHY

Manuscripts

Historical Society of Pennsylvania

Thomas A. Biddle Collection

Chaloner and White Papers

Clifford Papers

Coates and Reynell Papers

Stephen Collins Letterbook (Daniel Parker Papers)

Conarroe Autograph Collection

Henry Drinker Papers

Forges and Furnaces Account Books

Benjamin Fuller Letterbooks and Account Books

Gratz-Croghan Papers (Etting Collection)

Robert Henderson Letterbooks and Account Books (see also New York Public Library)

Michael Hillegas Letterbook

Hollingsworth Collection

Joshua Humphreys Papers

Abel James Papers; Thomas Pleasants Papers; Henry Drinker Papers (Thompson Collection)

Owen Jones Papers

Benjamin Marshall and Brothers Waste Book (in Christopher, Jr., and Charles Marshall Ledger)

Christopher Marshall Letterbook and Diaries

Thomas McKean Papers

Massachusetts Papers, Board of War Letters

Deborah Morris Papers (Coates and Reynell Papers)

Robert Morris Letters (Dreer Collection)

George Nelson Diary

Pemberton Papers

Penington Papers

Penn-Physick Manuscripts (Penn Manuscripts)

William Pollard Letterbook

The items in this bibliography do not include the sources used solely for prices presented in Appendix Table 1. The account books and newspapers used for that purpose are listed at the foot of each year. Sources with no location given may be found at the Historical Society of Pennsylvania.

Robert Proud Letterbook
Reed and Forde Papers
Daniel Roberdeau Letterbook (Roberdeau Buchanan Collection)
William and John Sitgreaves Correspondence (Thomas A. Biddle Collection, Letterbook No. 12)
William Smith Letterbook
Richard Vaux Diaries
Pelatiah Webster Account and Letterbook
Wharton Papers
Thomas Willing Correspondence (Balch Collection)

Library of Congress

James Abeel Letterbook
Ephraim Blaine Accounts and Correspondence
Stephen Collins Account and Letterbook
John Davis Papers
Dutilh and Wachsmuth Letterbook
John Holker Collection
Matthew Irwin Journal of Accounts
Robert Morris Official Diary
Woolsey and Salmon Letterbook

New York Public Library

Clymer-Meredith-Reed Papers
Constable-Pierrepont Papers
Robert Henderson Letterbook
Robert Morris Papers

Miscellaneous

Andrews and Eliot Letters (Massachusetts Historical Society)
James and John Cox Letterbook (Industrial Research Department)
Henry S. Drinker (private papers)
John and Henry Drinker Account Book (Industrial Research Department)
Durham Furnace (Bucks County Historical Society)
Stephen Girard Letters (Girard College)
Kuhn and Kuhn; Kuhn and Risberg Letterbooks (Bucks County Historical Society)
Minute Book of United Company of Philadelphia for Promoting American Manufactures (Wetherill Collection, Industrial Research Department)
Simeon Perkins Diary (University of Toronto)
Joseph Price Diary (Montgomery County Historical Society)
Shinkle and Graff Accounts (Industrial Research Department)
Smith Manuscripts (Ridgway Branch Library)

Books

Anderson, *Historical and Chronological Deduction of the Origin of Commerce,* revised by Mr. Coombe, Dublin, 1790

Andrews, Charles M., *The Colonial Background of the American Revolution,* Yale University Press, New Haven, 1939

Balch, Thomas, editor, *Letters and Papers Relating Chiefly to the Provincial History of Pennsylvania,* Crissy and Markley (privately printed), Philadelphia, 1855

Bezanson, Anne, Robert D. Gray, and Miriam Hussey, *Prices in Colonial Pennsylvania,* University of Pennsylvania Press, Philadelphia, 1935

Biddle, Henry D., editor, *Extracts from the Journal of Elizabeth Drinker, 1759-1807,* J. B. Lippincott, Philadelphia, 1889

Bining, Arthur C., *British Regulation of the Colonial Iron Industry,* University of Pennsylvania Press, Philadelphia, 1933

Burnett, Edmund C., editor, *Letters of Members of the Continental Congress,* The Carnegie Institution of Washington, Washington, D. C., 1921-36

Byars, William Vincent, editor, *B. and M. Gratz, Merchants in Philadelphia, 1754-1798,* The Hugh Stephens Printing Co., Jefferson City, Mo., 1916

Cheyney, Edward P., *Commerce, Navigation and Ship-Building on the Delaware River,* official document, Pennsylvania Department of Internal Affairs, Harrisburg, 1891

Collections of the New York Historical Society for the Year 1878 (Publication Fund Series), New York—printed for the Society, 1879

Colonial Records—Minutes of the Council of Safety; Minutes of the Provincial Council of Pennsylvania; Minutes of the Supreme Executive Council of Pennsylvania, published by the State, Harrisburg

Commerce of Rhode Island, 1726-1800, Massachusetts Historical Society, Boston, 1915

Correspondence of the Late President Adams, Everett & Munroe, Boston, 1809

Coxe, Tench, *A View of the United States of America,* Philadelphia, 1794, Reprinted for J. Johnson, London, 1795

Eddis, William, *Letters from America, Historical and Descriptive; Comprising Occurrences from 1769 to 1777, Inclusive,* Printed for the author and sold by C. Dilly, in the Poultry, London, 1792

Ford, Worthington Chauncey, editor, *Journals of the Continental Congress,* Government Printing Office, Washington, D. C.

Gray, Lewis Cecil, *History of Agriculture in the Southern United States to 1860*, The Carnegie Institution of Washington, Washington, D. C., 1933

Hamilton, John C., editor, *The Works of Alexander Hamilton*, Charles S. Francis & Co., New York, 1851

Johnson, Victor Leroy, *The Administration of the American Commissariat during the Revolutionary War*, dissertation in History, University of Pennsylvania, 1941

Journals of the House of Representatives of the Commonwealth of Pennsylvania, volume 1, printed by John Dunlap, Philadelphia, 1782

Massie, Joseph, *A State of the British Sugar Colony Trade*, Printed for T. Payne, London, 1759

Parsons, Jacob Cox, editor, *Extracts from the Diary of Jacob Hiltzheimer of Philadelphia, 1765-1798*, Wm. F. Fell & Co., Philadelphia, 1893

Pennsylvania Archives—1st series, volumes 5 to 11, Philadelphia, 1853-55; 2nd series, volume 1, Harrisburg, 1896

Posthumus, N. W., *Inquiry into the History of Prices in Holland*, E. J. Brill, Leiden, 1946

Reed, William B., *Life and Correspondence of Joseph Reed*, Lindsay & Blakiston, Philadelphia, 1847

Southey, Thomas, *Chronological History of the West Indies*, Longman, Rees, Orme, Brown, and Green, London, 1827

Sparks, Jared, editor, *The Writings of George Washington*, Harper and Brothers, New York 1847

Statutes at Large of Pennsylvania from 1682 to 1801, Harrisburg, 1897

Sumner, William Graham, *The Financier and the Finances of the American Revolution*, Dodd, Mead & Co., New York, 1891

Webster, Pelatiah, *Political Essays on the Nature and Operation of Money, Public Finances, and Other Subjects, Joseph Crukshank*, Philadelphia, 1791

Wharton, Francis, editor, *The Revolutionary Diplomatic Correspondence of the United States*, Government Printing Office, Washington, D. C., 1889

Newspapers and Magazines

American Museum, or, Universal Magazine

Bulletin of the Friends Historical Society

Gentleman's Magazine and Historical Chronicle, London

Journal of Economic and Business History

Maryland Historical Magazine

Maryland Journal and Baltimore Advertiser

Pennsylvania Evening Post

Pennsylvania Gazette
Pennsylvania Journal and Weekly Advertiser
Pennsylvania Magazine of History and Biography
Pennsylvania Packet
Political Science Quarterly

INDEX